SEX-ROLE STEREOTYPES
Traditions and Alternatives

SEX-ROLE STEREOTYPES
Traditions and Alternatives

Susan A. Basow
Lafayette College

Brooks/Cole Publishing Company
Monterey, California

Consulting Editor:
Lawrence S. Wrightsman, University of Kansas

Brooks/Cole Publishing Company
A Division of Wadsworth, Inc.

Printed in the United States of America

10   9   8   7   6   5   4   3   2   1

Library of Congress Cataloging in Publication Data:

Basow, Susan A   1947–
    Sex-role stereotypes.

    Includes bibliographies and index.
    1. Sex role.   2. Stereotype (Psychology)
I. Title.
HQ1075.B37   305.3   80-19086
ISBN   0-8185-0394-7

Acquisition Editor: *Claire Verduin*
Manuscript Editor: *David Armstrong*
Production Editor: *Marilu Uland*
Interior Design: *Jamie Sue Brooks*
Cover Design: *Stanley Rice*
Illustrations: *Lori Heckelman*
Typesetting: *Graphic Typesetting Service, Los Angeles*

To my parents, Faye and Phil,
and to Jay, with love

PREFACE

Masculinity. Femininity. These words engender clear pictures of two opposite sets of behavior and personal attributes. To some degree, we all know what these characteristics are. In fact, one of the most impressive aspects of these images is the extent to which we Americans share them. Men should be strong, rational, aggressive; women should be weak, emotional, submissive. And yet, to what extent do these images fit the majority of real-life people? That is, do men and women really conform to these images, or are these images stereotypes? If men and women do not conform to the stereotypes, how did such stereotypes come into being? Once established, how are the stereotypes maintained and transmitted? Once transmitted, how do these stereotypes affect women and men in our society? Once affected by the stereotypes, how does one break free, and toward what does one change? This book is dedicated to answering these questions.

The following chapters will demonstrate that there is little physical or psychological evidence to support gender stereotypes as clear-cut distinctions between the sexes. Yet the stereotypes are firmly entrenched in our individual and cultural psyches and are passed to future generations directly and indirectly via every socializing agent in society (parents, teachers, the media, religion, and so on). The effects of these stereotypes are pervasive, intense, and generally damaging to all individuals (both women and men), to their relationships, and to society as a whole. To break free of stereotypes is a difficult yet beneficial process, which is aided by the new concept of androgyny, which is a flexible integration in one person of masculine and feminine attributes.

To explore these areas, this book is divided into five parts: Part One explores the stereotypes; Part Two discusses the current findings in the area of sex similarities and differences; Part Three deals with the origins of the stereotypes; Part Four delves into the effects of the stereotypes; and Part Five considers alternatives to the stereotypes.

This book is clearly a viewpoint book. I feel very strongly that the sex-role stereotypes are imposed by society, not by physiology. People differ, yes. But they do not differ in most cases on the basis of sex. In those cases where sex differences are found, they arise mostly in interaction with a particular situation. Thus, this book takes an interactionist point of view with regard to sex-role behaviors; they are a product of the person as well as the situation. This point of view runs throughout the book. I hope that by putting this bias up front, I can aid the reader in evaluating in a more objective manner the material presented.

This book is designed to be used as a text in courses on sex roles, sex differences, gender, and women's or men's studies. It can also be used as a supplement in broader psychology, sociology, or interdisciplinary courses that have units on sex roles, sex differences, or male-female relations. It is written for the advanced undergraduate or graduate student who has some familiarity with basic social-science concepts and research methods.

One particularly useful aspect of this book is the exercises included in the Instructor's Manual, which highlight the content of the chapters and bring the information home to the student. The material discussed in the book is relevant to all of us; the exercises help make this connection more direct and explicit.

I would like to acknowledge the help and support I have received in planning and writing this book. The idea for, and basic organization of, the book came from my courses in masculinity/femininity at Trenton State College (1975, 1977) and in the psychology of sex roles at the University of Maryland, Far East Division (1976–1977). My appreciation goes to my students and to Drs. Tony DiGiorgio, R. David Young, and Joseph Arden, who supported my developing such courses. Special thanks go to the Brooks/Cole staff, particularly Claire Verduin and Bill Hicks, for their continuous encouragement. Brooks/Cole's consulting editor Larry Wrightsman and reviewers Harriett Amster of the University of Texas at Arlington, Janis Bohan of Metro State College, Suzanne Kessler of the State University of New York at Purchase, Virginia O'Leary of the American Psychological Association, and Abigail J. Stewart of the Radcliffe Data Resource and Research Center were instrumental in helping to polish and refine the book from its rough beginnings. And, of course, my sincerest thanks to my friends and family, particularly Jay K. Miller, for their unfailing support despite my short temper and long hours.

Susan A. Basow

CONTENTS

INTRODUCTION

1 Sex-Role Stereotypes

A boy and his father were involved in a serious automobile accident. The father was killed instantly; the son was severely injured. An ambulance rushed him to the nearest hospital, and a prominent surgeon was summoned to perform an immediate operation. Upon entering the operating room, however, the surgeon exclaimed "I can't operate on this boy. He's my son." Question: how can this be?

If this apocryphal story is unfamiliar to you, and you came up with answers involving a stepfather, adopted father, reincarnation, a mistake, and so on, you are part of the majority of Americans who think of surgery as a male occupation. The answer to the above riddle is simple: the surgeon is the boy's mother. The fact that most people do not guess that answer demonstrates the pervasiveness and strength of certain sex-role stereotypes—in this case, occupational ones.

This book will examine sex-role stereotypes—their bases, transmittal, consequences, and alternatives. It will be argued that such stereotypes are based on few actual sex differences and that, more importantly, such stereotypes seriously limit individual functioning and have a negative effect on relationships as well as on society.

DEFINITION

There are other sex-role stereotypes in our daily lives besides the occupational ones. For example, if you were giving a toy to a child, would you give a doll to a boy or to a girl? a catcher's mitt? a chemistry set? a coloring book? Such choices tap our basic assumptions about boys and girls, males and females. Although for a particular child your choice may not reflect the typical female/male pattern of responding to the above questions, how about your response for an unknown boy or girl? If that distinction made a difference, you have come face-to-face with the meaning of the term *stereotype*. According to Wrightsman (1977), a stereotype is "a relatively rigid and oversimplified conception of a group of people in which all individuals in the group are labeled with the so-called group characteristics" (p. 672). That is, stereotypes are strongly held overgeneralizations about people in some designated social category. Such beliefs tend to be universally shared within a given society and are learned as part of the process of growing up in that society. Not only may stereotypes not be true for the group as a whole, since they are oversimplifications (most boys may *not* want a chemistry set), but they also are unlikely to be true for any specific member of the group (Johnny Doe, in particular, may not want a chemistry set). Even when a generalization is valid (that is, it does describe group averages), we still cannot predict an individual's behavior or characteristics. For example, if we know that men are taller than women, we still don't know necessarily that Jane Doe is shorter than John Doe. Stereotypes, since they are more oversimplified and more rigidly held than such generalizations, have even less predictive value.

When we speak of sex-role stereotypes, we are speaking of those oversimplified conceptions pertaining to our behavior as females or males. A *role* is "a cluster of socially or culturally defined expectations that individuals in a given situation are expected to fulfill" (Chafetz, 1978, p. 4). Thus, roles are defined by society, are applied to all individuals in a particular category, and are well-learned responses by individuals. For example, the masculine role is currently defined by American society as involving aggressiveness, independence, nonemotionality, and so forth. It is applied to all individuals labeled male and is learned by the person during his early socialization experiences. The same is true with the feminine role. The fact that the definitions of the terms *masculinity* and *femininity* are different in different cultures and have changed over time, even in American culture, demonstrates their learned, as opposed to innate, nature. Thus, what we term masculine and feminine is not linked in any biological sense to being a male or a female but rather is established by society.

For example, in the United States, dentistry is viewed as a male profession; and, indeed, most dentists today are men. In Sweden and Russia, however, most dentists are women, and the profession is viewed as a female one. Clearly, then, the skills involved in dentistry are not inherently male or female related but are so labeled by a society.

Children in every culture need to learn their roles and the behaviors that go with them. They need to learn what a child, a student, a brother/sister, son/daughter, man/woman should do. With sex roles, as with other roles, the expectations are not always clear, nor does everyone adopt them to the same degree. For example, the male role in many lower-class families involves being physically aggressive and settling disagreements by a show of physical strength; in many middle- and upper-class homes, the expectation for men is to be verbally and intellectually aggressive and to settle disagreements through the use of reasoning powers. Yet there are many lower-class men who disdain physical violence and many upper-class men who use it. The former group, particularly, are likely to be accused of not being "masculine" enough. Such charges reveal the operation of specific role expectations.

Combining the definition of *stereotype* and the definition of *role*, we can view sex-role stereotypes as the rigidly held and oversimplified beliefs that males and females, by virtue of their sex, possess distinct psychological traits and characteristics. Such overgeneralizations tend to be widely shared in a particular culture and rigidly held. It is worth noting, however, that not all researchers agree on this definition. Ashmore and DelBoca (1979) do not think stereotypes are by definition rigidly held or that they imply consensus. Our definition refers primarily to cultural stereotypes, and Ashmore and DelBoca prefer to draw a distinction between personal and cultural stereotypes. A personal stereotype refers to "structured sets of inferential relations that link personal attributes to the social categories female and male" (Ashmore and DelBoca, 1979, p. 225). In this sense, sex-role stereotypes can be viewed as a type of implicit personality theory. As such, the topic fits in with a wide range of research and theory on psychological processes.

Since roles are learned, there is always the possibility that they can be unlearned and the definitions of the roles themselves redefined. The possibility of such changes is important to bear in mind as we examine the specific sex-role stereotypes in more depth.

EVIDENCE OF SEX-ROLE STEREOTYPES

There is considerable experimental evidence to support the existence of sex-role stereotypes in the United States. Studies conducted during the late 1960s and early 1970s with nearly 1000 males and females (Broverman, Vogel, Broverman, Clarkson, & Rosenkrantz, 1972; Rosenkrantz, Vogel, Bee, Broverman, & Broverman, 1968) have demonstrated that there exists strong agreement about the differing characteristics of men and women. This consensus is found regardless of the age, sex, religion, educational level, or marital status of the respondents. More than 75% of those asked agreed that 41 traits clearly differentiated females and males. Table 1-1 lists these traits in the two categories suggested by statistical analysis: 29 male-valued items (Competency Cluster) and 12 female-valued items (Warmth-Expressiveness Cluster). Although these studies are somewhat dated, more recent research (for example, Ashmore & DelBoca, 1979; Foushee, Helmreich, & Spence, 1979; Gilbert, Deutsch, & Strahan, 1978; Tunnell, 1979) still finds that both sexes view the typical man and woman as distinctly different from each other on such masculine and feminine traits.

There are a number of problems with studies of sex-role stereotypes, however. One problem relates to the methodologies of the studies themselves (Cicone & Ruble, 1978). Asking questions about how males differ from females may yield information about the attributes that are viewed as differentiating the sexes but not necessarily about how people see typical males and females themselves. In other words, most questionnaires ask about relative, rather than absolute, beliefs. For example, males and females may be thought of as similar in honesty, intelligence, and helpfulness but different in aggressiveness and warmth. Since only the differences are considered, the similarities are minimized.

Table 1-1
Stereotypic Sex-Role Items (Responses from 74 College Men and 80 College Women)

Competency Cluster: Masculine Pole Is More Desirable	
Feminine	Masculine
Not at all aggressive	Very aggressive
Not at all independent	Very independent
Very emotional	Not at all emotional
Does not hide emotions at all	Almost always hides emotions
Very subjective	Very objective
Very easily influenced	Not at all easily influenced
Very submissive	Very dominant
Dislikes math and science very much	Likes math and science very much
Very excitable in a minor crisis	Not at all excitable in a minor crisis
Very passive	Very active
Not at all competitive	Very competitive
Very illogical	Very logical
Very home oriented	Very worldly
Not at all skilled in business	Very skilled in business
Very sneaky	Very direct
Does not know the way of the world	Knows the way of the world
Feelings easily hurt	Feelings not easily hurt
Not at all adventurous	Very adventurous
Has difficulty making decisions	Can make decisions easily
Cries very easily	Never cries
Almost never acts as a leader	Almost always acts as a leader
Not at all self-confident	Very self-confident
Very uncomfortable about being aggressive	Not at all uncomfortable about being aggressive
Not at all ambitious	Very ambitious
Unable to separate feelings from ideas	Easily able to separate feelings from ideas
Very dependent	Not at all dependent
Very conceited about appearance	Never conceited about appearance
Thinks women are always superior to men	Thinks men are always superior to women
Does not talk freely about sex with men	Talks freely about sex with men

Warmth-Expressiveness Cluster: Feminine Pole Is More Desirable	
Feminine	Masculine
Doesn't use harsh language at all	Uses very harsh language
Very talkative	Not at all talkative
Very tactful	Very blunt
Very gentle	Very rough
Very aware of feelings of others	Not at all aware of feelings of others
Very religious	Not at all religious
Very interested in own appearance	Not at all interested in own appearance
Very neat in habits	Very sloppy in habits
Very quiet	Very loud
Very strong need for security	Very little need for security
Enjoys art and literature	Does not enjoy art and literature at all
Easily expresses tender feelings	Does not express tender feelings at all easily

From "Sex Role Stereotypes: A Current Appraisal," by I. Broverman, S. R. Vogel, S. M. Broverman, F. E. Clarkson, and P. S. Rosenkrantz, *Journal of Social Issues*, 1972, *28*(2), 59–78. Copyright 1972 by the Society for the Psychological Study of Social Issues. Reprinted by permission of the author and publisher.

In addition, most studies of sex-role stereotypes use checklist responses rather than self-generated descriptions. Checklists encourage responding from one's beliefs about the characteristics of males and females rather than from one's actual experience with the sexes. Thus, less stereotyping is found when people are asked to give their own description of males and females than when they are asked to check an adjective list (Frieze & Strauss, 1976, in Cicone & Ruble, 1978). Thus, the research on stereotypes may present an exaggerated picture of people's beliefs about the sexes. With that caution in mind, however, it is still notable how consistent the stereotyped differences are. Women are most often characterized as being warm, expressive, and people oriented; men are seen as active, levelheaded, dominant, and achievement oriented.

When people in the Broverman and Rosenkrantz studies were asked to rate the social desirability of each trait, the researchers found that the masculine poles were considered by both men and women to be more socially desirable than the feminine poles for any adult, regardless of sex. It is possible that this negative bias regarding women may be an artifact of the specific items the Broverman group used. However, the fact that these 41 traits were themselves chosen as particularly characteristic of the sexes from a larger number of traits suggests that there may indeed be an uneven evaluation of the two sex roles.

Other researchers have found similar evidence of a negative bias toward feminine traits, although one investigator, Sandra Bem (1974), also found that a few feminine traits were rated more highly than any masculine ones (for example, "sensitive to the needs of others"). On the balance, however, more negatively valued traits are typically attributed to the feminine role than to the masculine role. The implications are far reaching. How does it feel to be thought of as submissive, very emotional, easily influenced, very sneaky, and not at all ambitious? How does it feel to share the feeling that such traits are undesirable? How does it affect one's self-image, one's opinion of women, and one's attitude toward female professionals? Such consequences of the sex-role stereotypes will be examined in Part Four.

The traits listed in Table 1-1 reveal another common finding related to sex-role stereotypes: the characteristic traits for men and women are commonly viewed as being opposite each other. Thus, whereas males are thought of as dominant and objective, females are thought of as submissive and subjective. This all-or-none distinction may have been a function of the questionnaire used by the Broverman group. The items were presented as two end points on a line, and each respondent was asked to check where on the line the typical male or female could be placed. Thus a female could only be rated as either submissive or dominant, not as more or less submissive, or more or less dominant. (See Brannon, in press, for an excellent critique of such studies.) Even when responses are free form (for example, Chafetz, 1978), nearly identical lists and distinctions emerge; for example, males are strong, females weak; females are emotional, males are unemotional. Furthermore, Foushee and colleagues (1979) found that most people think that masculinity and femininity are negatively related—that is, that being low on masculine traits implies being high on feminine traits.

Despite the fact that people think of sex-typed traits as being opposite each other, research that has correlated individual scores on the masculine and feminine scales has found little relationship between the two (S. Bem, 1974; Spence & Helmreich, 1978). How masculine someone scores is unrelated to how feminine he or she scores. Thus, the bipolar model of masculinity and femininity, which postulates that instrumentality and expressivity fall at opposite ends of a single dimension, is incorrect.

The all-or-none categorizing of sex-role traits is misleading. People just are not so simple that they either possess all of a trait or none of it. This is even more true when trait dispositions for groups of people are examined. Part A of Figure 1-1 illustrates what such an all-or-none distribution of the trait "strength" would look like: all males would be strong, all females weak. The fact is, most psychological and physical traits are distributed according to the pattern shown in Part B of Figure 1-1, with most people possessing an average amount of the trait and fewer people having either very much or very little of that trait. Almost all the traits listed in Table 1-1 conform to this pattern. To the extent that females and males may differ in the average amount of the trait they possess (which needs to be determined empirically), the distribution can be characterized by overlapping normal curves, as in Part C of Figure 1-1. Thus, although most

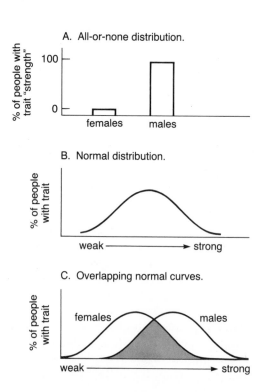

Figure 1-1

Three types of distributions for the trait "strength"

men are stronger than most women, the crosshatched area indicates that some men are weaker than some women and vice versa. The amount of overlap of the curves is generally considerable.

Another attribute related to overlapping normal curves is that differences within one group are usually greater than the differences between the two groups. Thus, there is more variation in the strength trait within a group of men than there is between the "average" male and the "average" female. Most of the stereotypic traits in Table 1-1 fit this pattern. For example, although males on the average may be more aggressive than females on the average, there may be greater differences among males than there are between males and females.

This concept of overlapping normal curves is critically important in understanding sex-role stereotypes because it undermines the basis of most discriminatory regulations and laws. Although most men are stronger than most women, denying women access to jobs requiring strength simply on the basis of sex is unjustified, because *some* women are stronger than some men (see crosshatched area in Part C of Figure 1-1). Thus, if most of the stereotypic traits are actually distributed in normal curves along a continuum (that is, people may be more or less dominant, more or less submissive) rather than distributed in an all-or-none fashion—dominant *or* submissive— then setting up two opposite and distinct lists of traits for females and males is entirely inappropriate and misleading.

Not only is it inaccurate to view traits as all-or-none; it may also be inaccurate to view personality in trait terms altogether. Despite their popularity, trait theories of personality have little empirical validity. People are simply not as consistent in their behavior across a variety of situations as one might like to believe. Mischel (1968) concludes that cross-situational consistencies rarely produce correlations greater than $+.30$. That is, a person does not usually exhibit the same trait to the same degree in every situation. Rather, human behavior is a function of both the person and the situation. The situation, in many cases, accounts for more than 90% of the variability in a person's behavior. For example, one's behavior during a church service or at a red light is almost entirely a function of the situation. As another example, how assertively a person acts depends not only on the person but on the situation itself. This can be readily verified from one's own experience. An individual can be very assertive in one situation (for example, in a class or group meeting) and markedly unassertive in another (for example, with a close friend).

Of course, some people are more consistent than others in their behaviors in general and with respect to specific behaviors in particular (D. Bem & Allen, 1974). That is, some people may generally be more predictable than others across a wide range of situations. For example, people who strongly identify with a sex role are more predictable since they more often act according to sex-role expectations than people who don't identify with such a role (S. Bem, 1975b). And some people are more consistent than others with respect to a particular behavior (for example, "You can always count on Mary to be assertive"). On the whole, however, the trait approach to personality needs to be modified. Specific people interact with specific situations and produce specific behaviors; generalized traits rarely apply.

With reference to sex-role stereotypes, then, it can be concluded that: (1) people cannot be viewed as simply collections of consistent traits, since situations are also important; (2) males and females specifically cannot be viewed as having unique traits that are opposite each other; and (3) whatever attributes are thought of as distinctly masculine or feminine are also possessed by at least some members of the other sex.

Therefore, if women and men are not accurately described as a collection of feminine and masculine traits, respectively, and, in fact, if the application of trait terms to personality is generally not appropriate, how can behavior be understood and how can the seeming differences in actual behavior between the sexes be accounted for?

ALTERNATIVE TO SEX TYPING

What is needed is a new conceptualization of personality that both allows and accounts for behavioral inconsistency. An answer may lie in the concept of *androgyny*, a term put forth by Sandra Bem denoting the integration of masculine and feminine traits within a single individual (S. Bem, 1974, 1975b, 1976). Androgynous people tend to characterize themselves, for example, as strongly understanding, compassionate, and affectionate *and* as strongly self-reliant, assertive, and independent. Sex-typed individuals, on the other hand, characterize themselves as strongly having *either* the first *or* last three characteristics but not all of them. The complex characteristics of androgynous individuals can be evidenced, depending on the situation, all in a single act or only in a number of different acts. Thus, a person may be an empathic listener when a friend has a problem, an assertive leader propelling a group to action, and an assertive and sensitive boss when an employee needs to be fired. Being androgynous does not mean being neuter or imply anything about one's sexual orientation. Rather, it describes the degree of flexibility a person has regarding sex-role stereotypic behaviors.

Androgynous individuals can also be contrasted with another group, the undifferentiated (Spence et al., 1974). People who fall into this category generally ascribe a balance of masculine and feminine traits to themselves but only to a limited degree. They do not perceive themselves as strongly having any traits. Thus, although they are not sex typed, such individuals are clearly different from the androgynous group.

The concept of androgyny, which will be discussed in greater depth in succeeding chapters, suggests a new way of looking at behavior and also serves as an alternative to strict sex typing. Most individuals (current estimates range from 40% to 66%), however, still describe themselves as possessing traits more characteristic of one sex than the other; that is, they are categorized as either sex typed or cross-sex-typed. These percentages may be a function of the method of categorization used, there being no absolute cutoff points for the categories of androgynous and sex-typed individuals. Rather, the cutoffs are based on the median scores of a particular sample. Still, the fact that a goodly number of people describe themselves as operating in terms of the sex-role stereotypes gives one pause. If the stereotypes are indeed overgeneralizations and oversimplifications, and if people cannot justifiably be described by trait terms in general, why do so many people characterize themselves in sex-role stereotypic terms?

BASES OF SEX-ROLE STEREOTYPES

Perhaps these stereotypes have some empirical validity; that is, perhaps there are real differences in behavior between the sexes that the stereotypes just exaggerate. This approach suggests that the differences exist first and that the stereotypes simply reflect them. In this case, what have been called stereotypes would not be stereotypes at all—that is, simplified overgeneralizations—but simply generalizations. It is only if a trait is not strongly possessed by a particular sex but is perceived by others as being possessed by that sex that the trait can be called a stereotype.

A study by Unger and Siiter (1975) examined this question and found that, at least in the area of values, most of the sex-role stereotypic traits were indeed oversimplifications and exaggerations of minor group differences. Polling 240 college students, Unger and Siiter found a striking agreement between males and females on the values they considered most important for themselves and members of the same sex. For example, both men and women felt it was important to be honest, responsible, and broadminded, and they thought other individuals of their sex felt similarly. Thus, the strong sex differences suggested by the sex-role stereotypes did not fit self- or same-sex perceptions. When it came to predicting the values of members of the other sex, however, the stereotypes operated quite strongly. Women exaggerated the importance of achievement-oriented values for men, and men, to the same degree, exaggerated the importance of nurturant-oriented values for women. Such misperceptions of the other sex (that is, views of the other sex as believing more strongly in stereotyped values than they actually do) can have far-reaching effects. Sex-role stereotypes, thus, may not be based on statistically significant differences between the sexes but, at best, are exaggerations of a grain of truth. Other researchers (for example, Gilbert et al., 1978; Spence et al., 1975) have also found that students exaggerate the number and magnitude of differences between the sexes.

EFFECTS OF SEX-ROLE STEREOTYPING

Rather than reflecting real behavioral differences, then, it is more likely that belief in the stereotypes may give rise to some behavioral differences. If the stereotypes function as part of the sex-role expectations, then people will learn them and be influenced by them. Even though sex-typed distinctions between the sexes may not fit individuals, stereotypes themselves have power as standards to which to conform, against which to rebel, or with which to evaluate others.

One way stereotypes operate is by setting up a *self-fulfilling prophecy*. If females are viewed as having more negative characteristics than males, some females may view themselves this way and may, in fact, develop those very characteristics. For example, if females are expected to be less rational than males, some may view themselves that way and not participate in problem-solving activities or take advanced math courses, since such behaviors are not sex-role appropriate. As a result, some females may indeed develop less problem-solving abilities than some males who have had those experiences, thereby fulfilling the stereotypes. Such beliefs can powerfully influence behavior in either a negative way, if the expectations are negative, or positive way, if the expectations are positive (Snyder, Tanke, & Berschend, 1977).

Another way sex-role stereotypes affect us is through *impression management*. All of us, at some level, want to be socially acceptable, at least to some people. To the extent that we desire such approval, we may engage in impression-management strategies in order to obtain it. That is, we will try to present ourselves (our image) in a way that we think is acceptable to another person. Zanna and Pack (1975) found that female Princeton undergraduates would present themselves as extremely conventional women when the ideology of a desirable male partner was conventional and as more liberated women when his ideology was nontraditional. When the man was viewed as undesirable, his views did not have much impact on the images presented by the women.

In a similar study by von Baeyer, Sherk, and Zanna (1979), 53 female undergraduates acted as job applicants and were interviewed by a male confederate who supposedly held either traditional or non-traditional views of women. The women who saw the traditional interviewer presented themselves in a more traditional way (they wore more makeup and clothing accessories, talked to and gazed at the interviewer less, and gave more traditional answers to a question concerning marriage and children) than the women who saw the nontraditional interviewer. These changes were unrelated to the women's own degree of sex typing. Thus, one way the sex-role stereotypes function is to define expected sex-role behavior and thereby shape people's self-presentations. This is as true for men as it is for women. As the stereotypes change, so might sex-role behaviors. Such changes, however, may simply define new images rather than reflect a general reduction in impression management.

In recent years, sex-role stereotypes have been undergoing change. For example, Pleck (1976a) points out that males traditionally have been expected to be instrumental, focusing on achievement, lacking in interpersonal and emotional skills, and relating to women in a dominant way. The modern version of the male role requires more interpersonal and intellectual skills than physical strength, as well as an egalitarian companion-style relationship with women. Yet men's emotional expressiveness is still restricted, and work is still the primary determinant of a man's self-esteem. Thus, although the content of the stereotype may be shifting (see also Dubbert, 1979; Tavris, 1977), some stereotypes of masculinity remain. Similarly, Gilbert and colleagues (1978) found that, although descriptions by college students of the ideal woman and man tended to be more androgynous than in the past, such descriptions still remain sex typed. This was especially true of the ideal-woman description given by college men. To the extent that individuals, male or female, are stereotyped, realization of their full human potential in all its complexity will be impeded.

LOOKING AHEAD

Where do these stereotypes come from? What are the differences and similarities that exist between the sexes? How many of the differences are innate and how many are learned? These questions are important to examine before looking at the actual effect of these stereotypes on people's lives.

RECOMMENDED READING

Bem, S. L. The measurement of psychological androgyny. *Journal of Consulting and Clinical Psychology*, 1974, *42*, 155–162. A description of the development of the Bem Sex Role Inventory for the measurement of androgyny and sex typing.

Brannon, R. Measuring attitudes toward women (and otherwise): A methodological critique. In J. Sherman & F. Denmark (Eds.), *The futures of women: Issues in psychology*. N.Y.: Psychological Dimensions, in press. An excellent critique of measurement studies.

Cicone, M. V., & Ruble, D. N. Beliefs about males. *Journal of Social Issues*, 1978, *34*(1), 5–16. A current appraisal of the male stereotype and how it is measured.

CURRENT
FINDINGS

An infant girl is in the babbling stage of development. An observer laughingly remarks, "A typical female. You can't keep them from talking."

After hearing how his son was sent home from school for being disruptive in class and fighting with other boys, a father remarks, with a smile, "Well, boys will be boys."

In both these incidents, certain assumptions are made regarding emotional and behavioral differences between females and males. Boys are assumed to be more active, unruly, and aggressive; girls are assumed to be more emotional, talkative, and passive. Our very use of the term *opposite sex* implies that females and males are diametrically different from each other not only in their sex but in their behaviors as well. In order to understand these stereotypic expectations, it is important to know what differences between the sexes actually do exist—that is, on what the stereotypes are based. Are any of the stereotypic differences listed in Chapter One based on fact? If so, which ones are factually based and to what degree? This section will attempt to answer these questions by examining the current findings related to male and female characteristics in four major areas: physical, cognitive, social, and sexual.

Controversy often surrounds even the most mundane of "facts," and what is accepted today may be questioned tomorrow. Human behavior is not fixed; it is not a direct product of biological factors. Therefore, since the environment can exert a major influence on behavior, research results are often quite complex and, at times, inconsistent. The clearest summary statement that can be made is that nearly all behavior is a function of situational forces that may interact with biological predispositions. The relative weighting of the two components varies with the particular behavior, the particular person, and the particular situation, as well as with more general cultural factors.

Because the research on sex-role stereotypic behaviors and characteristics is so complex, some attention to research problems is needed before the findings themselves can be looked at in detail. The remainder of this introductory section will examine such problems. By necessity, the discussion will be brief. The interested reader is encouraged to read Mary Parlee's critiques (1973, 1978) for further elaboration of research problems.

RESEARCH PROBLEMS

In many of the studies reported in this book, certain research problems occur that serve to qualify the reported results. Problems regarding basic assumptions of the researchers, choice of subjects, experimental design and methodology, and interpretation of the results are liable to occur in any research area. The areas of sex-role behaviors and sex differences are particularly vulnerable to such problems, since these areas are very personal and, in many ways, political.

It is thus necessary to highlight some of the possible problems, so that the reader can keep them in mind in reviewing the research presented in this book.

Basic Assumptions

Perhaps the most basic problem in examining the research on sex differences is the underlying assumption that sex differences exist and that these differences are important. As Kaplan and Bean (1976) point out, since researchers study areas already thought to reflect male/female differences, such as hormonal cyclicity, the data reflecting these differences may be exaggerated. For example, much research has been done on the effect of female hormone cyclicity on moods; very little has been done on the effect of male hormones (Parlee, 1973; Ramey, 1972). Thus we get an exaggerated picture of a male/female dichotomy and a limited understanding of the full range of human potential.

This emphasis on sex differences, as opposed to similarities, is further perpetuated by the policy of most journals to publish only statistically significant findings. The null hypothesis, meaning that there is no difference between groups, can never be proved. The strongest statement that can be made is that the null hypothesis cannot be rejected. Therefore, findings reflecting no difference usually do not get reported in the literature. Additionally, since journals have limited space, they have to reject a high percentage of submitted articles, and they naturally tend to accept those with positive findings. Signorella, Vegega, and Mitchell (1979), in studying sex-related variables in research published from 1968 to 1970 and from 1975 to 1977, found an increase in the number of studies testing for sex differences. Such an increase may result in more chance findings of differences being reported.

Another basic assumption is that sex differences can be attributed to either nature (biology) or nurture (environment). Thus, some studies are designed to demonstrate that postpartum depression has a purely biological basis (for example, Treadway, Kane, Jarrahi-Zaded, & Lipton, 1969); others, that it is purely cultural (for example, Melges, 1968). As Rosenberg (1973) and others have noted, it is nearly impossible in human beings to separate biology from environment since socialization begins at birth. Clearly, these two factors interact in the area of sex differences as well as in most other areas of human behavior. Research is needed to uncover the way this interaction occurs for particular behavior patterns for males as well as for females.

Choice of Subjects

Research problems arise in choosing whom to study. Some researchers have used animals, since human experimentation in the biological area presents serious ethical and practical problems. The choice of which animals to study, however, is often a product of the experimenter's assumptions and biases. Thus, rhesus monkeys, who show different behaviors by sex, are studied more frequently than gibbons, who do not show such differences; yet gibbons are evolutionarily closer to humans than rhesus monkeys (Rosenberg, 1973). The ability to generalize findings with animals is also questionable, since humans are unique in their development of the neocortex and of the plasticity of their behavior (Ramey, 1972; Rosenberg, 1973). Human behavior is extremely modifiable by experience. Although there may be similarities in behavior between humans and animals, the antecedents of the behaviors may be quite different.

Subjects may be selected to fit preexisting assumptions. For example, in examining the impact of menopause on women, one study simply excluded from the sample all women who worked, apparently on the ground that such women were "deviant" (Van Keep & Kellerhals, 1975).

Studying people with some abnormality or who need some form of treatment is also problematic, since, by definition, these are individuals whose development differs from normal. Women who consult doctors for menstrual problems, for example, are a select group and cannot be assumed to represent women in general. Other people may be brought up differently because of parental knowledge of their problems, or research may be designed to specifically highlight their differences (for example, Stoller, 1968). Such problems limit the ability to generalize findings.

The cultural relativity of many findings is important, too. Thus, although Tiger (1969) argues that greater male strength and size determine male dominance, this has not been supported in other cultures (for example, Mead, 1935). Physical activity and nutrition are often of greater importance than sex in determining physical attributes (Barfield, 1976), and religion has been found more important than hormones in determining menstrual discomfort (Paige, 1973). In addition, most studies use White middle-class subjects, often college students, which also limits the ability to generalize the findings.

Some behaviors seem to be situation- or age-specific. Thus Maccoby and Jacklin (1974) found that boys are more active in the presence of their peers, especially male peers, than are girls or than are boys when alone. This may contribute to the conflicting data on activity level. Similarly, Landers (1977) found that menstrual problems may be age related, although this variable is rarely even reported in research studies. Clearly, such variables are important to control and need to be borne in mind when generalizations are made from research findings.

A major problem in many studies is the lack of an adequate control group. For example, female behavior during the menstrual cycle has been extensively studied but rarely compared to male behavior. Dan (1976) demonstrated that, although females increased their activity preceding ovulation, there were no differences between wives and husbands in overall variability of activities. Similarly, although Dalton (1969) found correlations between premenstrual phase and commission of certain asocial behaviors, such as crimes and suicide, these behaviors were still less common in females than in males.

Design

Related problems in design are the lack of precise objective definitions of the behavior studied, selective perception of raters, and shifting anchor points. This last problem refers to the fact that we often evaluate male and female behavior differently. For example, what is seen as active for a boy may be different from what is seen as active for a girl. This may also depend on the rater (Maccoby & Jacklin, 1974). The use of different definitions of a behavior as a function of the sex of the ratee may also be a function of the sex of the rater. Imprecise measures of behavior may also limit a study's findings. Besides the premenstrual syndrome having various definitions, actual physiological measures of cycle phase have varied enormously from study to study, some relying on self-reports, others relying on varying physiological measurements taken at varying intervals (Parlee, 1973). The fact that the testosterone level has been difficult to measure in males may have contributed to the lack of attention paid to it (Hatton, 1977).

Four of the major research designs used in studying sex differences have serious limitations (see Parlee, 1973, for a more detailed summary):

1. Correlation studies do not demonstrate causation, although they are frequently interpreted that way by unsophisticated readers and, at times, by researchers themselves. Thus, a correlation between anxiety and the premenstrual phase has led many to assume that hormones determine mood in females, although such a relation may be caused by a third variable such as expectation of amount of flow (Paige, 1971). The causation also may occur in the opposite direction. For example, anxiety can bring on menstruation (see Parlee, 1973).

2. Retrospective questionnaires suffer from reliance on an individual's memory. They may also selectively lead the respondent to provide certain information, for example, by asking only about negative mood changes as a function of menstrual phase.

3. Self-reports or observations have serious problems with socially desirable responding. As an example, males may be reluctant to admit mood changes, since they contradict societal sex-role stereotypes. These methods also have a problem with selective perception or selective reporting by the respondent. For example, only negative mood changes may be observed or admitted in females, since that is the cultural and/or the experimental expectation (Ivey & Bardwick, 1968; Koeske & Koeske, 1975; Ruble, 1977).

4. Thematic analysis of unstructured verbal material is also vulnerable to the subjects' socially desirable responding, especially when they know the purpose of the study (for example, Ivey & Bardwick, 1968).

An important problem in all psychological research, especially in this area, is the effect on the results of the experimenter's beliefs. Rosenthal (1966, 1968) has ingeniously demonstrated that in unconscious, nonverbal ways, experimenters can influence the outcome of an experiment to conform to the experimental hypotheses. Thus, in studies in which the experimenter expects to find moods varying with menstrual phase, she or he may indeed find them (Moos et al., 1969; Ivey & Bardwick, 1968). Since most researchers have been male, they unconsciously may have misperceived certain situations with humans and animals to put males in the better light. Reading some of Harlow's (1962) observations of the behavior of monkeys sometimes resembles viewing a soap opera with the females "scheming" and acting "helpless" and the males acting "intelligently" and "strongly."

Using an appropriate baseline, or standard, when measuring sex differences is imperative but not frequently found. Thus, Parlee (1973) argues that an interpretation of a midcycle syndrome of positive traits and behaviors (that is, improved performance and feelings about oneself during the ovulatory period of the menstrual cycle) is as justifiable as a premenstrual syndrome of negative traits (that is, impaired performance and negative moods directly preceding menstruation). Such an interpretation has rarely been offered.

Interpretation

Statistical reporting and analysis are often a function of an experimenter's hypotheses and biases. To illustrate, although Dalton (1969) found that 27% of her female subjects got poorer grades before menstruation than at ovulation, she ignored the 56% who had no changes and the 17% who actually improved.

Another reporting problem arises in reviews such as those by Garai and Scheinfeld (1968) and Maccoby and Jacklin (1974). Although the studies that were reviewed varied greatly in quality, both reviews simply tabulated the results without giving greater emphasis to the better research. Therefore, a finding of a high percentage of studies reporting no difference in an area may be due to there being no difference, or it may be due to a large number of inadequate experiments. More use of the statistical technique of meta-analysis is needed in order to truly integrate the findings in this area. Cooper (1979) conducted a meta-analysis of the conformity research summarized by Maccoby and Jacklin. He reached somewhat different conclusions and also clarified some important issues and interactions.

Stephanie Shields (1975) has documented how interpretation of facts has sometimes determined the facts themselves. When the frontal lobes of the brain were regarded as the main area of intellectual functioning, research studies found men had larger frontal lobes, relative to the parietal lobes, than did women. When parietal lobes were regarded as more important, the findings themselves changed. Men now were "found" to have relatively larger parietal lobes, relative to their frontal lobes, than did women. Today, there is no firm evidence of sex differences in brain structures or proportions.

In examining the studies on male and female behaviors and characteristics, it is important to be aware of the many research problems that can invalidate the results. With these cautions in mind, the current findings will now be examined.

2 | Physical Characteristics

The examination of the differences and similarities between the sexes in the area of physical characteristics requires a clear understanding of some complicated physiological phenomena. How sex is determined needs to be understood, as do the specific areas in which sex differences have been found or suggested: anatomy, physiological processes, physical vulnerability, and activity levels. Since some people cite biology as the ultimate justification for stereotypes such as "Boys will be boys" or "Girls are just naturally more passive than boys," it is necessary for us to understand just what is biologically "given" and how biology and the environment may interact.

SEX AND GENDER

To begin an examination of the physical differences between the sexes, it is important to understand the distinction between sex and

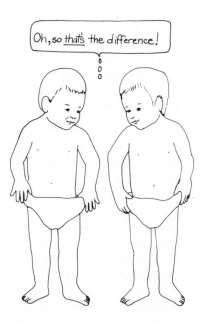

Figure 2-1
The basic sex difference.

gender. *Sex* is a biological term; people are either male or female depending on their sex organs and genes. *Gender* is a psychological and cultural term, referring to one's subjective feelings of maleness or femaleness *(gender identity)*. Gender may also refer to society's evaluation of behavior as masculine or feminine *(gender role)*. It is quite possible to be genetically of one sex with a gender identity of the other. Such may be the case of people born with ambiguous reproductive structures (anatomical *hermaphrodites*) or with other unusual physical conditions. A mismatch between sex and gender identity also occurs in *transsexuals,* who often report feeling "trapped in the wrong body" (Kessler & McKenna, 1978; Stoller, 1968).

This distinction between sex and gender, explored in the research of John Money and others (see Money & Ehrhardt, 1972, for an excellent review), is important precisely because it points out that one's behavior—indeed, one's basic identity as a female or male—is not directly determined by one's genes or hormones; that is, by one's biological sex. Through the study of sexually anomalous individuals (people born with ambiguous sex organs or with organs that do not correspond to their genetic sex), it becomes clear that "the predominant part of gender-identity differentiation receives its program by way of *social transmission* from those responsible for the reconfirmation of the sex of assignment in the daily practices of rearing" (Money & Ehrhardt, 1972, p. 4, italics added). That is, a person's gender identity, for the most part, conforms to the sex according to which the parents rear that person, regardless of the person's genes or hormones or sexual equipment. In fact, some researchers view gender as a completely social construction, independent of objective criteria (see Kessler & McKenna, 1978, for an explanation of this type of analysis).

How sex can be viewed as a social construct will be clearer after examining the variables that determine one's biological sex. For most people, the determination of sex seems strikingly simple and obvious. The *obvious* refers to one's external genitalia. Other criteria are internal genitalia, hormones, and chromosomes. Although these indices are usually in concordance, in some cases they are not. It is these unusual cases, these sexual anomalies, that shed light on the process of sexual differentiation.

Chromosomes

Usually, two X chromosomes produce a female, and an X and a Y chromosome produce a male. This initial sex determination occurs at the moment of conception and remains the only difference between male and female fetuses until the sixth to eighth week after conception. At this time, the internal reproductive organs develop from an undifferentiated state. Generally, if a Y chromosome is present, the gonad (sex gland) of the fetus will develop into a testis; if a Y chromosome is not present, the gonad will develop into an ovary. Thus, the basic course of development is female in the sense that female sex organs will develop unless a Y chromosome is present. This fact has led some writers (for example, Sherfey, 1974) to state that the fundamental form is female; males represent a deviation. To form a male, something must be added: in the fetal stage, a Y chromosome; in the next stage of development, the hormone androgen.

Besides the normal genetic patterns of XY for males and XX for females, anomalies occasionally occur in which individuals are produced with just one X chromosome (XO), three Xs (XXX), an extra Y (XYY or XXY), or other variations. Again, the presence or absence of the Y chromosome determines the development of the sex organs. A person with either an XYY- or an XXY-chromosome pattern will develop a testis, and an XO or an XXX person will develop an ovary.

The influence of genes on behavior is not always clear. The fact that males typically have just one X chromosome makes them susceptible to any recessive X-linked disorder they might have inherited, such as color blindness and hemophilia. Females, having two X chromosomes, are usually protected by the second X chromosome from developing such recessive disorders. Of course, if both X chromosomes carry such an ailment, the female will also manifest the disorder. In other cases, however, the female will merely be a carrier of the disorder. This genetic process has been thought to account partially for males' greater physical vulnerability.

Hormones

Prenatally, hormones have been found to be extremely important in the sexual differentiation of a fetus. After the first six to eight weeks of embryonic development, the internal reproductive organs (testes or ovaries) develop in response to either the presence or absence of the Y chromosome. Once these organs develop, hormone production begins, and further differentiation of the fetus occurs. Figure 2-2 shows the ensuing sexual differentiation.

During the third prenatal month, if the hormone testosterone (one of the androgens) is produced, the male external organs (urethral tube, scrotum, and penis) and the male ducts (seminal vesicles, vas deferens, and ejaculatory ducts) will develop, and the female ducts will regress. If testosterone is not produced, female sex organs (labia minora, labia majora, and clitoris) and female ducts (uterus, fallopian tubes, and upper vagina) will develop, and male ducts will regress. Once again, unless something is added—in this case, the hormone testosterone—female structures will develop. Anatomical development of the female fetus does not seem to require the female hormones (McCoy, 1977). The critical period for this development occurs between the second and third prenatal month.

If hormone production is impaired or hormones are externally administered to the mother during this critical period, an infant with sexual anomalies may develop (Money & Ehrhardt, 1972). Thus if a genetically female fetus is exposed to androgens, structural development will proceed along male lines; that is, male external sex organs will develop. This occurs in the *adrenogenital syndrome,* caused by excessive fetal androgen production signaled by an abnormally functioning adrenocortical gland, and in *progestin-induced hermaphroditism.* This latter disorder arises in some cases in which the mother is given the synthetic hormone progestin early in pregnancy to avert the

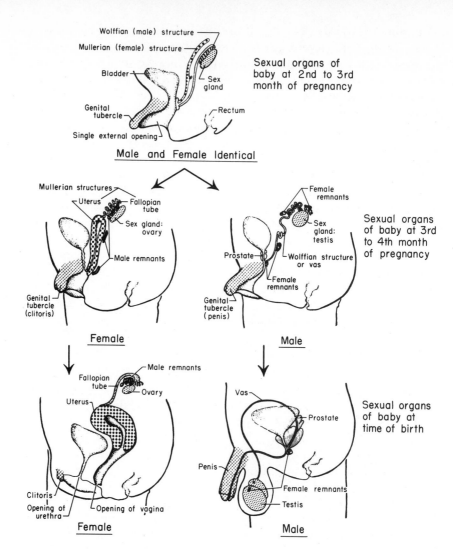

Wolffian (male) structure

Mullerian (female) structure

Bladder

Genital
tubercle

Single external opening

Sex
gland

Rectum

Sexual organs of
baby at 2nd to 3rd
month of pregnancy

Male and Female Identical

Mullerian structures

Uterus — Fallopian
tube

Sex gland:
ovary

Male remnants

Genital
tubercle
(clitoris)

Female

Female
remnants

Sex
gland:
testis

Prostate

Wolffian structure
or vas

Female
remnants

Genital
tubercle
(penis)

Male

Sexual organs
of baby at 3rd
to 4th month
of pregnancy

Male remnants

Fallopian
tube

Uterus

Ovary

Clitoris

Opening of
urethra

Opening of vagina

Female

Vas

Prostate

Penis

Female remnants

Testis

Male

Sexual organs
of baby at
time of birth

Figure 2-2
*Sexual differentiation
in the human fetus.
Note the early
parallelism of sex
organs. From* Man
and Woman, Boy
and Girl, *by J. Money
and A. A. Ehrhardt.
Copyright 1972 by
The Johns Hopkins
University Press.
Reprinted by
permission.*

danger of a miscarriage. Conversely, if a genetically male fetus is deprived of the androgens either through an inherited androgen insensitivity or through a metabolic error, a female system will be produced. From these cases it is clear that genes only predispose, not guarantee, the development of the corresponding reproductive structures.

The effects of prenatal hormones on later behavior is a subject of debate. At this time, it appears that prenatal hormones, by affecting certain areas of the brain, may influence the ease with which certain behaviors are acquired. The behaviors themselves would still be markedly affected by environmental factors (Money, 1978; Reinisch & Karow, 1977).

During the critical period for the differentiation of the external sex organs, another major differentiating development occurs, at least in animals, in response to the presence or absence of testosterone (Money & Ehrhardt, 1972). This differentiation is in the brain, in the area called the *hypothalamus*. This region is located at the base of the brain and controls the release of hormones at puberty by the attached pituitary gland. When testosterone is present during this prenatal period, the pituitary will function at puberty to cause a regular production of androgens and sperm. The presence of testosterone causes the pituitary gland to function at puberty with low levels of continuous hormone release. When testosterone is absent during the prenatal period, the pituitary will function at puberty to cause high levels of cyclical hormonal activity, which result in ovulation and menstruation. These differences in pattern of hormone production do not appear until the full functioning of the pituitary gland at puberty, yet the patterns seem to be set during the second to third month of gestation. The effect on performance and emotions of such differences in hormonal patterns is negligible in most cases and unclear in others (see "Physiological Processes" below). Again, hormonal errors during this critical period of gestation will affect pituitary functioning at puberty unless corrective hormones are administered after birth. It must be emphasized, however, that most of the evidence for brain differentiation is based on work with animals. Such differentiation in humans remains speculative at this time.

According to the above information, after eight weeks male and female fetuses can be differentiated by hormonal production. After birth, however, and until the child is about eight years old, hormonal production is negligible. Hormones, therefore, do not differentiate the sexes during this period. At puberty there is an increased production of all sex hormones in both sexes. Males generally have a greater increase in androgen production than do females, and the production of androgens becomes fairly regular and continuous. Females generally have a greater increase in estrogen and progesterone production at this time than do males, and this production becomes cyclic (the menstrual cycle). Hormones at this time result in the development of the secondary sex characteristics, such as facial and ancillary hair, enlarged genitals, and deeper voice in males, and development of breasts and menstruation in females.

It is important to note that these hormone differences are not absolute. Both sexes have all the hormones, and, like most other attributes related to human functioning, individuals differ greatly in the relative amounts and proportion of the sex hormones they possess. An overlapping normal curve distribution for all hormones demonstrates that some genetic females may have more androgen than some genetic males, at least some of the time. The 1968 International Olympic Committee ignored this fact when it decreed that all females must pass a "femininity test" consisting of chromosome analysis. The validity of the test relies on the premise that a genetic male has larger amounts of the hormone testosterone, which seems to be related to greater strength and muscle mass, than does a genetic female. But we have just seen that this premise is not always valid. Distinctions between the sexes based on hormonal production are proportional, not absolute (Goy, 1970; Money & Ehrhardt, 1972).

Genitalia—Internal and External

The external sex organs are the primary means by which sex is determined at birth. Males have an external penis and scrotum; females, a clitoris and vagina. Until the second to third month of pregnancy, however, the external genitalia, as well as the internal reproductive organs and tracts, are in an undifferentiated or *bipotential* (either sex) state (see Figure 2-2). Differentiation begins during the second to third month as a result of the presence or absence of the Y chromosome, which determines the internal organ development. Differentiation then proceeds during the third month as a function of the presence or absence of the hormone testosterone, which determines the external organ development. At each stage, development can go either way—toward the male form or toward the female form. That is, development is bipotential.

This bipotentiality continues at birth. With the doctor's pronouncement, based on external genitalia, that the infant is a boy or a girl, two different patterns of infant-adult interactions begin. These differentiating behaviors can be observed in the giving of blue or pink blankets, in the naming and handling of the infant, and in verbalizations to the infant. Again, it is the sexually anomalous individual who sheds light on the development of gender identity. Studies of hermaphrodites, pseudo-hermaphrodites (those born with external genitalia of the other sex), and children who suffered from surgical accidents that affected their genitals (for example, damage to the penis during circumcision) vividly demonstrate that the single most important variable in the development of gender identity is the sex of assignment; that is, the sex one's parents raise one to be (Money & Ehrhardt, 1972). This influence can override other influences of genes, hormones, and external organs and demonstrates very fundamentally how plastic and malleable is human behavior.

A striking example of the bipotentiality of the human infant is the case of identical twin boys, one whose penis was severely injured by an electrical needle during circumcision (Money & Ehrhardt, 1972). Rather than attempt reconstructive surgery, which would have been complicated and time consuming and would have had a low probability of success, the doctors recommended that the boy be given an artificial vagina, which was a simpler operation, and be raised as a girl. The parents agreed, and follow-up studies at ages 5–6 showed the two children to be clearly differentiated in terms of activities, toy preferences, and mannerisms as a result of different child-rearing practices. In fact, these children were more clearly differentiable than are most girls and boys. So much for the determinative influence of genes and prenatal hormones on behavior.

As for other stages of development, there is a critical period for the postnatal development of gender identity—up to 18 months or the time the child acquires language (Money & Ehrhardt, 1972). This identity becomes consolidated by ages 3 to 4, depending on the consistency of child-rearing experiences. Any attempt to change sex assignment after a child has acquired language is usually unsuccessful and may lead to later emotional problems. It is interesting, in this regard, that transsexuals do not seem to have formed a gender identity of their biological sex at this stage. Whether this deficit is due to parental upbringing, to other external factors, or possibly to a prenatally determined predisposition is unclear at this time (Bardwick, 1971; Finney, Brandsma, Tondoro, & Lemaistre, 1975; Money & Ehrhardt, 1972).

Having detailed the differentiation of sex in a fetus and in an infant and examined some problems that may arise, it remains to be emphasized that for the vast majority of infants all physiological sex characteristics are in agreement. That is, most babies with female external genitalia also have female internal genitalia, have an XX chromosome pattern, and will produce a preponderance of female sex hormones at puberty. Of these indicators, the external genitalia are the most important since they determine the sex of assignment. It is the sex of assignment that has been found critical in determining an individual's gender identity.

The research in this area has two major implications. The first is that the nature/nurture question is moot in the area of gender development as well as in virtually all aspects of human functioning. What is in question is the relative weights of the experiential and physiological influences. Money's studies (1963, 1972; Money & Ehrhardt, 1972) demonstrate that postnatal experiential factors can override prenatal, physiological ones.

The second implication is that human beings are bipotential in their psychosexual identity and behavior at each stage of development. Which path (male or female) is followed at each stage depends on both the internal and external environment. A fetus can develop male or female gonads, depending on its chromosomes; male or female external genitalia and possibly brain (hypothalamic) differentiation, depending on its hormones; and a male or female gender identity, depending on sex of assignment. There is a critical period for each stage of development to occur, after which the male or female path is relatively fixed. The sex of the infant is fixed by birth; its gender, by 18 months.

PHYSICAL FUNCTIONING

Physical differences do exist between the sexes, although their implication for behavior is unclear. First let us examine the actual findings. We will look specifically at anatomy, physiological processes, brain organization, physical vulnerability, and activity levels. It is important to remember the tremendous amount of overlap in virtually all human traits and characteristics.

Anatomy

Clearly, the most basic difference between the sexes at birth lies in their external genitalia. These organs usually determine the sex of assignment, and some writers, especially Freud, think they determine the personality structure of the child as well ("anatomy is destiny";

see Chapter Five). Although the possibility of getting pregnant, as opposed to impregnating, probably has meaningful consequences for one's personality, these consequences will surely vary with the individual, the family, the culture, and other external forces to such a degree that a mere deterministic explanation is simply untenable.

The sexes also typically differ in size and weight at birth, males generally being slightly larger (Tanner, 1972). Females have a wider pelvic outlet and tend to have a greater body fat-to-muscle ratio than do boys at all ages (Barfield, 1976; Hatton, 1977). These differences all increase significantly during and after puberty and contribute to males' generally having more strength, more ease in running and overarm throwing, and poorer ability to float and withstand cold. These are average differences, of course, and may also be a function of athletic training (C. H. Brown, 1977). The army found in 1977 that, when 825 women were given regular basic training and compared to men, there was little difference in relative performance (WEAL, 1977). Another example of the effect of training is the fact that, in the 1979 New York Marathon, the time of the female winner, Grete Waitz, although 16 minutes slower than that of the male winner, was better than that of any of the men who ran in the 1970 race.

These relative differences in size and strength may have accounted for certain sex-role distinctions in the past, such as certain forms of hunting that required strength, but they certainly have little importance in our modern technological society. Most work that formerly required brute strength is now performed with the aid of equipment, levers, and push buttons.

Physiological Processes

Generally, females mature faster than males. This difference can be observed as early as the seventh week of embryonic life and continues through puberty. For example, girls generally reach puberty two years earlier than do boys (Barfield, 1976; McCoy, 1977). Girls also tend to have a slightly lower metabolic rate and consume fewer calories than do boys. Males generally tend to endure physical exertion better than females, but this ability is also a function of amount of exercise (Barfield, 1976; Hatton, 1977).

There do not seem to be major differences in sensation, although females may have a slight edge in sensitivity to touch and pain (Barfield, 1976; McGuinness & Pribram, 1978; Maccoby & Jacklin, 1974). The research on smell and taste is unclear. Levels of estrogen have been found to relate to the ability to detect and differentiate smells. Some females evidence superior smell acuity after puberty, which may vary with menstrual cycle phase (Hatton, 1977; Maccoby & Jacklin, 1974; Reinisch, Gandelman, & Spiegel, 1979). Most research finds no differences in vision or audition (Maccoby & Jacklin, 1974), although recent work with electrical potentials in the brain suggests that women may be more sensitive to visual stimuli (Goleman, 1978).

One major process in which the sexes do differ is in hormonal functioning and production after puberty. Differences occur in actual hormone levels, in the pattern of secretion, in the sensitivity to particular hormones, and in the sources of hormone production (gonads or adrenals). Males tend to have continuous androgen secretion; females have cyclical hormonal fluctuations as part of the menstrual cycle. The different patterns of hormonal production represent reproductive fertility for the adolescent and result in the development of secondary sex characteristics (for example, facial hair in males, breast development in females).

Menstrual Cycle. The menstrual cycle has been the focus of much research and will consequently be described in some detail. The beginning of the cycle, which averages 28 days but which may range from 20 to 35 days, is usually set at the day menstruation begins. From that time, estrogen production increases to a high point around the 12th day. During this first part of the cycle, the lining of the uterus thickens to prepare it to receive the fertilized egg. On the basis of a 28-day cycle, an egg is released from an ovary around the 14th day and travels down a fallopian tube to the uterus. During its transit, if the egg encounters a sperm, it will most likely become fertilized. The fertilized egg will then become embedded in the thickened lining of the uterus. If fertilization does not occur, estrogen production decreases, and production of progesterone increases. Both hormones drop precipitously a few days before actual menstruation (the shedding of the uterine lining) begins. A new cycle then starts. Figure 2-3 charts the hormonal changes for one average 28-day cycle.

These hormonal changes that occur during the menstrual cycle may be related to some physical changes, but there are large individual differences in this area (Barfield, 1976; Dan, 1979; Landers, 1977). Most common are reports of fluid retention and slight weight gain premenstrually and increased basal temperature and smell acuity around ovulation (Barfield, 1976; Dan, 1979; Hatton, 1977). Diane

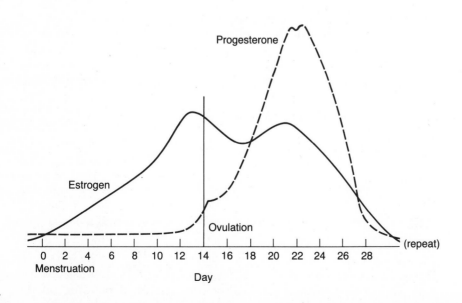

Figure 2-3
*Hormone levels
during the menstrual
cycle (28 days).*

Ruble (1977) has found, however, that even physical-symptom reports can be heavily affected by psychosocial factors. She found that,
by misleading college undergraduates as to their actual cycle phase,
she could obtain reports of severe physical symptoms, such as water
retention and pain, if the subjects believed they were premenstrual,
even though they were not really in that phase. Thus, learned associa-
tions or beliefs could lead a woman to exaggerate or overstate a
feeling. Such results must temper any conclusions based on self-
report data regarding the magnitude of menstrual-related changes as
well as the physiological bases of such changes.

Much attention has been paid to the psychological changes, especially of mood, thought to be associated with the menstrual cycle.
Although most of the research in this area has serious deficiencies in
design or interpretation (see Parlee, 1973, and "Research Problems"
in the introduction to Part Two), some general conclusions can be
drawn. Some females do experience an increase in anxiety premenstrually (Dalton, 1969; Golub, 1976; Ivey & Bardwick, 1968), although
such anxiety seems related more to the amount of the anticipated
flow than to the hormone levels themselves (Paige, 1971). Some
females do experience an increase in hostility levels premenstrually
that may be related to the amount of a certain chemical, monoamine
oxidase (MAO), in the blood (Paige, 1971). (MAO increases with progesterone levels and has been implicated in certain affective disorders.) Other personality changes that occur during the cycle appear
to be exaggerations of existing traits and may occur at any time of the
month, not just premenstrually (Landers, 1977). Indeed, the only general statement that can be made is that all females do not show
similar changes with reference to their menstrual cycle; rather, they
show only those consistent with the individual's own behavior pattern (see also Moos, Kopell, Melges, Yalom, Lunde, Clayton, & Hamburg, 1969).

More to the point, the variability of moods in females has not
been found significantly different from the variability of moods in
males matched for life-styles. Dan (1976) found that, when husbands
and wives kept track of their daily moods over a period of months,
there were no significant differences in moods between spouses. This
occurred despite the fact that the wives were experiencing hormonal
changes related to their menstrual cycle. Indeed, environmental
events and social variables have been found to account for more of the
variance in mood than does cycle point (Landers, 1977; Paige, 1973;
Ruble, 1977).

Despite the above facts, both men and women do believe that
negative moods are related to the premenstrual phase and attribute
and interpret such moods accordingly (Clarke & Ruble, 1978; Koeske
& Koeske, 1975). This expectation may become a self-fulfilling
prophecy, either creating the moods themselves or causing them to be
more noticed. Positive moods, because they are not expected, may
pass unnoticed, thereby preventing disproof of the belief. The existence of a premenstrual syndrome (variously defined to include such
things as cramps, mood swings, irritability, and/or depression) has
been reported in as few as 15% of the studies, depending on the

definition and measurement techniques utilized (Paige, 1973). With such a range of findings, the existence of such a syndrome is questionable and certainly not predictable. Neither are the effects of hormones during menopause, pregnancy, and the postpartum period any clearer or more predictable. Again, individual differences and the importance of social factors inveigh against any clear, simple linkage between hormones and moods or behavior (Bart, 1972; Melges, 1968; Treadway et al., 1969).

Another example of this complicated relationship is the finding that women's sexual desires appear to peak around ovulation for all but two groups of women: those taking oral contraceptives, suggesting a hormonal link, and those using the rhythm method of birth control, suggesting a psychological factor (Adams, Gold, & Burt, 1978).

The interest in the hormonal cycle and its correlates in females has obscured the fact that cycles are a part of all living things (Hatton, 1977; Luce, 1971). It would therefore be surprising if males were somehow immune to this basic biological process. This neglect of males is evidence of how societal stereotypes (males are "unemotional" and "rock-steady") may affect the questions researchers ask. Since males have no external indication of cycles like menstruation, such questions have been easy to ignore. Those few studies that have examined this area have indicated that male behavioral and mood variability does exist, but its determinants and pattern are unclear (Dan, 1976; Doering, Brodie, Kramer, Becker, & Hamburg, 1974; Petersen, 1979; Ramey, 1972, 1973). Testosterone levels, correlated with aggression in some animals, do not have a clear causative effect and, in some cases, may be a result of aggressive behavior (Rose, Gordon, & Bernstein, 1972; Rose, Holaday, & Bernstein, 1971). In humans, the findings regarding the effects of hormones on males have been mixed (Doering et al., 1974; Persky, Smith, & Basu, 1971; Ramey, 1973). The clearest statement that currently can be made is that further study is needed.

Androgens have been associated with increased libido, or sexual desire, and increased erotic reactivity, but this is true for both females and males (Money, 1963; Money & Ehrhardt, 1972; Rosenberg & Sutton-Smith, 1972) and is not a consistent finding even in animals (M. Rosenberg, 1973). To the extent that males, on the average, have larger amounts of androgen than females, some may argue that the male sex drive is greater. As will be discussed in Chapter Five, human sexuality is so much a function of learning and of social forces that a simple, biologically deterministic approach would be completely inappropriate. In addition, it is worthwhile to repeat that individuals differ in androgen levels and the distributions for females and males overlap.

Brain Organization

Since 1974, research has accumulated suggesting that men's brains may be organized differently from women's for certain tasks and activities. It had previously been suggested that each side of the brain was specialized and functioned differently. Language and language-related skills were thought of as being contained in the left hemisphere; nonverbal and spatial skills, in the right hemisphere. More recent research suggests that although this may be true for right-handed men, it does not seem true for left-handed individuals or for most women (Bryden, 1979; Goleman, 1978; Kupke, Lewis, & Rennick, 1979; McGlone, 1978). Females' brains appear to be less specialized than males' brains, at least on verbal and spatial tasks. That is, for most females, performance of verbal and spatial tasks seems to involve *both* hemispheres. Females may therefore have greater flexibility between hemispheres (Jorgenson, Davis, Opella, & Angerstein, 1979; Witelson, 1976). Females' brains may also become selectively more activated than do those of males while performing certain skills. These findings suggest that women do not perform two cognitively different tasks at the same time as well as men do. They may, however, be better cognitive specialists, performing one task with more focused attention (Goleman, 1978; Witelson, 1976).

These differences in brain organization may be genetic, or they may be influenced by different sex hormones (Bryden, 1979; Carter & Greenough, 1979; Goleman, 1978; McGuinness & Pribram, 1978). Even if such differences are somehow inherent from birth, differential treatment still will affect drastically how each sex develops. In particular, socialization appears to influence the type of cognitive strategies each sex develops. These strategies may then interact with cerebral organization (Bryden, 1979).

The evidence in this area is still tentative and may prove artifactual. Furthermore, the implications of the findings are unclear. Differences in brain organization may contribute to differences in verbal, mathematical, and visual-spatial skills, which are discussed in the next chapter. However, it should be kept in mind that all such differences are average differences, not absolute ones.

Physical Vulnerability

Another physical area that has been thought to differentiate the sexes is physical vulnerability. At every stage of life, males are more vulnerable than are females to disease, physical disorders, and death (Barfield, 1976; J. Harrison, 1978). The life span of females is nearly universally longer than that of males. In the United States in 1977, the average female life span was 77.2 years; the average male life span, 69.3 years (U.S. Bureau of the Census, 1979). In 1900, the average life span for women and men was 48.3 and 46.3 years, respectively. Although the X and Y sperm appear to be produced in equal numbers, between 108 and 140 males are conceived for every 100 females. At birth, the ratio of males to females in the United States is reduced to between 103 and 106 to 100. In India the ratio is 98 males to 100 females. This lower birth rate of males is accounted for by the fact that four times as many males as females are miscarried or stillborn and that 54% more males than females die of birth injury. Of those born, 18% more male infants have congenital malformations than do female infants. By ages 20 to 25, females outnumber males (Hatton, 1977).

Males are also more vulnerable than females to a wide range of physical handicaps that are genetically linked. As was previously discussed, because males have one X chromosome, if that chromosome carries genes related to any one of a possible 62 specific recessive disorders, ranging from hemophilia to color blindness, males will manifest it. Females, with a second X chromosome to balance out the abnormal one, would not develop the disorder. Males are also more susceptible to degenerative and infectious diseases and to death from them. During the first year of life, one-third more males die, primarily from infectious diseases, than do females (Barfield, 1976).

Males also show a greater incidence than females of a wide range of developmental problems, ranging from enuresis to minimal brain damage and autism. Stuttering is two to ten times as common among males; reading disabilities are four to six times as common, depending on how *disability* is defined, to cite two examples (Harris, 1977; Maccoby & Jacklin, 1974).

In examining the major causes of death in 1972, Harrison (1978) found that in four of the five major causes—the four being diseases of the heart, malignant neoplasms, accidents, and influenza and pneumonia—the death rate for males exceeded the death rate for females. Only in deaths from cerebrovascular diseases (the third most frequent cause) did the rate of female deaths exceed that of males. The 1975 data presented in Table 2-1 show an identical pattern. In addition, certain other causes of death show a strikingly high male-to-female death ratio: homicide caused the death of more than four times more males than females; bronchitis, emphysema, and asthma killed more than three times more males; suicide resulted in the death of more than two and a half times more males; and cirrhosis of the liver took twice as many males. Even the injury rate for males is 44% higher than the rate for females (*Stars & Stripes*, March 25, 1976).

This greater physical vulnerability of males goes against one of our most basic stereotypes—that of the strong male and weak female. Perhaps the stereotype needs to be restricted to muscular strength, although muscle strength is distributed normally in the population, indicating that some females are stronger than some males. Perhaps the stereotype refers to the greater strength surviving males must have over their less fortunate brothers. Or perhaps the stereotype of strength is a cognitive defense against this very vulnerability.

It is important to examine possible explanations for this difference in physical vulnerability. It has been suggested that, because the basic fetus is female and something—chromosome and gonadal hormones—must be added to make the fetus male, more can go wrong with the developing male embryo (Barfield, 1976; Money & Ehrhardt, 1972; Oakley, 1972; Reinisch et al., 1979). Other evidence suggests that female hormones may be protective. Risk of heart disease, for example, increases in females as estrogen decreases (Barfield, 1976); progesterone has anticonvulsive properties (Oakley, 1972). It may be

Table 2-1
Major Causes of Death (1975 data)

	Percentage of All Deaths	Ratio of Males to Females
Diseases of the heart	37.8	1.33
Malignant neoplasms	19.3	1.26
Cerebrovascular diseases	10.2	0.81
Accidents	5.4	2.49
Influenza and pneumonia	2.9	1.27
Diabetes mellitus	1.8	0.73
Cirrhosis of the liver	1.7	2.03
Arteriosclerosis	1.5	0.73
Bronchitis, emphysema, and asthma	1.4	3.36
Certain causes in infancy	1.4	1.44
Suicide	1.4	2.78
Homicide	1.1	4.26

From data in *Vital Statistics of the U.S. 1975* (Vol. 2). U.S. Dept. of Health, Education and Welfare. Washington, D.C.: U.S. Government Printing Office, 1977.

that ability to withstand infection is transmitted via the X chromosome or that females' lower metabolic rate contributes to their superior capacity for survival (Hatton, 1977; McCoy, 1977; Oakley, 1972).

Another possible explanation for superior female survival is that males may be more active, more subject to stress, and therefore more likely to have accidents, to be exposed to germs, to die of stress-related diseases, and to be victims of war. We shall see in the next section that the research on exploratory behavior does not support the explanation that boys are more active than girls simply because of biology. Nonetheless, it is true that male children are usually allowed more freedom of movement than are females and are often encouraged to take risks and be more aggressive, thereby increasing their exposure to accidents and illnesses.

Harrison (1978) and others (especially Jourard, 1971) have asserted that it is the male sex role itself that is dangerous to men's health. The emphasis on conformity to the male role and on achievement may give rise to anxiety about failing. This anxiety may lead to the development of certain compensatory behaviors that are health hazardous. Examples include taking risks, exhibitions of violence, smoking, and excessive consumption of alcohol. Other aspects of the male role encourage the development of aggressive, competitive behaviors, also known as Type A, or coronary-prone behaviors. Additional stress occurs because males are expected not to show their emotions and therefore must suppress most feelings. All of these patterns would lead to the major causes of death listed in Table 2-1. In fact, Waldron (1976) has estimated that three-quarters of the difference in life expectancy between males and females (currently about 8 years) can be attributed to sex-role related behaviors. One-third to one-half of the difference is due to smoking alone.

Thus we see an example of the negative effects of our socialization practices on males. Indeed, as females begin to experience many of the same stresses and behaviors that males do, like smoking, their susceptibility to stress-related diseases also increases (Barfield, 1976; Horn, 1975; Waldron, 1976). As an example, 15% of both teenage girls and boys now smoke, and in the last three decades deaths from lung cancer among women have increased fourfold because women have taken up the smoking habits of men (Brody, 1979).

Yet, across a variety of cultures with different stresses, males still seem to die earlier and have a greater incidence of chromosomal abnormalities than do females (Fitzgerald, 1977). It seems likely that a biological predisposition interacts with social factors in unclear ways to make males more physically vulnerable.

Activity Levels

Studies investigating the amount of activity shown by male and female infants have been plagued by methodological problems, an example being the definition and measurement of activity, and thus have produced inconsistent results (Maccoby & Jacklin, 1974; McCoy, 1977). Generally, females and males during infancy evidence equal amounts of total activity; but males show more large body movements, and females show more refined and limited movements. This difference in type of movement may be due to the differing rates of maturation of females and males.

Male infants tend to be more fretful and wakeful than females. Although in some cases this tendency may be a result of more male birth problems or the effects of circumcision (Barfield, 1976; Maccoby & Jacklin, 1974; Unger & Denmark, 1975), a recent well-controlled study by Phillips, King, and DuBois (1978) found a similar disparity between female and male fretfulness. During the two days following birth, 14 uncircumcised males and 15 females matched for physical and demographic variables were observed, and males evidenced significantly higher levels of wakefulness, facial grimacing, and low-intensity motor activity (hand and foot movements) than did females. This difference in fretfulness has implications for parent/infant interactions, since an infant's irritability may lead to decreased parental contact (R. Q. A. Bell, 1968; Lewis & Weinraub, 1979; Mitchell, 1968; Segal & Yahraes, 1978). Research on parent/infant interaction is unclear, but it does suggest another way biology and culture may interact.

As children and adolescents, males tend to be slightly more active than females in regard to participation in rough-and-tumble play and physical exertion (Maccoby & Jacklin, 1974; Tauber, 1979). This is true of other primates as well (Harlow, 1962, 1965). Females are also active but in different activities—for example, playing house and hopscotch—thus making a quantitative distinction difficult (Fitzgerald, 1977). Such differences may be a function more of socialization than of hormones.

Some writers suggest that androgen may be involved in activity levels. This involvement is indicated by the increased display of tomboy behavior (more physical activity) in females who experienced prenatal androgen produced either internally, as in the adrenogenital syndrome, or externally, as when the mother is given progestin to avoid a miscarriage (Money & Ehrhardt, 1972). Since masculinization of the genitals also occurs in some of these cases, it is possible that the parents of these children may have expected more such behaviors in these girls, thereby subtly reinforcing them. Additionally, since most females engage in tomboy behaviors (current estimates range from 51% to 78%, according to Hyde, Rosenberg, & Behrman, 1977), the use of this index to define a "masculine" activity pattern is highly questionable. However, a recent follow-up study of children between the ages of 8 and 14 whose mothers had received estrogen and progesterone during pregnancy has lent further support to the hypothesis that prenatal hormones may affect a child's activity level. Dr. Anke Ehrhardt (1979) found that the prenatally exposed children displayed less rough-and-tumble play than children who had not been exposed to such hormones. Dr. Ehrhardt cautions, however, that the way a child is reared is still more important than any hormonal effects.

SUMMARY

The physical underpinnings of sex-role stereotypes are complex. We have seen that even sex differentiation is not simple. It occurs in stages, first influenced by chromosomes, then by hormones prenatally, then by genitalia and socialization postnatally. At each stage, the developing fetus is bipotential; that is, it can develop along either female or male lines. The most critical factor in gender identity (one's concept of oneself as a male or a female) is culture, which can override the biological factors, as demonstrated in cases of sexual anomalies. We need not argue about nature or nurture. It is quite clear that an interaction occurs, with nature predisposing and nurture either reinforcing or contradicting that predisposition.

This interaction is true in the areas of physical functioning as well. Although, on the average, males tend to be bigger and stronger than females, nutrition and athletic training can decrease the gap. In physiological processes, females tend to mature faster and are slightly more sensitive to touch and maybe to smell than males, and they have cyclical hormonal fluctuations after puberty. The consequences of these differences are dependent on socialization and societal expectations, as depicted clearly in the research on menstrual cycle and the lack of research on male cycles. Particular mental functions may be organized more specifically in male brains than in female brains. Males tend to be more physically vulnerable to disease, death, and physical disorders than females, although these differences can also be affected by the environment. Differences in activity levels may exist after the second year of life, but this, too, depends on the environment and the researcher's definition of activity.

In summary, the only "basic irreducible elements of sex differences which no culture can eradicate, at least not on a large scale, [are that] women can menstruate, gestate and lactate, and men cannot" (Money & Ehrhardt, 1972, p. 14).

RECOMMENDED READING

Goleman, D. Special abilities of the sexes: Do they begin in the brain? *Psychology Today*, 1978, *12*(6), 48–59 *ff*. An excellent summary of recent research on sex differences in brain functioning.

Harrison, J. Male sex role and health. *Journal of Social Issues*, 1978, *34*(1), 65–86. A persuasive argument describing how the male sex role is hazardous to men's health.

Money, J., & Ehrhardt, A. A. *Man & woman, Boy & girl*. Baltimore: Johns Hopkins University Press, 1972. A fascinating, albeit technically written, book of how one's sexual identity develops.

Parlee, M. B. The premenstrual syndrome. *Psychological Bulletin*, 1973, *80*, 454–465. A thorough critique of research in the area.

3

Cognitive Abilities

- Boys are smarter than girls.
- Girls can't do math.
- Boys are more analytical than girls.
- Girls are better at simple repetitive tasks, like filing; boys, at 'higher level' tasks, like making decisions.

These misconceptions of the cognitive abilities (the thinking and reasoning powers) of the sexes are widely held in our culture (see also Figure 3-1). Despite the popularity of such misconceptions, however, research has provided little support for these hypothesized sex differences. In fact, few clear-cut differences between the sexes have been found in any cognitive behavior.

This chapter will examine the current status of the research in this area. First, we will review the findings, and then we will examine alternative explanations of these findings.

CURRENT FINDINGS

Comparisons of male and female performance have been made in the areas of learning and memory, intellectual abilities, cognitive strategies, and creativity. We will examine each area in turn.

Learning and Memory

One common belief is that girls learn best by simple memorization or association (that is, by rote), and boys by some advanced form of reasoning. Maccoby and Jacklin (1974), in their comprehensive review of more than 2000 books and articles, concluded that, in the area of learning and memory, there is no sex difference. Both boys and girls are equally capable of responses calling for inhibition of various responses, such as saying the word "red" when the letters b-l-u-e are written in red ink and the instructions require naming the color, and both are equally proficient in simple repetitive tasks. McGuinness and Pribram (1978), after a similar review of the current literature, conclude that women process information faster than men, particularly in tasks, like neurosurgery, that require rapid choices. That one

Figure 3-1
Stereotyped picture of a cognitive sex difference, from a pencil package. (Courtesy of Reliance Pen & Pencil Corp.)

sex finds some things easier to learn than does the other sex is a difference that relates to familiarity and interest, not to ability.

Intellectual Abilities

Are boys smarter than girls? According to the research, the answer is no. There are no known differences between males and females in overall intelligence after age 6, an unsurprising finding, since IQ tests were specifically designed to eliminate sex differences (Maccoby & Jacklin, 1974; Stewart, 1976). That is, test items were selected that specifically did not show differential responding by males and females, because it was assumed there were no sex differences in intelligence. There are differences in intellectual performance as a function of sex-role conformity, however. Nonconformity to sex-role stereotypes is positively related to IQ scores (Maccoby, 1966). Thus, the more assertive and active the female, the greater her intellectual abilities and interests; the less active and aggressive the male, the less developed his physique and the greater his intellectual abilities and interests. Here is a possible example of how conformity to sex-role stereotypes may limit one's capabilities.

In studies of specific abilities, only three differences appear fairly consistently: girls excel in verbal skills, and boys excel in quantitative and visual-spatial skills. Even these differences are small, however, and do not show up until after age 8 (Maccoby & Jacklin, 1974; McGuinness & Pribram, 1978). No differences have been found in concept mastery or reasoning abilities. Unfortunately, the literature abounds with studies of the differences, not the similarities, so that a reader gets the impression that these differences are large and very important.

Verbal Skills. Clearly, verbal skills are salient in our society, but, since there is considerable overlap in verbal performance between the sexes and since studies are sometimes contradictory, one wonders why only the differences are stressed. Research on ways to close the gap is also underrepresented.

Overall, females have been found to excel in a wide variety of verbal abilities (L. J. Harris, 1977; Maccoby & Jacklin, 1974; McGuinness & Pribram, 1978). They acquire language earlier than boys, as measured by acquisition of phonemes, amount of vocalization in infancy, age of use of first word, vocabulary size, articulation, comprehensibility, and fluency. From age 3 to about age 11, sex differences are minimal. After that time, including old age (Cohen & Wilkie, 1979), females again excel in grammar, spelling, word fluency, comprehension, and production, although, again, the size of the difference is small. The exception to this pattern of fluctuating female superiority is the population of underprivileged children, where females maintain their advantage throughout childhood. This female advantage in underprivileged groups may result from the exaggeration of males' general physical vulnerability through poor nutrition and medical care. For boys, the frequency of reading problems and speech difficulties is greater than for girls throughout the school years, although this may be due more to emotional-behavioral problems than to verbal ones.

One might expect, given that females as a group have higher verbal abilities than do males, that more women than men would be employed in language-related occupations, such as writing and publishing. That this is not the case demonstrates how elements other than ability, such as social and political factors, play a major role in people's vocational choices.

Quantitative Abilities. In the area of quantitative abilities, there are few sex differences in mathematical achievement until about the seventh grade (ages 11–13) except among underprivileged children, where girls are superior (Fox, Tobin, & Brody, 1979; Hilton & Berglund, 1974; Kreinberg, 1976; Maccoby & Jacklin, 1974). After that age, males generally move ahead, although there is wide variation, and differences in achievement are very small (Fennema & Sherman, 1976; Stewart, 1976; Wise, 1978). Differences in math-related behavior are clearer, however. Most girls stop taking mathematics as soon as it becomes optional in high school (Fennema & Sherman, 1977; Kreinberg, 1976), and their scores on the mathematical portion of the Scholastic Aptitude Test are consistently lower. (In 1974, girls scored 46 points lower than boys on the 600-point scale; *U.S. News & World Report*, October 20, 1975, p. 54.) In a study of freshmen at one of the top universities of the country, the University of California at Berkeley, Sells (1973) found that only 8% of the women, as compared to 54% of the men, had taken four years of high school math. Yet Wise (1978), in a longitudinal study, found that high-school-math achievement played a significant role in the development of math-related careers over the entire period from high school to age 29. Many women, thus, are effectively shut out of many possible careers.

It is interesting to note, however, that, although mathematical competence has been viewed as essential not only for obtaining "good" jobs but also for full participation in our society by all citizens, little research or programmatic work has been done to increase the mathematical competence of those with deficiencies, mostly females. In contrast, millions of dollars have been spent on remedial reading programs for those deficient in reading, mostly male. Such are the ways of a "nonconscious ideology" of sex discrimination (Bem & Bem, 1970).

Visual-Spatial Abilities.   In the area of visual-spatial abilities, males excel after age 8 and maintain their advantage through old age (Cohen & Wilkie, 1979; Keogh, 1971; Maccoby & Jacklin, 1974; McGuinness & Pribram, 1978; Petersen, 1976). These abilities refer to the visual perception of objects or figures in space and the way they are related to each other. Such perception usually requires some mental transformation of the object, as in disembedding a visual figure from its context (Embedded Figure Test) or in solving mazes. The Rod-and-Frame Test (see Figure 3-2) also taps this ability, sometimes referred to as *field dependence* or *field independence* (Witkin, Dyk, Faterson, Goodenough, & Karp, 1962).

In the Rod-and-Frame Test, the subject must adjust a luminous rod inside a luminous frame to the true vertical. Both the frame and the rod are tilted, and, since the room is darkened, the subject has few

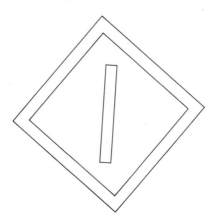

Figure 3-2
*The Rod-and-Frame
Test used to measure
field dependence and
field independence.
The center rod must
be aligned to the true
vertical despite the tilt
of the frame.*

cues with which to align the rod. Those who are accurate in their judgment of the true vertical are termed field independent; those who are inaccurate are termed field dependent (theoretically, they are assumed to be influenced by the frame or "field"). In general, females tend to be field dependent; males, field independent (Witkin et al., 1962). More recent work casts doubt on this simple distinction. Furthermore, the terms *dependent* and *independent* suggest the possibility of interpretive bias.

Field independence, since it involves responding to a stimulus without being distracted by its context, actually refers to more than visual-spatial ability. It is the same ability used in selective listening, such as listening to one voice in a noisy room, and in tactual discrimination, such as feeling a certain pattern amidst many others. This qualification has frequently been overlooked, however, and many researchers glibly equate visual-spatial ability with field independence, and field independence with general analytic ability. Thus, one hears that males are more "analytic" and females more "global" in their reactions to a variety of problems.

Analytic Ability. In research focusing directly on analytic ability, the findings have been quite complex and confusing. In one controversial study, Broverman and associates (1968) argued that females perform better on simple, overlearned perceptual-motor tasks that involve little thinking, whereas males perform better on tasks requiring inhibition or perceptual restructuring—a "higher" cognitive process. Following this argument, some might conclude that women are more suitable for typing and filing and men for managing businesses. The Broverman group also attributed these differences in cognitive processing to hormonal differences.

Numerous critics have attacked the assertions made by Broverman and colleagues (Dan, 1979; Maccoby & Jacklin, 1974; Parlee, 1972; Unger & Denmark, 1975). Among the many problems found in the work of the Broverman group are the following: the group selected and interpreted only those studies that conformed to their hypothesis, ignored the tremendous amount of overlap in male and female performance, and confused analytic functioning with a basically perceptual phenomenon—visual-spatial ability. As Julia Sherman (1967) points out, key measures of analytic cognitive functioning such as the Embedded Figures Test and the Rod-and-Frame Test are substantially related to space perception, and it is in this latter area that sex differences arise. There are no differences in analytic ability when verbal or auditory materials are employed, nor when spatial ability is controlled (Petersen & Wittig, 1979).

Males' general superiority in visual-spatial ability is one sex difference that appears, after age 8, across social classes and in most cultures. This ability, utilized in engineering and architecture, is positively related to performance in math and science courses and is negatively related to performance in language courses (Fennema & Sherman, 1977; Petersen, 1976). Even so, there are considerable individual differences here, too, making career assignments on the basis of sex totally unfounded.

Cognitive Strategies

How do males and females approach the solution to a problem? There has been some suggestion in the past of sex differences in cognitive strategies in problem solving, but these differences may be based on differential visual-spatial abilities (Keogh, 1971; Maier & Casselman, 1970; Sherman, 1967). Boys, when presented with a pattern to reproduce, performed better and utilized more visual cues than did girls. It may be that females use a general, less specialized strategy than do males for solving cognitive problems (Carter-Salzman, 1979). Allen and Hogeland (in press) found that, while both sexes use the same pattern of approaches to problems, women use spatial strategies less effectively and give up more easily than do men. These findings suggest that training may be effective in improving female performance. Berger and Gold (1979) have found that, among individuals under age 25, sex differences in problem solving no longer exist (see also Gold & Berger, 1978). These researchers suggest that the more supportive atmosphere in recent years for female achievement and the reduced emphasis on male achievement have served to eliminate sex differences in this area. Other research has indicated that sex differences can be minimized by changing the testing conditions, the problems used, or the sex of the experimenter (Hoffman & Maier, 1966) and by controlling for occupational affiliation (Berger & Gold, 1979).

Creativity

Another area in which cognitive differences have been thought to exist is creativity. A problem here is with the definition and tasks used to measure the construct. When creativity is measured by the number of responses produced to a stimulus (for example, "List all the possible uses of a paper cup") or by the uniqueness of the response, females are superior if verbal materials are used. No sex difference is found if nonverbal materials are used (Maccoby & Jacklin, 1974). When creativity is measured by career accomplishments, however, males excel, since most awards and recognition go to males.

Creative performance may be negatively related to sex typing in males—the less masculine one is, the more creative (Weitz, 1977). Sex typing and creativity do not appear to be related for females, although Lott (1978) found that nonstereotyped 4-year-olds of both sexes showed greater ideational fluency than sex-typed children. Ideational fluency (how many uses one can find for an object) is one component of creativity. As was noted previously, Maccoby (1966) found a similar relationship between sex typing and intelligence (the less sex typed, the more intelligent), yet creativity and intelligence are not themselves related. These findings imply that sex typing affects cognitive abilities both directly and independently.

EXPLANATIONS

Explanations for the differences between the sexes that are fairly consistently found in verbal, quantitative, and visual-spatial functioning fall into two main categories: those invoking predominantly physiological processes and those invoking predominantly social ones. Any explanation must take into account that most differences do not show up until after 8 years of age and that there is considerable overlap between the sexes for all differences mentioned.

Physiological Factors

Physiological explanations have centered on four mediating processes or on combinations of them: chromosomes, hormones, differential hemispheric processing, and maturation.

Chromosomes. The only cognitive sex difference that may have some genetic component is visual-spatial ability, but the evidence is contradictory. From studies of family members and twins, and on the basis of predictions made from genetic distributions, inferential evidence has accumulated that genetic control over this ability may be recessive and carried on the X chromosome or indirectly related to handedness (Carter-Saltzman, 1979; Maccoby & Jacklin, 1974; Petersen, 1976; Stafford, 1961, 1976). (See Vandenberg and Kuse, 1979, for an excellent review of this research.) Since males have one X chromosome, more males than females are likely to demonstrate this ability. The proportion of females showing high skill should be the square of the proportion of males showing high skill. For example, 50% of males might demonstrate visual-spatial ability compared to 25% of females. More recent evidence, using larger samples, has not fully supported the X-linked hypothesis (Bouchard & McGee, 1977; Sherman, 1978; Sherman & Fennema, 1978; Vandenberg & Kuse, 1979). In addition, there are a number of controversial issues involved in research in this area (Vandenberg & Kuse, 1979; Wittig, 1979). For example, the requirements for definitive studies have rarely been met, the statistical techniques commonly employed have not always been the most appropriate, and corrections for age have not often been made.

Even if genetic factors operate here, the contribution of cultural and environmental factors is not ruled out, since genetic transmission of a trait is quite complex and the gender differences mentioned are only sex influenced, not sex limited. The latter qualification means that, even though more males than females have good visual-spatial ability, not all males do. Furthermore, the actual demonstration of ability is a function more of contextual factors than of innate ones. A glance at any engineering school will demonstrate that females account for far less than one-third the student population. Thus, individual predictions cannot be made on the basis of group differences. These findings cannot be used to justify educational discrimination on the basis of sex.

In other areas of cognitive functioning, no sex-linked differences have been strongly supported, although both verbal ability and intelligence do show significant degrees of inheritability. Aliotti (1978) argues that reading—specifically the ability to acquire and process language fluently—is a sex-linked, inherited trait. The correlations involved are not as high as for visual-spatial ability, however, and social factors seem to be more clearly implicated (Maccoby & Jacklin, 1974). Although some researchers have suggested that quantitative abilities are X-linked (for example, Stafford, 1972), no clear supporting evidence is available (Sherman & Fennema, 1978).

Hormones. Explanations relying on hormonal processes to explain cognitive differences have been complex, largely because the operation of hormones themselves is complex. Overall, there is very little evidence of a direct contribution of adult hormonal levels to sex differences in cognitive performance, although pubertal levels may be important (Barfield, 1976; Dan, 1979; Maccoby & Jacklin, 1974; Petersen, 1976; Reinisch et al., 1979). There is also little evidence for an indirect effect of hormones on the central nervous system, as Broverman and colleagues (1968) have suggested (Parlee, 1972; Unger & Denmark, 1975). However, Petersen (1979) reviews research that suggests that sex hormones may be necessary for the manifestation of spatial ability in both sexes and perhaps for fluent production of words in males. For example, there appears to be a relationship between somatic type, which is assessed by measuring such things as body shape and muscle-to-fat distribution—all presumably related to hormone action—and spatial ability. Androgynous physical characteristics (that is, characteristics that are neither strongly masculine nor strongly feminine) are related to good visualizing ability, whereas extremely feminine and extremely masculine physical characteristics are related to poor visualizing ability. Furthermore, for males, extremely masculine somatic characteristics are associated with better fluent production than spatial ability. No relationship between somatic type and fluent production exists for females.

The effect of hormones on cognitive performance—such as it is— may begin prenatally, not in any direct way (Baker & Ehrhardt, 1979; Barfield, 1976) but indirectly through the influence of prenatal hormones on brain functioning (McGuinness & Pribram, 1978; Petersen, 1979; Reinisch et al., 1979). Sex hormones may act on different parts of the brain. Such action may then affect the brain's sensori-motor processes, which may later affect its cognitive processes. We shall now examine these differences in brain functioning.

Brain Functioning. Since left-cerebral-hemispheric functioning is generally associated with language ability and right-cerebral-hemispheric functioning is associated with spatial skills, different hemispheres may be dominant in each sex or the hemispheres may function differently in each sex. Such differences might account for the reported sex differences in verbal and visual-spatial abilities. Evidence related to this hypothesis has been rapidly accumulating but is still sketchy (see Barfield, 1976; Bryden, 1979; Carter-Saltzman, 1979; Goleman, 1978; L. J. Harris, 1977; Kupke et al., 1979; Levy, 1976; McGlone, 1978; McGuinness & Pribram, 1978; Witelson, 1976).

As was noted in Chapter Two, the simplistic localizing of functions in the two brain hemispheres is no longer clearly supported.

Brain functioning now appears more complex than previously thought, in large part because of possible sex differences in brain organization. Although a simplistic sex division on the basis of hemispheric dominance has not been substantiated, there is some indication that the left hemisphere is more highly specialized in females than in males (Carter-Saltzman, 1979; Levy & Reid, 1977). Since females mature faster than males, the functional specialization of language in the left hemisphere may occur earlier for them, giving females a lead in childhood language skills. Owing to this earlier lead, girls may use language more in their processing of their environment, whereas boys develop language abilities later than other cognitive abilities. Since boys' shift to linguistic skills occurs later, more language-related disorders may arise, as has been found. The finding that there is a higher correlation between verbal abilities and spatial skills for girls than for boys supports this hypothesis, as do findings that spatial ability is related to the degree of lateralization. Eventually, language may play a more important role in a female's intelligence and in her social interactions than in a male's, as some evidence suggests.

Davidson and colleagues (1976) report that males may excel on tasks that require use of both hemispheres simultaneously, while women do well on tasks that require suppression of one hemisphere. Goleman (1978) summarizes other research that also suggests that the sexes may have differential brain functioning, with females being more cognitively specialized than males but having less lateralization of skills. Thus, it may be easier for women than men to perform tasks that combine spatial and linguistic skills, such as "reading" a person's facial expressions. It also may be easier for women to focus attention on one particular task.

This line of research is suggestive but certainly not conclusive at this time. The precise relationship between degree of hemispheric specialization and performance of a particular skill is still an open question, and not all results have been confirmatory (for example, Sherman, 1979; Waber, 1979; see also Bryden, 1979, for an excellent review of the issues involved). Also, even if sex differences in brain organization were in some way inherent, social factors could still be important in the development of particular abilities. Acceptability of, motivation to use, and strategies in implementing a behavior are all affected by the environment. And, since the differences cited are average differences, it is likely that differential reinforcement by the environment can keep such differences to a minimum, if it were so desired.

Maturation Rates. Another physiological process that might account for sex differences in cognitive abilities is differential maturation rates. In her research, Deborah Waber (1976, 1977) found that, regardless of sex, late maturing children scored better than early maturing children on spatial-ability tasks. No relationship was found between performance on verbal tests and maturational rate. With early maturers, predominant use of the left hemisphere before localization is fully complete may interfere with an individual's ability to handle spatial information. Waber's findings that late maturers have more localized speech centers than early maturers substantiate the hypothesis that early maturers do not have as great a degree of brain specialization as do late maturers. Since males usually mature later, they may have a different brain organization that leads to sex differences in verbal and spatial abilities. Waber (1979) argues that, rather than viewing neuropsychological maturation as a linear process of increasing hemispheric specialization, it would be more accurate to view neuropsychological maturation as a process of repeated reorganization of functions. The developmental changes are qualitative as well as quantitative.

It is important to note that not all research supports Waber's hypotheses. Petersen (1976) did not find a relationship between cognitive performance and early-versus-late maturers. Furthermore, since degree of brain lateralization may be established at birth or soon after (Bryden, 1979; Petersen, 1979), there may be no causal relationship between maturation rate and degree of lateralization. Still, an important part of Waber's work is the use of early and late maturers of both sexes, demonstrating again that the difference in maturation between the sexes is not all or none. The sexes can be viewed as being "differentially arrayed along continuous biological dimensions" (Waber, 1979, pp. 183–184). Many individual differences occur that may override a sex difference.

Environmental Influences

Numerous environmental factors have been suggested to account for the few cognitive sex differences. (See Nash, 1979, for an excellent review of the research in this area.) The environmental factors can be divided roughly into those that focus on differential treatment by parents and other socializing agents and those that focus on societal expectations.

Differential Treatment. The essence of the hypothesis that differential treatment accounts for cognitive sex differences is the suggestion that sex-appropriate behavior is shaped by parents and others through the delivery or withdrawal of reinforcements. These reinforcements are often social in nature; hence, this position has been termed the *social-learning approach*.

Picture a parent holding a 3-month-old infant. First picture the infant as a girl; then picture the infant as a boy. If your picture changed, you understand the basis of the differential-treatment approach.

Evidence of differential parental treatment according to the sex of the child has been substantial although not unquestioned (Barfield, 1976; Harris, 1977; L. W. Hoffman, 1972; Kagan, 1964; M. Lewis, 1972; Maccoby & Jacklin, 1974). Males appear to be handled more often and more vigorously than females during the first six months of life, whereas females are more frequently vocalized to, especially by mothers. More frequent parental vocalizations to daughters may *lead to* increased vocalization on the part of female infants. Conversely, these differences in parental treatment may *result from* female infants' more frequent vocalizations. Evidence for both positions is available, and it is highly likely that these factors interact to strengthen each other from the earliest days of the child's life.

Other socializing behaviors related to cognitive sex differences involve providing different experiences for girls and boys. A number of researchers (Denier & Serbin, 1978; Serbin & Connor, in press; Sherman, 1967) have found that play with certain "boy's" toys (blocks, climbing toys, trucks, and Tinker Toys) is related to the development of spatial, rather than verbal, abilities for preschoolers of both sexes, whereas play with certain "girl's" toys (dolls, crayons, kitchen utensils, paints, and board games) is related to higher verbal, rather than visual-spatial, skills. Since both sexes generally play mostly with sex-appropriate toys, it is easy to see how differential abilities may develop during grade school. At later ages, some "girl's" activities—such as jigsaw puzzles, weaving, or making macrame—do help develop spatial skills; but these activities are not as closely related to high spatial ability as are two "boy's" activities—using hand tools and building models (McDaniel, Guy, Ball, & Kolloff, 1978). Thus, females are generally at a disadvantage in developing visual-spatial skills.

Boys also generally receive more practice in, and reinforcement for, problem-solving behavior from parents and teachers than do girls, making them more familiar with such activities and more proficient at them (Beck, 1977; Block, 1973; Coates, 1974). Problems arise in determining whether experience is a determinant or a result of demonstrated proficiency or interest (Maccoby & Jacklin, 1974). It is clear, however, that a genetic predisposition toward good visual-spatial ability could interact with the environment to maximize or minimize the development of that ability. Sherman (1976) has found that training can improve visual-spatial ability for girls.

Differential treatment by parents, teachers, and peers is particularly apparent with regard to mathematics achievement. Fox and colleagues (1979) reviewed the literature and concluded that sex-related differences in this area are primarily the result of differential social conditioning and expectations. Boys are directly and indirectly encouraged to pursue the study of mathematics, they have more self-confidence with regard to math, and they perceive mathematics as more potentially useful than do girls. In this regard, Fennema and Sherman (in press) found that a positive attitude toward success in mathematics was a strong predictor of whether eighth-grade girls took four years of college preparatory mathematics. This attitude was not an important predictor for males.

Sex-Role Expectations. The importance of sex-role expectations in the display of cognitive differences is demonstrated indirectly by the finding that these differences do not occur in an all-or-none fashion; that is, all girls aren't good at reading. Neither do the differences occur immediately from birth, nor do they occur only at the time of pubertal hormone production. Rather, they appear at a time when socialization processes are increasing (after age 8). Other support for the importance of sex-role expectations comes from the literature on cultural differences, sex-role stereotypes, androgynous individuals, and conditioned anxiety.

Although cross-cultural studies of cognitive differences have been scanty, there is some evidence that female superiority in language skills may not occur in every culture (Harris, 1977). In cultures where reading is considered to be male-appropriate (for example, England and Germany), males' reading and vocabulary performance is generally superior to that of females (Brimer, 1969; Johnson, 1973–1974; Preston, 1962). Visual-spatial ability, the only difference with a strong genetic link, does not differentiate the sexes in at least one culture—Canadian Eskimos. There, perhaps not coincidentally, autonomy is encouraged for both sexes (Berry, 1966; Coates, 1974; MacArthur, 1967). It is also possible, of course, that Eskimos may have different gene frequencies than Caucasians. However, other cross-cultural research also supports the link between permissive child-rearing practices, particularly by mothers, and good analytic visual-spatial ability (Dawson, 1967).

Additionally, some differences are related to social class. As noted previously, in populations of underprivileged children, girls maintain their advantage in verbal and quantitative abilities throughout childhood. This advantage may be due to the effects of poor medical care and malnutrition on physiological functioning (boys being more physically vulnerable than girls), to different child-rearing practices, or to differential reinforcement of behavior by peers and by the school environment. All three explanations have received some support (Harris, 1977; Maccoby & Jacklin, 1974), and all three involve some environmental mediation.

Sex-role stereotypes also influence how males and females behave. Picture the winner of a seventh-grade spelling bee. Now picture the winner of a seventh-grade math contest. If the first was a girl and the second a boy, you are well aware of sex-role expectations in cognitive abilities. As expectations, the stereotypes may operate as self-fulfilling prophecies by affecting the values and expectancies of success in a particular cognitive area (Nash, 1979). Beginning in the second grade, American children perceive socio-verbal and artistic skills as feminine, and they perceive spatial, mechanical, and athletic skills as masculine. Beginning around puberty, mathematics and science also are perceived as masculine areas of achievement (Hills, Hobbs, & Verble, 1974; Nash, 1975, 1979). It is probably not coincidental that the ages at which sex typing of achievement areas begins correspond to the ages at which cognitive sex differences begin— after age 8 for verbal and visual-spatial abilities and after age 11 for quantitative abilities.

The expectation that boys and girls will excel in different academic areas is held not only by students but by parents and teachers as well. The effect of teachers' expectations is particularly apparent in studies demonstrating that males perform better when tested and/or taught by males, particularly when verbal materials are presented, and females perform better when tested and/or taught by females. Female mathematical performance is also facilitated when problems describe experiences with which females are more familiar, such as cooking as opposed to baseball (Hoffman & Maier, 1966; Nash, 1979; Pedersen, Shinedling, & Johnson, 1968; Shinedling & Pedersen, 1970). Dwyer (1979) summarizes research that shows the important role of tests in producing sex-related differences in cognitive performance. Clearly, if ability were the sole determinant of performance, such variables would not influence the outcome.

The importance of expectations is also apparent in studies of non-sex-typed individuals. Creative female mathematicians have been found to be more rebelliously independent and rejecting of outside influence than their male counterparts (Helson, 1971). Creativity in male artists has been associated with an integration of feminine sensitivity and intuition and masculine action and determination (Hammer, 1964). Maccoby (1966) has found optimal intellectual functioning to be associated with sex-role nonconformity. Thus, nonconformity to the sex-role stereotypes may underlie some of the wide individual differences in cognitive abilities. The relationship between degree of sex typing and cognitive ability is not a simple one, however. Nash (1975, 1979) found that masculine adolescents of both sexes performed better than feminine adolescents on visual-spatial tasks. For girls, however, the relationship with superior visual-spatial performance was determined by ideal-self, not actual-self, descriptions. That is, boys who rated their actual selves as masculine and girls who rated their ideal selves as masculine performed the best on spatial tasks. Nash (1975) suggests that it may be too anxiety-producing for girls who are masculine sex typed actually to rate themselves as masculine.

Related to Nash's (1975) idea regarding role conflict is the finding that both sexes frequently develop anxiety about achieving in sex-inappropriate fields. Sheila Tobias (1976) and others have documented the significant amount of math-centered anxiety in young women—anxiety often directly reinforced by teachers. Males also are anxious about math but seem to have better coping skills and higher frustration tolerance for it than do females (Fuchs & Weissbrod, 1978). This difference in coping may be due to males' perceiving the relevance of math for their future careers more than do females. Or it may be due to differential expectations regarding coping. Boys are expected to cope with math; girls are not (Fox et al., 1979). For both sexes, confidence in learning mathematics is an important predictor in determining which high school students take four years of college preparatory mathematics (Fennema & Sherman, in press).

Similarly, males have been found to fear success in "feminine" areas. In school, this may mean not performing well at all, especially in the language and verbal areas. Boys experience intense pressure not to do anything vaguely feminine (think of the horrible epithet "sissy"!). Such pressures start during grade school and may account for some of the sex differences in verbal skills found at that time (Maccoby & Jacklin, 1974).

SUMMARY

In examining a wide range of cognitive sex differences, the only consistent findings lie in general female superiority in verbal abilities after age 11 and in general male superiority in quantitative abilities after age 11 and in visual-spatial abilities after age 8. There are no differences in how the sexes learn, in overall intelligence, in analytic ability, or in creativity (unless measured verbally). There may be some differences in cognitive strategies in certain situations.

A variety of physical and environmental explanations have been suggested to account for the three differences that have been found. Physiologically, genes have been implicated only in visual-spatial ability and only in some studies. Such genes seem to be recessive and carried on the X chromosome. Hormones do not appear directly involved in cognitive functioning, although prenatal androgen exposure may produce differential brain functioning. The effects of differential brain functioning and of differential maturation rates on cognitive processes are unclear at this time, although preliminary findings are provocative.

One environmental factor that seems to be involved in the three cognitive differences is differential treatment by parents. There are, of course, wide individual and class differences in child-rearing practices. A direct effect of particular parental practices on particular cognitive skills has not been demonstrated. Other evidence of the importance of environmental factors can be found if one examines sex differences in societal expectations of cognitive performance. Such differences are demonstrated by finding cultural differences in cognitive functioning, by examining specific sex-role stereotypes and their behavioral consequences, by studying those individuals not strongly sex typed, and by demonstrating conditioned anxiety in people who engage in activities deemed appropriate for the other sex.

Some sort of interactional hypothesis seems warranted. It seems likely that some biological predisposition, possibly genetic in the case of visual-spatial ability, interacts with the environment to determine whether the ability itself will be actualized. The environment can either reinforce or discourage such actualization, depending on the behavior's sex appropriateness in that society. The fact that most sex differences are not apparent in early childhood and emerge before puberty undercuts a purely physiological explanation. Expectations of performance shape a child's behavior, and these expectations vary along sex lines.

An important question to keep in mind as we continue to look at reported sex differences involves the implications of such differences. Since individual differences are so broad and since adult achievement and performance involve so much more than pure ability, no clear-cut predictions on the basis of sex are possible. The similarities between the sexes are as notable as, if not more notable than, the differences.

RECOMMENDED READING

Harris, L. J. Sex differences in the growth and use of language. In E. Donelson & J. E. Gullahorn (Eds.), *Women: A psychological perspective.* New York: Wiley, 1977, pp. 79–94. An overview of research in the verbal areas.

Maccoby, E., & Jacklin, C. N. *The psychology of sex differences.* Stanford, Calif.: Stanford University Press, 1974. A comprehensive examination of the research on sex differences in cognitive and social areas. Annotated bibliography.

Sherman, J. *Sex-related differences in cognition: An essay on theory and evidence.* Springfield, Ill.: Charles C Thomas, 1978. An incisive critique of research in the cognitive areas.

Wittig, M. A., & Petersen, A. C. (Eds.). *Sex related differences in cognitive functioning: Developmental issues.* New York: Academic Press, 1979. An excellent compilation of recent findings on cognitive sex differences and of explanations, primarily the biological, for such differences.

4 | Personality and Social Behavior

Generally, when we talk about masculinity and femininity, we are talking about certain personality and social characteristics. Females are seen as very emotional, very submissive, very talkative, very aware of others' feelings, and so forth; males are seen as possessing opposite traits. Figure 4-1 exemplifies one part of the stereotype.

In examining the factual bases for stereotypes in the areas of personality and of social behavior, a number of difficulties arise. First is the problem, discussed in Chapter One, of thinking of traits as consistent characteristics of an individual in all situations at all times. As has been noted, there is little support for this assumption.

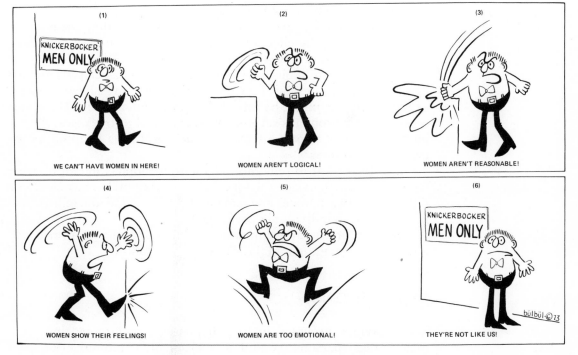

Figure 4-1
Illustrative sex "difference" in personality? (Copyright 1973 by Bülbül. Reprinted by permission.)

Situational factors interact with individual factors in determining behavior, and this is especially the case with social behaviors. For example, a person in isolation is not assertive. Assertive behaviors occur in a social setting and depend on that setting for their expression.

There is also the problem of definitions. Although cognitive differences, such as verbal ability, can be measured by a variety of paper-and-pencil tests (for example, spelling, reading comprehension), it is much more difficult operationally to define and measure concepts like *dependence*. An operational definition gives information regarding how a particular construct can be measured. *Dependence*, for example, can be measured in terms of *clinging behaviors*, *social responsiveness*, *number of friends*, and so forth. To illustrate, if one researcher looks at clinging behaviors of preschoolers and another looks at the number of friends a group of 8-year-olds have, the results would be difficult to compare. To complicate matters further, some researchers do not state explicitly which definition they used in their research, making comparisons among studies difficult (Maccoby & Jacklin, 1974).

Differently aged subject groups are also a problem when comparing study results, especially if developmental issues specifically are not discussed. This is particularly troublesome, since so much research is done with college students, generally aged 18 to 22. Results are often generalized to "all adults." Developmental issues are even more salient for children. Thus, comparisons of help-seeking behavior in children revealed sex differences for 3- to 6-year-olds but not for 7- to 11-year-olds (Whiting & Edwards, 1973).

Another problem that interferes with understanding the bases of the stereotypes is the effect of social expectations on an individual's behavior. This effect may take the form of a self-fulfilling prophecy, or it may be reflected in observer bias. For example, since girls are not expected to be aggressive, they do not develop aggressive behaviors, or their behavior might be mislabeled or misinterpreted. These and other research problems severely handicap an objective researcher (if one exists). It is important to keep such problems in mind as we evaluate the studies.

Also important to remember is the tremendous amount of overlap in behaviors between the sexes. This overlap makes any clear-cut difference between males and females difficult to find and of little use in predicting an individual's performance.

We turn first to an examination of current findings. A review of alternative explanations of these findings will follow.

CURRENT FINDINGS

The behaviors discussed in this chapter can be grouped into four major areas: personality and temperament, communication patterns, person-related behaviors, and power-related behaviors. Each of these areas will be examined in turn.

Personality and Temperament

The term *personality* refers to the distinctive character of an individual, whereas *temperament* refers to emotional mood or disposition. Both areas have been assumed to have sex differences. Most personality theorists, however, emphasize individual, rather than sex-specific, differences. (Freud and the neo-Freudian theorists are exceptions but their position will be discussed in the next chapter.) For our purposes here, a brief look at personality development as related to sex typing will prove more instructive.

Behavior Development. As was noted in Chapter One, people generally are in a great deal of agreement as to what constitutes the sex-role stereotypes. These stereotypes are learned by ages 3 to 5, although children do not necessarily behave accordingly (Maccoby & Jacklin, 1974). Of interest here is the common finding that boys are behaviorally sex typed much earlier and more strongly than are girls. Between ages 3 and 11, it is very unusual for boys to prefer activities or toys ascribed to girls. On the other hand, it is quite common for girls to choose "boys'" toys and activities as often as, if not in preference to, those ascribed to girls. In fact, between ages 6 and 9, most girls prefer "male" activities, perhaps because such activities have also been rated as more interesting and more fun (Donelson, 1977a).

From grades 6 to 12, however, there is increasing consistency between self-descriptions and sex-role expectations (Donelson, 1977a). By adolescence, these female/male distinctions strongly appear and have been variously labeled by different writers. Parsons and Bales (1955) speak of expressive (emotional, people-oriented) and instrumental (active, doing) orientations. R. Carlson (1965) speaks of people (other-involved) and individualistic (self-involved) orientations. Bakan (1966) speaks of communion (involving cooperation and receptivity) and agency (involving self-assertion and ego enhancement) orientations. These similar terms all describe stereotypic sex differences in personality and social behavior, but the research findings just cited refer only to self-descriptions and ideal self-descriptions, not to behavioral differences. With sex-role stereotypes being as pervasive as they are, it is not surprising that most people want to see themselves as behaving in sex-role appropriate ways. Whether they actually behave this way is a different matter.

Another issue concerns developmental aspects. Although most research concentrates on children and college students, personality development appears to be a continuous process. Yet few studies have examined data on adults. Martha White (1979), in studying 162 female nurse practitioners (median age 29), found that most of her sample rated themselves as high in both communion and agentic competencies; that is, they presented a more androgynous picture than younger samples generally do. Thus, it may be that people become more integrated or less subject to stereotypic thinking as they age. Daniel Levinson's (1978) developmental study of men's lives suggests a similar pattern for men. More work in this area is needed.

With regard to temperament, females have often been thought to be more passive than males. As Maccoby and Jacklin (1974) note, however, this term *passivity* has a variety of possible definitions: submissiveness, lack of sexual interest, dependence, inactivity, and so on. Because it covers such a broad range of behavior, passivity per se will not be examined here. From the research on the possible components of passivity, however, it is clear that there is little support for the assumption that females are uniformly more passive than males.

Emotionality.   In the area of emotionality (another vague term), studies of infants show no differences in frequency or duration of crying during the first year, although there is some indication that, after three months, boys may cry more, yet receive less attention from their mothers for their crying, than do girls (Maccoby & Jacklin, 1974; Moss, 1967; Phillips et al., 1978). The situations that occasion emotional outbursts are different for boys and for girls from ages 3 to 5. Boys react most to frustration situations, conflicts with adults, and fear-inducing situations; girls respond most to conflicts with other children. Girls also decrease their total emotional responsiveness at a faster rate than do boys (Fitzgerald, 1977; Maccoby & Jacklin, 1974).

In terms of fearfulness, the evidence is contradictory, partly due to different measurement techniques. Regarding infants' fear of strangers, which occurs in less than 50% of all infants (Fitzgerald, 1977), males more frequently evidence this fear, although females respond more intensely and at an earlier age to it. Observational studies of behavior do not show females, in childhood and adolescence, to be more timid than males of that age, although teacher ratings and self-reports usually do show more timidity in females (Maccoby & Jacklin, 1974). A problem with self-reports, as was noted in Chapter Two, is that people tend to respond in a socially desirable way, or they may respond to the demand characteristics of a situation. Thus, girls may be more likely to admit to fear or anxieties because such admissions are more socially acceptable from them and more expected of them.

In test-taking situations, females generally have higher anxiety levels than males, which condition may interfere with complex problem solving (Maccoby, 1966; Unger & Denmark, 1975). This anxiety in test-taking situations may be related to deviation from sex-role norms (achieving on a test may be viewed as unfeminine) rather than from chronically higher levels of anxiety in females. If this explanation were true, males who engage in cross-sex activities should also be more anxious. Bem and Lenney (1976) have found support for this prediction with college students.

A curious aspect of research in this area is defining emotionality as *fear* or as *the number of emotional upsets*. Emotions, of course, cover a wide range of feelings, including hostility. Yet, although more males display hostile feelings than do females, males are rarely termed "emotional," as illustrated in Figure 4-1. Again, a sexist bias in research questions, definitions, and conclusions is apparent.

In general, then, we cannot conclude simply that females are more emotional or more timid than males. Early childhood studies show few consistent differences between the sexes; after early childhood, differences that emerge seem more a consequence of sex-role stereotypes rather than a basis for them. In this regard, it is interesting to note that Buck (1977) found that boys between ages 4 and 6 increasingly inhibited and masked their overt reactions to emotion-producing situations (in this case, slides depicting emotion-laden scenes). Girls, however, continued to respond relatively freely to such situations. Such differences, becoming more extreme during adolescence, clearly conform to sex-role stereotypes of females as being emotional. As noted, this may mean only that more females than males show their emotions, not that more females have emotions. Cherulnik (1979) concluded from his research with undergraduates that, although women may be more emotionally expressive than men, especially facially, women do not appear to experience emotions more strongly than men. Evidence of this difference in emotional disclosure shows up clearly in sex differences in communication patterns.

Communication Patterns

The stereotype of female emotionality may be related to the greater frequency with which females display or communicate their emotions. The area of communication is an extremely important one in the study of sex differences, since most of our information and knowledge of others comes through their verbal or nonverbal cues. Until recently, however, few researchers have examined sex differences in this area. In ground-breaking work, Nancy Henley (1977; Henley & Thorne, 1977) has found sex differences in communication patterns to be pervasive in both verbal and nonverbal behaviors.

Verbal Communication.   Contradicting the "talkative female" stereotype, Henley found that males talk more and for longer periods of time than do females. Males interrupt other speakers more, control conversations more as to topic, make more jokes, and speak less in standard English (that is, they use slang more). Females talk at a much higher pitch, ask tag questions (for example, "Isn't that so?") rather than make statements, allow themselves to be interrupted, listen more, and disclose more personal information to others. Differences in content of conversation are not clear because males and females often engage in different activities and occupations. The only general statement regarding content that can be made is that males are more often talked about by both sexes, perhaps a reflection of their greater importance or interest. Thus, we see that males tend to dominate verbally, whereas females tend to listen more and to disclose intimate information about themselves more. Henley's work has been supported by numerous other studies (see Haas, 1979, and Parlee, 1979, for recent overviews).

The finding that women are more self-disclosing than are men relates specifically to intimate topics, such as personality and bodily matters. On such topics as opinions, interests, and work, men disclose more than women (Rosenfeld, Civikly, & Herron, 1979). Research incorporating measures of androgyny has found that it is specifically masculine males, not androgynous males, who markedly limit the personal information they reveal (Lombardo & Levine, 1978).

Nonverbal Communication. In studies of nonverbal behavior, the observed sex differences are of even greater importance than in the verbal behaviors just noted, since the impact of nonverbal communication is so much stronger and so much more subtle than verbal communication (Henley & Thorne, 1977). Generally, females are more restricted in their demeanor and personal space, have more frequent eye contact during conversations (but avoid eye contact otherwise), smile more when it is unrelated to happiness, touch less but are touched more, and are more sensitive to nonverbal cues than are males (Deaux, 1976; Frances, 1979; Hall, 1978; Henley, 1977). This last finding may be more complex than stated. Rosenthal and DePaulo (1979) have found that women are more "polite" in their reading of nonverbal cues than are men; that is, females are superior only in decoding nonverbal cues when such cues are nondeceptive. Furthermore, although females in general seem more accurate in interpreting nonverbal cues, especially in interpreting cues relating to negative affect, a more specific pattern of this ability is revealed when measures of sex typing are included. Both androgynous- and feminine-typed groups are more accurate in the assessment of nonverbal behavior than are masculine-typed groups (Fischer & Grande, 1978). Since more females than males are feminine typed, a sex difference is usually found.

The differences in nonverbal behavior clearly reflect the sex-role stereotypes of females displaying more submission and warmth and males displaying more dominance and high status cues (Frieze & Ramsey, 1976). Such findings are particularly striking, since these behaviors usually are not controlled consciously and are therefore difficult to change.

These sex differences in communication patterns may relate to the status differences between the sexes and to different needs for affiliation and power. Since females (or feminine- and androgynous-sex-typed individuals) generally use more self-disclosure, display greater eye contact and smiling behavior, have smaller personal space, and exhibit greater listening and attending skills than males, they generally facilitate close personal interactions. Rosenthal and colleagues (1979) have determined that people who are more skillful at decoding nonverbal cues are more effective in their interpersonal relationships. Since more women have this skill and use it politely, their proficiency in interpersonal situations would be strengthened. Males (or masculine-sex-typed individuals), who have greater domination of conversations, space, and touching, and have minimal self-disclosure, would generally impede close personal interactions but would facilitate interpersonal control. These differences in spheres of influence (personal interactions versus power interactions) again reflect stereotypic differences.

Person-Related Behaviors

As noted above, females generally are assumed to be more concerned with person-centered interactions than males, who are assumed to be more concerned with power-centered interactions. Although this generalization is true to some extent (Deaux, 1976), both types of interactions are composed of a wide range of behaviors, and not all of these behaviors show clear-cut sex differences. Person-centered interactions encompass such behaviors as dependency, affiliation, empathy, nurturance, and altruism.

Dependency. Dependency is a trait commonly associated with females. As with passivity, however, dependency has multiple meanings and is neither clearly unitary nor clearly the opposite of independence (Sherman, 1976).

When dependency is defined as seeking the presence of others or as resistance to physical separation, no consistent sex difference for this trait emerges during the childhood years, although parental behavior toward the child may differ at different periods (Fitzgerald, 1977; Maccoby & Jacklin, 1974; Moss, 1967). Males may receive more physical contact during the first six months; females seem to receive more contact after that time.

When dependency is defined as social interest or social responsiveness, some differences do appear, although they are subtle. Maccoby and Jacklin (1974) found no consistent differences during the first two years of a child's life in social responsiveness to either live people, faces, or voices. Similarly, Etaugh and Whittler (1979) found that preschool boys and girls did not differ in their ability to remember the faces of their peers. A few frequently reported studies, however, do find females to be more sensitive to social cues (Bardwick, 1971; McGuinness & Pribram, 1978). During childhood and adolescence, boys appear more sociable than do girls in the sense that they have more friends, chat and play with them more frequently, show off with them, and depend more on them for values, support, and activity (Lott, 1978; Maccoby & Jacklin, 1974; Strommen, 1977). Young girls are more likely to play alone or to relate to nearby adults. Although there may be some similarity in friendship patterns for the sexes (Kandel, 1978), the relationships themselves seem qualitatively different during childhood and adolescence. Girls have fewer, but more intense, friendships that provide emotional support in personal crises. Boys have more friends of a less intimate nature (a "gang") who provide support in case of conflict with adults.

This tendency of males to form groups has rarely been defined as dependency, however. Rather, it sometimes has been glorified as the basic element of society (see Tiger, 1969). Tiger argues that males have an innate tendency to bond together and form close groups and suggests that this bonding serves to maintain social order and accounts for male leadership and all-male clubs. However, although males do tend to have more friends, female friendships appear closer than male friendships. And no sex difference has been found in the tendency to belong to single-sex groups (Booth, 1972).

Thus, there is no evidence that females are more dependent than males when dependency is defined as proximity seeking or social responsiveness. An argument can be made that boys are more dependent when dependency is measured by numbers of friendships. These findings again illustrate the frequently biased nature of research questions and definitions.

In a cross-cultural study of 3- to 11-year-old American, Western European, and African children (Whiting & Edwards, 1973), younger girls (ages 3 to 6) were found to be more dependent than boys only when dependency was defined as seeking help and physical contact. Older boys (ages 7 to 11) were more dependent when dependency was defined as seeking attention. Lott (1978), in her study of 4-year-old New Zealanders, found that children of both sexes smiled, asked for help, and followed adult instructions with equal frequency. Again, the importance of consistent research definitions cannot be sufficiently stressed.

Affiliation. When interest in, and concern about, other people is assessed after childhood, females tend to show a greater interest in affiliation and more positive feelings about social interactions than do males (Deaux, 1976; Ickes & Barnes, 1977; Maccoby & Jacklin, 1974). For example, when adolescents were asked to rank a number of concerns in the order of the importance they felt each had for them personally, both sexes ranked identity and sexuality as the top two items. For the third item, however, a sex difference appeared. Girls ranked interpersonal relationships as the third most important concern to them, whereas boys ranked autonomy third (Strommen, 1977). It has already been noted that females express feelings more, verbally and nonverbally, and are more perceptive of the nonverbally expressed feelings of others than are males. Thus, there does seem to be a sex difference here, corresponding to sex-role expectations, although it does not show up until adolescence and is thus more likely to be a consequence, not a cause, of the sex-role stereotypes.

Interestingly, this greater "need" for affiliation on the part of females has led many to assume that females are more dependent on males for love and fulfillment than males are dependent on females. Men actually fall in love more quickly and easily, become more upset at the end of a relationship, are more likely to remarry, and generally are in worse emotional and physical shape when unmarried than are women (for example, Gove, 1973, 1979). Thus, simple generalizations of females "needing" others are unwarranted.

Empathy. One component of empathy is the degree of sensitivity to others' thoughts and feelings. Females and feminine-sex-typed individuals, as it was previously discussed, tend to be better than males and masculine-sex-typed individuals at interpreting nonverbal cues, perhaps because they have greater eye contact or because they take more of an interest in people. When other forms of empathy are examined, however, as in responding to people with problems or in describing the feelings or plans of characters in a story or picture, no consistent sex differences emerge (Bem, Martyna, & Watson, 1976; Maccoby & Jacklin, 1974; Olesker & Balter, 1972). Rather, people tend to be more accurate about people of the same sex and about situations with which they are familiar. Sex typing plays a part here, too. Masculine-sex-typed people appear less empathic than either androgynous- or feminine-sex-typed people (Bem et al., 1976), paralleling the findings for nonverbal communication. If one views empathy as a positive trait, masculine sex typing is a handicap.

Nurturance. Females traditionally have been thought to possess exclusively the capability of nurturing others—facilitating the development of others or, more generally, helping others. This belief has been an outgrowth of the fact that only women can bear and nurse children. Since only women can bear and nurse them, it might follow that women must "naturally" be more qualified to take care of them and, by extension, take care of others. The problem with this assumption is twofold. First, there is no evidence at all of a maternal instinct. Second, there is no evidence that females are consistently more nurturant than are males. In responses to infants and other vulnerable creatures, males and females have been found capable of equally nurturant behavior (Bem et al., 1976; Donelson, 1977a; Maccoby & Jacklin, 1974).

The important variables related to nurturant behaviors seem to be (1) contact with a newborn during a critical period after birth (first 24 hours), (2) experience (females are usually given more preliminary practice with such behaviors—for example, playing with dolls, babysitting), and (3) sex-role expectations. For example, Bem and colleagues (1976) found that androgynous college men were just as responsive to a kitten and to a human baby as were college women, but masculine-sex-typed men were not as responsive. Thus, sex typing may restrict nurturing behavior in males. Supporting this is a finding by Berman (1975) that males respond with more facial expressions to pictures of infant monkeys when their ratings are private than when they think their ratings will be made public. Another interesting finding in the Bem study is that, when nurturant behavior necessitated active initiation of a response, feminine-sex-typed college women were less nurturant than androgynous women and androgynous men. Thus, because feminine women are behaviorally constricted in instrumental functioning, they were less able to be nurturant when the situation also required assertion.

The fact that women are more likely to be in nurturant roles in our society (mothers, nurses, social workers, and so forth) is more a consequence of sex-role stereotypes than a direct reflection of any fundamental sex difference in nurturing ability. As Whiting and Edwards (1973) found in their cross-cultural study, differences in nurturance did not show up until ages 7 to 11, and then they were a clear function of differential socialization pressures.

Altruism.   Since females are expected to be more concerned about others, one might also expect them to be more altruistic—that is, to live and to act for the good of others, as in helping someone in distress. The research in this area shows no consistent sex differences (Crawley & Basow, 1979; Deaux, 1976; Maccoby & Jacklin, 1974). In her study of 4-year-old New Zealanders, Lott (1978) found no sex difference in the frequency with which the children helped one another or shared. The important variables here are (1) the nature of the response required (men are more likely than women to help if some initiative on the part of the respondent is required), (2) the sex-role appropriateness of the task (males are more reluctant to engage in sex-role inappropriate activity), and (3) the sex of the person requiring help (opposite-sex helping behaviors are more likely than same-sex ones).

Power-Related Behaviors

In the area of power-centered interactions, males generally are thought to outperform females. Such interactions encompass the behaviors of aggression, assertion, dominance, competition/cooperation, and independence/compliance.

Aggressiveness.   Of all assumed sex differences, the one most common and strongly held assumption concerns males' greater aggressiveness. Although this assumption has been repeatedly substantiated across many situations and cultures (Maccoby & Jacklin, 1974), it is not without qualification. A primary qualification is again in definition. Moyer (1974) has differentiated at least eight different types of aggression, some of which are more common in females. Of the different types, boys tend to aggress in physical and destructive ways, girls in verbal and disobedient ways (Barfield, 1976). Even these generalizations concerning this sex difference in mode of expressing aggression may be restricted to findings from self-reports (Frodi, Macaulay, & Thome, 1977). Males also tend to be more aggressive than females when some form of initiative, such as getting up to do something, is required; no difference occurs when just a response, such as pushing a button to deliver a shock after having been shocked by the target person, is called for (Deaux, 1976).

   Another problem with research findings about aggression is differentiating behavioral aggression from both the ability to aggress and the propensity to aggress. Although males seem to have a greater readiness to respond in aggressive ways (Maccoby & Jacklin, 1974), they still must learn the behavior and choose to display it. Whereas readiness to aggress may be physiologically based, the learning and performance of aggressive acts are definitely socially based. As Bandura (1973) has demonstrated, girls learn aggressive behavior to about the same degree as boys but are more inhibited in performing those behaviors. When the social situation allows it, however, girls exhibit the same amount of aggression as boys (also Frodi et al., 1977; Lando, 1976). Important variables are sex of victim and observer, empathy, guilt, aggression anxiety, and amount of provocation.

In general, though, across a wide range of behaviors and cultures, males do exhibit a greater amount of aggression than do females, beginning at ages 2 to 3 (Barfield, 1976; Maccoby & Jacklin, 1974; Whiting & Edwards, 1973). The considerable amount of overlap in these behaviors is important to keep in mind, however. Some girls may be more aggressive than some boys. These sex differences are consistent with training differences and do not necessarily imply that females are without any aggressiveness or are submissive or passive. As has been noted above, given appropriate social conditions, females can be just as aggressive as males.

The implications of this finding are not clear, since, in industrialized societies, physical aggressiveness does not necessarily help one survive or achieve high status. Rather, physical aggression may be maladaptive for the individual as well as for society if it leads to violence and crime. These societal effects of aggression will be discussed in Chapter 12.

Assertiveness. Although the terms *assertiveness* and *aggressiveness* are frequently confused, they refer to different behaviors. Whereas aggressiveness refers to behaviors meant to put another person down, assertiveness refers to the ability to speak up for oneself while continuing to respect the other person. Assertiveness can also be differentiated from passivity, which, in this regard, refers to letting oneself be put down by someone else (Alberti & Emmons, 1970; Phelps & Austin, 1975). In the few studies of this variable, females have been found generally to be less assertive than males. We previously noted that women let men dominate conversations, allow themselves to be interrupted, and are less likely to initiate actions. This general lack of assertiveness may be true only for sex-typed women, however. Thus, Bem (1975a) found feminine college women to have difficulty refusing a request even when it was tedious, time consuming, and unimportant. Androgynous women and men did not have this trouble.

Assertiveness is an important area of research. While many of the positive aspects of power, such as standing up for one's rights, displaying leadership, and so forth, have been associated with the trait of aggressiveness, they are really assertive behaviors. Since aggression may be biologically based, some people have assumed that males more "naturally" are leaders. This is totally unwarranted, since most leadership behaviors involve assertiveness, and assertiveness is definitely learned and has been successfully taught (Alberti & Emmons, 1970).

Dominance. The image of males as the more dominant sex is strongly held in our culture. Think of the standard picture of our prehistoric ancestors—a caveman dragging a cavewoman about by the hair. Dominance refers to a relationship in which one member of a group has control and influence over the behaviors of others (Frieze & Ramsey, 1977). As noted in the discussion of communication patterns, males clearly dominate conversations and physical space. Males also dominate when behaviors are related to physical toughness and force, as in children's play groups. However, even here there is a considerable amount of overlap between the behavior of the sexes (Maccoby & Jacklin, 1974). These early differences in dominance may be related to differences in aggression. As adults, men tend to be more manipulative than women (for example, more Machiavellian), although this seems a consequence, not a cause, of the stereotype, since children show no sex difference in these behaviors (Maccoby & Jacklin, 1974).

In laboratory settings and in society at large, males more often are leaders in mixed-gender, cooperative, and task-oriented groups. By adolescence, leadership has little to do with force and much to do with status, norms, and expertise. As some researchers have argued (for example, Deaux, 1976; Lockheed & Hall, 1976), males generally have higher status than females, and this higher status structures the power and prestige of a group unless steps are taken to alter the power structure. Becoming a leader depends upon being seen as a leader. One group of researchers (Porter, Geis, & Walstedt, 1978) found that women simply were unlikely to be seen as leaders in mixed-sex groups despite the presence of customary leadership cues, such as sitting at the head of the table. This was true regardless of the observer's sex, sex typing, or feminist ideology. Such perceptions, then, appear to be cultural stereotypes that operate on a nonconscious level.

Similarly, Golub and Canty (1979) found, in a dyad situation, that when college women were paired with male peers, only one-third of the women assumed leadership despite there being no difference in the dominance scores of the two people as measured by the California Personality Inventory. However, 60% of these same women did assume leadership when paired with other women. Again the findings suggest that sex role, rather than dominance, is related to leadership in mixed-sex groups.

It is not true that women are simply less task-oriented or less active than men or that they naturally assume a more social-expressive role rather than an instrumental role in a group (Deaux, 1976; Lockheed, 1975a; Lockheed & Hall, 1976). Rather, peer interactions and expectations for competence tend to socialize males and females to play different roles in groups. With appropriate interventions (see Lockheed & Hall, 1976), this imbalance can be remedied, and females can be equally effective as leaders.

Competitiveness. According to sex-role stereotypes, males are generally more competitive than females. This is certainly true in sports and perhaps in business, but, in laboratory settings, sex differences are not found consistently (Deaux, 1976; Kahn, 1979; Maccoby & Jacklin, 1974). In observations of young children's behaviors, sex differences in competitiveness also generally do not appear (Lott, 1978). Moely, Skarin, and Weil (1979) found an interesting developmental pattern in their study of competitive and cooperative behavior in children aged 4 to 5 and 7 to 9. Both sexes in the younger age group were most competitive with other-sex partners; in the older age group, however, only girls retained this response selectivity. Boys aged 7 to 9 showed a general tendency to compete regardless of partner sex and instructional set.

What do emerge from a variety of studies are differing patterns of performance for the sexes, with males being more likely than females to be concerned with winning, especially if money is concerned, and in surpassing an opponent. Females appear more concerned than males with interpersonal aspects of the situation, such as minimizing losses (Deaux, 1976). These differences, of course, parallel sex-role expectations of instrumental versus expressive behaviors, and they probably reflect the marked differences the sexes experience in athletic training and play activity. These general differences in group performance can also be changed depending on the nature of the task, group composition, significance of the behavior, training, and so forth (Deaux, 1976; Kahn, 1979; Lockheed & Hall, 1976; Maccoby & Jacklin, 1974).

Independence/Compliance. Both Eagly (1978) and Maccoby and Jacklin (1974) conclude from their reviews of the literature that, across all subject matters and sources of influence, females are not more compliant, suggestible, or conforming. Earlier research had suggested that females were more conforming in attitude-change studies (for example, Asch, 1956). More recent research has demonstrated that such findings depend on the task itself, on whether there is group pressure, and on the sex typing of the individual (Bem, 1975b; Cacioppo & Petty, 1979; Cooper, 1979; Deaux, 1976; Eagly, 1978; Sistrunk & McDavid, 1971).

When a task is familiar or sex-role appropriate, both sexes show independence; when it is unfamiliar or sex-role inappropriate, both sexes are more likely to conform. When there is no group pressure, females are no more likely to conform in their opinions than are males; when group pressure exists, and in face-to-face encounters, females are more likely to conform than are males in order to preserve social harmony. The change appears more at the level of behavioral expression than at the level of a genuine change of opinion.

Bem found feminine-sex-typed college students conformed more than masculine and androgynous subjects on a judgment-of-humor task, although there was no overall sex difference. There is also no sex difference in the degree to which male and female college students are influenced by other people in making certain life decisions (Basow & Howe, 1979a).

Sex does interact with situations in such a way that, during childhood, girls comply more than boys with directives from parents and teachers; boys comply more than girls with peer pressure (Maccoby & Jacklin, 1974). It is possible that girls may be more socialized for adult approval than are boys. In any case, it does seem true that females receive more requests from adults than do boys, making the cause and effect sequence here very unclear.

Before we examine some of the explanations proposed for the sex differences found in personality and social behaviors, it is important to remember that findings of similarities actually outweigh findings of differences. In Lott's (1978) observation study of 4-year-old kindergarteners, she found that only 6 of the 41 specific social behaviors observed clearly differentiated boys from girls. Girls were more likely than boys to talk with, and smile at, adults, and boys were more likely than girls to chat with peers, follow a peer's lead, play roughly, and be noisy. In other behaviors, the similarities were greater than the differences.

Another important point to bear in mind is that there appear to be strong developmental patterns. For most behaviors, sex differences appear, if at all, only for certain age groups. Usually the pattern is for sex differences to increase with age, at least into college. Post-college adults have rarely been studied. Thus, the few sex differences that do appear are more likely a consequence of sex-role development than a cause of it and may be apparent only at certain ages.

EXPLANATIONS

Explanations for the most frequently found sex differences in personality and social behaviors can be divided into three categories: physiological, social, and status related.

Physiological Factors

Physiological explanations of social behavior differences have been used mainly to account for differences in aggression, dominance, and nurturance. They have centered on two basic factors—chromosomes and hormones.

Chromosomes. The only social behavior linked to chromosomes in any way has been aggression, and the evidence here is very unclear. The finding of a higher percentage of males with an extra Y chromosome (XYY instead of XY) in mental-penal institutions than in the general public gave rise to speculation that the extra Y chromosome may make these individuals hyperaggressive (Meyer-Bahlburg, 1974). Further studies did not support such a linkage. For example, such individuals did not commit more aggressive crimes than their XY counterparts, and males with an extra X chromosome (XXY) are comparable behaviorally to those with an extra Y chromosome (Barfield, 1976; Meyer-Bahlburg, 1974). Thus, the question of chromosomal influence on aggression is still unresolved. Indications are that environmental conditions may interact with abnormal genetic conditions to make certain deviant behavior patterns, including aggression, more likely.

Hormones. Male fetuses during the third prenatal month normally produce androgen, which sets the brain for a fairly regular production of hormones at puberty. Evidence from studies on animals and humans has suggested that testosterone (an androgen) is related to aggressiveness (Barfield, 1976; Maccoby & Jacklin, 1974; Money & Ehrhardt, 1972). This relationship is not clear-cut, however. Firstly, the relationship is not unidirectional. High levels of testosterone may increase aggressiveness, but aggressiveness may also increase testosterone levels (Rose, Gordon, & Bernstein, 1972). Secondly, the relationship between the two is not found in all animals, nor have significant correlations been found between testosterone level and hostility or aggression in human males (Doering et al., 1974; Moyer, 1974). Thirdly, studies of genetic females exposed to prenatal androgens (those with the adrenogenital syndrome) have found an increase in rough-and-tumble play and self-assertion, but not in aggression itself, in these females (Money & Ehrhardt, 1972). Not surprisingly, human behavior appears to be multidetermined.

On the other hand, sex differences in aggression in rhesus monkeys do seem to have a hormonal component, since even infants raised with cloth and wire "mothers" exhibit sex differences in aggressive play (Harlow, 1965). In addition, administration of hormones postnatally can sometimes increase aggression (Barfield, 1976).

The most parsimonious explanation of these findings is that prenatal exposure to androgen may predispose an individual to behave aggressively. Such a predisposition may increase sensitivity to certain stimuli, like rough contact, or may make certain patterns of reactions, such as large muscle movements, more rewarding and thus more likely to occur (Hamburg & Lunde, 1966). This predisposition may arise through the effect of androgens on the amygdala, a structure in the limbic system of the brain that appears to affect aggressive behavior. For this predisposition to be actualized, however, various social influences are needed.

The rise in premenstrual hostility for some females may have a hormonal basis since it coincides with low levels of both progesterone and estrogen and high levels of monoamine oxidase (Paige, 1971). The underlying process is not fully understood, however. Social factors are clearly involved, especially since the linkage between hormone level and hostility is inconsistent and there is such wide individual variation (Barfield, 1976).

To the extent that dominance is based on aggressiveness, dominance may be related to androgen production. However, Money and Ehrhardt (1972) found in their study of adrenogenital females that, although these girls did compete more in the dominance hierarchy of boys than did other girls, they did not compete for the top positions, a suggestion that social factors may also be operating. In addition, other researchers have found that aggression does not automatically lead to dominance, although the two may be correlated (Rose et al., 1971). In humans, as discussed above, dominance is more a function of status than of physical power.

In the area of maternal behavior, there is no evidence for an instinctual basis, even in animals. Rather, contact with the newborn during a critical period (in humans, the first 24 hours, especially the first 45 minutes, after birth) is necessary in developing or maintaining such behaviors (Bronfenbrenner, 1977; Maccoby & Jacklin, 1974; Money & Ehrhardt, 1972). This is true for men as well as for women. Money and Ehrhardt (1972) have argued that maternalism should really be termed parentalism, since both sexes can and do exhibit such behavior.

There is some indication, however, that it is easier to trigger the response of parental care in females than in males. This may be a function of prenatal hormonal history (Money & Ehrhardt, 1972). Specifically, exposure to androgens seems to inhibit such behavior. Although most studies have been done with animals, studies of adrenogenital females show them to be less interested in rehearsing parental behaviors, such as babysitting and playing with dolls, during childhood. This, of course, may be a function of competing athletic interests and/or socialization and not a consequence of prenatal hormone exposure. These girls do eventually marry and have children; so again the hormonal effect seems, at most, to make parental behaviors easier to learn. Hormones clearly do not make parental behaviors inevitable, as evidenced by numerous cases of child beating and infanticide in the general population. Nor do hormones prevent males from learning such behaviors.

Social Factors

Two general environmentally based explanations have been used to account for sex differences in social behavior: differential parental behavior and societal expectations.

Differential Treatment. As mentioned in Chapter Three, parents seem to respond differently to their male and female infants. This partly reflects parental sex-role stereotypes. For example, Rubin, Provenzano, and Luria (1974) found parental sex typing of infants to begin within 24 hours of birth. Differential parental responding may also occur in interaction with different infant behaviors. A female's faster maturation, lower irritability, and faster verbal development may make her more rewarding to her caretaker. Consequently, the interpersonal bond between child and parent may be strengthened. Studies have found that mothers give more visual and auditory stimulation and more physical contact to their infant daughters than to their infant sons (Fitzgerald, 1977). This stimulation and contact may serve to encourage an interpersonal orientation in young females. Males, on the other hand, whose nervous systems at birth are less developed than those of females at birth and who tend to be more active and irritable, may be less reinforcing of a caretaker's behavior. It has been found that mothers have less physical contact with male infants after six months of age than they did during the first six months. This may serve to make males less amenable to social reinforcement and more autonomous than are females (Fitzgerald, 1977; Moss, 1967).

For aggressive and nurturant behaviors particularly, parental training starts early (Barfield, 1976; Maccoby & Jacklin, 1974). Parents are more likely to give daughters, rather than sons, dolls and to ask them to babysit. Parents also seem more tolerant of aggression in their sons than in their daughters, although this varies with the type of aggression displayed and the object of the aggression. Somewhat surprisingly, Maccoby and Jacklin (1974) found that boys are actually punished more often for physical aggression than are girls. This may occur because boys engage in physical aggression more often than do girls.

In general, males seem to receive more intense socialization pressures during childhood than do girls (Maccoby & Jacklin, 1974). Such pressure may further their autonomous development and account for their greater reluctance to engage in cross-sex behaviors. This may be due to the greater importance placed on males or to the greater difficulty males have in inhibiting their predisposition to aggression. In any event, parental behaviors are clearly different for sons and daughters in many cases and may account for some behavioral differences.

Sex-Role Expectations. Of even greater importance than parental behavior is the influence of societal expectations, which parental behavior, of course, reflects. The fact that most differences in social behavior appear during childhood and increase with age indicates the strong role that learning and culture play in the development of differences.

Lott (1978) found that adults predicted 18 sex differences in the social behaviors of 4-year-old boys and girls. When observed, however, these children differed in only five of the predicted behaviors. Behaviors that were expected but not observed were disobedient and quarrelsome behaviors predominantly in boys and dependent, helpful, and pleasant behaviors predominantly in girls. Such differences in expectations may lead adults to treat the sexes differently, such as to treat girls as more dependent. This differential treatment may have direct and indirect effects; for example, it may lead girls to believe they cannot do things by themselves.

Numerous cross-cultural studies have illustrated the power of a society to modify the behavior of its constituents. Most surveys have found an emphasis on girls to be nurturant and responsible and on boys to be self-reliant, achievement oriented, and aggressive (Barry, Bacon, & Child, 1957; Block, 1973; Whiting & Edwards, 1973). These differences seem a function of a variety of social factors. Whiting and Edwards (1973) concluded that the sex differences they found across six cultures were a reflection of style (when dependency was defined as seeking help, it was feminine; when defined as seeking attention, masculine) and of task assignment (more away-from-home chores for males, more domestic chores for females) rather than a reflection of innate sex differences. In those cultures where girls do not engage in infant care as well as in cultures where boys do care for infants, fewer sex differences in behavior are found.

Similarly, in Margaret Mead's (1935) classic study of New Guinea tribes, one tribe was found where both sexes were aggressive as adults (Mundugumor); one, where both sexes were passive (Arapesh); and one, where females were aggressive and males passive (Tchambuli). Clearly, regardless of any physiological predisposition, society plays the determining role in the development of social behavior. Block (1973) has found that, in the United States more so than in England or Scandinavia, aggression in males and early and distinct sex typing in both sexes is encouraged.

Thus, even a behavior with a possible physiological basis, such as aggression, can be influenced by cultural norms, being either augmented or diminished. Other evidence indicates that this environmental and biological interaction is true with animals as well. Aggressive behavior is influenced by rearing, previous encounters, and amount of fighting experience (Hutt, 1972).

Connor, Serbin, and Ender (in press) studied the responses of fourth, sixth and eighth graders to stories in which a male or female character behaved aggressively, assertively, or passively. Differential degrees of approval for each behavior were found depending upon the sex of the story character engaged in the behavior. Assertive behavior was viewed as more desirable for males and passive behavior as more desirable for females. There were also sex differences in the way children responded to the three types of behaviors. There was greater approval by girls of passive behaviors and greater approval by boys of aggressive behaviors. These behaviors are thus perceived by children aged 9 to 13 as sex stereotyped. Such perceptions undoubtedly affect the way children evaluate their own behaviors and those of their peers.

In examining other social behaviors, the findings from research using measures of sex typing support the assertion that many of these behaviors are a function of sex-role socialization. Masculine-sex-typed individuals are lowest in self-disclosure, nonverbal sensitivity, empathy, and nurturance. Feminine-sex-typed individuals are lowest in assertiveness and independence (Bem, 1975b; Bem et al., 1976; Fischer & Grande, 1978; Lombardo & Lavine, 1978).

The different friendship patterns of boys and girls may reflect socialization pressures as well. Strommen (1977) argues that, because girls are expected to be more concerned about interpersonal situations, girls' friendships tend to be more intimate. Boys, who are pressured toward independence and assertion, tend toward less intimate friendships. Our culture's proscription against emotional expression in males further serves to limit the depth of their relationships. The cultural relativity of *emotionalism* can be seen by observing males from Mediterranean cultures. "Big boys don't cry" is not a universal message.

Status

One way to view sex differences in social behavior is to view them as a reflection of the differences in status between males and females. In this view, males are perceived as possessing higher status characteristics than females. The behaviors that the sexes develop are thus a function of this status differential and are not necessarily related to sex per se.

The first to propose this kind of analysis was Helen Mayer Hacker (1951), who compared women to other minority groups, specifically to Blacks. She found striking similarities in behavior (flattering or deferential manner, fake shows of helplessness/ignorance), ascribed attributes (inferior intelligence, irresponsibility), rationalizations of status (each has their "place"), discrimination (limits on job and educational opportunities), and problems (unclear roles, role conflict). This analysis is still valid more than 25 years later (Hacker, 1975) and has recently received experimental support from different lines of research.

As was discussed in the section on communication patterns, Henley (1977) has analyzed sex differences in verbal and nonverbal behavior as reflecting differences in status. These differences and her comparisons are summarized in Table 4-1. Thus, females' politeness, smiling, emotional expressiveness, smaller personal space, less frequent touching and talking, and greater frequency of being interrupted all reflect their subordinate status. Females' greater sensitivity to nonverbal cues may reflect a survival mechanism. Since a female's well-being is likely to depend on her "superior's" moods or desires, it is to her advantage to learn to read them well, especially since these "superiors" try to hide them.

Table 4-1

Gestures of Power and Privilege. (Examples of some nonverbal behaviors with usage differing for status equals and nonequals, and for women and men.)[1]

	Between Status Equals		Between Status Nonequals		Between Men and Women	
	Intimate	Nonintimate	Used by Superior	Used by Subordinate	Used by Men	Used by Women
1. Address	Familiar	Polite	Familiar	Polite	Familiar?[2]	Polite?[2]
2. Demeanor	Informal	Circumspect	Informal	Circumspect	Informal	Circumspect
3. Posture	Relaxed	Tense (less relaxed)	Relaxed	Tense	Relaxed	Tense
4. Personal space	Closeness	Distance	Closeness (option)	Distance	Closeness	Distance
5. Time	Long	Short	Long (option)	Short	Long?[2]	Short?[2]
6. Touching	Touch	Don't touch	Touch (option)	Don't touch	Touch	Don't touch
7. Eye contact	Establish	Avoid	Stare, ignore	Avert eyes, watch	Stare, ignore	Avert eyes, watch
8. Facial expression	Smile?[2]	Don't smile?[2]	Don't smile	Smile	Don't smile	Smile
9. Emotional expression	Show	Hide	Hide	Show	Hide	Show
10. Self-disclosure	Disclose	Don't disclose	Don't disclose	Disclose	Don't disclose	Disclose

[1] From *Body Politics: Power, Sex, and Nonverbal Communication*, by N. M. Henley. Copyright 1977 by Prentice-Hall, Inc. Reprinted by permission.

[2] Behavior not known.

Using a different approach, Lockheed and Hall (1976) have demonstrated persuasively that sex differences in activity, influence, and task orientation in small groups reflect differences in status, not simply differences in sex-role socialization. Sherman (1976) has argued that female sexual-caste prescriptions work in a circular fashion: they encourage females to become less competent than males, and this incompetence is then used to justify their inferior status.

One advantage of a status analysis rather than a role analysis is that it focuses attention on the dysfunctional aspects of power and prestige ordering, such as relentless competition and feelings of superiority/inferiority, without implying that all roles must be eliminated. It is not the roles themselves that are problematical; rather, it is the strict division along sex lines and the unequal statuses attached to them that create difficulties.

A second advantage of a status analysis is that it provides suggestions regarding how to alter the effects of a status characteristic. Thus, Lockheed and Hall (1976) summarize ways to increase females' performance in groups—for example, by reinforcing competent behavior of low status individuals. Henley (1977) also makes suggestions as to how to break down the *bodypower barrier*. For example, women can stop smiling when they are not happy and start staring people in the eye. Men can stop interrupting and start displaying some emotion.

SUMMARY

In this chapter, we have reviewed a wide range of social behaviors and have found very few clear-cut sex differences except for aggressiveness (more frequent in males) and for communication patterns (males tend to dominate). Most differences that appear in the literature seem to be differences in quality, not quantity, as in friendship patterns. There is a considerable amount of overlap in all areas surveyed.

In general, girls do not seem more fearful than boys, although they are more willing to admit fears; they are not more dependent when dependency is defined as seeking a caretaker or as number of friends. In fact, by the latter definition, boys are more dependent, since they have more friends and rely on them more for their values. Females do express a greater interest in affiliation during and after childhood than do males but they are not more responsive to social rewards.

In some areas, the data are too unclear to allow definitive statements to be made. Interactions between the situation and the sex of the participant or between the situation and the sex typing of the participant are the major findings in the following areas: competitiveness, compliance, assertiveness, empathy, nurturance, and altruism.

In reviewing explanations for the few sex differences, there is some evidence that a predisposition for aggressiveness is related to prenatal androgen levels and is thus more common in males. But the specific behaviors must be learned by each individual, and society can either encourage or discourage the development of behaviors in one sex or in an individual. Similarly, prenatal androgen exposure may inhibit parental behavior in adults, but this behavior is more clearly a function of learning than of hormonal predisposition.

Differences in verbal and nonverbal communication and in leadership patterns seem to reflect differences in the status of males and females in U.S. society. Male behavior is consistent with males' higher status; female behavior is consistent with the subordinate status of females.

The strong sex-by-situation and sex-typing-by-situation interactions for certain behaviors emphasize the influence of social forces (parental behavior and societal expectations), as do developmental patterns.

In summary, social factors and status factors seem to play the major roles in determining social behaviors and personality functioning. Biological predispositions, however, may be involved for aggression and nurturant behaviors in particular.

RECOMMENDED READING

Deaux, K. *The behavior of women and men*. Monterey, Calif.: Brooks/Cole, 1976. An excellent review of the research on social behaviors.

Eagly, A. Sex differences in influenceability. *Psychological Bulletin*, 1978, *85*, 86–116. A comprehensive review of research on social influence.

Henley, N. M. *Body politics: Power, sex, and nonverbal communication*. Englewood Cliffs, N.J.: Prentice-Hall, 1977. A fascinating analysis of our nonverbal behaviors, using a status analysis.

Whiting, B., & Edwards, C. P. A cross-cultural analysis of sex differences in the behavior of children aged three through eleven. *Journal of Social Psychology*, 1973, *91* (second half), 171–188. An examination of social behaviors in six cultures.

5 | Sexual Behavior

Perhaps no area in the study of sex differences and similarities is more clouded by misconceptions than is the area of sexual behavior. Part of this confusion is due to the very private nature of sexual experiences in our culture. Although a person's social behaviors are observed by many people, an individual's sexual behaviors are viewed by very few others—perhaps by only one other person in the course of a lifetime. This clearly limits factually based generalizations.

In the United States especially, there has been a taboo against talking about sexual feelings and behaviors. This is particularly true

Figure 5-1
A cartoonist's view of male and female communication about sex. (Copyright 1973 by Bülbül. Reprinted by permission.)

for females. This limits the information one can obtain from others. When one does obtain information from self-reports, it is difficult to know its accuracy, which is a general problem. Kinsey's surveys in the 1950s (Kinsey, Pomeroy, & Martin, 1948; Kinsey, Pomeroy, Martin, & Gebhard, 1953), Masters and Johnson's laboratory research (1966) in the 1960s, and Hite's survey of female sexuality (1976) and Pietropinto and Simenauer's survey of male sexuality (1977) in the 1970s have added tremendously to our knowledge of sexual functioning, but research problems still abound.

A major problem in sex research has been researcher bias. Since people have so many preconceived notions of sexual behavior, it is not surprising that these assumptions manifest themselves in the research questions asked. For example, women's reactions to visual stimuli have rarely been studied, since "everyone knows" women do not get turned on by erotica. Similarly, some researchers generalize about human sexuality from animal data despite the fact that nonhuman female primates have no hymen, no orgasm, no menopause, and no voluntary birth control. In addition, nonhuman primate sexuality is determined by the female estrus cycle (Oakley, 1972). The extent to which such researcher biases can influence our attitudes and beliefs is clearly demonstrated in the case of Freud, who postulated the vaginal orgasm as an index of a woman's psychological maturity. Despite the fact that there is no such thing as a vaginal orgasm (scientists now agree that all female orgasms result from clitoral stimulation), Freud was believed for 50 years and is still believed today by many people.

Another research problem is in the use of volunteers. As Abraham Maslow (in Seaman, 1972) demonstrated, people who willingly participate in sex research without financial compensation are usually freer in their sex lives than most people and are less inhibited and more self-actualizing. Consequently, surveys may be using biased samples. Masters and Johnson, however, did pay their subjects and carefully screened them for psychological abnormalities; so such bias in their studies is reduced. One might argue, however, that people who would allow their sexual behavior to be studied in a laboratory still constitute a quite unrepresentative sample.

Sex of the researcher is also an important variable. Male anthropologists often get data only on the male sex life in other cultures either because of their own bias or because females will not talk with them about sexual matters. Israel and Eliason (1971) found an effect of interviewer bias that resulted in each sex giving more traditional answers to same-sex interviewers. This bias certainly would affect survey responses.

Once results are obtained, the data are often interpreted according to prevailing assumptions. Although there is a striking amount of similarity in male and female sexual responses, only the differences have been stressed. Thus, based on the findings that more males than females engage in masturbation, it has been concluded that females are uninterested in sex for its own sake. Yet the same studies also show that more than half of the females do masturbate and achieve orgasm, contradicting the women-as-asexual image.

Keeping these research problems in mind, we will review the current findings regarding sexual behavior. This will be followed by an overview of some explanations proposed to account for the findings.

CURRENT FINDINGS

Perhaps the first area to consider is that related to the physiology of sexual responses. We will then examine the findings on sexual desires, responses to erotic stimuli, homosexuality, and masturbation.

Physiology of Sexual Responses

In Masters and Johnson's revolutionary work (1966), the authors shattered the myth of sex differences in sexual responding. In their laboratory study of 382 women and 312 men, they discerned four phases of human sexual response, each of which is virtually identical in males and in females. These phases are summarized in Table 5-1.

The four phases are as follows:

1. The *excitement* phase is characterized by sexual stimulation producing vasocongestion (filling of the blood vessels). This vasocongestion results in lubrication and clitoral erection in females in 5 to 15 seconds and penile erection in males in 3 to 8 seconds. This response occurs for any kind of effective sexual stimulation, physical or mental.

2. The *plateau* phase results in sexual tension increasing if effective sexual stimulation continues. Both sexes experience generalized skeletal muscle tension, rapid breathing, fast heart rate, and, in some, a body flush. In females, the clitoris retracts while remaining extremely sensitive to traction on the clitoral hood, the vaginal passageway constricts, and the inner two-thirds of the vagina balloons out. In the male, the glans of the penis increases in diameter and the testes are pulled up into the scrotum.

3. In the *orgasmic* phase, a sequence of rhythmic muscular contractions occurs about every .8 seconds, markedly reducing the vasocongestion built up by stimulation. Breathing increases at least three times normal, blood pressure increases by one-third, and heart rate more than doubles. In males, semen is ejaculated. In females, muscular contractions continue longer, and many females can have a further orgasm immediately with continued stimulation. This repeated orgasm is very rare in males.

4. The *resolution* phase completes the cycle, with muscular tension subsiding and the body gradually returning to its preexcitement state. The speed with which this occurs is related to the speed with which excitement occurred—the more slowly the excitement builds up, the more slowly it recedes. If orgasm does not occur, the resolution phase is prolonged, giving rise to a tense, uncomfortable feeling. This is true for both males and females. Males experience a refractory period in which they are temporarily unresponsive to sexual stimulation; females experience no refractory period.

Table 5-1

Four Phases of Human Sexual Response in Males and Females

Male	Female
Excitement Phase	
Erection of penis	Vaginal lubrication
Nipple erection	Nipple erection
Partial elevation of testes	Lengthening and distention of vagina
Plateau Phase	
Fast heart rate (100–175 beats per minute)	Fast heart rate (100–175 beats per minute)
Rapid breathing	Rapid breathing
Elevated blood pressure	Elevated blood pressure
Sex flush (25% incidence)	Sex flush (75% incidence)
Glandular emission of lubricating mucus from penis	Glandular emission of lubricating mucus into vagina
Sometimes deepened color change in head of penis (glans)	Vivid color change in labia minora
Increased circumference in ridge at the penile glans	Decrease in size of vaginal opening
Full elevation of testes	Elevation of uterus
	Retraction of clitoris
Orgasmic Phase	
Rapid breathing	Rapid breathing
Fast heart rate (110–180 beats per minute)	Fast heart rate (110–180 beats per minute)
Increased blood pressure elevation	Increased blood pressure elevation
Rhythmic penile contractions, beginning at .8 second intervals	Rhythmic vaginal contractions, beginning at .8 second intervals
Resolution Phase	
Return to normal breathing, heart rate, and blood pressure	Return to normal breathing, heart rate, and blood pressure
Loss of vasocongestive size increase in penis, scrotum, testes	Loss of vasocongestive size increase in vagina, labia majora, and labia minora
Rapid disappearance of sex flush	Rapid disappearance of sex flush
Perspiring reaction (33% incidence)	Perspiring reaction (33% incidence)
Refractory period—temporary loss of stimulative susceptibility	No refractory period—capable of repeated orgasm if stimulated

Data from *Human Sexual Response*, by W. H. Masters and V. Johnson. Boston: Little, Brown and Company, 1966.

These reactions occur in the same sequence regardless of the type of stimulation (manual, oral, genital) or the source of stimulation (fantasy, masturbation, homosexual stimulation, heterosexual intercourse). Intensity and duration of sexual responses vary. Women generally have more intense and quicker orgasms from manual clitoral stimulation, especially from their own stimulation, than from heterosexual intercourse. In fact, as Kinsey and colleagues (1953) found, during masturbation, a woman takes the same length of time to reach an orgasm as does a man—from two to four minutes. The fact that it usually takes a woman longer to achieve orgasm during intercourse is most often a function of poor coital technique and of poor communication between partners regarding what is most stimulating.

Masters and Johnson's research proved a variety of ideas about sexuality to be false. They found the following facts:

1. Women have sexual responses similar to men except that women are capable of multiple orgasms. This finding is contrary to the belief that women are less sexual than men or that they are even asexual.

2. Women arouse and reach orgasm as quickly as men when stimulation is appropriate, contrary to the belief that women are inherently slower to respond than are men.

3. Women, as well as men, respond with physical discomfort to not reaching an orgasm, contrary to the belief that an orgasm doesn't matter for a woman.

4. Women can achieve full sexual satisfaction without genital intercourse, contrary to the belief that a woman's sexual enjoyment depends on a man. Hite (1976) did find that, with vaginal penetration, orgasm is more diffuse (felt less specifically over wider areas of the body) than without it. This can be either more or less pleasurable for a woman, depending on individual preference.

5. Women have only one kind of orgasm, based in the clitoris, although contractions are felt in the vagina. This is contrary to Freud's distinction between a vaginal and a clitoral orgasm, the former, according to Freud, being more "mature."

6. The subjective experience of orgasm is essentially the same for females and males. This was confirmed in an experimental study in which people closely concerned with sexual behavior (for example, psychologists, obstetricians/gynecologists, medical students) were unable to distinguish the sex of a person from that person's written description of his or her orgasm (Proctor, Wagner, & Butler, 1974).

These findings have altered traditional thinking about female sexuality, but changes in awareness have come slowly. Hite (1976) found that, ten years after Masters and Johnson's research was published, many women still believe the traditional view of their sexuality, even though they know that they do not conform to it. She found that most women have more intense, quicker orgasms with masturbation than with intercourse but that they feel they should not do so. The consequences of holding a traditional view of female sexuality may be feelings of insecurity and inferiority (LoPiccolo & Heiman, 1977). As Hite notes, there is no great mystery about why a woman has an orgasm. The key is adequate stimulation, and, for most females, this is simply not supplied by intercourse, since clitoral stimulation, if it occurs, is usually indirect.

Sexual Desires

Another misconception resistant to refutation is that of men's stronger sex drives. It is important to differentiate among sexual desire, sexual interest, and sexual experience. Some evidence indicates that males generally have more sexual experiences (summing all types of experiences together) than do females (DeLora & Warren, 1977; Kinsey et al., 1948, 1953), but this is a function of age and social factors, such as social class. For males, the highest point of sexual activity occurs around the age of 18; for women, around the age of 30. Sexual activity also varies with marital status for females but not for males.

Few studies have directly examined women's sexual desires. From the studies that have dealt with female desires, confusing or contradictory results have emerged. There is some suggestion that women may have a peak of sexual desire at a specific phase of their menstrual cycle. For some women, the peak corresponds to their ovulatory phase; for others, the menstrual phase (Adams, Gold, & Burt, 1978; Money & Ehrhardt, 1972). This finding is far from conclusive and depends, at least in part, upon the form of birth control used.

Mancini and Orthner (1978) studied recreational preferences among more than five hundred middle-class wives and husbands. They found that wives were more likely to prefer reading a book to sexual and affectional activity (37% preferred the former; 26%, the latter). Husbands, on the other hand, preferred sexual and affectional activities over attending athletic events and reading books (45%, 41%, 33%, respectively). If women are less interested in sex than are men, Hite (1976) suggests that it is most likely because they do not expect to achieve orgasm from it. Intercourse may not be a particularly satisfying experience for many women. The fact that this dissatisfaction results from inadequate stimulation and not from a personal or female-related defect is usually neither known nor acknowledged.

Since the 1950s, there has been an increase in premarital sex among women to the extent that, of married couples 18 to 24 years of age, 95% of the males and 81% of the females have had premarital sex (Hunt, 1974). This can be compared to 92% of the male, and 65% of the female, partners in married couples in the age group of 25 to 34 years old. Hopkins (1977), in his review of surveys conducted between the 1930s and the 1970s on the sexual behavior of adolescents, concludes that a larger number of college-age people are sexually experienced now than in earlier generations. There has been a greater increase in the incidence of premarital intercourse for college females than for males (from about 25% of all college females in the mid-1960s to about 70% to 85% in the mid-1970s), although most surveys still report a higher absolute incidence for males. These findings suggest that the younger generation of women may be more interested in sex, or at least its manifestation in intercourse, than previous generations. These findings also suggest that societal expectations regarding women's sexual activities have changed. Glenn and Weaver (1979), in analyzing survey responses of more than 10,000 people from 1972 to 1978, concluded that society has indeed become more permissive of premarital sexual activity. This permissiveness was most marked for individuals aged 18 to 29 and for those with more than 12 years of education. Virginity is no longer a necessity for marriage for young women, and, therefore, fewer feel compelled to retain it or to say they have retained it.

Interestingly, men's interest in sex may be less important than once was believed. In a recent survey of 1,990 men conducted by Louis Harris and Associates for Playboy Enterprises (reported by Brozan, 1979), slightly less than half (49%) of the men surveyed considered sex as "very important" for life satisfaction. Of greater importance, in order of preference, were health, love, peace of mind, family life, work, friends, respect from others, and education. Only religion and money, in that order, figured lower than sex.

Yet, despite the above findings—the more permissive attitudes regarding sex and the nearly equal numbers of males and females currently engaging in sexual activity—the belief persists that men have stronger sex drives than do women (Byrne, 1977; Gross, 1978). Since the male sex drive is believed to be stronger than the female drive, sex is perceived by both females and males as being more important and enjoyable for men than for women. This belief is particularly evident in married and dating couples (see reviews by Gross, 1978; Peplau, Rubin, & Hill, 1977; Rainwater, 1965).

Males usually do seem to take the lead in heterosexual activities, both in initiating sexual contact and in controlling the sexual interaction itself (Gagnon & Simon, 1973; Masters & Johnson, 1979; Peplau et al., 1977; Safilios-Rothschild, 1977). Women appear to exert more negative control; that is, they may resist or encourage sexual advances but may not initiate them. This double standard regarding sexual initiative still remains strong, although attitudes about its acceptability may be changing (Komarovsky, 1976; Peplau et al., 1977). Peplau and colleagues (1977) suggest that such sexual role playing persists because it serves to structure sexual interactions and facilitates interpreting behavior.

Meaning of Sex. Regardless of similarities or differences between the sexes in sexual interest, there does seem to be an important difference between males and females in the meaning attached to sex (see Athanasiou, Shaver, & Tavris, 1970; Gross, 1978; Hite, 1976; Peplau et al., 1977; Tavris, 1973). Females generally connect sex with feelings of affection and closeness; males often see sex as an achievement, an adventure, a demonstration of control and power, or a purely physical release. Various studies have found that women generally have fewer partners than do men. Their first experience is usually with someone with whom they are romantically involved. They are also more likely to use sex to get love, rather than using love to get sex. This is true before, during, and outside marriage and for homosexual relationships as well as heterosexual ones. Hite (1976) found also that the chief pleasures of sex and intercourse for women are the shared feelings, the emotional warmth, and the feeling of being wanted and needed, not the physical sensations per se. Men, on the other hand, tend to isolate sex from other aspects of relationships and are more likely than women to view any heterosexual relationship in a sexual-romantic framework (Gross, 1978). Other studies question these conclusions, however. Pietropinto and Simenauer (1977), after surveying over 4000 men, conclude that most men, like most women, prefer having love and sex together, although men, perhaps, are more likely to separate them. Masters and Johnson (1979) found that, contrary to belief, both heterosexual men and heterosexual women are preoccupied with attaining orgasm, especially when contrasted with homosexuals of both sexes.

These differences in the meaning of sex may be due to the fact that intercourse often is not satisfying for females or is less satisfying than is masturbation. Hence, the secondary gains of intimacy may be the only benefit some females experience. These differences may also be a function of the different socialization experiences for males and for females in our society. As Gross (1978) and others have noted, sex is commonly viewed as a major proving ground of a male's masculinity. Quantity, more than quality, is stressed, with many negative consequences as a result.

Some of the negative consequences manifest themselves in sexual dysfunction. For males, problems with impotence or premature ejaculation often arise from pressure to perform and from an exclusive goal orientation, both being parts of the male role. As Masters and Johnson (1974) note, this very pressure can be self-defeating. In females, sexual dysfunction often takes the form of inability to have an orgasm. In the past, such women were termed *frigid*. Now they are called *preorgasmic*, since it is understood that, with proper stimulation, any female can have an orgasm. Instruction on self-stimulation has been markedly effective in this regard. Modern sex therapists treat sexual problems more as learning and communication problems than as a reflection of physiological problems, although the latter sometimes occur. These physiological problems, too, can be successfully treated.

Response to Erotic Stimuli

Another strong belief in our society is that males are sexually aroused, especially by visual stimuli and by their own fantasies, more frequently and more easily than are females. This belief regarding arousal is part of the male stereotype of a stronger sex drive. In fact, females do get aroused by erotic material, and females do have sexual fantasies.

Research on reactions to erotic stimuli generally has used only male subjects or has used materials with explicit sexual content aimed almost exclusively at heterosexual males. Hence, accurate data on female responsiveness have been minimal. However, a few well controlled studies have confirmed that females do respond to erotic and erotic/romantic stimuli (stories, pictures, films) with levels of arousal equal to that of males (Byrne & Lamberth, 1971; Fisher & Byrne, 1978; Heiman, 1975; Masters & Johnson, 1966; Schmidt, 1975; Schmidt, Sigusch, & Shafer, 1973). In one study (Schmidt & Sigusch, 1973), from 80% to 91% of the men were aroused, while 70% to 83% of the women were aroused, with considerable intragroup differences in responding. There is some suggestion that males may respond more than women to posed pictures of the other sex, but this may be due to differences in pictures or to differences in experience. Certainly the female form has been pictured more frequently in sexual poses in advertising and pornography than has the male form. (See Figure 5-2.) Fisher and Byrne (1978) found that the females in their experiments had less contact with erotica and had more negative beliefs about it than did the males. Despite these differences, when actually exposed to erotic films, the sexes reported equal levels of arousal.

A problem with some of the older studies (for example, Kinsey et al., 1948, 1953) is that they relied purely on self-reports. As Heiman (1975) documented, women sometimes do not know when they are physiologically aroused, or else they feel reluctant to report this arousal. This reluctance may be due to conditioning and also to the fact that female sexual arousal (vaginal lubrication) is much less noticeable to the woman herself than is male arousal (erection) to the man.

Another finding from more recent studies is that females do not respond more to romantic stories than to erotic ones, as Kinsey had hypothesized. Rather, both sexes respond most to explicit sex stories, women sometimes responding more than men (Fisher & Byrne, 1978; Heiman, 1975).

In regard to erotic fantasies, it appears that both sexes are able to arouse themselves through fantasy (Heiman, 1975), and the majority of both sexes do arouse themselves in this way (Hariton, 1973; Kinsey

Figure 5-2
Example of the female form used for advertising unrelated products. (Courtesy of Sanders Bootmakers.)

et al., 1948, 1953). The great popularity of Erica Jong's *Fear of Flying* (1973) may reflect women's identification with the heroine's sexual fantasies.

Homosexuality

Although it is difficult to obtain precise figures, in our culture, more males than females are apt to have had a homosexual experience or be exclusively homosexual (Athanasiou et al., 1970; Hunt; 1974; Kinsey et al., 1948, 1953).

One difficulty in obtaining precise estimates derives from the fact that homosexuality is not an exclusive identification. Homosexuality and heterosexuality are points on a continuum of sexual orientation, with many points in between. For example, some people have homosexual fantasies but have had no corresponding experience; some have had a homosexual experience but prefer heterosexual ones; and so on. Consequently, classifying people as either heterosexual or homosexual depends on the definitions of these terms that are used. The number of people in each category will vary accordingly. Another difficulty in obtaining accurate figures is that, since homosexuality is such a stigma in our society (Lehne, 1976; Morin & Garfinkle, 1978), many people are reluctant to admit to engaging in any homosexual behaviors.

It does appear, however, that sexual attraction between same-sex members is common and that, by age 45, approximately one-third of all men and one-fifth of all women have had at least one homosexual experience (Hunt, 1974; Kinsey et al., 1948, 1953). The number of exclusive homosexuals after age 15—from 3% to 5% of all males and from 1% to 2% of all females—is much smaller than the figures cited above for homosexual experiences (Athanasiou et al., 1970; Hunt, 1974; Kinsey et al., 1948, 1953). These findings are approximate.

In our culture, there is a greater stigma attached to male homosexuality and greater persecution of male homosexuals than is the case with their female counterparts (see Morin & Garfinkle, 1978, for a review of such studies). This difference in social opinion may reflect the greater importance and status our society attaches to anything "masculine." Therefore, a deviation from masculine behavior is more disapproved of than is a deviation from feminine behavior. Supporting evidence for this hypothesis comes from the observation that, among male homosexuals, it is those who are more effeminate who receive the most harassment and disapproval, even from other homosexuals (Chafetz, 1978).

Although homosexuality is often considered a mental disorder (the American Psychiatric Association removed it from its classification system only in 1973), most controlled research has indicated that homosexuals as a group are as emotionally stable as heterosexuals. (See Riess & Safer, 1979, for a review.) In fact, some homosexuals may have even stronger ego controls than heterosexuals (Freedman, 1975; Thompson, McCandless, & Strickland, 1971). Yet, psychotherapists still tend to view a hypothetical client (male or female) who holds a homosexual orientation as less psychologically healthy than an identical person with a heterosexual orientation (Garfinkle & Morin, 1978). When emotional problems *are* found in individuals with a homosexual orientation, one major cause of those problems often is the heavy stress under which such individuals are placed by an anti-homosexual society.

Interestingly, sex differences in homosexual behavior seem to reflect the same sex differences in sexual functioning as was previously noted for heterosexuals. Males tend to have more sex with more partners and in the context of more short-term relationships than do females (Athanasiou et al., 1970; Bell & Weinberg, 1978; Kinsey et al., 1948, 1953). Male homosexuals also tend to act on their sexual feelings earlier than do female homosexuals (Riddle & Morin, 1977), just as heterosexual males act earlier than do heterosexual females. Female homosexuals appear to emphasize the importance of emotional attachments over sexual behaviors more than do male homosexuals (de Monteflores & Schultz, 1978), again in keeping with the heterosexual pattern.

These same patterns are found as well for bisexuals (those who relate sexually to both males and females under some circumstances) (Blumstein & Schwartz, 1977). These results concerning homosexuals and bisexuals indicate that sex-typed sexual behaviors occur regardless of the sexual orientation of the person.

Masturbation

Sex differences are also found when individuals sexually stimulate themselves—that is, in masturbation. More males engage in masturbation more frequently than do females, although, with increased sexual awareness on the part of females, these numerical differences seem to be changing (Mosher & Abramson, in press). Virtually all men and two-thirds of all women have masturbated (Hunt, 1974; Kinsey et al., 1948, 1953). The fact that some women never masturbate is important in light of the findings that masturbation is strongly related to the ability to have coital orgasms (Kinsey et al., 1953).

EXPLANATIONS

Since sex is necessary for the reproduction of the species and since it involves many physiological responses, some researchers lean toward a physiological explanation of sexual behavior. Others stress psychosocial factors and status differences. As will be demonstrated, all these factors interact. The strongest factors, however, seem to be the environmental ones.

Physiology

"Men are just naturally more interested in sex than women." "Men's urges are stronger, you know." These comments reflect the belief that physiological factors underlie differences in sexual behavior. Explanations invoking physiological processes center on hormones, anatomy, and evolutionary development.

Hormones.   Sexual interest, or libido, for both males and females has been related both prenatally and postnatally to the hormone androgen (Barfield, 1976; Money & Ehrhardt, 1972). Androgen secretion appears to lower the threshold of arousal and to increase the energy with which sexual activity is pursued in both humans and animals. Even in animals, however, social factors and past experience play the more important role (Barfield, 1976). In humans, behavior is more variable and freer from direct hormonal control than is the case with animals. Consequently, the effect of experience is even greater. Even in individuals who reach puberty earlier than usual due to hormonal changes, sexual behavior still appears at the appropriate age and in the appropriate way (Hamburg & Lunde, 1966). Therefore, although generally higher androgen levels in males may tend to lower their arousal threshold, social factors could either encourage or discourage related sexual behavior. In our society, such behaviors are encouraged in males but not in females. It bears repeating that there is wide individual variation in androgen secretion, and some females secrete more androgen than do some males.

Changes in women's sexual desires as a function of menstrual cycle, although not consistently found, have been related by some researchers to changes in hormones (for example, Adams et al., 1978). However, the data have been contradictory, and social factors have been so important that no definitive statement can be made at this time. For example, a peak in desire premenstrually may relate to anticipated sexual abstinence during menstruation, to increased vasocongestion, or to the unlikelihood of conception at that time (Barfield, 1976).

There is no known correlation between homosexuality and either prenatal or postnatal sex hormones (Barfield, 1976; Money & Ehrhardt, 1972). Genetic females (those with two X chromosomes) who were exposed to androgen prenatally are no more likely to be homosexual than females not exposed to androgen during that period. Although hormones may affect the amount of sexual energy, they do not affect the choice of sex partner. For this and other aspects of sexual behavior, learning and social factors are the most important.

Similarly, the age difference in sexual peaks for males and females does not appear to be due to any difference in hormones. It is now generally agreed that such peaks reflect differences in social training.

Anatomy.   The fact that males and females have different sex organs has been held by some to account for the sex differences in sexual behavior. By this reasoning, the greater visibility and accessibility of the penis (as opposed to the clitoris) and the use of the penis in urination may orient a boy to handling it and discovering its pleasurable qualities. This may account for males' greater likelihood of masturbation (Bardwick, 1971; Gagnon & Simon, 1973). At puberty, a male's attention is further focused on his genitals by the increased frequency of erections and by the start of seminal emissions. Female genitals, on the other hand, are easier to ignore, often remaining unlabeled (referred to only as "down there"), and their signs of arous-al are subtler. As Heiman (1975) found, some women misread their physiological arousal. This may occur because females have relative-ly less experience in producing and identifying such states than do males, since they tend to masturbate less than males. Furthermore, since masturbation is clitoral, it would be difficult to imagine vaginal intercourse as pleasurable. Puberty for females is marked by men-struation, which has reproductive, rather than sexual, significance and which is often surrounded by fear or mystery. Thus, anatomical differences may lead to differences in attention being paid to genita-lia. This differential attention may be further socialized into two different scripts (behavioral blueprints) concerning sexual behavior for males and females (Gagnon & Simon, 1973; Laws & Schwartz, 1977).

Freud (1905, 1924a, 1924b) spelled out the anatomy-is-destiny approach quite comprehensively and is most closely identified with it. In brief, he posited that a child's sex-role development is based on unconscious reactions to anatomical differences. When a little boy (age 3 to 6) discovers that a female does not have a penis, he becomes afraid of losing his. This *castration anxiety* forces him to repress his desire for his mother and to identify with his father. By identifying with the father, the little boy's fear of punishment is reduced, since he believes that the father would not punish someone so much like him. This male form of resolution of the *Oedipal complex* leads to the de-velopment of a strong superego (through fear of punishment) and a strong male sex-role identification.

A little girl, on the other hand, upon discovering she does not have a penis, envies a male and feels inferior. She rejects her mother and looks to her father for a replacement penis. The resolution of her Oedipal complex occurs when she accepts the impossibility of her wish for a penis and compensates for it by desiring a child. This *penis envy* on the part of females has enormous consequences for their personality development, according to Freud. He concluded that, firstly, females have weaker superegos than males, since their Oedi-pal complex is resolved by envy, not fear. Secondly, he concluded that females feel inferior to males and consequently develop a personality characterized by masochism, passivity, and narcissism. Thirdly, he believed that females give up their clitoral focus in masturbation and begin to prepare for adult gratification via vaginal stimulation.

Freud's theory has been criticized on a variety of grounds. What concern us here are the criticisms of penis envy and its conse-quences. As was noted previously, there is no evidence that females are more passive or masochistic than males, or that they have inferior superegos. In addition, the vaginal/clitoral orgasm differentiation is incorrect. All orgasms are clitorally based regardless of stimulation. There is also no evidence that little girls believe they are anatomical-ly inferior to boys or that they blame their mothers for lack of a penis, and so on. Freud's theory reflects a strong male bias: he regards sexuality itself as male, he bases his theory on a patriarchal society, and he assumes that everyone recognizes a penis as inherently superior (see Millet, 1970, for an interesting critique). If young girls do envy boys, they more likely are envying males' higher status and greater power rather than the male anatomical appendage (Horney, 1922). Furthermore, an equally persuasive argument can be made for male *womb envy*. This envy is theoretically manifested in the way males develop rituals and develop a greater achievement orientation as compensation for their inability to conceive (see Bettelheim, 1962; Chesler, 1978; Collins, 1979). Thus, although anatomy may influence an individual's sexual development, Freud's "destiny" edict is greatly overstated and very male biased.

Evolution. Before leaving physiological explanations, the explanation based on evolutionary development merits consideration. Mary Jane Sherfey (1974) argues that women have a biologically based inordinate sexual drive. As evidence, she cites women's potential for multiple orgasms, and she includes the fact that the more orgasms a woman achieves, the more she can achieve. This sexual capacity may have evolved because the more erotic primates bred more and therefore reproduced more than the less erotic primates. In humans, however, women's inordinate sexual drive had to be suppressed if family life and agricultural economies were to develop, since the female sex drive interfered with maternal responsibility and the establishment of property rights and kinship laws, all elements vital to modern civilization. Thus, Sherfey (1974) describes how men had to suppress female sexuality in order to establish family life and maintain their own position of power and the power of patriarchy.

There are many problems with Sherfey's theory. In the first place, there is no conclusive evidence that female hypersexuality ever existed, even in tribal hunting societies (Tavris & Offir, 1977). Also, her theory cannot account for societal differences. As we shall see, female sexuality is not universally suppressed. In addition, the theory itself reflects a curious patriarchal bias in which men are viewed as coming to the rescue of society and in which women are viewed, in terms of their sexuality, as being unable to control themselves. Thus, although provocative, Sherfey's theory remains in the realm of speculation. It does highlight, however, the greater, often unused, potential that females have for sexual enjoyment.

Another type of explanation based on evolutionary development is the sociobiological one. Donald Symons (1979) has argued that differences in sexual conduct between women and men relate to different reproductive strategies in the sexes. These different strategies ultimately are dependent on the differences between sperm and egg cells. Because men produce a large number of sperm, their reproductive strategy is to have many sexual partners and transient relationships. Women, because they have a small supply of eggs and must carry a child for at least 9 months, require stable relations with a good provider. Symons' arguments, albeit provocative, involve much speculation and ignore contradictory evidence that is currently available. Symons also bases his entire explanation on sexual conduct in the United States, despite the fact that sexual behavior varies widely in different cultures. Therefore, although his explanation has a certain simplistic appeal, it does not appear to be well substantiated.

In sum, physiological factors do not clearly explain male and female sexual behavior. Psychosocial factors also need to be examined.

Psychosocial Factors

Evidence for the importance of psychosocial factors in the development of sexual behavior comes from three major sources: personality correlates and learning, sex-role expectations, and cross-cultural studies.

Personality Correlates and Learning. The fact that social factors influence sexual behavior can be seen in the studies of personality correlates. Oakley (1972) summarizes research that shows that the more assertive and self-confident the individual (male or female), the greater is that person's capacity for sexual fulfillment. Thus, contrary to Freud's hypotheses, unconventionally assertive women are the sexiest; passive and conforming women, the least sexy or sexually satisfied (Maslow, 1942; Seaman, 1972). Clearly, more factors than anatomical ones are at work here. Similarly, other studies (for example, Bell, 1971) have found that, with women, sexual satisfaction is directly related to the level of education attained.

The importance of learning in sexual behavior is illustrated by the finding that the ability to respond sexually, for both sexes, is at least partly a function of experience (Kinsey et al., 1948, 1953). Since women begin all forms of sexual activity later than men, their peak of sexual activity occurs later.

Sex-Role Expectations. In our society, as in most societies, females and males have different sexual scripts (Gagnon & Simon, 1973; Laws & Schwartz, 1977). In the United States, parents expect the adolescent son, but not the daughter, to have overt sexual activity. They therefore are more restrictive of the daughter's behavior, which retards her sexual experimentation (Oakley, 1972; Schofield, 1968). Consequently, adolescent rebellion in girls usually consists of sexual "offenses," whereas adolescent rebellion in boys usually does not involve sex. In fact, the labeling of adolescent female sexual activity as deviant or as an offense is itself an example of the sexual double standard. Such behavior in adolescent males is expected and often encouraged. For adolescent females to have sexual experiences, they often deliberately have to reject their families. This is not true for boys.

Because females can become pregnant, their socialization typically emphasizes this consequence of sexual activity. Females usually learn about sex as connected to reproduction, family life, and emotional ties. They are thereby trained to think about "catching" a mate, using sex as a bait if necessary. Females' limited sexual exploration, combined with their minimal experience with masturbation, may cause some females to mature without having had any sexual gratification. It therefore may be difficult for them to connect heterosexual sex activity with pleasure. Female sexuality is never spoken of as valuable or worthwhile in and of itself, but only as a means to an end. Many females learn to use their sexuality in this way and become quite manipulative. One-fourth of the women answering a survey in *Psychology Today* magazine reported using sex to bind a person into a relationship; two-thirds admitted to faking an orgasm to make their partner feel good and avoid rejection (Tavris, 1973).

The devaluation of female sexuality is also evident in our double standard of shamefulness (Gullahorn, 1977a). Female genitals are either unlabeled or derogatorily labeled (for example, "down there," "cunt"). Girls are encouraged to conceal "their privates" with clothes, leg positions, and deodorant. It is therefore not surprising that some women never touch their genitals nor learn to masturbate.

Boys, on the other hand, are taught to view sex as a way of proving their masculinity. This emphasis reflects the pressure on males to consistently achieve in all areas of their lives (Fasteau, 1974; Gross, 1978; Gullahorn, 1977). In the sexual area, this may result in the males' trying to "score"—that is, have many sexual experiences with many partners and, for the "modern" male, bring their partners to many orgasms. Numbers matter, not the quality of the experience. This exclusive goal orientation may be a result of early male mastur-batory experiences in which the focus is solely on producing an orgasm. As a result of this achievement focus, females are often viewed solely in their sexual roles (for example, "a piece of ass"), and sex itself is viewed as a conquest rather than as a form of communica-tion. (See Figure 5-1.) In the 1973 (Tavris) survey previously cited, over half of the men that were questioned admitted to using decep-tion in order to have sex.

Males are also expected to be in control, to take the lead, in sexual areas particularly. This control may sometimes be a burden. In one study (Carlson, 1976), nearly half of the husbands felt that the responsibility for sexual initiation should be equal between husband and wife. Yet women feel uncomfortable as the initiator, perhaps because they sense men's ambivalence about losing control (Komar-ovsky, 1976; Safilios-Rothschild, 1977). The pressure to appear in charge may also make men hesitant to reveal ignorance or uncertain-ty, thereby inhibiting open communication between partners about sexual interactions (Gross, 1978; Masters & Johnson, 1979).

The consequences of the male sexual role are many. The unstated permission to masturbate may limit male sexuality to the genitals and make sex entirely goal oriented, thus limiting the pleasure of a sex-ual experience. The constant pressure to achieve may lead to impo-tence, since anxiety is inconsistent with sexual arousal (Julty, 1972; Masters & Johnson, 1970). Yet, if sexual difficulties occur, a man is more likely to be censured by other men for his "inadequacies" than is a woman with similar difficulties to be censured by other women (Polyson, 1978). Women do not show this same negative attitude to-ward sexually troubled men, although men may not be aware of, or believe, that. Thus, open communication with one's partner is re-stricted.

If we consider the two different cultural scripts for males and females, we can better understand why more males express interest in, and participate in, sexual activities than do females. They must be more interested if they are "real men." Sex for many is another area of achievement or of power, unconnected to feelings of intimacy. Similarly, we can understand why some women never learn to enjoy their own sexuality. They haven't had the experience, and, besides, they shouldn't enjoy it if they are "good girls." Sex is all right only in the context of a relationship, only as a means to an end. These expectations, or cultural scripts, combine with both a societal preoccupation with sex and a social taboo against talking about sex, especially for females. The results are serious misunderstandings, dishonesty ("scoring," "faking it"), and a lack of full sexual enjoyment for both sexes, particularly for females. Hence, we find greater numbers of women who can achieve orgasm through masturbation rather than through genital intercourse.

Liberating men from their stereotype as sex agents and liberating women from their stereotype as sex objects will result in a sexuality based on authentic concern for the persons involved, whether it be part of play, affection, or love. This form of sexuality will undoubtedly be deeper and more rewarding for those concerned than the manipulative form of sexuality we now often have.

Cross-Cultural Studies. Nowhere can the social bases of our sexual behavior be more clearly seen than in comparisons with other cultures. When different cultures have different forms of sexual behavior, it is apparent that these behaviors cannot have primarily a physiological basis. In observing such behaviors in a wide range of cultures, enormous variability has been found.

Cultures vary on a number of factors related to sexual behavior:

1. The amount of sexual play permitted between children varies between cultures. For example, Trobrian Islanders (Malinowski, 1932) and the Yolngu in Australia (Money & Ehrhardt, 1972) encourage such play; the U.S. strongly discourages it.

2. The permissibility of intercourse before marriage is strongly encouraged in Mangaia, Polynesia (Marshall, 1971), and by Pilagá Indians in Argentina (Money & Ehrhardt, 1972), but is strongly discouraged in the Batak culture of northern Sumatra (Money & Ehrhardt, 1972) and in the U.S.

3. The latitude of sexual activity after marriage varies widely, from strict monogamy among the Batak, to serial monogamy in the U.S., to extramarital relations in Mangaia.

4. The importance attached to sexual activity itself ranges from highly desirable, as in the Truk Islands (Malinowski, 1932) and among Mangaians, to very unimportant and secondary, as among the Arapesh of New Guinea (Mead, 1935).

5. The extent to which sexual desire is seen as dangerous varies from the Manus (Malinowski, 1932), who encourage restraint, to the Balinese, who view the sex drive as very weak (Malinowski, 1932).

6. The acceptance of homosexuality differs from encouragement during certain ages in the Batak culture, to acceptance by American Mohave

Indians (Devereaux, 1937), to nearly total rejection in the U.S. and Nicaragua.

7. The expectation of sex differences in sexual behavior ranges from no expectation of a difference, as in Southwest Pacific societies like Mangaia (Marshall, 1971), to an expectation that the female sex drive is stronger, as among Trobriand Islanders and the Kwoma and Mataco (Malinowski, 1932), to an expectation that the male sex drive is stronger, as in Latin America.

In those societies where the sexes are seen as equal in sexual potential (for example, Mangaia), the sexes do not have different sexual peaks, sex is not linked necessarily to love for women, and frigidity and premature ejaculation are rare. Thus, the cultural relativity of our sexual sex-role standards and their consequences are readily apparent.

Status

Another way of explaining sex differences in sexual behavior is by examining the differences in status and power between the sexes in our culture. We live in a patriarchy, in which men hold economic and material power. This holds several direct consequences for sexual behavior.

One major consequence of patriarchy, as Millet (1970) points out, may be that, for females to obtain economic and material security, they must barter their sexual availability either through marriage or prostitution. Thus, females may use sex as a means to an end, subordinating their own desires to those of the male, distorting their self-image and personality in the process. Men end up distrusting women and being afraid of getting "hooked." Hite (1976) found that, for several reasons, women were very reluctant to create their own orgasms either through masturbation or by requesting certain behaviors from their partner: habit, fear of losing their man's "love," and, especially, fear of economic recrimination. In our marriage laws, a woman is required to have sexual intercourse with her husband; she need not enjoy it, and many do not enjoy it. If a woman is financially and emotionally dependent on a man, she is not in a good position to demand equality in bed.

Another consequence of patriarchy is men's control of women's biological functioning. Laws and institutions regulating contraception, pregnancy, and childbirth are made and run by men. Thus, women are prevented from controlling their own bodies. Their sexuality remains tied to their reproductive functioning, whereas men's sexuality is not tied to reproduction. This may limit more than a woman's sexuality—such dependence limits career and educational plans as well. Since the late 1960s, there have been increasing challenges to this aspect of patriarchy, but the continuing battle over abortion laws and contraceptive availability indicate that the struggle is far from over.

Patriarchy also restricts female behavior and activities, including sexual behavior. This is clearly shown by the various conceptions of sexuality and of healthy, versus dysfunctional, behavior held by scholars throughout Western history (LoPiccolo & Heiman, 1977). For example, Freud (1924b) wrote that "masturbation at all events *[sic]* of the clitoris is a masculine activity, and the elimination of clitoral sexuality is a necessary precondition for the development of femininity."

Women's major role in our culture has been to serve the needs of others, particularly the needs of men and of children. Thus, women have been oriented to satisfy men's sexual needs without any thoughts about their own needs or about any expectation of reciprocity. The double standard of sexual behavior is very ingrained in America. Men are supposed to need, want, and enjoy sex; women are not supposed to do any of these things. As Hite (1976) notes, "Lack of sexual satisfaction is another sign of the oppression of women" (p. 420).

A related consequence for females of a patriarchal society is defining sexuality using the male as the norm. Thus, sexuality in our culture is *phallocentric;* that is, sex is defined as genital intercourse and male orgasm. Female satisfaction occurs in foreplay or in afterplay, if it occurs at all, but it is not the main point of sexual activity (Rotkin, 1972). Many people still believe in vaginal orgasms because such orgasms require a penis; a clitoral orgasm does not have that requirement. Other evidence of phallocentrism can be seen in the following facts: (1) A female generally is considered to be a "virgin" as long as she has not had genital intercourse; (2) the clitoris usually is defined as a miniature penis rather than the penis being defined as an enlarged clitoris, though the latter definition is phylogenetically more accurate (see Chapter Two); (3) premature ejaculation is sometimes viewed as the cause of female frigidity, although the penis does not provide the best mode for producing female orgasms.

The effects of phallocentricity are far-reaching for females and for males. Females often give up expecting sexual satisfaction and use sexual contacts to secure affection and security rather than for sexual pleasure. Or they feel guilty about their desires and think they are abnormal, immature, and so on. Men, on the other hand, are under increased pressure to identify themselves with their penis, and some see in it the answer to all problems. (See Figure 5-3 for one example.) Thus, any sexual difficulty for either the male or the female partner reflects on the male's masculinity, on his psychological effectiveness, and on his personal identity (Julty, 1972; Polyson, 1978). In addition, as females increase their substitute demands of love and commitment, males become more confused, more guilty, and more alienated. This further reduces compatibility (Masters & Johnson, 1974; Rotkin, 1972).

One way to avoid these consequences is to redefine sexuality. The clitoris needs to be recognized as equal with the penis as a center of human sexuality. Females need to be recognized as having separate sexual centers for gratification (clitoris) and for reproduction (vagina). Whereas reproduction requires intercourse, gratification does not, although intercourse may well provide secondary pleasures. A liberation from constricting sex roles is needed as well as is a change

Figure 5-3
An often proposed solution to female unhappiness. (Copyright 1973 by Bülbül. Reprinted by permission.)

in the patriarchal system. As Masters and Johnson (1974) note, "The most effective sex is not something a man does to or for a woman but something a man and woman do together as *equals*" (p. 84).

SUMMARY

It can be said, in summary, that there are some similarities between the sexes in sexual behavior, and there are some differences. Male and female sexual responses are virtually identical with one exception: females are capable of multiple orgasms, and most males are not. Both sexes have sexual fantasies and become aroused by erotic material, although most material is aimed solely at heterosexual males. In our culture, males are generally more sexually active and express greater interest in sex than do females, although females are far from inactive. Fewer females than males have orgasms. Orgasms experienced during masturbation are generally more intense for females than those experienced during intercourse. There is generally a qualitative difference in sexual behavior for males and females—sex tends to be tied more to love and affection for females and more to achievement for males. A minority of individuals of both sexes partake in some homosexual activity, and sex differences in such activities are similar to those for heterosexuals. More males engage in homosexual activity and in masturbation than do females.

Physiological factors do not adequately account for the differences between males and females in sexual behavior, although they may provide the basis for different socialization experiences. Culture puts a value on certain behaviors and characteristics, endowing some characteristics with more status and more power than others. In most cultures, males have the power. From the different experiences and scripts for the sexes, different sexual behaviors develop.

RECOMMENDED READING

Gross, A. E. The male role and heterosexual behavior. *Journal of Social Issues*, 1978, *34*(1), 87–107. A review of research relating sexual behavior to the male sex role.

Hite, S. *The Hite report: A nationwide study of female sexuality.* New York: Macmillan, 1976. A controversial survey with interesting first-person comments.

Masters, W., & Johnson, V. E. *Human sexual response.* Boston: Little, Brown, 1966. Also, *Human sexual inadequacy.* Boston: Little, Brown, 1970. Two of the seminal works in the area of sexual functioning.

Peplau, L. A., & Hammen, C. L. (Eds.). Sexual behavior: Social psychological issues. *Journal of Social Issues*, 1977, *33*(Whole No. 2). Recent research in the area of sexual behavior relating to social psychology.

Safilios-Rothschild, C. *Love, sex, and sex roles.* Englewood Cliffs, N.J.: Prentice Hall, 1977. An informative analysis of the relationship among love, sex, and sex roles.

PART TWO: SUMMARY

After reviewing the current findings related to sex differences and similarities, certain general conclusions can be stated. Summary Table 1 summarizes the information in the physical, cognitive, personality, social, and sexual areas.

Table 1. Summary of Sex Comparisons

Physical

Anatomy: Females have a uterus, ovaries, a clitoris, and a vagina. Males have testes, a penis, and a scrotum. Males tend to be bigger and more muscular.

Processes: Females mature faster, have slower metabolism. Differences in sensation are unclear; females may be more sensitive to touch, pain, and visual stimuli. Hormonal production is cyclic in females after puberty (ovulation and menstruation); it is mostly continuous in males.

Brain organization: Females may have less localization of function than males and may be cognitive specialists.

Vulnerability: Males are more vulnerable to disease, physical disorders, and early death.

Activity level: There are no differences in the amount of activity, although differences in type of movements and activities are found.

Cognitive

Learning and memory: No difference.

Intelligence: No difference in level of intelligence.
   Verbal: Females tend to excel up to age 3 and after age 11.
   Quantitative: Males tend to excel after age 12.
   Visual-spatial: Males tend to excel after age 8.
   Analytic: No difference.
   Concept mastery: No difference.

Cognitive style: Differences are unclear.

Creativity: No difference with nonverbal material; females tend to excel with verbal material.

Personality and Temperament

Self-description: Females are more people-oriented; males are more achievement-oriented.

Emotionality: No difference during childhood.

Fears: The evidence is contradictory; females report more fears.

Social Behavior

Communication patterns.
  Verbal: Males dominate.
  Nonverbal: Males dominate; females may be more sensitive to cues.
Person-centered interactions
  Dependency: No difference depending on the definition used.
  Affiliation: No difference during childhood. After adolescence, females tend to be
    more interested in people.
  Empathy: No difference depending on the situation and the person.
  Nurturance: No difference depending on experience.
  Altruism: No difference depending on the situation and the person.
Power-centered interactions
  Aggression: Males tend to be more aggressive after age 2.
  Assertiveness: Differences are unclear; depends on the situation and the person.
  Dominance: Differences are unclear; males may be more dominant depending on
    the situation.
  Competition and cooperation: Differences are unclear; males may be more com-
    petitive depending on the situation.
  Compliance: No difference depending on the situation and the person to whom
    compliance is required.

Sexual Behavior

Response: No difference; females are capable of multiple orgasms.
Interest: Males express more and have more experiences. Meaning of sex may be
  different for the two sexes.
Response to erotica: No difference.
Homosexuality: Reported more in males.
Masturbation: Reported more in males.

As the table indicates, there are very few clear-cut differences between males and females. Males, compared to females, tend to be more physically vulnerable, aggressive, and sexually active, to excel in visual-spatial and quantitative skills after age 8, and to dominate communications. Females, compared to males, tend to mature faster, to have cyclic hormonal production, to have less localized brain functions, to excel in verbal skills after age 11, to be more interested in people after adolescence, and to be capable of multiple orgasms.

Far more numerous than the areas of sex difference are the areas in which no overall sex differences have been found. These areas include activity level, audition, learning, memory, general intelligence, analytic ability, concept mastery, creativity, self-esteem, emotionality, dependence, empathy, nurturance, altruism, compliance, suggestibility, sexual responsiveness, and response to erotica.

In a few areas, the differences are unclear, such as sense of touch, pain, vision, and smell; cognitive style; fearfulness; assertiveness; dominance; and competition and cooperation.

Of the few sex differences that seem to exist, the differences themselves are small, and there is wide individual variation. The distribution of these behaviors for the sexes overlaps considerably. Thus, the differences in Summary Table 1 reflect group averages and are not predictive of individual behavior.

Another important finding that appears in examining research on sex differences is the tremendous importance of situational and personal factors, such as social expectations, the nature of the task, the presence and characteristics of other people, the age of the subjects, and, especially, the sex typing of the subjects. In most cases, these variables interact with an individual's sex in determining performance. Such situational factors need to be acknowledged more and trait terms need to be relied upon less.

It is important to note that many of the sex differences that are found do not appear until adolescence or later. This suggests that they might be a consequence, rather than a cause, of the sex-role stereotypes.

In looking at explanations of the differences, environmental factors (learning, expectations, and status differences) seem to be the most powerful influences on sex differences, although biological predispositions may play a role in some cases. Even in these cases, however, nature and nurture interact, with environmental factors usually overpowering the biological factors, shaping the behavior to conform to cultural expectations. We are all born with different physical, intellectual, and emotional potential, but these differences are not distributed by sex. The potentials that become actualized depend on the environment in which we are raised. And social factors in our environment often do differ on the basis of sex.

The question remains as to why the sex-role stereotypes discussed in Chapter 1 remain and are so strongly believed when there is little factual basis for them. To understand stereotypes' tenacity, one needs to understand the nature of stereotypes themselves. Once believed, stereotypes become confirmed and strengthened whenever someone behaves in the expected way. For example, whenever a female expresses fearfulness, an observer may remark "That's just like a woman." The observer's belief in the stereotype then becomes stronger. On the other hand, when someone acts in a way contrary to the observer's expectation, instead of weakening the stereotype, the behavior in question is more likely to go unnoticed or to be classified as an exception. Thus, if a female does not act fearful, an observer might simply brush off the observation as unusual ("Oh, she's different"), if an observation is made at all. The stereotype itself remains inviolate and protected from refutation. Thus, we have the case where active athletic behavior on the part of girls is called atypical ("tomboyish") despite the fact that the majority of girls behave that way.

To challenge stereotypes, we need to get to the individual before he or she learns them; that is, we need to change the content of our sex-role socialization. In the next section, we will review how sex-role socialization occurs and how very difficult instituting such change would be.

ORIGINS OF SEX-ROLE STEREOTYPES

As was shown in Part Two, there are few basic differences between the sexes aside from the purely physical. Given that few differences are inherent, how do sex-role stereotypes get transmitted to members of a society? The following three chapters are devoted to answering this question.

Before examining the transmission of stereotypes from one generation to another, we might first ask how the stereotypes began. Did a division of traits, behaviors, and activities always exist between the sexes? If so, on what was a division based, since there are so few innate differences between the sexes and since the sex-role stereotypes themselves differ cross-culturally? Does such division necessarily imply differing statuses? To answer these questions, anthropological evidence is needed as well as an evolutionary perspective. These will be covered in Chapter Six.

Given an evolutionary background, we then can examine how children develop their sex roles and how they learn the sex-role stereotypes appropriate to their culture. *Socialization* is the process by which children are inculcated with the values and mores of their society. Three different theories of how sex-role socialization occurs, together with evidence regarding specific socializing agents, are reviewed in Chapter Seven, and various socializing forces are discussed in Chapter Eight.

Evolutionary Derivations

A survey of a broad cross-section of cultures over the course of human history reveals that a division of labor between the sexes is nearly universal. The precise division, however, varies from one society to another, as does the rigidity with which such divisions are held (Blumberg, 1977, 1979; J. K. Brown, 1976; Friedl, 1975; Murdock & Provost, 1973). In most cultures, males are primarily responsible for hunting, fishing, and warfare, and females for gathering foods, cooking, and child care. Yet this division is not true for all cultures. For other activities, such as preparing soil and tending and harvesting crops, the cultural variations are considerable.

In this chapter, we will examine briefly the sex-based labor division patterns in various societies. Explanations proposed to account for the patterns will also be reviewed. How these patterns relate to the status of females and males within a society is another important question that will be discussed.

PATTERNS OF LABOR DIVISION

In nearly all cultures, women and men perform different tasks. The exact division of tasks depends on three factors: the particular subsistence base of a society, the supply of and demand for labor, and the compatibility of the needed tasks with child rearing. This last factor accounts for the fact that women's contributions to the subsistence activities of their society vary more than men's. Across all cultures, however, women contribute about 44% of their society's subsistence (Blumberg, 1977).

In this section, we will examine the various patterns of labor division by sex as a function of the technoeconomic base of the society. There are four major bases: hunting and gathering, horticulture, agriculture (wet and dry), and industry. Societies based on hunting and gathering and on horticulture are characteristic of almost all of the last three to four million years of human history, and in most of these societies, women were the primary producers (Blumberg, 1979).

Hunting and Gathering Societies

In hunting and gathering societies, which are the original form of social grouping, both sexes may work together to hunt and gather where game is close; this is the case, for example, with the Mbuti pygmies of the African Congo. Where game is available at a distance and vegetables are available nearby—as among the !Kung Bushmen of Africa—the sexes are segregated. Men hunt and provide protein for the group; women gather roots and berries, thereby contributing most (60–80%) of the food supply. This pattern is the most common. Where hunting is the only food source, men provide all the food. This pattern, which is found, for example, among the Eskimos, is quite rare (Friedl, 1975). Except in the latter case, women are generally full economic partners in hunting and gathering societies. Relations between the sexes tend to be warm, cooperative, and egalitarian, and women tend to be unrepressed sexually (Blumberg, 1977). This type of society apparently characterized all human groups for several million years—98% of all human history (Blumberg, 1979; Collins, 1979).

Most hunting and gathering societies have been nonterritorial and have focused around the activities of both men and women, not solely around men as has sometimes been claimed (see Gough, 1975). For example, in the !Kung society, groups of siblings and their offspring of both sexes band together, share food with all members of the group, and migrate to a new setting when any conflict arises (Lee, 1972). In such a society, women enjoy high status, relative autonomy, and some ability to influence group decisions (Kolata, 1974). Fathers also tend to have a great deal of contact with children, including infants (Collins, 1979).

Horticultural Societies

Societies in which food is cultivated by hoe emerged in the Middle East about 10,000 years ago and are primarily found today in sub-Saharan Africa and islands of the Pacific. Here, the amount of subsistence contributed by women is a direct function of the amount of warfare in that society and of certain natural environmental conditions (J. K. Brown, 1976; Sanday, 1973). In general, because hoe cultivation is compatible with child care, women tend to make the predominant contribution. A 1974 study of the African economy estimated that 70% of the cultivation is in the hands of women (Economic Commission for Africa, 1974, cited in Blumberg, 1977). Since neither sex automatically controls food, there is considerable flexibility in sex roles and equality between the sexes on certain life options. These societies also tend to have the most egalitarian (as opposed to male-dominated) sexual ideology (Blumberg, 1977).

Agrarian Societies

When a group begins to lay claim to land and increase its food supplies through plow cultivation and the domestication of animals, certain social changes occur as well. Since land becomes property to be owned, defended, passed on, and bartered, inheritance factors, such as legitimacy of offspring, become very important. Thus, with the rise of agrarian societies five or six thousand years ago in the valleys of the Tigris-Euphrates, Nile, and Indus rivers, patriarchy (societal organization based on the supremacy of the father in the family and the reckoning of descent and inheritance in the male line) and men's control of women's sexuality became firmly established. Women were not to engage in any sexual activity with men other than their husbands in order to ensure the legitimacy of their children. Consequently women's behaviors and lives became more restricted.

In the overwhelming majority of agrarian societies, men tend to dominate the division of labor (Blumberg, 1979). The division seems to be based on the fact that, since plow cultivation is more efficient, such work generally requires fewer people than does horticulture. In addition, since the activities required for plow cultivation range far from home, they are generally not compatible with child care. The !Kung offer a case in point (Kolata, 1974). Although foragers for over 11,000 years, more and more of the !Kung have now begun to live in agrarian villages since the 1960s. In 1974 fewer than 5% were still nomadic hunter-gatherers. Their society has changed dramatically as a result. Women have less mobility and contribute less to the food supply. Children now play in single-sex and -age groups as opposed to all playing together. Such segregated play encourages segregated roles. Aggression has increased because of such segregation, less supervision by adults, and less ability to leave the area. Fertility has also increased because of earlier age of menarche as a result of changing diet. All these factors have led to a marked drop in women's status.

In cultures that use wet irrigation—for example, for the cultivation of rice, as in Southeast Asia and Indonesia—more labor is required in a smaller area. There, women (at least those of the lower class) contribute a great deal to the economy in the paddies and the market place. Consequently, their status is relatively high. In dry agrarian regions, however—for example, in northern India and the Middle East—there is a surplus of labor, and women's economic importance is minimal. This, too, is reflected in their status (Blumberg, 1977).

In sum, the status of women in agrarian societies is low because of patriarchy, male dominance, and the division of labor. Interestingly, every one of today's industrialized societies sprang from an agrarian base (Blumberg, 1979).

Industrial Societies

The Industrial Revolution, begun about 1800 in England and northwest Europe, transformed basically agrarian societies but did little to change the status of women. In fact, the position of women declined as men took over tasks formerly done by women and transferred these tasks from the home to the factory (Boserup, 1970).

Since factory work is not compatible with continuous child care, women were not encouraged to do such work except when their labor was needed and/or when they needed the money. Thus, it was mostly poor women who worked and then mainly in low-status sweat-shop activities. Women were viewed as a cheap and often nonessential labor pool. Today, although women constitute from one-quarter to one-half of the labor force in industrialized societies, they are often still viewed the same way (Blumberg, 1977).

Although birth control and modern child-care and educational practices free a mother from having to pay constant attention to these functions, such traditional activities are still often used to bar women from equal employment opportunity and equal pay. To some extent, then, industrialized society's low view of women's productivity and status may be a carry-over from its agrarian heritage. Attitudes have not yet caught up with current realities.

EXPLANATIONS OF LABOR DIVISION

Why are men almost always the hunters and warriors and women the gatherers and domestics? The reason for the nearly universal division of labor by sex has, at various times, been attributed to physical, psychological, and functional factors.

Physical and Psychological Factors

The *physically* based explanations argue that, because men are "naturally" bigger and stronger and women are "incapacitated" by childbearing, men are assigned the more strenuous, dangerous, and important societal activities. M. Harris (1977b) has gone so far as to say that a woman's most "essential characteristic" is her ability to make eggs, and this ability lays the groundwork for all differences between women and men in all societies for all times.

The difficulties with this explanation are numerous: (1) Physical differences between the sexes do not exist until puberty, and they vary considerably. In fact, such differences are often a function of different activities rather than a cause of them. (2) Motherhood does not require giving up work. (3) Women's activities require a great deal of physical strength and energy (for example, carrying water or lifting a 30-pound child). (4) Women generally do contribute substantially to a society's economic base. (5) In some societies, parenthood restricts male activities. For example, in some extreme cases, fathers—not mothers—are expected to have labor pains and a long recovery period after birth (Paige & Paige, 1973).

However, the bearing and nursing of children do have significance for what women can do in societies where life expectancy is short, no efficient birth-control methods are available, and the family is entirely responsible for the socialization of its young. In most primitive societies and in India until 1920, the average age at death was 20. Until about 1800, the average age at death in most countries was only 35 (Youssef & Hartley, 1979). In such societies, women spend most of their lives either pregnant or breast-feeding. Thus, women's activities must be compatible with simultaneous child care.

Another physically based explanation relates to how the brain is organized (Goleman, 1978). As was noted in Part Two, females appear to have superior verbal skills and ability to read nonverbal cues.

These characteristics seem well suited to the traditional mother's role and may be based on nonspecific localization of function in female brains. Males, in contrast, appear to have superior visual-spatial skills and greater aggression—traits that are appropriate to roaming in search of food and that may be based on more specific localization of function in male brains. Division of labor, then, may have followed from these genetic blueprints. Even though society has changed radically from that of hunters-gatherers, evidence for this blueprinting can still be found. This explanation is based on much speculation; a sex difference in perception of nonverbal cues is not that clear, nor are any of the sex differences absolutes. Furthermore, the understanding of brain organization and localization of functions is very limited at this time. This type of physical explanation is nonetheless intriguing.

Similarly, explanations invoking *psychological* differences between the sexes as justification for the division of labor are unsupportable. There is no evidence of basic psychological differences between females and males. Mead (1935) and other cross-cultural researchers have noted that the sexes are quite variable on a number of different traits—jealousy, dependency, artistic interests, aggressiveness, and so on. Specific cultures may encourage the development of different traits in females and males, but these differences then are culturally, not biologically, derived.

Functional Factors

Functional explanations of the division of labor between the sexes stress the practicality of such divisions for a society. Claude Lévi-Strauss (1956) suggests that, by having men and women responsible for different tasks in a society, mutual dependency between the sexes is established. This dependency serves to strengthen marriage and family ties. Although interesting, this theory does not account for the specific division of tasks by sex (J. K. Brown, 1976).

Another functional explanation involves women's child-bearing capacity (Blumberg, 1979; J. K. Brown, 1976; Friedl, 1975). Since women do bear and nurse children, it is more functional to have them perform tasks which are compatible with such activities in societies where no alternative exists. Because hunting, fishing, and warfare occur irregularly, last for unpredictable lengths of time, and require long-distance travel, these activities are not very compatible with child bearing and early child care. Carrying young children around for a long distance is cumbersome, and leaving them home to be cared for by others is unfeasible when the children are still nursing.

In addition, it would be impractical to train everyone to become hunters. Game is an uncertain commodity. Therefore, some members of society must be responsible for a more reliable food supply, such as berries and roots. Since foraging activities, hunting small game, and cultivating the land are perfectly compatible with child bearing and early child care, women became primarily responsible for these food-producing activities. Men, in turn, were assigned other tasks, perhaps by default.

In accordance with such functional explanations is a theory put forth by Owen Lovejoy to explain the emergence of *bipedalism*—the ability to walk on two legs instead of on four (in Rensberger, 1979). Lovejoy theorizes that such an ability became evolutionarily functional as our human ancestors bonded together to form a nuclear family in order to raise several children at once. This bonding was encouraged by a combination of ecological and demographic factors. There was a consequent need for one partner to bring food to the other from a wide geographic area. Food sharing was facilitated by having free hands. Thus, bipedalism evolved. However intriguing this theory might be, at this time such a theory still is being hotly debated.

Thus, the most persuasive explanation of the division of labor involves an interaction of functional distinctions between the sexes and the environmental conditions of specific cultures. Tasks are divided according to the compatibility of tasks with child care, the subsistence base of the society, and the labor supply and demand.

Another factor has been proposed to account for the division of labor between the sexes throughout history—the factor of status or of prestige. Since a status difference can be a cause, a concomitant, or a consequence of the division of labor, a closer examination of this complex variable is warranted.

STATUS AND ITS RELATION TO THE DIVISION OF LABOR

Men having a higher status than women in terms of power and prestige is a nearly universal occurrence. Even in modern societies in which women hold what we, in the United States, would consider high-status jobs, their actual status is low. For example, most doctors in Russia are women, but practicing medicine is considered a low-status job there.

The status differential between the sexes seems to have existed, in varying degrees, since prehistoric times (M. Harris, 1977b). Does this status differential arise from the division of labor between the sexes, or does the differential give rise to the division of labor? There is evidence for both of the above positions. Figure 6-1 gives a humorous example of one way status and labor division are related.

Status as a Cause

Marvin Harris (1977a) proposes that male supremacy existed since prehistoric times as a way to counter the threat of overpopulation and to counter the threat of depletion of resources that such overpopulation would bring. Warfare was one means of controlling overpopulation as well as of controlling the resources. Because, during prehistory, muscle-powered weapons (clubs, bows, and arrows) were relied upon and because of the greater average strength and height of the human male, men were everywhere the principal, if not exclusive, combatants. To prepare to risk one's life in battle took years of mental and physical training via competitive sports and physical ordeals. Since a female's life cycle after puberty was constantly interrupted by pregnancy and breast feeding, males were the logical sex to undergo such training.

The consequences of only males' being responsible for warfare were enormous. To get males to risk their lives and their comfort, a powerful system of rewards and punishments was needed. Sex was the reward; ostracism, the punishment. "If wives and concubines were to be the chief inducement for men to become masculine, women had to be trained from birth not for combat but for acquiescence to male demands" (Harris, 1977b, p. 117). Patriarchy, patrilocality (place of residence determined by males), exchange of women, polygamy, aggressiveness in males, passiveness in females, and male chauvinism and supremacy all follow from assigning responsibility for warfare solely to males.

The division of labor in other areas of society followed the initial division for combat. Harris further states that males' hunting specialty arose from their warfare training. The weapons of hunt were the same as the weapons of war. Therefore, women were assigned all the remaining tasks. Since maleness was associated with power and prestige through warfare, whatever men did was considered of high status. Since females were trained to be subordinate, whatever they did was considered of low status. This relationship between male status and female status continues into the present. Touhey (1974) found that the status of an occupation declined when respondents (female and male) thought more females than males would enter that occupation in the future. When more males than females were predicted as entering an occupation, the status of the occupation increased. Although more recent replications of Touhey's study using expectations of changing sex proportions have not found the same results (for example, Suchner, 1979), the bias still appears to exist when actual increases in proportions of women in various occupations occur.

Since Harris sees the threat of overpopulation and the assignment of warfare exclusively to males as the cause of male supremacy,

Figure 6-1
One relationship between status and the division of labor. (B. C. by permission of Johnny Hart and Field Enterprises, Inc.)

he foresees the development of safe contraceptives and the integration of women into the military as the way to end this domination by males. Not everyone shares his optimism or his thesis. In the first place, as previously noted, not all societies were focused around warfare or hunting, nor were all societies patrilocal. Secondly, men's relatively greater strength may have been a consequence of men's roles as warriors and hunters and not a cause of the role assignment. Thirdly, some control over contraception, although unrefined, did exist in some primitive societies. For example, the !Kung of Africa breast-feed each child for about four years (Friedl, 1975). Breast feeding often inhibits ovulation, thereby facilitating a certain amount of spacing between children. Of course, nursing itself does impose some restrictions on a woman's activities. On the whole, however, Harris's thesis is provocative.

Sherry Ortner (1974) suggests another way status factors may have affected the division of labor. She believes that people tend to put a higher value on things they can control than on things they cannot control. Thus, all activities that are regulated by humans (activities of a society, such as hunting) are viewed as more valuable than all activities regulated by nature (for example, childbirth). Since women, by virtue of their reproductive functions, are more controlled by nature than by their culture, their work and their status as people become devalued. Men, who do not seem as subject to natural forces as do women, are considered to be more in control of themselves. Therefore, they and their activities become more highly valued. Although Ortner's thesis is suggestive, it, too, is far from confirmed.

From the above, it is clear that status factors may play a role in assigning tasks within a society. Status may also accrue from task divisions, depending upon which sex is dominant in a task.

Status as a Consequence

The degree to which a woman contributes to the economic base of her society generally parallels her status in that society; that is, the greater her contribution, the higher her status, up to a point. As was noted above, female contributions tend to be greater in horticultural societies than in other societies. Their status in horticultural societies also tends to be higher than in other societies. In agrarian societies, in which women's contributions are low, their status is also low. Yet this relationship is not perfectly linear. Even when women contribute greatly to a society, their status still tends to be lower than men's.

A key factor in determining status levels is the control of the most valued resources (Blumberg, 1979; J. K. Brown, 1970, 1976; Sanday, 1973, 1974). Blumberg (1979), in examining 61 preindustrial societies, found that participation in production, by itself, was not directly related to control of certain life options, such as freedom to initiate and end a marriage. The strongest influence on female equality was women's relative degree of economic control over the group's productive resources and surpluses. For example, Iroquois women have an unusually high status in their society. They contribute about 50% of the subsistence of their society (basically vegetables, fish, and game). But in other societies in which women contribute more, as in the Tikopia and the Azande societies, their status remains low (Sanday, 1974). What differentiates the Iroquois from these other groups is that, in the past, the Iroquois women also controlled the distribution of food because their men were frequently away hunting or at war for years at a time (J. K. Brown, 1970). Being in charge of food distribution was a form of power, and Iroquois women used this power in political areas as well. In societies where women do not have control of the food distribution, even though they contribute 60% to 70% of the food supply, their status is low. In most societies, it is usually game that gets distributed among tribal members. Since men are in charge of hunting, they are generally in charge of the food distribution. The vegetables and berries gathered by women are usually directed more toward family, rather than toward tribal, consumption (Friedl, 1975). Hence, women generally have less power than men.

Blumberg (1979) also has found that the economic power of women in a society is further enhanced by their being strategically indispensable and by kinship arrangements that take females into account. Strategic indispensability arises when there is no reserve labor pool—such as slaves or homemakers—when specific expertise is needed, and when work is autonomous as in the case of African marketing. In societies where inheritance passes through the mother's side of the family or where the family residence is with the wife's family, women also tend to have considerable economic power. Economic power can be translated into political power and into some immunity to physical force. Thus, for full sexual equality, economic power by women is imperative.

In modern societies, the same pattern of economic power seems to exist as has been described for more primitive cultures. Since men are assigned the role of breadwinner, they usually are in charge of the distribution of their earnings. Even if the wife works, men's generally higher salaries mean the men still are in control. The battle for equal pay for equal work has important ramifications for the balance of power in a family, as both opponents and supporters of the equal-pay position are well aware.

Another reason men have had more power and status may be that they are in charge of the relatively more vital and rarer resources. Since protein can be considered more vital and rarer than vegetables, and since meat is protein, men's contributions from hunting have been more highly valued than women's contributions from gathering.

Men's status also may have been greater because of the dangers involved in the male activities of hunting and fighting. Since such activities were vital for tribe survival, making them more important may have compensated men somewhat for taking the risks ("Oh, my hero!"). Since warfare has been a male province in all societies, even in modern ones, the same compensation of high status for warfare also may have continued.

Thus, males' high status can be viewed as both a cause and a consequence of the division of labor between the sexes. The legacy of male dominance, however, has continued far past its initial justification.

SUMMARY AND OVERVIEW

The difference in status between the sexes, so visible in our society, seems to be a carry-over from the division of labor in societies that preceded ours. This division of labor was initially necessary because of women's child-bearing function and was determined by environmental conditions. Thus, the precise activities allocated to women were determined by the activities' compatibility with child care, with the supply and demand of labor, and with the subsistence base of the society. In hunting and gathering societies, men were the hunters; women, the gatherers. Men had slightly higher status because their activities were more dangerous, more vital for their tribe's survival, and because their activities gave men more power in the distribution of the food. But women and their economic contribution were very important. In horticultural societies, females generally contributed a great deal and also tended to have high status. Because males were the warriors, however, their status still tended to be higher. In agrarian societies, women's economic contribution dropped, as did their status. In industrialized societies like our own, the division of labor and the lower status of women have continued despite the fact that such divisions and status levels no longer are justified culturally.

Thus, although child bearing is an unchangeable sex difference, the implications of this biological fact are different today in the United States than they were in previous times in other societies. With the advent of birth control, women no longer need to become pregnant frequently and unpredictably. Most women now use some form of birth control, plan on having fewer children, and are having them at a later age than in the past (Hoffman, 1977). Because of smaller family sizes and longer life expectancies, motherhood, if entered at all, occupies a much smaller proportion of an American woman's life than it used to. In advanced countries, less than one-seventh of a woman's average lifetime is spent bearing children (Yousef & Hartley, 1979). In addition, since many child-care responsibilities previously borne by the family alone are now borne by society, such as by schools and day-care centers, there is no longer any justification for a division of labor based on sex.

One implication from the above brief survey of labor division and status is that, although productive labor does not automatically lead to equality, it does lead to economic power, at least in the form of control of a paycheck. This economic power, in turn, is the strongest determinant of a woman's freedom and status. Economic power is not, however, the only determinant. Political and military power are of even greater importance in determining the status of members of a society. Women's presence in these areas is just beginning.

Blumberg, R. L. A paradigm for predicting the position of women: Policy implications and problems. In J. Lipman-Blumen & J. Bernard (Eds.), *Sex roles and social policy: A complex social science equation*. Beverly Hills, Calif.: Sage Publications, 1979, 113–142. An interesting analysis of the ways in which status, sex, and the division of labor are related. A theory of sex stratification is proposed, and policy implications discussed.

Friedl, E. *Women and men: An anthropologist's view*. New York: Holt, Rinehart, & Winston, 1975. A cross-cultural survey of the behaviors and tasks assigned to the sexes.

Harris, M. *Cannibals & kings*. New York: Random House, 1977. A fascinating, albeit controversial, examination of how societal needs shape the norms and mores of a society and the behaviors of the sexes in particular.

7 | Socialization: Theories and Agents

In Part Two, a strong case was made for the overriding importance of socialization over biological factors in determining an individual's sex-typed behaviors. In Chapter Six, the origins of the sex-role stereotypes were found to be rooted in the division of labor based on economic and biological conditions present in a society. Although such a division based on sex is no longer either practical or necessary, the traditional pattern remains and gets transmitted to each succeeding generation as part of its socialization. Since socialization is such an important factor, it is productive to examine more closely how such a socialization process occurs, who the socializing agents are, and what other forces operate.

In this chapter, three major theories of gender identity development—psychoanalytic theory, social learning theory, and cognitive-developmental theory—will be reviewed and evaluated. As with other research in this area, the evidence is complex and contradictory, partly because of methodological problems and partly because of the complexity of human development itself. In general, some combination of the above theories is needed to account for the complex interaction among biological factors, the learning environment, and the level of cognitive development of the child. Reviews of research on the major socializing agents, which include parents, teachers, and peers, will follow, along with a summary of their influence. Chapter Eight will focus on the influence of other socializing forces in American society.

THEORIES

There are three major theories of sex-role development—psychoanalytic, social learning, and cognitive developmental. Each emphasizes different aspects of development and makes different predictions as to the sequence of development.

Psychoanalytic Theory

Psychoanalytic theory stresses the importance of biological (including anatomical) factors and parental identification. As was discussed in Chapter Five, through the resolution at age 5 to 6 of the Oedipal conflict brought on by the recognition that only boys have penises, children become motivated to identify with the same-sex parent. Each child is thought to have incestuous desires that cause guilt and anxiety. Each views the same-sex parent as either responsible for the absence of a penis, in the case of girls, or able to remove the penis, in the case of boys. Identifying with the "aggressor" is thus a way to allay this anxiety. The fear of penis removal is considered stronger for males than is penis envy for females, since girls have already "lost" the coveted penis. Consequently, males' sex-role identity is viewed as stronger than females' sex-role identity. For Freud, same-sex identification is critical for healthy adjustment and for the development of masculine and feminine personalities. He viewed the sequence of development as innate and biologically based, proceding from an awareness of the anatomical sex difference to identification with same-sex parent and eventually to adoption of sex-typed behaviors.

There is little empirical support for the above assertions of psychoanalytic theory. We have already reviewed evidence of the nonuniversality of Freudian personality concepts, stages, and interpretation (see Chapter Five). In addition, contrary to psychoanalytic predictions that females should have a weaker identification with their same-sex parent than do boys, Lynn (1979) cites research which shows the reverse to be true. It is true that more females than males prefer other-sex activities (for example, Connor & Serbin, 1978; Lynn, 1959), but interpretations other than "penis envy" are more likely. Some females may prefer male-related activities because of males' generally higher status and greater power. Or they may prefer such activities because of the intrinsic qualities of the activities themselves. For example, engaging in sports or playing with an Erector Set simply may be more fun than playing with dolls.

The prediction that identification with the same-sex parent is critical for mental health also has not been verified. Williams (1973) studied high school senior girls and their identification with their parents. She found that those who identified with ascendant-dominant fathers were the healthiest with respect to personality functioning when compared to those who identified with retiring, passive mothers. According to psychoanalytic theory, the passive mothers are traditionally feminine. Thus, for high school girls at least, androgynous roles are healthier than stereotypic roles, contrary to predictions. Spence and Helmreich (1978) also have found that the most healthy homes (those in which children are able to function effectively and achieve a sense of worth) are homes in which both parents are perceived as androgynous. Following closely in this same rating for health are homes in which only one parent is perceived as androgynous. Therefore, psychoanalytic theory does not satisfactorily account for the development of an individual's sex-role identity.

Social Learning Theory

One theory that contrasts strongly with the psychoanalytic approach is *social learning theory*. Instead of viewing gender identity as an innate, biologically determined development, social learning theory views gender identity as a product of various forms of learning. This theory, put forth by Mischel (1966), Bandura and Walters (1963), Lynn (1969), and others, emphasizes the importance of the environment on a child's sex-role development. The child learns his or her role directly through differential treatment, rewards, and punishments, and indirectly through observational learning and modeling (see Figure 7-1).

Figure 7-1
*Social learning by
direct instruction.*

If a boy is punished for clinging and is rewarded for working on his own and doing things, he is more likely to develop autonomous and independent behavior than is his sister who receives the opposite treatment. In addition, because powerful, nurturant, and similar models are most likely to be imitated (Bandura, 1969), children tend to model their same-sex parent (the one most similar to themselves), thus learning sex-role-appropriate behavior through observation.

According to the social learning theory, since sex typing begins at birth, same-sex modeling precedes, and gives rise to, the formation of a stable gender identity. Because different behaviors get reinforced and modeled by the different sexes, children develop an awareness of the two sex roles. Their own behavior becomes shaped to accord with one of these roles, and they then develop a stable gender identity. In other words, "I do girl things; I must be a girl."

Lynn (1959, 1969), in an expansion of this theory, posits that, since the father is frequently absent from the home and since masculine-sex-typed activities are not directly observable by the child, boys have a more difficult time than girls in establishing their sex-role identity. They are forced to develop a more abstract identification with the male role, while girls identify directly with their mothers, who are observable. This early abstraction may account for sex differences in cognitive style and in males' greater attachment to a culturally defined masculine role. Although cognitive style differences have not been found consistently and can be better explained by differences in experience (see Chapter Three), there is some support to Lynn's hypothesis that a son's identification with his father is qualitatively different from a daughter's identification with her mother. For example, Lynn (1979) has summarized studies finding greater mother-daughter similarity than father-son similarity. Also, boys clearly attend to same-sex models, when available, although girls do not always do so (Connor & Serbin, 1978; Grusec & Brinker, 1972). Boys also may imitate same-sex models more closely than do girls (Perry & Bussey, 1979). Girls may be more flexible, since they are less consistently reinforced than are boys for imitating only same-sex adults (Kagan, 1964).

Support for social learning theory comes from studies indicating that knowledge about sex-role stereotypes increases with age from ages 2½ to 8 (see, for example, Nadelman, 1974). In one study (Vener & Snyder, 1966), children 5 years old were found to have an 84% accuracy rate in matching certain artifacts with adult sex roles (for example, "Who uses lipstick? Who smokes a pipe?"). Even children 2½ years of age showed 75% accuracy, although another study (Myers, Weinraub, & Shetler, 1979) found less than chance accuracy in children under age 3. The examples used in the studies, of course, assumed a clear dichotomy in usage of items. Such an assumption may be unwarranted, especially when stereotyped behaviors are becoming more flexible. Also supportive of social learning theory are findings that the number of sex-typed traits increases with age (Silvern, 1977).

Although there is much evidence that people can and do learn through reinforcement and imitation, social learning as the sole explanation of the development of sex-role identity is insufficient. Firstly, like all learning theories, social learning theory views the child as relatively passive in the learning process. Other evidence suggests complex parent-child interactions. For example, if female infants begin vocalizing earlier than males, parents may respond with more vocalizations to females. This parental response further reinforces the infants' vocalizations, and a sex difference in language development may ensue.

Secondly, research on direct reinforcement has been equivocal. Clearly, it would be impossible for parents consistently and deliberately to reward and punish each behavior according to its sex-role appropriateness. Maccoby and Jacklin (1974), reviewing a large body of research, concluded that, at least in parental self-reports and in laboratory observations, there is surprisingly little differentiation in parent behavior according to the sex of the child. The one exception to this finding is that boys are subject to more intense socialization pressures than are girls. Some differences in parent behavior do emerge outside laboratory settings, but not enough differences occur to account for the clear differences in sex-role expectations that boys and girls have.

Thirdly, a problem with social learning theory exists concerning the importance placed on imitation of the same-sex parent in the acquisition of sex-role behavior. Although identification can account for the acquisition of more behavior than can differential treatment, the evidence again is only partially supportive. Maccoby and Jacklin (1974) found that children do not always select same-sex models, that they do not necessarily resemble the same-sex parent, and that the sex-typed behavior, such as it is, is not a direct copy of adult behavior but tends to be more stereotyped and exaggerated.

The criticism regarding the extent of imitation by a child of his or her parents recently has been addressed by Perry and Bussey (1979). These researchers demonstrated that the imitation process is more complex and abstract than previously assumed. Children learn sex-role appropriate behaviors by observing differences in the frequencies with which female and male models, as groups, perform various behaviors in given situations. Children are more likely to imitate a model if that model usually displays sex-appropriate behavior than if that model usually does not display such behaviors. Hence, a child may imitate a same-sex parent but only if the parent is seen as representative of other members of his or her sex. Since Perry and Bussey's modification of social learning theory involves a significant amount of abstracting ability, such as in noticing that the sexes differ in their frequency of performing some behaviors, a child's cognitive capacities need to be fairly well developed for this imitation process to occur. It is important to note that Perry and Bussey tested their hypotheses using 8- and 9-year-old children. Factors other than imitation must be involved in earlier sex differences.

Age is a crucial factor in sex-role behavior acquisition. There is a trend toward same-sex modeling that increases from grade school through high school and adulthood, especially for boys (Connor & Serbin, 1978; Flanders, 1968). These findings agree with Perry and Bussey's (1979) reformulation of social learning theory. However, the degree of sex stereotyping also varies with age in the opposite direction. Whereas first- and third-graders were found to have stereotyped images of occupations appropriate for women and men, fifth-graders had fewer occupational stereotypes (Garrett, Ein, & Tremaine, 1977). In fact, stereotyped sex-role behavior is most pronounced between ages 4 and 5 (Mussen, 1969). After these ages, definitions of appropriate sex-role behaviors become less rigid, especially for girls (Lynn, 1959). Social learning theory would predict increasing strength of stereotypes with age, since there would be increased exposure to the stereotypes.

Social learning theory does offer an explanation of how modeling and reinforcement may interact, with the former process being involved in the acquisition of behavior and the latter determining the performance of the behavior. For example, Bandura (1965) found that boys were more likely than girls to act aggressively after viewing an aggressive model. When incentives for behaving aggressively were introduced, however, the sex difference was wiped out. This study demonstrates that both sexes may learn aggressive responses, but girls are less likely to perform them because of previous experience and knowledge of what is appropriate. Similarly, Perry and Bussey (1979) found that 8- and 9-year-old children were unaffected by the sex of a model in recalling a model's behavior, even though the sex of the model was an important variable with regard to whether the children actually imitated a behavior.

What is needed is a theory that can take into account the different cognitive abilities of young children. These abilities are likely to mediate any experiences young children have. Cognitive-developmental theory provides one way of acknowledging these factors.

Cognitive-Developmental Theory

Cognitive-developmental theory, put forth by Kohlberg (1966), emphasizes the active role of the child in acquiring sex-role behaviors. As Piaget has delineated, children go through various discrete stages in their cognitive development. They first perceive the world in relation to their sensorimotor abilities, such as crawling and sucking. Then they learn how to categorize the world. Later they become capable of performing concrete operations on that world as in taking both the height and width of an object into account when estimating its size. Finally, they become capable of abstract reasoning, but not until after age 8. A child's reality, then, is qualitatively different from an adult's.

Based on Piaget's theory of stages of cognitive development, Kohlberg (1966) argues that the way children learn their sex role is a function of their level of understanding the world. Before age 5, children do not have an understanding of physical constancy. For example, they don't understand that water poured from a narrow glass to a wide glass is still the same amount of water. Therefore, before age 5, they cannot have a firm gender identity. After that age, however, the permanence of gender is grasped, and this self-categorization (one's label of self as girl or boy) becomes an organizing focus of future behaviors. The child begins valuing same-sex behaviors and attitudes and begins devaluing opposite-sex ones. He or she then seeks out models and situations in accordance with this categorization in order to remain self-consistent; that is, after establishing what they are (female/male), children look around to find out what people with that label do. It is at this point, when gender identity is already established, that a child may identify with the same-sex parent, reversing the sequence proposed by social learning theorists. This identification is not important to cognitive-developmental theorists, however. A child can acquire information about appropriate sex-role behaviors from many sources—adults, peers, stories, TV, and so forth. Table 7-1 contrasts Kohlberg's proposed sequence of development with that proposed by psychoanalytic and social learning theorists.

Table 7-1

Theoretical Models of Gender-Identity Development: Sequence of Events

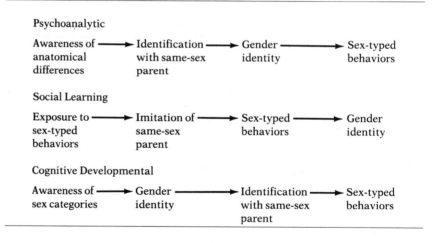

Psychoanalytic

Awareness of → Identification → Gender → Sex-typed
anatomical   with same-sex   identity   behaviors
differences   parent

Social Learning

Exposure to → Imitation of → Sex-typed → Gender
sex-typed   same-sex   behaviors   identity
behaviors   parent

Cognitive Developmental

Awareness of → Gender → Identification → Sex-typed
sex categories   identity   with same-sex   behaviors
                             parent

Because their cognitive development is still tied to concrete operations, children aged 6 to 7 often have very simplistic and exaggerated pictures of the two sex roles and have sharp sex-role stereotypes. It is only with further cognitive development that these stereotyped conceptions can become modified to incorporate exceptions and personal preferences. Thus, a cognitive-developmental theorist would explain the findings of Garrett and associates (1977) that fifth-graders held fewer occupational stereotypes than did first- and third-graders by suggesting that the older children were at a cognitively more sophisticated level of classification competency than were the younger children. They were able to use multiple classification schemes and did not need to rely on extreme either/or categories.

Jeanne Block (1973) has taken Kohlberg's model beyond early childhood. She has attempted to sketch out later stages of sex-role development based on Loevinger's (1966, 1970) stages of ego development (see Table 7-2). Kohlberg's model primarily relates to the first three stages of sex-role conception in Table 7-2—development of gender identity, self-enhancement, and conformity. Block suggests that after the third stage of conformity and stereotypes comes the conscientious level at which sex-role definitions become moderated by concepts of responsibility and duty. At the next level of autonomous behavior, conflicting masculine-feminine aspects of the self become acknowledged and must be integrated. At the highest, or integrated, level, masculine and feminine traits and values are integrated into an individualized androgynous sex-role definition. Although everyone does not reach the highest level of maturity, those who do, do seem to be androgynous (Block, 1973; Waterman & Whitbourne, 1979).

Direct support for cognitive-developmental theory has been limited, and, although a number of its predictions have been borne out, this theory, too, is insufficient to account for the entire process of sex-role development. Some support for Kohlberg's theory comes from studies that find that children, boys more so than girls, do value their own sex more highly. This facilitates the modeling process. For example, McArthur and Eisen (1976) found that over 90% of nursery school children preferred same-sex characters of a story. When asked why they had this preference, the children usually indicated some form of identification with that character (for example, "because I'm a girl [boy]"). Since children view same-sex characters as more similar and more likeable, it is not surprising that they imitate them.

Geller and colleagues (1979), in studying preschoolers, first-graders, and third-graders, also found that the children had a positive evaluative bias toward same-sex individuals. This bias was associated significantly with the amount of time a child spent attending to same-sex adult models presented on videotape. Thus, Kohlberg's predictions related to same-sex preference and selective attention were supported, at least through ages 4 to 9. Such findings, however, could also support social learning theory.

The age at which gender identity is established is critical in cognitive-developmental theory. Although there is strong evidence that, by age 6, gender identity is firmly established, a significant amount of sex typing does seem to occur before this age. Thus, Money and Ehrhardt (1972) found that changing a child's assigned sex up to age 2 was easy, but after age 4 it was usually unsuccessful. Also, as was noted in Chapter 3, by nursery-school age, children do prefer same-sexed toys, boys more so than girls, and they are quite knowledgeable about sex roles (Garrett et al., 1977; Lewis & Brooks-Gunn, in press; Maccoby & Jacklin, 1974). In fact, in children as young as 20 months of age, sex-typed toy preferences have been observed (Fein, Johnson, Kosson, Stork, & Wasserman, 1975). Infants as young as 18 months of age correctly label adults on the basis of gender 90% of the time (Lewis & Brooks-Gunn, in press). The age at which children actually acquire a sex-role identity is further complicated by the suggestion that Kohlberg's age estimates may be inaccurate. Lewis and Weinraub (1979) point out that Kohlberg's estimates were based on data that may have confounded gender knowledge with language sophistication.

Table 7-2
Loevinger's Milestones of Ego Development and Extrapolations to Sex-Role Development

Stage	Loevinger's Milestones of Ego Development			Sex-Role Development Extrapolated
	Impulse Control	Interpersonal Style	Conscious Concerns	Conceptions of Sex Role
Presocial/symbiotic Impulse-ridden	—	Autistic, symbiotic	Self versus nonself	—
	Impulse-ridden, fear of retaliation	Exploitive, dependent	Sexual and aggressive bodily feelings	Development of gender identity, self-assertion, self-expression, self-interest
Self-protective (formerly opportunistic)	Expedient, fear of being caught	Exploitive, manipulative, wary	Advantage, control, protection of self	Extension of self, self-extension, self-enhancement
Conformity	Conformity to external rule	Reciprocal, superficial	Things, appearance, reputation, self-acceptance	Conformity to external role, development of sex-role stereotypes, bifurcation of sex roles
Conscientious	Internalized rules, guilt	Intensive, responsive	Differentiated inner feelings, motives, self-respect	Examination of self as sex-role exemplar vis-à-vis internalized values
Autonomous	Coping with conflict, toleration of differences	Intensive concern for autonomy	Differentiated inner feelings, role concepts, self-fulfillment	Differentiation of sex role, coping with conflicting masculine-feminine aspects of self
Integrated	Reconciling inner conflicts, renunciation of unattainable	Cherishing of individuality	All of the above plus identity	Achievement of individually defined sex role, integration of both masculine and feminine aspects of self, androgynous sex-role definition

From "Conceptions of Sex Role: Some Cross-Cultural and Longitudinal Perspectives," by J. H. Block, *American Psychologist*, 1973, 28(6), 512–526. Copyright 1973 by the American Psychological Association. Reprinted by permission.

There is evidence for a rapid and early increase in the accuracy of gender differentiation and labeling from ages 2 to 5 as well as evidence for important cognitive development changes relating to the recognition of gender constancy during ages 2 to 8 (Kohlberg, 1966). For example, prior to achieving gender constancy (say, at age 4), children might say that a pictured girl would be a boy if she wore "boy's" clothing or had a "boy's" haircut. After constancy is achieved, however, the pictured girl would still be considered a girl no matter how she looked or what she wore.

Slaby and Frey (1975) have identified three sequential aspects of gender identity formation related to a child's cognitive development. This process of gender identity formation begins around age 3 with an awareness that two sexes exist, followed by an awareness that gender remains the same over time (stability). This awareness of stability is then followed by an awareness that gender remains fixed across a wide range of situations and behaviors (constancy). This constancy, critical for the attainment of true gender identity, occurs between the ages of 4½ and 5½. As gender constancy increases, children spend more total time attending to models. Sex-typed preferences also increase after age 6 (Emmerich, Goldman, Kirsh, & Sharabany, 1977). These findings support Kohlberg's cognitive-developmental theory.

It is possible, of course, that early sex typing is due to differential reinforcement, whereas later sex typing, after ages 5 to 6, may be due to modeling. Cognitive-developmental theory, although not ruling out learning principles, subordinates them to the cognitive processes occurring in the child's mind. It is also possible that sex-role preference and adoption are not the same as sex-role identity. This will be further commented upon below.

Another problem with cognitive-developmental theory is that Kohlberg used only male examples and interviews to support his theory (Weitz, 1977). Thus, the theory can explain why boys should see a physical size difference between men and women and learn to value it and, by extension, other males. But how do females learn to value the female role? The generally positive aura surrounding nurturing experiences may help females gain a positive image of their sex, although it does seem true that there are more females who prefer male-related activities than there are males who prefer female-related activities. In any case, the cognitive-developmental model has not specifically addressed this problem.

Integration

Some coordination of the three theories discussed above seems required to account for the complexity of sex-role development. Such a coordinated explanation would include an active role for children in developing concepts of masculinity and femininity and in organizing their world consistent with their level of cognitive development. In this process, differential treatment by primary socializing agents and observation of different models all add to the information the child gathers about appropriate sex-role behaviors. Interacting with this input are the affectional bonds formed with one or both parents and any biological predispositions the child may have. The process of identification itself may be different for females and for males.

While such a comprehensive theory has yet to be clearly delineated, Kagan (1964) has suggested one such combination theory. For his theory, the central concept is a sex-role standard comprised of culturally approved characteristics for males and females—that is, the sex-role stereotypes. With the ability to discriminate between the categories of male and female, the groundwork is laid for the acquisition of sex-typed responses through social learning and through identification with the same-sex parent. Actions in accordance with the standard receive external reinforcement and self-reinforcement. Motivation to comply with the standard is therefore very strong. Children learn fairly early (between ages 2 and 4) what the stereotypes are, as we have seen. When children perform certain sex-appropriate behaviors, as a girl playing with a doll, they are likely to receive reinforcement ("See how nicely Janie plays"). If they perform sex-inappropriate behavior, children are likely to receive either a negative comment ("Boys don't play with dolls") or no comment at all. Since children are assumed to desire positive reinforcement, they become motivated to perform sex-appropriate behaviors. Once they have the sex-role standard in mind, children can even reinforce themselves for behaving appropriately.

Kagan's theory adds an organizing cognitive schemata (the sex-role standard) and an affective dimension (motivation) to social learning theory and thus has much to offer as an integrated approach. As it stands, however, it is too sketchy to explain all behavior or to make clear predictions.

Two other recent formulations regarding the acquisition of sex roles deserve attention. Anne Constantinople (1979) proposes a model of sex roles as rules and analyzes the acquisition of sex roles as similar to the process of pattern recognition in speech and vision. First a child must disembed sex-related stimuli from all others in the environment. The acquisition of language, which occurs around 18 months to 2 years of age, is an important adjunct to this process. Observational learning and direct tutelage, as proposed by social learning theory, add to the labeling process and can account for the acquisition of the distinctive features of sex-role patterns. These patterns then build up certain expectancies and categories of sex-role appropriate behavior, as explained by cognitive-developmental theory. Children then realize that not only do they belong to one sex, but that the same rules and expectancies that apply to others of their sex also apply to them (Perry & Bussey, 1979). Children need the cognitive structure of simple rules, a need that may account for the marked stereotyped behavior in young children (for example, Garrett et al., 1977). More complex rules and subtle discriminations develop with age. Constantinople's (1979) model integrates data from a number of areas, but it still needs considerable development before it can account satisfactorily for the complicated process of sex-role acquisition.

Phyllis Katz (1979) has proposed a model of sex-role acquisition which, although very general, goes beyond all previously mentioned approaches. Katz views the acquisition of sex-role behavior as a gradual process beginning in infancy and continuing throughout life. There are three levels to this process. At Level I, a child must learn what is appropriate behavior for a male or female child. This learning occurs in three stages: (1) infancy (ages 1 to 2), in which a child learns there are two genders and learns how to correctly categorize self and others; (2) preschool (ages 2 to 6), in which a child actively learns sex-appropriate activities and attributes, and acquires gender constancy; and (3) grade school (ages 6 to 12), in which a final elaboration of child sex-role activities occurs and a base is laid for adolescent development. At Level II, the adolescent acquires concepts about what is appropriate behavior for a male or female adult. This period is divided into early and late adolescence. The final level, Level III, is where individuals behave in ways deemed appropriate for male and female adults across the life span. Although Katz's approach is theoretical, it does serve to highlight the overemphasis on the preschool period in the other theoretical positions. Katz's model, however, does not add any further clarification of the process by which sex-role acquisition occurs during the first 8 years of life.

RESEARCH PROBLEMS

Clear empirical support of any of these theories has been difficult to obtain because of the many research problems in the area. Discussed in previous chapters were problems of assumptions, definitions, methodology, choice of subjects, and interpretation. These are equally present in the area of sex-role development. A few examples will suffice.

Although all theories use sex-role identity as a key concept, the term *sex-role identity* is not *defined* the same by all researchers. As Lynn (1959) notes, there are important distinctions to be made among the following terms: (1) *sex-role preference*, the desire to adopt certain behaviors associated with one sex, which is measured by asking the child, (2) *sex-role adoption*, the performing of behaviors characteristic of one sex, which is measured by observation, as of play behavior, and (3) *sex-role identification*, the actual incorporation of a role and the unconscious reactions characteristic of it, which is measured by figure drawings and parent-child similarities. These measures may be independent of each other and may operate differently for girls and for boys (Ward, 1969). Thus, girls can prefer male activities and toys and adopt male behavior, like wearing pants and playing ball, and still have a female identification, as in drawing themselves as a female. This, in fact, seems to be true more often for girls than is its complement for boys (Lynn, 1959; Maccoby & Jacklin, 1974; Ward, 1969). Thus, males are generally considered to be more strongly sex-typed at an earlier age than are girls. Studies that do not use these distinctions are confusing. Experiments using toy preference as a measure of sex-role identity actually are measuring only sex-role preference, which is another dimension altogether. This preference may develop early, beginning by age 2, whereas true gender identity may develop later, around age 5 to 6, as Kohlberg suggests.

Another research problem lies in the *measurement* instruments used. For example, the It Scale for Children (D. G. Brown, 1956), a projective test frequently used to measure sex-role preference, may be biased in the male direction. The "neutral" stick figure has been found to be more easily interpreted as a male figure, which may account for the frequent findings of girls' "preferring" male sex-role activities. They may simply be matching a perceived male figure with male activities and not indicating their own preference at all (Fling & Manosevitz, 1972).

Another serious methodological problem is the frequent use of *self-reports* of both parents and children. When people describe behaviors related to sex roles, it is often difficult to separate out socially desirable responses from an individual's true preferences or behavior. Thus, studies that find few parental differences in admitted treatment of sons and daughters (see Maccoby & Jacklin, 1974) may reflect more a parental ideal than actual parental practices. In addition, much parental behavior may occur beyond the parents' level of awareness or even intention and is thus difficult to measure.

Similarly, *laboratory studies* of parent-child interactions may not reflect what actually goes on in the home. Bronfenbrenner (1977) concludes from surveying a number of studies that interactions in the laboratory are substantially and systematically different from those in the home. Laboratory settings tend to increase anxiety and decrease behaviors showing social competence. This effect may be even more profound on lower-class families, for whom the laboratory setting is especially likely to be anxiety arousing. For example, parents may be so anxious about doing the "right" thing or being a "good" subject that they may refrain from punishing their child in the laboratory, although they do so at home. Thus, generalizations from laboratory observations may be quite limited. These and other research problems should be kept in mind as the research related to socializing agents is presented.

SOCIALIZING AGENTS

Clearly, because of the prolonged interaction, the differences in power, and the intense bonds between parents and children, parents serve as the initial and major socializing agents in our society. The term *parents* here refers to a child's biological parents or to anyone who has major caretaking responsibilities, such as a grandparent or a regular baby-sitter. Little research has been done with these latter groups, although similar socialization procedures probably operate.

A child also receives input from people outside the home. Once school begins, teachers and peers become increasingly important. These agents will be examined following a discussion of the role parents play in the socialization of children.

Parents

In order to understand how parents transmit sex-role stereotypes to their children, it is important to look at parental treatment, at the role of the father, at cross-sex effects, and at parent-child interactions.

Parental Treatment.   Parents are aware of the sex-role stereotypes and begin to apply them to their child at the moment a sex determination is made. Rubin, Provenzano, and Luria (1974) interviewed 30 first-time parents within 24 hours after their child's birth and found that a significant amount of sex typing already had begun. Girls were seen as softer, finer, and littler; boys, as firmer, stronger, and more alert. These differences were posited despite the fact that hospital data indicated that the infants did not differ on any health or physical measure. Fathers made even more stereotyped ratings of their newborn than did mothers, a finding that has received confirmation in other studies (e.g., Block, 1973; Lynn, 1979). Perhaps because a father's contact with a newborn is generally less than is a mother's or maybe because males generally are concerned more about sex roles than are females, fathers fill in their lack of knowledge with more stereotyped expectations. In any case, it seems clear that sex typing and sex-role socialization begin at birth and may affect the way parents actually treat their children. If boys are viewed as stronger, they may be handled more roughly than girls, and girls may be protected more. There is some evidence that this does occur (Frisch, 1977; Hoffman, 1977). Infant girls also are expected to be cuter than infant boys, and this expectation may affect the evaluation as well as the treatment of an infant (Hildebrandt & Fitzgerald, 1979).

Actually, sex typing may begin even before birth in the form of differential preference for, and value attached to, a male or female child. Hoffman (1977) and Williamson (1976) summarize data to show that, in the United States today, most couples prefer male children to female children and base this value preference on assumed sex differences, such as boys carrying on the family name and girls helping around the house. Although such preference for males is considerably less in this country than in other countries, especially in less developed areas like Asia and India, a striking difference remains that cannot help but be reflected in the way the sexes are treated by their parents.

In studying how parents actually treat their children, a somewhat confusing picture emerges. Strong differences in sex typing are not found consistently. However, depending on the population studied and method used, certain differences do emerge. Parents perceive girls as more vulnerable and fragile and treat them accordingly. They dress the sexes differently (girls wear dresses; boys, pants), assign different household tasks (girls help set the table; boys help Dad in the yard), and provide different toys in line with the sex-role stereotypes (toys for girls, like dolls, relate to the mother role; those for boys, like trucks, the work role). Parents strongly discourage their children, especially boys, from engaging in other-sex activities. Picture Johnny playing with a dollhouse and tea set. Imagine his parents', particularly his father's, reactions. Parents encourage boys' independent explorations and pressure them more for achievement. They give boys both more praise and more punishments than they give to girls (Hoffman, 1977; Maccoby & Jacklin, 1974). The direct effects of these differences on a child's behavior are not always apparent. However, the steering of girls to dolls and of boys to trucks, for example, and the generally more intense socialization that boys receive cannot fail to convey some message to a child struggling to organize his/her world. This message may be that boys are more important, since more attention is paid to them. Also, the message may be that the sexes are really opposite, since strong distinctions are made between them. Such behaviors by parents toward children may also lead to some of the sex differences discussed in Part Two.

In addition, although parents say they treat their daughters and sons similarly, they do admit to having different expectations of females and males and to having different emphases in child rearing (Block, 1973; Katz, Bowermaster, Jacobson, & Kessell, 1977; Maccoby & Jacklin, 1974). By reanalyzing data from the Berkeley Growth Study, a 40-year longitudinal project, Block (1973) found that socialization values for boys at all ages emphasized agentic qualities—achievement, competition, control of feelings, and concern for rule conformity. Socialization for girls emphasized communal aspects—developing and maintaining close interpersonal relationships and expression of feelings. Key parent-child issues also differed by sex of child. For boys, key issues were authority and control; for girls, relatedness, protection, and support. In both cases, the father appeared to be the more sex typed of the parents, making greater differentiation of the sexes than did the mother. These value differences may be communicated in more subtle ways than can be measured in a laboratory or by a questionnaire. One way these value differences may be communicated is through parental reactions to their children's behavior. Parents have been found to react more positively when sex-typed toys were used by children of the appropriate sex, especially boys, than when they were used by the other sex (Fagot, 1977a; Russell, Waller, James, & Ames, 1978).

In other studies, race and class have been found to be important mediators of sex-role socialization (see Hess, 1970; Lynn, 1979; Weitzman, 1975). Lower-class families tend to differentiate between the sexes even more sharply than do middle-class families, and they tend to be particularly restrictive toward girls. Black parents tend to socialize their daughters to be more independent than do White parents, and Blacks seem to use a different female stereotype, that of the "strong Black woman," in their training (Ladner, 1971; Lynn, 1979; Wallace, 1979). Such differences need to be borne in mind in examining research findings, especially since most of the research has been on middle-class Whites. The ability to generalize such findings, therefore, may be limited.

In general, according to all studies of parental behaviors, boys seem to have the more intense socialization. Compared to girls, they receive more pressure against engaging in sex-inappropriate behavior, they receive more punishment and also more encouragement and praise, and they receive more attention in general (Donelson, 1977a; Fling & Manosevitz, 1972; Hartley, 1959; Maccoby & Jacklin, 1974; Spence & Helmreich, 1978). Girls receive intensified role pressures from puberty on, but these are centered around their sexual identity and around finding a mate (Donelson, 1977a, 1977b; Katz, 1979).

Why this differential pressure exists is not clear. As Maccoby and Jacklin (1974) suggest, perhaps males' greater strength and aggressiveness make their adequate early socialization much more important. Or perhaps males simply are more valued, and, therefore, more attention is paid to them. This is supported by findings regarding parental sex preferences. Another reason for differential pressure involves the greater demands of the masculine sex role. To get a child to accept the masculine role, as in suppressing his feelings, socialization must be intense. Or perhaps establishing a male identity is harder to do because of absence of male models; so socialization must be more intense to compensate.

The explanations with the most support involve the differential value being placed on the male sex role and the greater demands attached to it. The rigidity of the male sex role can be seen in the four basic themes of masculinity (Brannon, 1976): (1) rejecting all "feminine" behaviors and traits, (2) being strong, competent, and independent, (3) acquiring success and status, and (4) demonstrating aggressiveness and daring. Regardless of which explanation for differential pressures is accepted, such differential pressures have important consequences for a child's personality development and the child's relationships with others. These consequences will be discussed in Part Four.

Aside from specific treatment, however, the behavioral characteristics of the parents also influence a child's sex typing. Both Kelly and Worell (1976) and Orlofsky (1979) investigated the relationship between college students' current sex typing and certain behaviors of their parents when the students were 16 years old. Despite the limitations of retrospective reports, the results are interesting. Both sets of researchers found that the important family characteristics were somewhat different for females and males. For males, parental warmth and involvement were the critical factors in determining their sex typing; for females, cognitive encouragement and consistent discipline were most important. However, Kelly and Worell's (1976) findings differ considerably from those of Orlofsky (1979) with regard to the particular parental patterns found.

Kelly and Worell (1976) found that androgynous males had two parents who showed warmth and emotional involvement. Feminine males had only one parent—their mother—who showed such behaviors. Masculine males did not experience warmth or emotional involvement from either of their parents. Undifferentiated males also did not experience such behaviors and, in addition, received little encouragement for cognitive activities. Thus, parental warmth seems the critical variable for sex typing in males. Orlofsky (1979), while generally confirming the parental pattern for androgynous males, found that feminine males received rejection from both their mother and father, not just their father, as Kelly and Worell (1976) had found. Orlofsky also found that masculine men had nurturant but sex-typed fathers and that undifferentiated men tended to occupy an intermediate position on many of the scales. A key finding of Orlofsky was that the father's influence seemed to be more important than the mother's influence in the sex-role development of the male.

The pattern of parental behaviors in the sex-role development of females again shows marked differences. Kelly and Worell (1976) found that androgynous females, as opposed to other sex-typed females, reported the greatest encouragement of cognitive activities, greater maternal warmth, and less paternal permissiveness. Feminine females received little intellectual encouragement. Masculine females reported strong cognitive encouragement from both parents, especially the father, and rather lax discipline. Undifferentiated females received little cognitive encouragement and stricter maternal control, although their mothers tended to be less involved. Thus, for sex typing in females, cognitive encouragement and discipline seem most important. Again, Orlofsky (1979) basically confirmed these findings for androgynous, feminine, and undifferentiated females but found marked differences for the masculine women. In his study, masculine women had strongly masculine fathers and received considerable rejection and lack of involvement from both parents. Orlofsky also found that the mother's influence seemed to be more important than the father's influence in the sex-role development of the female.

The major difference in the findings of Kelly and Worell (1976) and Orlofsky (1979) centers on cross-sex-typed individuals. Why these differences occurred is not clear, except that the two studies used different measures of sex typing. Kelly and Worell used the PRF-ANDRO scale (Berzins, Welling, & Wetter, 1978); Orlofsky used the BSRI (Bem, 1974). From both sets of results, however, it seems clear that parents do influence the sex typing of their children, but they do so in different ways for females and for males. Spence and Helmreich (1978) also found a strong relationship between parent behaviors and attitudes and the sex typing of their children. The relationship is complex, however, and depends, in part, on the sex typing of the parents themselves. Families with one or both parents being androgynous were rated highest in parental warmth and supportiveness and in encouraging achievement and a sense of self-worth in the children. Undifferentiated couples were rated the lowest in the above qualities; the traditional masculine-feminine couples were rated at an intermediate level.

These last three studies (Kelly & Worell, 1976; Orlofsky, 1979; Spence & Helmreich, 1978) indicate the importance of both parents in a child's development. Yet traditionally, the father role generally has received short shrift. It will therefore be instructive to focus on the father role in some detail.

Father's Role.   Fathers, as specific socializing agents, have rarely been studied in the past. As with other aspects of sex-role research, preconceived notions about the "naturalness" of maternal behavior has led many fathers to avoid child care and has led many researchers to avoid studying fathers. Results from research conducted with fathers demonstrate that fathers are indeed important for their children's development, especially the children's sex-role identity development, academic achievement, and moral development (see Collins, 1979; Lamb, 1976a, 1979; Lynn, 1974, 1979; Spence & Helmreich, 1978). There are some problems with earlier studies, however. Few were of actual fathering behavior (Kotelchuck, 1976). Rather, most of these studies were conducted with children whose fathers were absent. Unfortunately, social class differences between father-absent and father-present homes were seldom taken into account (Biller, 1974). More recent research suggests that the key factors in father-absent homes may be the additional stresses a family experiences when a father is absent rather than the absence per se (Herzog & Sudia, 1974; Shinn, 1978).

The effect of fathers on the sex-role identity development of their children actually is unclear. Most studies have focused on the father's role as an identification figure or as a model for his son. With few exceptions, the literature has failed to support the hypothesis that masculine fathers will have masculine sons or that boys raised in father-absent homes will be less masculine (Biller, 1976; Herzog & Sudia, 1974; Lamb, 1976b; Maccoby & Jacklin, 1974). Such studies are complicated by methodological problems with the techniques used to assess masculinity and similarity as well as by failure to control for important variables, such as socioeconomic status. Fathers do seem to be the primary role models of young boys, but only when the fathers are nurturant and the father-child relationship has been affectionate (Biller, 1976; Lamb, 1976b). Orlofsky (1979) found that a father's behavior was more important than a mother's in determining the sex typing of a male. Spence and Helmreich (1978) found that males were more likely to exhibit the socially desirable characteristics of their fathers than of their mothers. Females, on the other hand, were likely to exhibit desirable characteristics of either parent regardless of their sex-role appropriateness. Thus, fathers do appear to have a particular influence on their sons as well as on their daughters.

Somewhat surprisingly, the impact of fathers on the sex-role development of their daughters has been found to be quite strong, particularly when contrasted with paternal effects on sons. Femininity of daughters is greatest when fathers are nurturant and participate actively in child rearing. In addition, acceptant relations between fathers and daughters seem critical for the daughters' personality development and for heterosexual behaviors in particular (Biller, 1976; Fleck, Coffey, Malin, & Miller, 1978; Hetherington, 1972; Lamb, 1976b; Lynn, 1974).

Cross-Sex Effects. The finding that, in some areas, fathers have particularly strong effects on daughters rather than on sons is paralleled by findings that mothers have particularly strong effects on sons rather than on daughters. These cross-sex effects have been found to be stronger than the sex of the child alone in influencing parent-child interactions; that is, all sons are not treated one way and all daughters another. Cross-sex effects also appear stronger than the sex of the parent alone in influencing parent-child interactions; that is, all mothers do not treat children one way and all fathers treat them another. Rather, it appears that mothers tend to treat their sons, and fathers tend to treat their daughters, in specific and different ways.

In general, fathers tend to be more favorable towards, and permissive with, girls in regard to aggressive, dependent, and achievement behaviors than they are with boys. For mothers, the opposite is true—they tend to be more favorable towards, and permissive with, boys than with girls (Gurwitz & Dodge, 1975; Maccoby & Jacklin, 1974; Rothbart & Maccoby, 1966). Somewhat contradictorily, Bearison (1979) found that parents tend to be most role conscious and rule conscious with their offspring of the other sex. Thus, fathers tend to reinforce sex-role stereotypes in their daughters and mothers tend to reinforce such stereotypes in their sons. These differences appear as early as the first grade. Parents were also found to cuddle other-sex newborns more than same-sex ones (Rubin et al., 1974). Since mothers are often the only parent studied, these results may account for the predominant findings in the literature that boys receive more praise, are subject to stricter socialization, and are held more at birth than are girls. In the home, with father present, these effects may be counterbalanced. However, since most fathers do not spend an equal amount of time with their children as do mothers, girls may grow up receiving less positive treatment and more restrictiveness than do boys in general. As noted above, there is some evidence that this is the case (Maccoby & Jacklin, 1974).

The reasons for this cross-sex effect are unclear, but it may result from a variety of sources. It may be a reaction to the other-sex child as a member of the other sex, or it may be a reaction to the same-sex child as a rival. It may also be a reminder of the parents' own negative impulses, which they then punish (Rothbart & Maccoby, 1966). In any case, such effects certainly need to be taken into account in drawing conclusions about parental behavior.

Parent-Child Interactions. Another major consideration regarding parents as socializing agents is the interaction between the child and the parent. Research has shown that such exchanges go two ways: not only does a parent shape a child's behavior, but child characteristics can influence a parent's behavior as well (see Bronfenbrenner, 1977, for a theoretical discussion of such interactions; also Segal & Yahraes, 1978). Studies have found that parents tend to handle male infants more frequently than females at 3 weeks of age, but the reverse is true for infants at 6 months of age (Moss, 1967). Parents also tend to vocalize more to female than to male infants (Cherry & Lewis, 1976; Goldberg & Lewis, 1969; Lewis, 1972). These parental behaviors may stem from the greater fussiness of male infants and from the more frequent vocalization of girls. When infant fussiness was controlled for, some of these sex differences disappeared (Moss, 1967). It is thus possible that the greater fussiness of male infants leads to greater maternal contact, but, when such comforting does not quiet the child (as it seems not to), mothers begin cuddling less. This, in turn, may encourage earlier independence in sons than in daughters. Similarly, girls' earlier and greater vocalizations may be more reinforcing for the parent and may lead to more parental vocalization to daughters than to sons, further reinforcing the difference.

Additional interactions also are likely to occur. Bronfenbrenner (1977) discusses studies that find the parent-infant interaction to be influenced by the presence or absence of the other parent, siblings, and others. The sex of siblings may also be important. Tauber (1979) found that cross-sex play amongst 8- and 9-year-olds was more common among children who came from single-sex families than among those coming from both-sex families. Her finding lends support to the idea of role diversification in families. Human behavior functions as part of a whole system, each part of which undoubtedly influences another.

Teachers

However influential parents and other household members may be in the child's development, once school begins, other people share the responsibility for socialization. Teachers, in particular, are important.

From the time a child starts school, which for some children occurs as early as 3 years of age, teachers provide additional messages regarding sex-role development through provision of activities, reinforcement, modeling, and subtler forms of communication. In most cases, these messages reinforce those received at home, strengthening the sex typing. Even when teacher messages contradict parental messages, their influence is enormous and sometimes is greater than parental influence, especially if the messages are supported by other socializing forces.

In general, teacher influence has been found to be very strong, albeit very subtle. In an observational study of 15 nursery school teachers by Serbin and colleagues (1973), the teachers were found to reinforce boys for being aggressive and girls for being dependent. Teachers responded three times more often to boys who were disruptive than to girls. They also responded more to girls who clung or stayed nearby than to boys who exhibited similar behaviors. Teachers also actually taught boys more than girls. Boys were given more individualized instruction, thereby making them more capable of fending for themselves and more capable in problem solving. In general, boys were given more attention for their behavior, whether such behavior was appropriate or not. Fagot (1978b) also found that nursery school boys were given more positive feedback from their teachers than were girls for engaging in tasks appropriate to academic behaviors. For girls, only sex-stereotyped behaviors brought consistent positive feedback from teachers.

The greater attention and encouragement given to boys have been found related to problem-solving ability (Hess & Shipman, 1967) and may explain boys' greater mathematical skills. The lack of accurate and continuous feedback for girls may interfere with girls' realistic appraisal of their abilities. It may also interfere with the development of self-confidence and of achievement motivation. The indirect reinforcement of aggressiveness in boys may also explain the higher incidence of behavior and learning problems in school-age boys than in girls, since such behaviors interfere with learning.

In elementary school as well, boys receive most of their positive feedback for their academic behavior and most of their negative feedback, or criticism, for their nonacademic behavior—such as making noise (Dweck & Bush, 1976; Dweck, Davidson, Nelson, & Enna, 1978). For girls, the reverse pattern has been found: girls receive most of their positive feedback for nonacademic behaviors—such as doing neat work—and most of their negative feedback for academic work. The consequences of this pattern of teacher behaviors are quite serious: girls learn to give up on academic work after a failure more quickly than do boys. This learned helplessness by girls may stay with them throughout their school years.

These differences in teacher behavior, supported by other studies (for example, Cherry, 1975; Etaugh & Harlow, 1975; Guttentag & Bray, 1977; Harrison, 1974), parallel those found in parents. Boys receive more attention, more praise, and more punishment than do girls. These findings are especially striking because teachers were not aware that they were treating boys and girls differently (Guttentag & Bray, 1977; Serbin et al., 1973). Without awareness, changing such differential practices is impossible.

The generally favorable treatment of male as compared to female students may be restricted to a White population. Taylor (1979) found that Black males, when compared with females of both races and with White males, received the most unfavorable teacher treatment, such as the fewest response opportunities. Since the students in Taylor's study were hypothetical, actual student characteristics could not account for the differences in teacher behavior. Thus, race may interact with sex in affecting teacher behavior. Unfortunately, very few studies have even examined race as a variable.

Teachers do admit to believing that boys and girls behave differently and need to be treated differently. In addition, teachers have been found to interpret a child's behavior as a function of the child's sex (Guttentag & Bray, 1977). For example, Rotter (1967) found, using different vignettes, that boys were rated by teachers as more active, more gregarious, more leaderlike, and more accepted by their peers than were girls, although the behaviors that were judged were nearly identical. In addition, more teachers, especially females, admit to preferring male students, although teachers felt females were less of a discipline problem (Ricks & Pyke, 1973). Female teachers also were likely to rate fourth- and fifth-grade girls as higher than boys in self-esteem-related behaviors, although male teachers showed the opposite pattern (Loeb & Horst, 1978). Such beliefs and behaviors on the part of teachers undoubtedly affect the children's behaviors and feelings both about themselves and about each other. Perhaps female conformity in school (see Chapter Four) is an attempt to win teacher approval, a tactic which never quite succeeds.

Peers

Age-mates also serve as strong socializing agents. They become increasingly important during the school years. In many cases, peer pressure is stronger and more effective than parental or other adult pressure, particularly during adolescence (Chafetz, 1978; Coleman, 1961; Katz, 1979; Strommen, 1977). Even during preschool years, however, peers influence the sex-role behaviors of their friends.

Fagot (1978a) found that preschoolers gave fewer reactions, in general, and more negative reactions, in particular, to classmates who did not play much with either masculine- or feminine-sex-typed toys. (Fagot terms these children "androgynous.") In addition, boys who preferred feminine-sex-typed toys received less positive feedback and were more likely to play alone than were other boys in their class. The findings from this and other studies (for example Connor et al., in press; Fagot, 1977b, 1978b) suggest that children who adopt traditional forms of sex-role behavior are more socially acceptable to their peers than those who do not adopt traditional behaviors. This may be particularly true for boys, and it serves as another example of their more intense socialization and more rigid sex role.

Three behaviors, in particular, seem affected by peer responses —aggressiveness, assertiveness, and passivity. Connor and associates (in press) found that 9- to 14-year-old girls expect less disapproval from their peers for passive behavior and more disapproval for aggressive behaviors than do their male classmates. Such expectations were indeed justified. Assertiveness is also regarded as more desirable for males than for females. Such sex-role stereotypes may influence the way children respond to other children and may influence their willingness to use other children as models.

Beginning in preschool years, boys and girls increasingly separate into same-sex groups, a process which intensifies once a child enters school. As was noted in Chapter Four, boys tend to have larger friendship groups than do girls and tend to be more influenced by them. Hartley (1959) suggests that a peer group is more important to a male because he has to look to them for information about the male role, since adult males are less available than adult females. Since his peers have no better source of information than he, the information the child obtains is likely to be distorted and oversimplified. Males' conceptualizations of appropriate behavior therefore are often extremely rigid and stereotyped. Boys often feel great pressure to prove their masculinity through athletic skill, physical strength, acts of daring, and, later, sexual conquests (Chafetz, 1978; Fasteau, 1974; Hartley, 1959). The same pressure to prove their femininity does not exist for girls until adolescence, when they are often pressured to find a mate. Peer status for girls then becomes contingent on their popularity with boys (Chafetz, 1978; Weitz, 1977). For both sexes, sex-role-consistent behavior is a major factor in peer acceptance (Hartup, 1970).

SUMMARY

Children are strongly affected by socializing agents—parents, teachers, and peers—and generally learn the sex-role stereotypes early and well. By school age, children know what girls and boys "should" and "shouldn't" do and tend to behave accordingly, boys more so than girls. Boys tend to receive the more intense socialization pressures and consequently behave in more stereotyped ways than do girls. One future implication of this differential socialization pressure is that androgyny may be more difficult for males, since they are more committed to the masculine stereotype.

Both directly and indirectly—through modeling and reinforcement—and as a function of their level of cognitive development, children are steered toward different modes of behavior. Boys are steered toward the agentic—achievement, competition, independence—and girls toward the communal—nurturance, sociability, dependence.

Although the effects of socializing agents are enormous, socializing agents alone cannot account for the entire socializing process. Children formulate their conceptions of sex roles from a wide range of social forces acting on a more impersonal level, such as from the media, from the educational system, from religion, and so forth. It is to an examination of these forces that we now turn.

RECOMMENDED READING

Bronfenbrenner, U. Toward an experimental ecology of human development. *American Psychologist*, 1977, *32*(7), 513–531. A review of the complex interactions among the many variables that affect child development.

Lamb, M. E. (Ed.). *The role of the father in child development.* New York: Wiley, 1976. An excellent collection of articles by the most prominent researchers in the area of paternal effects on children.

Lynn, D. B. *Daughters & parents: Past, present, and future.* Monterey, Calif.: Brooks/Cole, 1979. General review of the research on parental influences on the development of women.

Maccoby, E., & Jacklin, C. *The psychology of sex differences.* Stanford, Calif.: Stanford University Press, 1974. Contains a review of child development theories and the research, to 1974, on parental treatment of children.

8 Socialization: Social Forces

A 6-year-old child is overheard by her mother explaining to a friend that only boys can be doctors and only girls can be nurses. The mother remarks "But, Sally, you know I'm a doctor." Sally replies "You're no doctor; you're my mother."

This story illustrates not only the simplistic categories children use to understand their world but also the fact that children acquire information about the world from sources outside the home. This chapter examines the sex-role messages the child's world contains.

That social contexts are crucial in understanding human behavior has been amply demonstrated by social psychologists. Naomi Weisstein (1969) notes, in particular, the following findings. Under certain nonthreatening, innocuous conditions, people can be made nearly to kill other humans, while under other conditions they cannot be made to do so (Milgram's obedience experiments, 1965). People appear to react to their state of physiological arousal, induced by adrenalin, with either euphoria or anger depending upon their expectations and the behavior of another person (Schacter & Singer, 1962). Students can sometimes get better grades if their teachers expect them to be intelligent (Rosenthal & Jacobson, 1968). Given these findings, Weisstein concludes that "a study of human behavior requires a study of the social contexts in which people move, the expectations as to how they will behave, and the authority that tells them who they are and what they are supposed to do" (Weisstein, 1969, p. 58).

The influence of social contexts need not be direct or, in fact, deliberate. As Daryl and Sandra Bem (1970) suggest, this training of people to know "their place" is a function of a nonconscious ideology that can be seen most clearly in the socialization of the female. Whereas when a boy is born, it has been difficult to predict his life (job, interests, activities) 25 years later, when a girl is born, we could be fairly confident of how most of her time would be spent—in homemaking activities. Her individuality, her unique potential all have been irrelevant. The majority of women have ended up in the same role—homemaker—regardless of individual factors. If they have worked, they most likely have been in one of four low-status, low-salary jobs—clerk, salesperson, waitress, hairdresser—and have done homemaking in addition. This restrictiveness has not been true for males.

An examination of the social context in which a child develops is thus important to fully understand how sex-role stereotypes and sex-role expectations develop and are maintained. Messages about sex-role-appropriate behavior can be found in our language, play activities, the media, school, religion, and the workplace. Of all, language is perhaps the most subtle.

LANGUAGE

From the moment a child begins to understand the spoken word, she or he also begins to receive messages about the way society views sex roles. Sexism in the English language takes three major forms: ignoring, labeling, and deprecating (Henley & Thorne, 1977; Lakoff, 1975).

Ignoring

The most striking way of ignoring females is by using the masculine gender to refer to human beings in general—for example, "chair*man*;" "best *man* for the job;" "*man*kind;" "the working *man*;" "everyone should do *his* best." This use of the male term to refer to all humans makes maleness the norm and femaleness the exception. That people do, in fact, perceive the use of the masculine form to refer predominantly to males has been demonstrated by a number of researchers (Moulton, Robinson, & Elias, 1978; Schneider & Hacker, 1973). For example, when college students were asked to make up a story about the average student in a large coeducational institution, 65% who had read the pronoun *his* told a story about a male. In contrast, only 54% told male stories when the pronoun encountered was *their*, and only 44% told male stories when the pronoun was *his or her* (Moulton et al., 1978). Clearly, then, the use of male pronouns is not sex-neutral. It allows many people to ignore the female half of the population.

Labeling

Language also defines women by labeling what is considered to be the exception to the rule ("*lady* doctor," "*career* girl"), thereby reinforcing occupational stereotypes. Females are defined by the groups with which they are linked—"*women* and children"—and the order in which they are usually referred to—"he and *she*," "boys and *girls*"—that is, in second place. Women also are predominantly referred to by relationships. When they marry, they lose their name (identity) and take on that of their spouse; thereafter, they are "Mrs. John Doe." Until recently, marriage ceremonies pronounced a couple "man and *wife*." He maintains his personhood; she becomes a role. Women also are referred to as possessions, as in "pioneers moved West, taking their *wives* and children with them."

Deprecating

A third sexist aspect of language is the way it deprecates women. One way to do this is by trivializing them ("poet*ess*," "girl" for woman).

Another way to deprecate women is to sexualize them. For example, *dame* and *madam* have double meanings, while their male counterparts, *lord* and *sir,* do not. A third means of deprecation is to insult women. One researcher found 220 terms for a sexually promiscuous woman, compared to 22 terms for a sexually promiscuous male (Henley & Thorne, 1977). A fourth form of deprecation is depersonalization ("chick," "piece of ass," "cunt," "broad").

Even the American Sign Language system used by most deaf people in this country mirrors sex-role stereotypes. References to men and masculine pronouns refer to the top portion of the head. This part of the body is also the reference point for signs depicting intelligence and decision making. References to women and feminine pronouns, on the other hand, are signed in the lower part of the face, the part of the body associated with signs for the emotions and feelings (*Psychology Today*, Feb. 1979, p. 98).

As was noted in Chapter Four, the sexes also are thought to use language differently. Lakoff (1975) suggests that women more than men use tag questions ("It's hot, isn't it?"), qualifiers ("maybe," "I guess"), and compound requests ("Won't you close the window?" rather than "Close the window"). These three speech style differences are assumed to indicate a lack of assertiveness and more politeness on the part of females. The evidence regarding the existence of sex differences in these three areas is inconsistent (McMillan, Clifton, McGrath, & Gale, 1977; Newcombe & Arnkoff, 1978). However, there is evidence that speakers who do use the "female" speech style are more often viewed as less assertive, more polite, and warmer than speakers who use the "male" speech style (Newcombe & Arnkoff, 1979). Furthermore, children are taught that girls do not curse, talk too loudly, or issue demands but that boys do. This greater permissiveness for boys is reflected in male dominance in verbal and nonverbal interactions—talking more, interrupting more, and touching more, and more often using a familiar form of address (first name, "honey") when talking to a female than would a female talking to a male (Henley, 1977).

Changing Language

These aspects of the English language convey to young children important messages—that females are less important and less interesting than males, that males are dominant and forceful—that are reinforced by other aspects of socialization. To begin to change these stereotypes, our language and our use of it must change. (See Blaubergs, 1978, for a review of types of changes). Publishers are finally beginning to issue guidelines for eliminating sexism in writing (Scott, Foresman & Co. was among the first in 1972). For example, use "he or she" instead of "he;" recast pronouns into the plural ("their" instead of "his"); neuterize occupation terms ("police officer" instead of "policeman"). Changes in our use of language clearly can be done. Witness the change of the word "Negro" to "Black" and the acceptance of "Ms." by most businesses and organizations. It may be hard to change, it may be awkward until a new habit develops, and it may be superficial compared to needed economic and social changes. But it is important. As Blaubergs (1978) notes, "Although language may be only one of the reflections of societal practices, nevertheless it is a reflection, and as such provides continuing inspiration for sexism" (pp. 246–247).

Social and linguistic changes are interactive, each promoting change in the other. For example, Munroe and Munroe (1969), in their study of ten cultures, found a significant relationship between structural sex bias in a culture, such as marital residence and inheritance regulations, and the proportion of male to female gender nouns in use. To develop an androgynous society, a more egalitarian language is needed.

PLAY

Language is only one vehicle through which sex-role stereotypes are taught. As soon as children start to play, they receive another lesson. Picture a group of children playing with blocks. Picture another group playing "house." What is the sex composition of these groups? Now picture a high school athlete who has just received a school letter for excellence in basketball. Does a boy or does a girl come to mind? From all these play activities—toys, games, and sports—children receive messages about sex-role-appropriate behavior that affect their lives.

Toys

As was noted previously, by the time girls and boys are 4 years old, they play with different toys and prefer toys identified with their sex. This is true for boys more so than for girls. Boys play with trucks, building blocks, robots; girls, with dolls, household goods, stuffed animals. In general, girls' toys do not make many cognitive demands or prepare girls for any occupational future except the role of motherhood. Boys' toys, on the other hand, tend to be more varied, expensive, and creative—for example, scientific kits (Hoffman, 1977). These differential experiences convey important occupational messages to young children. One message is that careers are not important for girls but are important for boys. Another message is that child care is not important for boys but is important for girls. One consequence of playing with different toys may well be the development of different abilities, such as verbal abilities for girls (playing "house" involves a great deal of talk) and visual-spatial and manual abilities for boys.

Games and Sports

The games that boys and girls play also differ. Girls spend more time in individual activities that require little competition and have few rules—for example, jumping rope, playing "house" (Hennig & Jardim, 1977; Lott, 1978; Maccoby & Jacklin, 1974). Sports considered appropriate for females, such as skating, swimming, and horseback riding, also have few rules and usually involve no competition. The emphasis is on quality of performance, not on winning. Boys, on the other hand, are more likely to play in situations that involve sociability and coordinated action (Lott, 1978). They also are strongly encouraged to play in highly organized, complex, competitive team sports such as baseball, football, and basketball. Through such team sports, boys learn how to set goals and work with others to achieve those goals. They learn a degree of emotional detachment necessary in choosing players for a team. Boys come to understand and respect rules, and they learn to be persistent. They also learn the importance of winning and come to view it as a personal or team achievement. Failure can be spread among team members, keeping the individual ego protected (Booth, 1972; Hennig & Jardim, 1977).

These games have direct consequences for future occupational performance. As David Riesman comments, "The road to the board room leads through the locker room" (*Time*, July 26, 1978, p. 59). Hennig and Jardim (1977), in their book on women in management, attribute male dominance of business to early sports experience. Males transfer to the business world in an effective way what they learned from team sports—competition, emotional detachment, teamwork, and ego protection from failure. Females, however, usually have not learned these things. They are not used to delegating responsibility, tolerating people who do not perform well, or focusing on winning. Hennig and Jardim found that women who have "made it" in the business world have one thing in common—they were raised free from sex-role stereotypes. Other research (see Rohrbaugh, 1979) has found that female participation in sports enhances females' general sense of confidence and well-being.

Sports and sport terms play another important role in future occupational performance. Many analogies used for business and political processes are based on sports—for example, *one-on-one*, *blitz*, *strike out*. People unfamiliar with the jargon, as are many women, are often at a loss to understand the messages being communicated. This lack of understanding further increases their difficulty in operating in traditionally masculine fields (Fasteau, 1974). In addition, many social activities and conversations revolve around sports, such as the business golf game, Monday night football. People who are not interested in, or are not familiar with, such activities, such as many women, often are left out.

In school, particularly in high school, the emphasis on male sports is often overwhelming, being totally disproportionate to sports' role in adult life. Coleman (1961) found that athletic performance was valued higher than academic performance, especially by freshmen, and that athletes were the most visible and most popular members of their student bodies. This emphasis on male sports to the exclusion of female sports is particularly evident in the budget allocations. An informal survey conducted by *Womensports Magazine* in 1974 (reported in *ER Monitor*, March–April, 1977, p. 11) found that, in high school, boys' budgets were, on the average, 5 times larger than girls'; in college, the men's budgets were 30 times larger than women's. Since then, there has been some slow improvement. In 1977–78, men's budgets in college were "only" 10 times greater (*Time*, July 28, 1978, p. 57).

This imbalance in sports budgets is just beginning to change as a result of the Title IX regulation of the Education Amendments Act of 1972, which prohibits schools and colleges receiving Federal funds from discriminating on the basis of sex in any educational program or activity. For example, the University of Georgia in 1977–78 spent $2.5 million for men's athletics and $120,000 for women's athletics. The allocation for women, however, was over 100 times greater than the $1,000 spent in 1973 (*Time*, July 28, 1978, p. 58). Regulations governing application of Title IX that went into effect July 21, 1978, were still weak, however. They did not require equal expenditures but required only that athletic *opportunities* be equal. Separate teams were allowed for contact sports or when team selection is based on competitive skills. Another problem with the regulations was that no affirmative action requirements were included to upgrade women's athletic programs. The Department of Health, Education, and Welfare's 1979 guidelines on college athletics, which may correct some of these problems, were only announced in December 1979 (Fields, 1979). They have yet to be put into effect. Thus, females in sports still remain handicapped by unavailable facilities, lack of encouragement, absence of role models, and parental and societal suppression of female competition (Agate & Meacham, 1977). Increasing visibility of female role models—Billie Jean King, Nancy Lopez, and Wyomia Tyus—hopefully will help. Figure 8-1 shows one way such models may help break down sex-role stereotypes.

There are some signs that women's participation in sports is increasing. Both *Ms.* and *Time* magazines ran cover stories about women and sports in June 1978. The number of high school girls participating in interscholastic sports in 1969–70 was 294,000; in 1978–79, the number was 1.8 million, a sixfold increase (Seidman, 1979). The Association for Intercollegiate Athletics for Women (A.I.A.W.), the counterpart of men's National Collegiate Athletic Association (N.C.A.A.), was formed in 1971–72 with 278 member schools.

Figure 8-1

How sports models can break down sex-role stereotypes. (Copyright 1973 by G. B. Trudeau/ distributed by Universal Press Syndicate. All rights reserved.)

In 1977–78, it had 825 active members, compared to 710 schools in the N.C.A.A. During 1977–78 more than 100,000 women, compared with 170,000 men, were taking part in intercollegiate sports. In professional sports also, the growth of women's participation has been phenomenal and can be measured in dollars. For example, in 1970 there was only $200,500 available in prize money on the tennis circuit. In 1980 the corresponding figure is projected to be $9.2 million (Seidman, 1979).

Although females' participation in sports is quickly approaching that of males' in numbers, the meaning of sports still may be different for the sexes. Reis and Jelsma (1978), in their survey of 48 male and 47 female college varsity athletes evenly distributed among four sports (basketball, lacrosse, swimming, and tennis), found that there were important differences in the way each sex approached sports. The males scored significantly higher than females on all questions dealing with the importance of competition; the females scored significantly higher than males on all questions dealing with the importance of social interactions. These responses parallel, and perhaps reflect, the stereotypic sex difference in interest areas. There were no significant sex differences in enjoyment of the sport or in the desire to perform well. The sex differences in attitudes toward sports may be related to the participants' sex typing. Myers and Lips (1978) found that feminine-sex-typed athletes may participate in sports for noncompetitive reasons whereas androgynous and masculine athletes may participate for competitive reasons. Unfortunately, the direct effect of attitudes on athletic performance was not examined. Other research on the consequences of participation in sports suggests that such participation is not always beneficial. Athletics can have a negative impact on people, especially when athletics is overemphasized. This negative impact has fallen differentially on males because more males than females engage in sports and because athletics is intimately related to the male sex role.

Negative Effects of Sports Participation

Although sports have long been thought to build character, Ogilvie and Tutko (1971) have shown that sports do not necessarily increase personality strengths. Rather, in some ways, athletic competition limits personality growth. Athletic stars tend to conform to the traditional male stereotype (strong, silent, competitive, aggressive), making it difficult for them to function in other than the athletic arena. Stein and Hoffman (1978) and others (Hyland, 1978; Simpson, 1978) further point out that the emphasis on, and preoccupation with, high-level performance and winning may cause an athlete to play while in great pain or when injured. The male role, however, does not allow him to either acknowledge or give expression to such pressures and pain. This puts great strain on the athlete and may cause lasting physical problems. Furthermore, the focus on top players (the star system) generates problems of cooperation among team members.

Those who participate in sports also may suffer from the intense male competition that can pervade nearly every encounter among men (Fasteau, 1974; Peck, 1976b). One consequence of this competition may be a feeling of inadequacy and self-hatred, since few males actually make it to the top and no male (or female, for that matter) can win all the time. This self-hatred and this competition also can generate an undercurrent of violence among men that they must learn to defend against and to use to their advantage. Such feelings mitigate against deep friendships among men and encourage males to constantly prove their masculinity in other ways.

Competition itself, especially if excessive, may not even be beneficial for athletic performance. Spence and Helmreich (1978) report research that shows that the most successful individuals are those with a high mastery orientation and a low competitive orientation. Reis and Jelsma (1978) also report on the possible disruptive effects that excessive competition may have on a group's performance and morale. Thus, it may be that the sex difference these latter researchers found in the meaning of sports—with male college athletes having a competitive orientation; female college athletes, a participative orientation—may work to the disadvantage of many male athletes.

For nonathletes, the pressure and strain of sports are even more severe. As Stein and Hoffman (1978) and others (for example, Fasteau, 1974; Pleck, 1976b) note, the overemphasis on male athletic skill can be devastating to boys with limited athletic ability or interest. One result of this overemphasis on sports is role strain and feelings of failure and inferiority for not living up to male sex-role expectations. Picture a clumsy boy who gets ridiculed for dropping the ball. One of the worst things he could hear would be "You play like a *girl!*" Such boys also get left out of many male groups and consequently may feel like, and be, outcasts. Another consequence for the nonathlete of the overemphasis on male athletic skill is total disdain for sports and feelings of distance from his body.

The intimate association between athletics and masculinity is especially obvious in the resistance expressed by males when females try to join their games. Figure 8-2 shows an example of such resistance as well as an involved participant's view. (These letters to the Editor were written in response to *Time's* cover story on women and sports.) The uproar over admitting qualified girls to Little League baseball teams and the concern about female "fragility" may reflect a belief in the masculinity-destroying prospects of female competition. To get beaten by a girl has been viewed as a major humiliation for boys because girls clearly are thought to be inferior. If they were not considered inferior their competition would be welcomed. The issue at the college level is more complex. A division of monies is at stake there in addition to the political and psychological ramifications.

Because athletics and the male sex role are so closely related, many women have hesitated to become involved in sports for fear of becoming, or being labeled, "masculine." Research (see Rohrbaugh, 1979) suggests, however, that some of the stigma attached to female participation in sports may be diminishing. Other research (Myers & Lips, 1978) has found that female athletes tend toward an androgy-

Your profiling women's participation in sports is like encouraging a snail to enter a foot race. Let's face it, women just aren't made right to enter a man's realm of sports.

They have cluttered up the baseball diamonds and football fields, and now they have invaded and completely tied up our handball courts with their sissy game of racquetball.

Thank you for your article on women in sports. I'm a twelve-year-old girl going to a school that doesn't really give girls a fair chance in sports. In eighth grade next year, I want to play flag football with the boys, but I'll never get permission from our school board or superintendent. Most of the boys try to discourage me and tell me to go back to cheerleading. Now, with the help of your article, I may be able to win over the boys and (I hope) the superintendent.

Figure 8-2
Two reactions to women in sports, the one on the left by a male, the one on the right by a female. (Letters to the Editor of Time *magazine in response to an article on women in sports. Copyright 1978 Time Inc. All rights reserved.)*

nous, rather than a masculine, sex-role orientation, although for male athletes the masculine sex type predominates. Thus sports can be, and perhaps should be, divorced from the male sex role.

MEDIA

Of all the sources of sex-role stereotypes, the media are the most pervasive. Television, books, films, songs, art—all communicate messages about sex roles that are far from subtle. Females and males are presented, for the most part, in stereotyped ways, usually with deviations from the stereotypes depicted negatively. Since the media both reflect and shape society, they are extremely influential, especially for young children who cannot clearly differentiate fantasy from reality.

Television

It has been estimated that children spend one-third of their lives at home and/or sleeping, one-third at school, and one-third in front of a TV set. Almost all households in the United States (98%) owned at least one television set in 1977, which represented more households than those that had indoor plumbing (Nielsen, 1978). TV usage averages over 6 hours a day in the average TV household. Half of the 12-year-olds in the country watch this amount or more, although the average child watches between 3 and 4 hours a day (Gerbner & Gross, 1976; Nielsen, 1978). By the time a child is 16, she or he has spent more time in front of a TV set than in a classroom. Children from blue-collar families and from minority groups spend even more time watching TV than White middle-class children. Consequently, whatever effects TV viewing has should be particularly strong for such children (Women on Words and Images, 1975a).

Children's Shows. The world that children see on TV is a sex-typed and male-oriented one. Children's TV, for example, has been found to depict twice as many male as female roles. The behaviors of the female and male characters are strikingly different, as are the consequences of these behaviors (Sternglanz & Serbin, 1974). Male characters are more likely to be aggressive, constructive, and helpful and to be rewarded for their action than are female characters. Females are more likely to be shown as deferent and as being punished for displaying a high level of activity. In general, female behavior has no environmental consequence. This pattern parallels the practices of socializing agents: males get more attention and reinforcement; females are usually ignored and are expected to be passive and sedate.

Even in educational and "innovative" programs like "Sesame Street," males and females are depicted as having different activities. Men's work is outside the home; women's work is inside (Bergman, 1974). Furthermore, the major characters on "Sesame Street," the Muppets, all have male names or voices or both. These puppets not only are the mainstays of the show but also are prominent in books, toys, and other commercial articles. As Stevens-Long, Cobb, and Goldstein (1978) have demonstrated, puppet figures can have tremendous influences on children's sex-typed behaviors. They found that children aged 4 to 6 would not play with non-sex-typed toys that had been labeled by two Muppets as appropriate only for the other sex. This behavior change occurred after only 5 minutes of TV exposure.

Prime-Time TV. Four separate groups have documented sexism on TV shows. One group, the U.S. Civil Rights Commission (1977), viewed TV programs from 1969 to 1974. Women on Words and Images (1975a), originally a task force of the National Organization for Women, analyzed 16 top-rated dramatic shows during the 1973 viewing season. A third study, conducted by George Gerbner and Nancy Signorelli for the Screen Actors Guild (L. Brown, 1979), monitored 1365 prime-time and Saturday-morning programs from 1968 to 1978. Dominick (1979) viewed 1314 TV programs between 1953 and 1977. All four studies found that, in prime-time TV, sex-role stereotypes abound. For example, 65% to 75% of all leading characters were White males. This percentage has remained relatively constant for 25 years. In exciting adventure shows, such as "Kojak," males constituted 85% of the major characters. Occupationally, twice as many jobs were depicted for the major male characters as for the major female characters. Males could be police officers, detectives, lawyers, doctors, psychologists, and so on. Working females were usually nurses, secretaries, or teachers. Men also were three times more likely than women to be depicted as wage earners, and women were more than twice as likely as men to be depicted as nonwage earners. Since the 1950s, the makeup of the television-depicted labor force consistently has shown no relationship to the real-life employment patterns of women. Blacks and other minority groups, both females and males, were scarcely represented at all on television. In a 1979 update, the U.S. Civil Rights Commission found no significant changes in the status of women and minorities on TV (Holsendolph, 1979). Figure 8-3 indicates some of the typical female roles on TV.

I am a psychotic/mute/Indian/ Chicana who is restored to normalcy and neatness by a young, attractive, white, middle class doctor from the east. (Lots of flashbacks showing me whipped, raped, and force-fed)

I am the sister/daughter of an unjustly imprisoned man or else the witness to a mafia crime. I am also the client of a blind freelance insurance investigator. I scream often and inopportunely. I always fall and twist my ankle when the investigator and I are fleeing the bad guys.

I am a black/white cop. I have a short snappy name. I am tough but feminine. I like to follow my own instincts about a case. This frequently gets me into trouble; I am inevitably rescued by my male, fellow officers, who are devoted to me . . . I never rescue them.

I am the woman behind the man. I spend a lot of time keeping dinner warm for my crusading policeman/coroner, lover/husband. Sometimes I nag about being left alone so much. Sometimes I am kidnapped by mafia thugs. This makes a welcome break in my routine.

Figure 8-3
Memorable television role models. (From I'm in Training to Be Tall and Blonde, *by Nicole Hollander. Copyright 1979 by Nicole Hollander. Reprinted by permission of St. Martin's Press, Inc.)*

Behaviorally, females were three times more likely than males to be depicted in a negative light, especially on adventure shows. For example, the only women in a number of "Kojak" episodes were prostitutes or dope addicts. Women also were twice as likely as men to show incompetent behaviors. For example, even in a show where a woman is the major character ("Police Woman"), she often must be rescued from a difficult situation by her male partner. Men, on the other hand, although depicted somewhat negatively on situation-comedy shows, are more than twice as likely as women to be shown as competent (independent, skilled, leaderlike, self-confident). Archie Bunker may be a ridiculous figure, but Edith is even more so. She's the one called a "dingbat." Men on TV also are more likely than women to be older, more serious, and more likely to hold prestigious jobs, such as Quincy. The family time concept was introduced in 1975 to eliminate violence and sex from programs shown between 7 and 9 P.M. A perhaps unintended byproduct of this concept was the increase in stereotypic female characters, especially in programs aimed at younger viewers (Peever, 1979).

In news programs, the percentage of female network news correspondents actually declined from 1977 to 1979 (Holsendolph, 1979). In network broadcasts from March 1974 to February 1975, the U.S. Civil Rights Commission (1977) had found that 79% of the newsmakers were White males, 10% White females, 8% nonwhite males, and 3% nonwhite females. It is easy to see how the image of females as unimportant can come across to the viewer.

Commercials.   The sex-role stereotypes are even more explicit in TV commercials than in regular programming (Pingree, 1978; Women on Words and Images, 1975a). In order of frequency, women are depicted as predominantly concerned with their appearance, their housework, and family matters. In contrast, men are more likely to be shown working, playing, eating, or being nursed. Relations between the sexes are portrayed in strictly traditional ways. For example, one detergent commercial shows a man engaged in bird-watching. A woman next to him notices grime on his shirt and repeatedly remarks in an irritating, sing-song voice "Ring around the collar." The scene immediately shifts to the aghast wife and her subsequent efforts to rectify the "humiliating" occurrence. Men are almost always (96%) the authoritative, dominant voice-overs in commercials, even when the products are aimed at women. Thus again, males are depicted as the competent working authority; females as vain homemakers and consumers.

Soap Operas.   In soap operas, viewed primarily by women, characters also are presented in traditional and stereotypic ways, although the subject matter has become more controversial in recent years. Women on such shows as "All My Children" and "Guiding Light" more often are depicted as nurturant, hopeless, and displaying avoidance behaviors than are men on these shows. Men, more than women, are depicted as directive and problem solving (Finz & Waters, 1976).

Summary. The message one hears on TV is that there are more men around than women and that men are more important, competent, dominant, authoritative, and aggressive than women. Women are depicted in far fewer situations, are less likely to be working, and more often are shown in a negative way. Modeling is an important process in sex-role development, and the models presented on TV are stereotyped to the extreme. Even adults may be affected. Being exposed to a constant barrage of a TV world of sex-role stereotypes may help to reinforce adults' own sex-role training. Even if one's training had been nontraditional, TV may encourage more traditional conceptions of the sex roles.

A legitimate question arises regarding the impact of TV on a person's attitudes and behaviors. Although there is still much controversy in this area, there is an increasing body of research that shows that TV's effects can be very significant, especially for children who, as a group, are not as skilled as adults in distinguishing fantasy from reality (*APA Monitor*, 1977; Eysenck & Nias, 1978).

In an interesting series of experiments at the University of Delaware, Florence Geis and colleagues (Geis, Jennings, Corrado-Taylor, & Brown, 1979; Geis, Jennings, & Porter, 1979; Jennings, Geis, & Brown, in press) have demonstrated the powerful effect TV commercials can have on college student viewers. These researchers first videotaped replicas of four network commercials showing traditional sex-role divisions. They then produced four matching commercials with the sex roles reversed. In their first study, Geis et al. found that the sex-role stereotypes depended more on role than on actor sex. For example, actors playing the authoritative role (males in the traditional version, females in the reversed-role version) were rated as more rational, independent, dominant, and ambitious than actors playing the supportive role. In their other studies, these researchers found that women who viewed the reversed-role version of the commercials later showed greater self-confidence, more independence of judgment, and higher achievement aspirations than women who viewed the traditional version. Since children see about 20,000 traditional commercials a year, it is clear how TV can contribute to important sex differences.

Perloff, Brown, and Miller (1978) summarize studies that document the effect of TV on children's conceptions of sex roles. Children, boys more so than girls, recognize sex differences in character attributes and identify with, and aspire to be like, same-sex TV characters. Sprafkin and Liebert (1978) report similar findings.

The amount of time children spend watching TV has been found to be directly and positively related to their degree of acceptance of traditional sex roles as early as kindergarten age (Frueh & McGhee, 1975; Gross & Jeffries-Fox, 1978). Parents' sex-role attitudes may be important factors here, as may be a child's intelligence. These factors may interact with the amount of TV viewing in such a way as to ameliorate TV's sex-typing effects (Perloff et al., 1978).

Children's sex-role attitudes have been found to be directly affected by media messages. Pingree (1978) found that, by showing third- and eighth-grade children commercials of either traditional women (housewives and mothers) or nontraditional women (professional business people), she could affect children's attitudes about women. All children, except eighth-grade boys, who saw the nontraditional commercials and who were told that the women were real people, became less traditional in their attitudes about women. And this was after only 5 minutes of viewing! Clearly, children can learn from TV, although what they learn may be unintentional and unpredictable. TV's effect may also vary as a function of the cognitive developmental level of the child (Perloff et al., 1978).

Books and Magazines

Sex-role messages are clearly found in children's books, in magazines, and in fiction. Each of these categories will be discussed in turn.

Children's Books. Women on Words and Images (1972, 1975b) has compiled impressive statistics on the world depicted in elementary school readers. Table 8-1 shows the results of both their 1972 survey of 2,760 stories in 134 books from 14 different publishers and their 1975 update using 83 readers published since 1972.

As shown in the table, 75% of the textbooks focus on male characters. Although there was some improvement in the number of female biographies and occupations presented in the 1975 update, the ratio of boy-centered to girl-centered stories increased further.

In addition to this quantitative male bias, there was also a qualitative male bias evident in both samples. Males predominated in situations with active mastery themes (cleverness, bravery, adventure, and earning money), and females predominated in situations with "second-sex" themes (passivity, victimization, and goal constriction). For example, Jane watches as John fixes a toy. This portrayal of the sexes has been found in studies of other children's books as well (Child, Potter, & Levine, 1946; Key, 1971; Saario, Jacklin, & Tittle, 1973; U'Ren, 1971; Walstedt, 1975). Even in prize-winning preschool picture books, females were greatly underrepresented, and their characterizations reinforced traditional sex-role stereotypes (Weitzman, Eifler, Hokada, & Ross, 1972). This stereotyping continues in textbooks throughout the school years. In fact, the stereotypes become

Table 8-1
Sexism in Children's Readers, 1972 and 1975

Content	1972	1975
Boy-centered stories to girl-centered stories	5:2	7:2
Male biographies to female biographies	6:1	2:1
Male occupations to female occupations	6:1	3:1
Adult male main characters to adult female main characters	3:1	*
Male animal stories to female animal stories	2:1	*
Male folk or fantasy stories to female folk or fantasy stories	4:1	*

* Not calculated in the 1975 update.
Data from *Dick & Jane as Victims*, by Women on Words and Images. Princeton, N.J., 1972, 1975.

even more pronounced with increasing grade level. Saario and associates (1973) report that, from first- to third-grade readers, the total number of female characters declined sharply, and the number of significant sex differences increased.

One of the tragedies of this situation is that such stories not only teach values but also influence behavior. McArthur and Eisen (1976) report that nursery school boys persist longer on a task (a measure of achievement motivation) after hearing a story depicting achievement behavior by a male character than after a story depicting the same behavior by a female character. The trend was in the opposite direction for girls. This change occurred after hearing just one story. Given that 75% of the central characters in children's books are males and that females, when depicted, are rarely shown in achieving roles, it is not surprising that women have been underrepresented in achieving roles in our society.

Magazines. In other written material as well, sex-role stereotypes abound. Magazines aimed at men focus on themes of sexuality *(Playboy)*, sports *(Field and Stream)*, and daring *(Road and Track)*. Franzwa (1975) found in her study of women's magazine fiction from 1940 to 1970 that the ideal female goal was to be a homemaker and mother. Women are shown as passive and dependent. Their lives revolve around men, and their activities are limited to the home (for example, *Family Circle*). More recent examinations of women's magazines, including *Ms.*, find a similar emphasis on women striving to please or help others (Ferguson, 1978; Phillips, 1978). However, Geise (1979), in her review of articles in *Ladies Home Journal* and *Redbook* from 1955 to 1976, did not find the female role restricted to home and family concerns. She found that positive attitudes toward female employment and political interests have increased in the last 20 years. However, a complete rejection of traditional sex roles is still unpopular.

Advertisements that appear in magazines also reinforce sex-role stereotypes. Erving Goffman (1977) found numerous examples of genderisms that illustrate the position of men and women in our society: function ranking (male taller, in front, and in authoritative position), ritualization of subordination (for example, a woman at a man's feet), snuggling, mock assault games, and an overabundance of images of women on beds and floors. Figure 8-4 is an example of function ranking—the man is pictured seated above, and leaning over, the woman.

Fiction. In the American novel, Snow (1975) found a consistent duality presented for women—purity versus evil, Dark Woman versus Fair Maiden (for example, Hawthorne's *Marble Faun*), American bitch versus Mother-savior (for example, Philip Roth's *Goodbye Columbus* and Steinbeck's *Grapes of Wrath*). Much more so than men, women are depicted symbolically and simplistically, perhaps because most writing in the past was done by men. Since the early 1970s, however, books by and about women have increased. The stories now often depict strong women and the changes the authors have

Figure 8-4
Example of function ranking in magazine advertising. Note how the man is seated above, and leaning over, the woman. (Photo courtesy of Kenyon & Eckhardt Advertising, Inc., New York.)

gone through with respect to their sex roles (for example, *The Woman's Room* by Marilyn French). Along with this more realistic trend, though, is another trend—the romantic historical novel, written and read primarily by women (for example, Victoria Holt's Gothic novels). In these stories, the heroine is usually helpless or dependent upon a man to bring meaning to her life, although recent heroines have been more nontraditional in attitudes and behavior than in the past (Weston & Ruggiero, 1978).

Popular books and fiction aimed at men, on the other hand (for example, James Bond thrillers), tend to present the male going off for some adventure, unencumbered by family ties. Themes of aggression predominate, and if females are presented, they are usually cast in a stereotyped sexual role (Weitz, 1977).

Films

Like books and television, films present stereotyped images of the sexes. As in the American novel, American films generally have presented two images of women. These were clearly exemplified in the 1950s and 1960s as the brainless sexpot (for example, Marilyn Monroe) and the feminine homebody (for example, Doris Day). It was only during the late 1930s and early 1940s, with the increased number of women in the labor force spurred by the Feminist movement of the 1920s and by World War II, that successful, achieving images of women emerged (as in the case of Katharine Hepburn). This ended when the war ended. When men reclaimed their jobs, women were pushed back to the home in films as well as in reality. The New Woman of the late 1960s and 1970s, although sexually active and more independent than her predecessors, usually has been depicted in a negative way, or she has been punished for her sexuality (Mellen, 1973). For example, in *Looking for Mr. Goodbar*, the main character gets killed by someone she met in a singles' bar. The spurt of films in the mid- and late-1970s presenting women as credible human beings, as in the movies *Alice Doesn't Live Here Anymore, An Unmarried Woman, Julia, Turning Point*, hopefully presages an acceptance of women's attempts to break out of the confines of their sex role (Mellen, 1978a; Wilson, 1977).

Cinematic images of masculinity, until recently, also have held strongly to the sex-role stereotype. Whereas the realms of domesticity and sexual allure have been reserved for women, those of aggression, as in Westerns, war, and gangster movies, moral superiority, and intelligence, as in detective and mystery movies, have been reserved for men (Weitz, 1977). Since the male stereotype has more positive characteristics than the female one and since male characters usually are developed to a far greater degree than are female characters because of their central role, men have not fared too badly in film. However, the overemphasis on violence and the depiction of superficial sexual encounters as the norm has tended to distort men's human characteristics. Mellen (1978b) argues that men, like Clint Eastwood and Charles Bronson, in some 1970s' films are even more violent and brutal than were their predecessors in older films.

At the same time, a new image of masculinity seems to be emerging—the emotionally competent hero (Starr, 1978). This new character is not the archetypal, old-fashioned hero, like John Wayne or Gary Cooper, or the intensely emotional hero, like Marlon Brando and James Dean, or the counter-culture antihero, like Dustin Hoffman and Jack Nicholson. Rather, he is strong and affectionate, capable of intimacy, unthreatened by commitment, and firm without being dominant. He is exemplified by Jon Voight in *Coming Home*, Alan Bates in *An Unmarried Woman*, and Kris Kristofferson in *Alice Doesn't Live Here Anymore*. Not coincidentally, the latter two films have been recognized as depicting women in nonstereotyped ways as well. However, in all the films, the heroines still meet their heroes, indicating that Hollywood is not yet ready for a woman who makes it on her own.

Popular Songs

In popular songs, sex-role stereotypes are again observable. Women are frequently depicted as deceitful, excessively emotional, sentimental, illogical, frivolous, dependent, and passive. Men frequently are depicted as sexually aggressive, rational, demanding, nonconforming, adventuresome, and breadwinning (Chafetz, 1978; Reinartz, 1975). For example, the Rolling Stones, in "Under My Thumb," sing about a woman's place in a relationship with a man. Billie Holiday's "My Man" depicts a woman pining for a man who beats her and treats her badly. In "Someone to Watch Over Me," a woman is looking for a paternal, dominant lover/husband.

This familiar dichotomy between male and female behavior can be extremely influential for adolescents who are developing their view of male-female relationships and of future opportunities. Adolescent girls may be even more influenced than their male peers, since, after puberty, girls have fewer alternatives presented to them regarding appropriate behavior and fewer outlets available for resisting the stereotypes (Hayakawa, 1955; Riesman, 1957).

Art

In art, too, females have been depicted in the double image of either virgin or whore, with characteristics of either purity or sexuality. In recent years, the latter image has prevailed, with females almost completely becoming erotic images, often in an obsessive or distorted way (Brown, 1975). For example, Tom Wesselman's *Great American Nude* is all grin and nipples and sprawl. Although male nudes also have appeared, they are more often presented as the ideal of humanity and not as objects of pleasure. For example, Michelangelo's paintings and sculptures of nude men emphasize their muscularity, solidity, and sense of proportion (as in the statue of David), whereas paintings of nude women, like Manet's *Olympia*, emphasize women's sensuality.

Of course, most artists have been male because of restrictions on training, encouragement, and economic support. Until this century, women were socially prohibited from seeing nude men. Drawing them was unheard of. It has recently come to light that many of the paintings signed "Anonymous" have actually been done by women (Glueck, 1977).

Summary

In all forms of media, sex-role stereotypes are conveyed often in the most exaggerated way. Since children are trying to understand sex-role-appropriate behavior and the world around them, they are especially vulnerable to these distorted images. That these images in no way reflect reality can be seen particularly in the media depiction of women and work. Although TV, magazines, and children's readers continually depict a world in which nearly all women stay at home as housewives, in the real world, most women work. Of women who have school-age children, 55% are in the labor force. Even women who do stay home are concerned about more than waxy buildup on their floors. The male image, too, is far from realistic. Boys generally do not fight grizzly bears, cannot solve all problems with a show of physical force, and certainly experience emotions other than anger. To the extent that children are aware of the discrepancy between the

TV world and their own experience, they are as likely to view their own experience, such as their working mother, as abnormal as they are to consider the TV image to be erroneous unless corrective measures are taken—for example, learning how to view TV with a skeptical eye.

SCHOOL

Unfortunately, the stereotypes perceived in the media are often echoed in another major socializing force in children's lives—school. As noted in the last chapter, teachers are a major source of sex-role stereotypes. Other aspects of school life are influential as well: textbooks, curricula, counseling, school organization, and general atmosphere. These factors come together to form a hidden curriculum on sex roles. This curriculum conveys the message, often without the conscious awareness of either the students or the teachers, that there are strong stereotypic sex differences.

Textbooks

The absence of women in textbooks is found increasingly through grade school, high school, and college. Weitzman and Rizzo (1974) found that women are rarely mentioned as important historical figures, as government leaders, or as great scientists. This stereotyping is most extreme in science textbooks, in which only 6% of the pictures include adult women. Even when a scientist like Marie Curie, who won two Nobel Prizes, is presented, her achievements are likely to be minimized. (One text described Madame Curie as a "helpmate" of her husband.) Even in college, there is a striking absence of women both in textbooks and in the curriculum (Banner, 1977). The absence of women in textbooks can encourage readers to view the field depicted, particularly science, as a prototypic masculine endeavor. This may discourage females from entering the particular fields being studied, thereby perpetuating the stereotypes portrayed.

Clearly, textbooks need to be rewritten with the elimination of sexism in mind. California was one of the first states to take systematic action in this regard, passing a code requiring a balancing of traditional and nontraditional activities for each sex in textbooks used in state schools (*ER Monitor*, March–April 1977, p. 8). Because California purchases huge quantities of books, the state's code is beginning to have impact in all states. Change is slow, however, since replacing texts is expensive. As was reviewed previously, even recent books incorporate stereotypes, although not to as great a degree as before.

Curricula

Who takes home economics? Who takes shop classes? Either formally or informally, the different curricula and activities prescribed for each sex are powerful conveyors of sex-role stereotypes. Beginning in kindergarten, activities usually are segregated by sex. Boys and girls play different games, form different lines, carry out different classroom tasks, and learn different things.

Differential curriculum requirements for girls and boys still are frequent. They serve automatically to limit the choices children can make both while they are in school and later in life. Although Title IX is beginning to break up this "tracking," many school systems, parents, and peers still exert informal pressure to keep it going. Until recently, in the seventh grade, girls took home economics, and boys took woodworking. In 1971, males predominated in agricultural courses (95%), technical courses (92%), and trade and industrial courses (89%). Females predominated in consumer and home-making courses (93%), home economic courses (85%), and office occupations courses (75%) (reported in Saario et al., 1973). Even in 1978, a nationwide study (*New York Times*, 1979) found that only 11% of the students in traditionally masculine vocational programs were female. This tracking system keeps students from learning many skills needed in their home as well as in their occupational lives. For example, girls don't learn how to make home repairs, and boys don't learn cooking and domestic skills. The consequences of this tracking are particularly pernicious, since such tracking prepares females for only a few jobs, which have low status and low salaries. In 1978, the median salary of working women was less than 60% of that earned by men.

The Education Amendments of 1976 to the Vocational Education Act of 1963 went into effect in October 1977. They should help change some of the inequities just discussed. The new law requires educational institutions to initiate programs to overcome sex discrimination and sex stereotyping in vocational education programs and to make all courses accessible to everyone. When given the opportunity, women do move into male-dominated, higher paying fields. For example, the number of bachelor degrees awarded women in the computer and information sciences area increased fivefold, from 4.6% in 1964–65 to 23.9% in 1976–77 (*American Education*, 1976; *Chronicle of Higher Education*, November 13, 1978, p. 13).

The kinds of curriculum changes that would decrease sex-role stereotyping have been of great concern. Marcia Guttentag and colleagues (1975, 1977) set up a 6-week curriculum designed to make kindergarteners and fifth- and ninth-graders more flexible in their assumptions about the sexes in occupational, familial, and socioemotional roles. These researchers designed curricula with the different developmental concerns and cognitive levels of the three grades in mind. Students read stories, saw films, acted out plays, and worked on special projects to accomplish the study's goals. Teachers were trained to use the materials and to treat boys and girls equally. The results were mixed. Attitude change was found to be a function of grade level, student sex, teacher attitude, background variables, and the particular stereotypes highlighted. Kindergarteners decreased their occupational stereotypes but not the socioemotional ones. Girls were more willing than boys to accept the nonstereotyped ideas. Ninth-grade girls showed the greatest decrease in stereotyped attitudes; ninth-grade boys showed the greatest increase in stereotyped attitudes. The key factor seemed to be the degree to which the teacher implemented the curriculum effectively. With an enthusiastic teacher, even ninth-grade boys changed to nonstereotyped views in many areas.

This study illustrates the complexity of the school environment. Changing curricula can be effective when implemented early and when the new curricula coincide with the teacher's attitudes. Modeling, however, may be more important than specific lessons in the acquisition and maintenance of sex-role stereotypes.

Counseling

In a variety of ways, school counselors support sex-role stereotypes. They do so by their career and personal counseling orientations and by their use and interpretation of achievement tests.

Vocational Counseling. Until the 1970s, different tests, scores, and interpretations for boys and girls were used in counseling and testing for aptitudes and interests. For example, the Strong Vocational Interest Blank had separate male and female versions (printed on blue and pink forms, respectively) with different occupations for each sex. The revised Strong-Campbell Interest Inventory removes some of the sex bias but still uses single-sex criterion groups for some occupations, such as language teacher (female) and photographer (male). Other attempts to eliminate sex bias in interest measurement also have not been entirely successful, although they show promise (for example, Lunneborg, 1979).

In addition, the problem of interpretation remains. Counselors often interpret test results on the basis of sex and provide verbal and nonverbal messages that discourage the student from pursuing nontraditional careers. For example, Thomas and Stewart (1971) found that high school counselors rated female clients who expressed an interest in traditionally masculine occupations as being more in need of counseling than women with more traditional interests.

A greater number of females than males graduate from high school with generally higher grades. Yet, fewer females than males have gone on to college. Such figures suggest a sex bias operating in career counseling (Astin & Harway, 1976). As education level increases, the proportion of women decreases. In 1976–77, 46% of all B.A.s and 47% of all M.A.s were awarded to women, as were 24% of the Ph.D.s and 10% of first professional degrees (*Chronicle of Higher Education*, November 13, 1978). College admission practices may contribute to these figures as well. There is some evidence that higher entrance examination scores and grade point averages have been required for women seeking admission than for men (Astin & Harway, 1976; *ER Monitor*, March–April 1977, p. 9).

Even available vocational materials have some bias. Women on Words and Images (1975c) analyzed 100 nationally distributed career education materials. In the materials, they found that males dominate the depicted field of work—five males to every two females. In the work force, the ratio is actually less than three to two. The occupations presented for each sex, for the most part, also were traditional and stereotyped. For example, men were depicted in administrative jobs, whereas women were depicted in clerical jobs.

Achievement Testing.   In addition to career counseling, counselors also are responsible for much of the achievement testing done in schools. In such tests, too, sex bias is present. Tittle and colleagues (1974; Saario et al., 1973) found frequent stereotypic portrayals in the content of test questions. For example, women were typically homemakers; men, responsible workers. There also was sex bias in the language used in the tests. Analysis showed more frequent use of male pronouns and referents than female pronouns and referents, since male characters predominated. Such a masculine orientation in tests has been shown to depress the scores of many females, thereby giving an inaccurate picture of their abilities. As with the findings on textbooks, stereotypic portrayals in achievement tests, particularly in the mathematics sections, intensify as grade level rises. Similar bias exists in college admissions testing programs and may account partially for the poorer performance of the average female than the average male on the mathematics portions of these tests.

Sex bias on the part of counselors is not surprising, since it is so prevalent in society at large. An investigation of counselor training (Astin & Harway, 1976) revealed three potential sources of sexism: (1) of all counselor educators, 85% are men, (2) textbooks used in counselor training appear biased, and (3) there is a paucity of courses on counseling girls and women as a group with special needs. Counseling procedures, then, are another part of the school environment which demonstrates a male bias. In a related area, Lacher (1978) notes that on the college level as well, academic advisors traditionally have been insensitive to the special concerns of female undergraduates.

Organization

From the very organization of the school itself, students receive messages regarding sex-role-appropriate behaviors and career opportunities. What they observe are men in positions of authority—coordinators, principals, superintendents—and women in positions of subservience—teachers and aides. The percentage of male teachers generally rises with grade level, as does their status, and the percentage of female administrators decreases. In a nationwide survey of public schools in 1978, women were found to account for nearly 70% of all classroom teachers but only 10% of all school administrators (*New York Times*, September 5, 1979, A16). In elementary schools, 89% of the teachers are women, while 82% of the principals are men. At the secondary level, 98.5% of the principals are male, as are 99.5% of school district superintendents (*ER Monitor*, March–April, 1977, p. 9). At the college and university level, more than 95% of the deans and presidents are men (*Do It NOW*, April 1977, p. 2).

The percentage of women on college faculties has remained low despite a great deal of talk about Affirmative Action. In 1977–78, the percentage of women on college faculties was 25.4%, slightly higher than 22.5% in 1974–75 (Dullea, 1977; National Center for Education Statistics, 1979). As rank increases, the percentage of women decreases. The percentage of women faculty by rank can be seen in Table 8-2.

Table 8-2
Percentage of Women Faculty by Rank, 1975–1976, 1977–1978

Rank	1975–1976	1977–1978
Instructor	47.2	50.6
Assistant professor	26.0	31.6
Associate professor	17.0	18.2
Full professor	9.8	9.5

Data from National Center for Education Statistics, 1979.

There are findings that female college teachers may be particularly important role models for female students in their choice of careers and in their productivity. Therefore, the small number of faculty females, especially in the higher ranks, is disturbing (Basow & Howe, 1979a; Goldstein, 1979; Tangri, 1972; Tidball, 1973). Without viable female career role models, female students may be further limited in their recognition of the career alternatives open to them.

Atmosphere

The number of women teachers in a school contributes to the total school atmosphere. And the school atmosphere is another way in which sex-role messages get communicated.

Elementary school classrooms primarily are the province of female teachers. Some writers argue that the predominance of women, plus the emphasis on obedience and conformity instead of on more active learning, makes the early school environment a feminine one (Fagot & Patterson, 1969; Sexton, 1969; Sugg, 1978). This feminine atmosphere may account for the many school difficulties that boys have, especially in the early years, since such an atmosphere goes counter to the socialization boys receive elsewhere. Researchers (Hill et al., 1974; Kagan, 1964) have found that children do classify reading as a feminine subject. Boocock (1972) suggests that this incongruence between the student role and the sex role for boys contributes to their generally poorer academic performance. In high school and in college, the student role and the sex role become more congruent because of the clearer linkage between academic achievement and future success. It is then that male academic performance substantially improves. The picture for females is nearly the reverse. In elementary school, there is no incongruence between the female sex role and the student role. Both roles require obeying adults and being orderly. Females, therefore, do well in elementary school. As school achievement becomes more competitive and linked to future career achievements, however, the two roles for females become increasingly incongruent. Females' academic performance consequently declines.

Research by Douvan, Kulka, and Locksley (reported in *Psychology Today*, December 1976, pp. 36–37) supports the hypothesis that high school actually may be tougher on girls than on boys. Girls showed a larger discrepancy than did boys in rating their own abilities and needs in comparison to what was expected of, and available to, them in their schools. Girls benefited less from academic achievements and from sports participation than did boys. The researchers concluded that schools seem to be particularly out of step with the aspirations of female students. Most high schools treat girls as career housewives, although less than 3% of the female students in 1978 actually chose that role as their sole or main interest (Association of American Colleges, June 1978, p. 3).

The thesis that elementary schools are feminine and that they "feminize" boys can be criticized on a number of grounds. Firstly, the writers who equate femininity with passivity and equate masculinity with activity tacitly accept stereotyped definitions of sex-role behavior. Secondly, there is much evidence, reviewed before, that boys actually receive more teacher approval, attention, and direct instruction than do girls. Thirdly, boys' poorer achievement in grade school may reflect the intense and often contradictory pressures on boys at that time. To be aggressive, independent, and athletic may be viewed as more important for a boy during grade school than is achievement. In any case, more empirical research is needed on the impact of teachers' behaviors upon sex-role development than is currently available.

There is evidence that when a school's sex-typing messages match those from a student's home environment, the messages are particularly powerful. Minuchin (1965) compared fourth-graders from traditional middle-class schools and homes (those stressing societal standards) with those from modern middle-class schools and homes (those stressing individualized development). The latter group, especially the girls, expressed less sex typing and more role openness than any other group. Those from traditional backgrounds, especially boys, were more sex-role typed in play, fantasies, and attitudes than any other group. When the two environments conflicted, families appeared more influential at the level of a child's fantasies, such as in boys' fantasies about aggression, and girls' fantasies about family concerns, but schools seemed more influential at attitudinal levels, as regarding sex-role preferences and opinions. Such interactions demonstrate how the learning of sex-role stereotypes can be either reinforced or mitigated by the school environment.

School, then, serves as a powerful socializing force, especially with regard to sex-role development. Another major force in some children's lives is religion.

To the extent that a child has any religious instruction, he or she receives further training in the sex-role stereotypes. Virtually all major religions of the world, including the Judeo-Christian religions dominant in America, have strong emphases on the two sexes acting in ways consistent with traditional patriarchal society (Andreas, 1971; Goldenberg, 1979).

In the Old Testament, God clearly is perceived as male, creating first a male human and then a female helpmate to be subservient to the male. The Adam and Eve story can be viewed as a rationalization of patriarchy. Because of Eve's gullibility and treachery, she brings about the downfall of Adam and of succeeding generations. Consequently, she is condemned to suffer childbirth, to work hard, and to be a faithful and submissive wife (Chafetz, 1978). In earlier versions of the Old Testament, however, God was depicted as creating a man (Adam) and a woman (Lilith) at the same time. Because Adam would not accord Lilith equal treatment, she went into exile, emerging, in later mythology, as the snake who tempts Eve (Rivlin, 1972). Such a version of the Creation gives a picture of the status of the sexes that is very different from the one currently promulgated.

In various references throughout the Bible, females clearly are depicted as secondary to males and are often the subject of derogatory statements, especially about their reproductive functioning (for example, menstruating women are "unclean"). In the New Testament, a double image of woman as Madonna (Virgin Mary) or whore (Mary Magdalene) is conveyed with all its double messages about female sexuality.

In the religious hierarchies, power and prestige have been reserved exclusively for males. Until recently, only males could be priests, popes, ministers, rabbis. The Catholic Church still does not have female clergy, although Roman Catholic women are now participating in the Mass as lectors and in the distribution of the Eucharist. Nuns also are becoming more visible and involved with the community and there is a strong movement for equality in the Church (Vecsey, 1979). In various Protestant and Jewish sects, female clergy have made some headway—the first female cleric was ordained in 1970; first female rabbi, in 1972; first female Episcopal priest, in 1976. Their position, however, is still controversial, and their numbers are few. For example, among all ordained Protestant clergy, women still account for only 4% (Association of American Colleges, 1979).

Another recent change in male-dominated religious messages has been the rewriting of hymns, creeds, and prayers to remove sexist words. In substituting *humanity* for *mankind*, *community* for *fellowship* and *brotherhood*, *Creator* for *Father*, and so on, the new guidelines should go a long way in reducing the predominance of male imagery in religion. But, as Dr. Bruce Metzger of Princeton Theological Seminary, revision committee chairperson of the Revised Standard Version of the Bible (due in the mid-1980s) has found, the committee cannot alter passages that reflect a historical situation in a "masculine-oriented" and "male-dominated" society (*New York Times*, June 5, 1977). Religions, as they currently exist, still reflect that male dominance and not all religious personnel want that dominance to change. In November 1979, the National Conference of Catholic Bishops failed to approve a resolution which would have removed sexist language from the Mass (Kaufman, 1979).

WORK

Children also perceive sex-role messages in the world around them, particularly with regard to what occupations people have. One key source of influence on children's future plans is the behavior of sex-role models. As has been noted above, the image children get from the media (TV, books, songs) and from school is one of men primarily as wage earners in a wide range of occupations and of women primarily as housewives and mothers. If women work, their range of occupations is extremely narrow. For example, in children's readers, males were depicted in 195 different occupations; females, in only 51, with one being a fat lady in a circus and another being a witch (Women on Words & Images, 1975b). These images certainly can influence what a child considers appropriate for males and females to do. These depictions are not accurate, since about half of all women work and 90% of all females will work at some point in their lives. Yet, real differences do exist in the occupations of women and men. This difference, too, influences children's future plans and their conception of sex-role-appropriate behavior.

In 1979, women comprised 42% of the labor force, but they were concentrated in a relatively small number of positions. The greatest concentration has been in predominantly low-paying, low-status, "female" jobs. In 1979, 53% of all working women were either clerical or service workers like waitresses. Only 16% of working women were employed in a professional capacity, and nearly 60% of these were either noncollege teachers or nurses (U.S. Dept. of Labor, 1979). Even when women achieve high-status positions typically held by men, they still are often depicted stereotypically. Figure 8-5 is an example of a newspaper's stereotyped portrayal of female politicians.

Children see the small number of women in certain professions and the small number of men in certain others and draw conclusions about which jobs are appropriate for themselves. In addition, seeing men in the higher-status, better paying jobs also affects children's conceptions of the status of the sexes. Since this is in line with other messages the child receives, it strengthens his or her sex-role stereotypes.

A somewhat encouraging note was sounded by Oullette and White (1978) in their study of the occupational preferences of first-, fifth-, eighth-, and eleventh-graders. They found that, at each grade level, the occupations chosen as appropriate for females tended to be nontraditional—that is, not socially identified with women. On the

Wynona Lipman

Barbara Curran

Marie Muhler

Pretty political

Time was when the presence — the mere presence — of a woman in the chambers of the State Legislature caused considerable raising of eyebrows, if not downright alarm.

But times, fortunately, have changed in Trenton and elsewhere around the nation's state capitol buildings.

When eyebrows are raised today, it may well be a woman legislator raising her own — such as in the case of Sen. Wynona Lipman (D-Essex).

And before New Jersey's lawmakers begin another day of debate and demur, it's not uncommon to witness typically feminine gestures from these assemblywomen:

Barbara Curran (R-Union) applying lipstick; Mary Scanlon (D-Essex) powdering her nose; Jane Burgio (R-Essex) combing her bangs, and Marie Muhler (R-Monmouth) applying a fresh scent of perfume.

Mary Scanlon

Photos by Edward N. Stiso

Jane Burgio

Figure 8-5

Stereotyped portrayal of female politicians. (From The Newark Star-Ledger, *May 16, 1978, p. 15. Reprinted by permission.)*

other hand, the occupations selected for males were almost entirely traditional. The researchers attribute their findings partly to the feminist movement and its emphasis on breaking stereotypes for females. Clearly, however, males need help, too, in breaking free from the confines of their role.

SUMMARY

What is most striking from this review of socializing forces is the consistency of the sex-role stereotypes conveyed. Through the structure of the English language itself, through play activities, media depictions, the school environment, religious messages, and career models, the two sexes are depicted as differing widely in behavior and status. Females are nearly uniformly characterized as unimportant, incompetent, passive, and nurturant homebodies and homemakers; males, as important, competent, active, and aggressive wage earners and athletes. Throughout a child's developing years, these images are emphasized through continuous repetition. With this type of socialization, the high degree of concordance found regarding the sex-role stereotypes is understandable. Everyone knows and agrees with the stereotypes despite the fact that there are few actual sex differences in behaviors and attitudes.

RECOMMENDED READING

Bem, S. L., & Bem, D. J. Case study of a nonconscious ideology: Training the woman to know her place. In D. J. Bem, *Beliefs, attitudes, and human affairs.* Monterey, Calif.: Brooks/Cole, 1970, pp. 89–99. A classic essay on how socialization affects our sex-role behavior.

Blaubergs, M. S. Changing the sexist language: The theory behind the practice. *Psychology of Women Quarterly*, 1978, *2*(3), 244–261. Suggestions and theories on how to change sexism in our language.

Stein, P. J., & Hoffman, S. Sports and male role strain. *Journal of Social Issues*, 1978, *34*(1), 136–150. An interesting discussion of how the emphasis on sports for males produces role strain for athletes and nonathletes alike.

Tuchman, G., Daniels, A. K., & Benét, J. (Eds.). *Hearth & home: Images of women in the mass media.* New York: Oxford, 1978. A good compilation of articles selected from a 1975 conference on women in the news media. Highlighted is the role of TV, magazines, and newspapers.

PART THREE: SUMMARY

In Part Three, an answer to the question of how sex-role stereotypes are acquired has been explored on two levels—evolutionary derivations and current socialization practices. Initially, the stereotypes arose from the division of labor by sex in previous societies as a function of the subsistence base of the society, the supply of labor, and the functional requirements of child bearing. Despite the fact that a division of labor is no longer functional or even practical, the stereotypes remain.

In each generation, a child experiences, from the moment of birth, socialization pressures based on her or his sex that, in most cases, incorporate the sex-role stereotypes. From parents, teachers, and peers and from the social forces of language, play, media, school, religion, and work, the child acquires a gender identity and a clear picture of distinct sex roles. This socialization process occurs through direct reinforcement, modeling, and imitation and as a function of the cognitive development of the child. Boys, especially, receive intense socialization pressures and are particularly strongly sex typed.

The consequences of such rigid sex-role images are numerous and, as will be shown in Part Four, almost overwhelmingly negative. This does not mean that children should not form a separate and distinct gender identity. Clearly, they need to do so as part of their developing self-identity and for future reproductive functioning, if they so choose. But, as Money and Ehrhardt (1972) note, nature supplies the basic, irreducible elements of sex differences (women can menstruate, gestate, and lactate; men, impregnate). Sharply differing behaviors for the two sexes are simply unnecessary to accomplish the goal.

> Provided that a child grows up to know that sex differences are primarily defined by the reproductive capacity of the sex organ, and to have a positive feeling of pride in his or her own genitalia and their ultimate reproductive use, then it does not much matter whether various child-care, domestic, and vocational activities are or are not interchangeable between mother and father [Money & Ehrhardt, 1972, p. 14].

What is being argued here is that rigid sex typing is neither necessary nor functional to the individual, to her or his relationships, or to society as a whole. Part Four will discuss these consequences in detail.

CONSEQUENCES OF SEX-ROLE STEREOTYPES

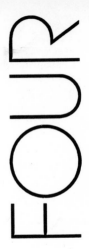

In the preceding chapters, the development of the gender stereotypes and their transmittal to successive generations were shown to occur despite little demonstrable support for the existence of the traits depicted by the stereotypes. Except for aggressive behavior and for mathematical and verbal abilities, the sexes differ very little during childhood; indeed, there appear to be more differences *among* members of a sex than *between* the sexes. Yet, once the stereotypes are acquired by age 5 or 6, certain sex differences sometimes do emerge. Since the acquisition of sex-role stereotypes by a child occurs through individual instruction, interpersonal observation, and more generalized social forces, it is important to examine the consequences of the gender stereotypes on these three levels—that is, on the personal, interpersonal, and societal levels.

Even if the existence and knowledge of the stereotypes—what females and males are "supposed to be" like—do not change behavior, they can have many consequences. As will be shown in the next four chapters, the effects of the stereotypes are far-reaching and, for the most part, are negative to both females and males.

9

Individual
Consequences

The effects of sex-role stereotypes can be seen most clearly on the individual level. The stereotypes affect an individual's self-concept, behavior, mental health, and physical health. In fact, there is almost no aspect of human functioning that the sex-role stereotypes do not, in some way, affect.

SELF-CONCEPT

> A great golf course is like a good woman. Beautiful . . . and a little bit Bitchy.
>
> —advertisement in a golf magazine

The quotation above reveals one concept of womanhood. Such conceptions of the sex roles are important insofar as they relate to an individual's *self-concept*—the way in which individuals view themselves. This concept incorporates several other concepts: (1) how one thinks of oneself, known by the term *self-esteem*, which itself incorporates self-acceptance and self-regard, (2) an estimate of one's abilities, referred to as *self-confidence*, and (3) a sense of control over one's life, including the *attributions* that one makes, called *locus of control*. These three aspects of self-concept—self-esteem, self-confidence, and locus of control—will be examined in some detail below, with the concept of the *ideal self* considered as incorporated within self-esteem. Other aspects of self-concept, such as self-image and body image, will not be discussed specifically. Findings in these last two areas, as well as in the areas that will be discussed, indicate that, overall, females have a somewhat more negative self-concept than do males (Donelson, 1977a; Loeb & Horst, 1978; Rosenkrantz et al., 1968).

Because the sex-role stereotypes contain many more negative characteristics of females than of males, as seen in this chapter's opening quote, such a finding of lower female self-concept should not be surprising. Yet it would not be correct to assume that all females have a more negative self-concept than all males in all situations. These findings depend on whether the sexes are comparing themselves to members of the same sex or to the other sex, on methodological variations in measuring the self-concept, and on what task is involved. A major variable in the findings concerns which aspect of the self-concept is being tapped—self-esteem, self-confidence, or locus of control.

Self-Esteem

When self-esteem (the degree of negative or positive regard one has for oneself) is examined, the sexes show surprisingly few differences. Maccoby and Jacklin (1974) and Loeb and Horst (1978) concluded, after examining a broad range of studies that used standardized paper-and-pencil questionnaires, that males and females from kindergarten to college generally indicate equivalent levels of self-esteem. This is surprising, since society seems to value men so much more than it values women. How then can females think of themselves equally as positively as do males? The answer involves four possibilities: developmental differences, different standards, sex typing, and the nature of the tests used.

Developmental Differences.   There is some indication that, starting in late elementary school, males may score increasingly higher than females in self-rated self-esteem (Loeb & Horst, 1978). This result, however, is not found consistently, partly because most studies do not analyze for age trends. The significance of this finding is also unclear. It is possible that boys inflate their self-esteem scores, whereas girls may not do so. This hypothesis concerning inflated scores is supported by the finding that, although fourth- and fifth-grade boys rated themselves higher in self-esteem than did their female classmates, teachers of these students rated the girls as higher in self-esteem-related behaviors (Loeb & Horst, 1978). (Problems with the measurement instrument will be commented upon below.) In general, studies that use different age samples may obscure possible sex differences.

Different Standards.   Another reason males and females do not differ in their levels of self-esteem may be because of their use of different standards for themselves; that is, females may compare themselves to the ideal female and males compare themselves to the ideal male, rather than both sexes comparing themselves to some absolute standard. In this case, both sexes would be accepting the roles society has assigned them and thus would have equal self-esteem.

The *ideal self* does seem to differ for men and women. Gilbert and colleagues (1978) found that college men pictured the ideal man as having more masculine than feminine attributes, as measured by the Bem Sex Role Inventory. Yet, although the ideal man was definitely sex typed to be masculine, he was more androgynous than the "typical" man. In contrast, college women pictured the ideal woman as androgynous—that is, having relatively equal masculine and feminine qualities. Women's ideal self-image was also more androgynous than the "typical" woman. Thus, there do seem to be different standards that the sexes may use to evaluate themselves. However, H.

Freeman (1979) found few differences in the needs that are thought to characterize the ideal male and ideal female, as rated by male and female college students.

Donelson (1977a) summarized research showing that adolescents who feel successful in the realm they consider appropriate (sociability for many girls; achievement and leadership for many boys) have high levels of self-esteem. The key seems to be what the person views as central to her or his self-concept. With adults, these personal standards may not correspond to the sex-role stereotypes. Although there is considerable evidence that there are different standards of behavior and personality for females and for males, the evidence is contradictory regarding the relationship between sex-role conformity and self-esteem, especially for females.

The key to understanding this area of self-concept seems to be to take into account both the discrepancy between the real and ideal self-concept and the salience of sex roles in the individual (Garnets & Pleck, 1979). Thus, for those for whom sex roles are important, sex-role conformity should be related to self-esteem. For those for whom sex roles are not that salient, there may be no relationship. Research has not yet examined the importance of sex-role salience as related to self-esteem.

Sex Typing.   Research, however, has investigated the relationship between sex typing and self-esteem. In general, the more masculine characteristics that are present, the higher the individual's self-esteem. There is some developmental trend in this regard.

By high school, self-esteem appears correlated with sex-typed role performance for both sexes (Carlson, 1965; Connell & Johnson, 1970). However, numerous studies of people in late adolescence and older have found that androgynous individuals—those who score highly on both masculinity and femininity—along with masculine-sex-typed individuals (both male and female), have the highest self-esteem (Antill & Cunningham, 1979; Bem, 1977; Doherty & Schmidt, 1978; Hoffman & Fidell, 1979; Spence & Helmreich, 1978; Spence, Helmreich, & Holahan, 1979; Spence, Helmreich, & Stapp, 1974, 1975; Stericker & Johnson, 1977; Watson, 1979). Feminine-sex-typed women have significantly lower self-esteem than do androgynous and masculine groups. The undifferentiated individual (low on masculinity and femininity) appears to have the lowest level of self-esteem. From these findings, one may conclude that the presence of strong agentic characteristics, as in androgynous- and masculine-sex-typed persons, seems positively related to self-esteem as an individual matures. This may reflect societal values on agentic, as opposed to communal or expressive, qualities. The strong relationship between sex typing and self-esteem may serve to obviate sex differences in this area.

Test Instrument.   Another possible explanation of the equal self-esteem levels found for females and males may lie in the test instrument itself. As Deaux (1976) reports, the questions used on self-esteem scales generally contain two distinct classes of items: those tapping *self-acceptance*, the degree to which one accepts oneself as one is, and *self-regard*, the degree to which one actively affirms one's worth and abilities. If females score higher on the former items and males score higher on the latter items, then their total scores would be equal, even though they are responding positively to different items. There is some indirect support for this interpretation. Females generally make more realistic estimates of their abilities and have lower aspirations than do males (Feather, 1969; Stein & Bailey, 1973). Using another indirect measure of self-esteem, Callahan-Levy and Messé (1979) found that females, from first-graders through college students, consistently paid themselves less for work done than did their male counterparts. These findings together suggest that females may have higher self-acceptance and lower self-regard than do males, at least as related to the abilities measured. Males, in contrast to females, have higher expectations of their abilities and tend to overestimate them (Crandall, 1969; Feather, 1969), suggesting a higher self-regard and a lower self-acceptance. One possible conclusion from these studies, then, is that, although the sexes do not seem to differ in overall level of self-esteem as measured by questionnaires, the bases for self-esteem may be different and may be related to sex typing.

Other evidence supporting the hypothesis that the sexes have different bases for self-esteem comes from a study by Stake (1979). After reviewing factor analytic studies of self-esteem measures, Stake concluded that self-esteem is multidimensional and that one clear factor is performance self-esteem. Using a new scale to measure only this factor in a college sample, Stake found significant sex differences. College women tended to have lower evaluations than college men of their abilities and performances across a wide range of achievement settings.

One contradictory piece of evidence regarding the hypothesis that the sexes have different bases for self-esteem comes from a nationwide study of high school seniors. O'Malley and Bachman (1979) found that, although females had slightly lower self-esteem than males, the relationship of self-esteem to educationally relevant measures was nearly identical in both sexes.

In summary, the sexes may have different bases for self-esteem, but this conclusion depends on how the bases of self-esteem are defined. When self-regard is a basis, sex differences usually occur.

Self-Confidence and Expectations

The research on self-regard, at least as related to task expectancy, is part of a considerable body of research on self-confidence. It is in this area that striking sex differences are observed. Males, on the average, consistently predict, over a wide range of ages and tasks, that they will do better than females predict for themselves (Crandall, 1969; Deaux, 1976; Donelson & Gullahorn, 1977a; Maccoby & Jacklin, 1974; Parsons, Ruble, Hodges, & Small, 1976). Males have higher expectations of themselves and more confidence than do females. Although this tendency leads many males to overestimate their abilities, it is also likely that it leads them to attempt more tasks. Such attempts give them more opportunities to increase their skill and to be rewarded. Females, who tend to underestimate their ability, may take themselves out of the running, refraining from attempting or continuing with new activities, thereby limiting their world and potential. They also tend to blame themselves for failures, which further exacerbates this tendency. It is important to note, however, that, although the sexes predict different levels of performance, there is little difference in actual performance. Differences appear, then, only in how the two sexes think and feel about their performance. Many girls seem to exaggerate negative aspects of a situation; boys, the positive aspects (Crandall, 1969; Donelson, 1977a). This may result in very real differences in the way the sexes evaluate current behavior and in the way they derive their expectancies of future performance. For example, in a recent study of more than 3,000 students at six top universities in the Northeast, women were found to underestimate consistently their academic ability and to have lower career aspirations than men, even though the grades of the women and men were relatively equivalent (reported in *New York Times*, December 10, 1978, p. 85).

The nature of the task used in testing is criticial in laboratory studies. Since most experimental tasks are masculine in orientation —that is, related to the masculine stereotype, such as achievement —it is not surprising that males have higher expectancies of their abilities and that females have lower expectancies. O'Leary (1974) summarizes research that shows a positive relationship between self-esteem and exhibition of sex-role-appropriate behavior. To the extent that an individual's self-esteem has incorporated the sex-role stereotypes, it is likely that that individual would be hesitant to engage in sex-role-inappropriate behavior. When the task is explicitly labeled "feminine" (even though it may be neutral), women are more confident that they will do well than if the task is labeled "masculine" or is unlabeled (Basow, 1980). When the task is labeled "feminine," women expect to do as well as men expect to (Deaux, 1976). The fact that women don't make higher predictions than do men may reflect the "masculine" nature of competency and achievement themselves.

Lenney (1977), in her review of the literature, concluded that, although females generally have less self-confidence than males, this is not the case in all achievement situations. Situational variables, such as specific ability area, availability of performance feedback, and the emphasis on social comparison, all affect females' self-confidence in such situations. When the ability tapped relates to feminine behaviors (such as social skills), or is simply labeled as "feminine," no sex difference in self-confidence in achievement settings is found. Similarly, sex differences disappear when clear performance feedback is available or when social comparison is not made salient.

While the sex difference in self-confidence is consistent and stable, its antecedents are unclear. One reason for this discrepancy may be a result of differential reinforcement history for females and males. Males may be rewarded for being confident; females may be rewarded for being modest about their abilities. Or this difference between the sexes in self-confidence may be caused by differential sensitivity to rewards and punishments on the part of females and males. A third possibility to account for the difference may be linked to the different cultural norms that permit females more than males to admit to low self-confidence. Evidence was reviewed in Part Three supporting all these factors, the most powerful of which is the first—namely, the differential behavior on the part of the major socializing agents in line with the sex-role stereotypes (Parson et al., 1976). For change to occur, then, the female stereotype must be divested at the most basic level—the family—of its implied incompetence. To do this requires deliberate efforts by parents not to reinforce the stereotypes and not to give subtle cues that convey lower expectancies for girls than for boys, such as showing excessive concern for girls' safety. Parents also must give appropriate feedback and strategies for improving performances and provide competent female models.

In general, the research on expectancies demonstrates that females have lower self-confidence than do males, especially in male-oriented situations and activities. This pattern could contribute to a negative self-image in some females.

Locus of Control

If you were given a choice between playing a game of luck, such as a "one-armed bandit" slot machine, or a game of skill, such as darts, which would you choose? Deaux and colleagues (1975) found that nearly 75% of the men studied chose a game described as requiring skill, whereas only 35% of the women did so. Women preferred games of chance, suggesting that they see themselves as less skilled than men and as having less control over the outcomes of their behavior.

Other research on locus of control (the expectation that one's behavior will lead to desirable goals and reinforcements) has found similar results (Hochreich, 1975; Lefcourt, 1976; Maccoby & Jacklin, 1974). The generally external locus-of-control orientation of females is associated with feelings of helplessness, with an avoidance of task-oriented behaviors, with fear of success, and with a preference for situations where luck, rather than one's degree of skill, determines the outcome (Deaux, 1976; Deaux et al., 1975; Rotter, 1966; Savage, Stearns, & Friedman, 1979; Throop, 1971).

The findings of sex differences in this area are neither consistent nor strong, however, depending on performance outcome (success or failure) and on the sex typing of the individual. For example, one study (Hoffman & Fidell, 1979) found androgynous- and masculine-sex-typed women to be more internally oriented than feminine women. Undifferentiated women were the most externally oriented. Jones, Chernovetz, and Hansson (1978), however, found no differences among women but found masculine men to be more internally oriented than androgynous or feminine men. Thus, there is a suggested relationship between masculinity and internal locus of control that is similar to the relationship between masculinity and self-esteem. At this time, however, such a relationship between sex typing and locus of control is not clear.

The relationship between performance outcome and *attribution* of control is somewhat clearer. Whether a person attributes a success to an internal or an external cause is largely a function of the person's sex. For example, when students are asked why they received a 90 on a test, females are more likely than males to say they were lucky, that the test was easy, that the teacher liked them, or that they studied very hard. Males are more likely to say they received such a high grade because they knew the material or because they were smart. In contrast, when a low grade is received, females are more likely to say it was because they didn't know the material or were "dumb," whereas males are more likely to say it was because the test was unfair, the teacher didn't like them, or because they didn't try.

In general, many females tend to attribute their successes to luck and their failures to lack of ability (Deaux & Emswiller, 1974; Deaux, White, & Farris, 1975; Dweck & Repucci, 1973; Frieze, 1975, 1978; Nicholls, 1975; Parson et al., 1976; Stein & Bailey, 1973). The picture for many males is the opposite—males tend to credit their successes to their ability and to credit their failures to luck. These tendencies are evident throughout the school years and become particularly striking in adolescence.

Adolescence is a time when socialization pressures become particularly intense for females, and they become anxious and concerned about both failure and success (Bardwick, 1971; Donelson, 1977b; Donelson & Gullahorn, 1977a; Katz, 1979; Locksley & Douvan, 1979). Adolescence is, of course, stressful for males as well, but the most intense period of socialization for them occurs earlier, during grade school. It is at this earlier time that boys must learn that being a male means not doing anything vaguely "feminine."

With the type of attribution process described above (attributing success to luck and failure to lack of ability), it is very difficult for some females to feel good about themselves. Without taking credit for their successes, females cannot increase their self-confidence. With continued personal blame for their failures, females can only decrease their self-confidence further. This, in turn, may lead to lower expectancies for future performance and to withdrawal from achievement situations, when possible, for many females. For example, Brewer and Blum (1979) found that feminine-sex-typed, female college freshmen felt less control over their achievement in mathematics and science than did male respondents or androgynous females. This lack of control on the part of "feminine" females was translated into a low expectancy of success in math and science courses. This low expectancy might discourage persistence and lead to fewer women enrolled in math and science courses. The causal relationship between sex-role identification and feelings of control over achievement was not found for nonmathematical courses, suggesting that course sex-typing may play an important role in such feelings of control.

Even when credit is taken for success, females more often attribute the success to effort ("I tried hard"), an unstable cause, rather than to ability ("I'm smart"), a more stable cause (Basow, 1980; Frieze, McHugh, & Duquin, 1976). With this type of attribution, also, success does not bolster self-esteem, since effort is not something on which one can really count.

In contrast to the female pattern of attribution, the attribution pattern of many males (attributing success to ability and failure to luck) protects self-confidence (and self-image) from failure and increases it with each success. This pattern may have negative consequences, too, by making it difficult for many males to learn from their mistakes or to admit failure. Frieze and colleagues (1976) found males, in general, to be more defensive than females following failure in sports events. In fact, this defensiveness was reinforced by their male coach. Another consequence of this pattern for many males is their increasing frustration when they discover that they have less ability than they had assumed. A male may unrealistically expect to receive a 90 on a test and be extremely disturbed and frustrated when a 70 is received instead. This frustration itself may have serious negative consequences, such as increased aggressive behavior.

Yet, such an attribution pattern does serve to increase males' continued striving. This, in turn, increases the probability of future success. Given the pressure on males to achieve, their self-protective attitude is facilitative (Donelson & Gullahorn, 1977a). Frieze (1975) has asserted that maximum self-esteem should be associated with the development of an external orientation for failure and an internal one for success. Girls need to be deliberately taught such a pattern—that is, to attribute their success to internal and stable causes, such as their ability—rather than to be taught to be "modest." They likewise need to be taught to attribute their failures to unstable, yet controllable, causes, like lack of effort.

Such attributions *can* be taught (see Dweck, 1975). It is a hopeful sign that some recent research (for example, Perez & O'Connell, 1979) has found that both high school and college males and females attributed success on an anagram task to internal factors and attributed failure to external ones. This finding, however, may have been a result of the verbal nature of the task, which may have made it appear more "feminine" (Feather & Simon, 1975).

Summary

The picture drawn with respect to the consequences of the sex-role stereotypes on males' and females' self-concepts is fairly consistent. Females, in general, tend to have a more negative image of themselves than do males; they have less self-regard, less self-confidence, and less feeling of responsibility for their successes. This negative self-concept is offset by their being more self-acceptant than are males. Males, on the other hand, tend to have a very positive, though somewhat unrealistic, self-image. They have a high regard for themselves, are overconfident of their abilities, feel responsible for their successes, and attribute their failures to external causes. They are, however, notably less self-acceptant. These varying self-concepts on the part of the sexes have direct consequences for behavior and for evaluation of others.

BEHAVIOR

Sex-role stereotypes, even if we do not conform to them, affect us directly as *standards* of behavior. They also affect us indirectly through effects on our self-concept. One consequence of the stereotypes can be seen in the flexibility of our behavior—that is, how comfortable and effective we are in engaging in a wide variety of behaviors. A more specific consequence of the stereotypes is the manner in which we engage in certain behaviors. One area of behavior that has been the focus of much study has been the area of achievement and achievement motivation. This area will be examined first, followed by a review of the research on behavioral flexibility.

Achievement

History books amply demonstrate that women have not been considered major contributors to Western Civilization beyond their role of reproduction and family matriarch. Although the reasons for this fact may lie in the biases of historians themselves, in institutionalized sexism, in the lack of effective means of birth control, and in other social forces, at least one reason may lie within the individual herself. The reason most often suggested for the discrepancy in achievement level between females and males is that females do not have as great a *need for achievement* as do males.

In school, girls generally outperform boys in all subjects. These differences narrow from elementary school to high school to college (Maccoby & Jacklin, 1974; Stewart, 1976). In high school, girls fall behind in certain subjects, including social studies, mathematics, science, and citizenship (*Time*, October 27, 1975, p. 60). While more girls graduate from high school than do boys, fewer go on to college, and still fewer go on to graduate and professional schools. Since there is no evidence that the sexes differ in intelligence, differences in school achievement more likely point to personality and social factors. Boys may find the student role incompatible with the stereotyped male role during childhood but find it increasingly compatible with the male role during adolescence. At that time, its linkage with occupational success becomes stronger and clearer. The reverse may be true for females, who are often actively discouraged from planning careers (Katz, 1979; Locksley & Douvan, 1979; Weitz, 1977).

Do men have a greater need for achievement than do women? Since the original work of McClelland and associates in 1953 on achievement motivation as measured by projective techniques, a vast amount of data has accumulated showing that males and females have equal amounts of motivation (summarized in Maccoby & Jacklin, 1974). Although sex does not seem important with regards to achievement motivation, sex typing does appear important. Spence and Helmreich (1978) found that androgynous individuals show the highest motivation, followed, in order of level of motivation, by masculine, feminine, and undifferentiated individuals. Olds and Shaver (1979) also found high masculinity to be strongly associated with certain aspects of achievement motivation.

Strong sex differences emerge, however, when achievement behavior is examined as a function of the achievement motive. The results of studies with males on the relationship between need for achievement and achievement behavior have been theoretically consistent. Yet, results with females show a contradictory and confusing picture. For example, males increase their need-for-achievement imagery as a function of "arousing" appeals to competence and mastery (McClelland, Atkinson, Clark, & Lowell, 1953); females do not increase in the same way (Lesser, Kravitz, & Packard, 1963; Veroff, Wilcox, & Atkinson, 1953). Male achievement behavior is a direct function of motive to achieve, expectancy of the consequences of success, and the value attached to such consequences; female achievement behavior is not a direct function of these factors (Atkinson & Feather, 1966).

As a result of the failure of many women to conform to the proposed theoretical model of achievement behavior, they simply were neglected from study for many years (an example of the sexist nature of science). More recently, however, sufficient data have accumulated that throw light on achievement motivation and on behavior in many females. The recent studies focus on problems with measurement, competing needs, fear of success, sex-role-appropriate behavior, and definitions of achievement.

Measurement. The standard measurement of achievement motivation has been based on projective techniques, such as stories about a picture card, has been scored using a system developed on male data, and has been collected in response to male competitive cues (O'Leary, 1974). Thus, it is not surprising that such measures do not predict well for many females, since many females may operate under a different definition of achievement than do many males. In addition, Entwisle (1972), summarizing the research on such projectives, found that the scoring categories did not cover the full range of the women's responses. This possibly may lower intercorrelations. Furthermore, the projective measure's low reliability (.30 to .40) may account for its lack of predictive validity. Helmreich and Spence (1978) developed a nonprojective questionnaire (Work & Family Orientation Questionnaire) to measure achievement motivation and aspiration. Although it is still being refined, validity studies have been impressive. Initial results demonstrate no sex difference in achievement motivation but positive correlations with masculine sex typing (see also Olds & Shaver, 1979). Hermans (1970) also has developed a nonprojective questionnaire to measure need for achievement, but his has not been much utilized. One study that did use it (Kissler, 1978) found a higher need for achievement among female workers than among male workers.

Competing Needs.   Problems with measuring achievement behavior in females also may have to do with some females having needs that compete with achievement needs for actualization. Speficially, research has focused on females' somewhat greater need for affiliation as compared to males' needs. Because females, as a group, are more needful of social approval, they supposedly do not strive to achieve. It is important to note here that, although some females may be more needful of social approval, there is no evidence to support the contention that females are more influenced than are males by social reinforcements (Maccoby & Jacklin, 1974). Nor is there anything intrinsically conflicting in the two needs. The important variable seems to be the consequences of achievement behavior. Thus, although males and females have similar needs for achievement, since females have a stronger need for affiliation and since achievement behavior in females is often socially disapproved, females may limit their own achievement. Recognition of this factor by Matina Horner (1968) transformed psychology's understanding of female achievement behavior by invoking another motive—a motive to avoid success.

Fear of Success.   Although not an entity unto itself, the concept of a motive to avoid success has added much to our understanding of achievement behavior. This motive, however, also has been the focus of considerable controversy, some of which is due to a misinterpretation of its nature (Horner, 1978). It will be instructive to review the development of the concept and then the controversy surrounding it. Used appropriately, it appears to be a meaningful and valuable construct.

Horner (1968, 1970, 1972) asked students to write stories about the following sentence: "After first term finals, Anne (John) finds herself (himself) at the top of her (his) medical school class." Horner found that roughly 65% of women college students, but only 10% of the men, told stories indicating fear of success. Fear of success was defined as denial of success, unhappiness about it, or negative consequences that followed it. For example, fear of success would be scored for responses such as the following: "A mistake has been made. Anne is not really at the top of the class" and "Anne is ugly, studies all the time, and will never get married." Not only did more females than males demonstrate this motive to avoid success using a projective technique, but Horner also found this fear to predict behavior in competitive achievement situations. Females high on fear-of-success imagery performed better in noncompetitive situations than did females low in such imagery. Males in general performed better in competitive situations. From these findings, Horner concluded that fear of success was "a stable personality trait" and was caused by the negative consequences expected to follow success.

As a result of the research that this concept generated, however, it soon became apparent that this simple, clear explanation was insufficient to account for all the data. The problems are multiple—methodological, empirical, and theoretical. (See Tresemer, 1977, for a review of the research.) Some of the criticisms, however, are based on a misunderstanding of the concept.

Methodological measurement of fear of success as a psychological trait has been markedly unreliable and lacking in validity. Research (see Condry & Dyer, 1976, for an excellent summary) has shown fear of success to lack consistency across various cues, across various cue contexts, and across judges. For example, when "Anne" is put at the top of her *nursing* school class (Alper, 1974) or when her medical school class is composed of 50% women (Lockheed, 1975b), women respond with less fear-of-success imagery. Horner (1978), however, never implied that fear of success functioned by itself. Rather, the critical factor is an expectation of negative consequences for success when one desires or expects success. Thus, in the nursing and coed-class situations, negative consequences might not have been expected.

A more serious problem with the measurement of fear of success is the finding of Sadd, Leneauer, Shaver, and Dunivant (1978) that fear of success is not a unitary concept. Factor analysis of five measures of fear of success and two measures of fear of failure revealed five separate factors, only one of which came close to Horner's definition regarding fear of success—that is, concern about the negative consequences of success. The other four factors were: self-deprecation and insecurity, test anxiety, attitudes toward success in medical school, and extrinsic motivation to excel. Unfortunately, Sadd et al. found the only factor to correlate highly with Horner's original measure was factor four, attitudes toward success in medical school—a very limited definition of fear of success, indeed.

Additionally, research on the *empirical* validity of Horner's measure of fear of success has been sufficiently contradictory to cast some doubt on it. Although there has been some tendency to find higher levels of this motive among women at elite, highly competitive colleges (Fleming, 1977), this is not a consistent finding. Nor is it always the case that such a fear actually reduces achievement attempts on the part of females (Condry & Dyer, 1976; Zuckerman & Wheeler, 1975). Studies involving mixed-sex competition demonstrate that women's achievement behavior is different in those situations than it is in same-sex competitive situations. However, such changes are not clearly related to fear of success (for example, Makosky, 1972; Swanson & Tjosvold, 1979).

The problem of predicting behavior based on fear of success may have resulted from the scoring system used. Horner revised her original system in 1973. The new empirically derived system (Horner & Fleming, 1977) involves the scoring of more subtle story sequences using six scoring categories rather than the previous present-absent ones. The scoring system also generally is more concerned with the avoidance of instrumental competence than with avoidance of success per se. Research using this newer measure has been much more promising (see Fleming, 1977).

A more telling criticism of fear of success involves the *theoretical* assumption that respondents are projecting their own motives onto the story. This assumption is the basis of all projective techniques. Horner had females and males write stories using only the same-sex character, Anne or John, since she assumed respondents needed a same-sex character to facilitate projection. When people respond to both Anne and John cues, however, males and females invoke more fear of success images for Anne than for John (Feather & Raphaelson, 1974; Juran, 1979; Monahan, Kuhn, & Shaver, 1974). Yet, a more recent study (Ashton, 1979) did not find a difference in stories told for the male and female cues by both male and female college students. These findings suggest that cultural stereotypes regarding appropriate achievement behaviors of females and males and regarding the actual consequences of such behaviors, not any deep-seated "motive," may be tapped by the stimulus cues. In fact, in the studies before 1979, when Anne was the cue, men told even more fear-of-success stories (68%) than did women (51%). In other words, more people may predict negative consequences for a female who is at the top of her medical school class than for a male because she is engaging in sex-role-inappropriate behavior and/or because such women actually do meet with more negative consequences than do their male counterparts. Fear of success as a motive may have little, if anything, to do with it.

Another criticism often aimed at fear of success as an explanation of female achievement behavior is that fear of success also occurs in many males. Horner (1978), however, never proposed that the motive to avoid success was either sex linked or related to a particular sex-role orientation, but rather, that it would arise in anyone whenever a desire or expectation of success was present alongside an expectation that success would have negative consequences. Research has indeed found that, under those conditions, males as well as females do seem to express such fears (Cherry & Deaux, 1978; Janda, O'Grady, & Capps, 1978; Perez & O'Connell, 1979; Tresemer, 1974). The specific cue used is the important variable. Tresemer, in his 1974 summary of related studies, found that the proportion of fear of success in women in many studies ranged from 11% to 88%, the median being 47%. In men, percentages ranged from 22% to 86%, the median being 43%.

Fear of success in females and males, however, may have different causes. In women, fear of success may be caused by fear of social rejection. In men, it may be due to questioning the value of success (Donelson, 1977a). That is, the stories women create seem to involve the social consequences of success (no dates, dislike by classmates), whereas the stories men create seem to involve the worth of success itself (the emptiness of achievement; not having any future goals).

In summary, there is little to support Horner's statement that fear of success is a stable personality trait, although there is evidence that it does arise in females and males in conjunction with specific expectations and values. Perhaps a more satisfactory explanation of the research findings can be made by viewing fear of success as a *situational variable*—that is, as a realistic appraisal of negative consequences that may result from success in specific situations. As will be shown, such an explanation can account for existing findings as well as for other problematic ones.

Sex-Role Appropriateness. The critical factor in understanding achievement behavior in men and women is the sex-appropriateness of the behavior. As was discussed in Chapter Seven, children learn by age 5 or 6 the cultural norms for sex-appropriate behavior and begin to alter their values, attitudes, and behaviors in response to them. Deviation from these norms has negative consequences both internally, in terms of anxiety and low self-concept, and externally, in terms of others' reactions. Research indicates that men show even more negative consequences in response to Anne's success in medical school than do women (for example, Monahan et al., 1974; Spence, 1974; Tresemer, 1974). Men also prefer to work alone rather than to work with their steady dates in competitive situations (Peplau, 1973). Therefore, given no other information, the fear of negative consequences as a result of success that many females have, at least in male-defined situations, may be quite reasonable, albeit counterproductive. For example, the behavior of female athletes in recent years suggests that many may feel that success threatens their femininity (Kaplan, 1977; Rohrbaugh, 1979). This ambivalence may limit their sports potential.

Bremer and Wittig (in press) provide further support for a situational interpretation of fear of success. They asked women and men to write stories about a woman who achieved success in one of four situations: a deviant or nondeviant occupation (engineering or nursing school) and a neutral or role-overload situation (married and no children or married and three school-age children). Significant effects of deviance and overload were found in fear-of-success imagery, but there was no effect of sex of participant; that is, males and females both told stories high in fear of success about the mother in engineering school, and both sexes told stories relatively low in fear of success about the wife in nursing school. Situational factors, specifically sex-role expectations, are a key to understanding achievement behavior.

Thus, more fear-of-success imagery and more blocking-of-achievement behavior may have been found in females because most studies have used male-appropriate achievement situations, such as medical school or competition. If achievement is defined in a female-appropriate situation, such as in nursing school or in feminine-defined tasks, the opposite results would be expected; that is, more males would be found restricting their achievement behavior and showing high fear of success. This prediction has received consistent empirical support. Numerous researchers have found that both sexes write more fear-of-success stories to gender-inappropriate cues than to gender-appropriate cues (Bishop, 1974; Cherry & Deaux, 1978; Glasser, 1974; Janda et al., 1978; Makosky, 1972). There have been occasional refutations, however (for example, Ashton, 1979), especially when different subject populations, different measuring instruments, and different statistical analyses are used.

Further support for a situational interpretation of fear of success comes from findings that, as the sex proportions of various occupations change, so does fear-of-success imagery. Perez and O'Connell (1979) tested high school and college students using cues of Tom or Diane in either law school or nursing school. The greatest fear-of-success imagery found was for Tom in nursing school, perhaps because men still constitute only about 5% of nursing school students, whereas women now constitute over 20% of law school students. Interestingly, college students demonstrated more fear-of-success imagery than did high school students, supporting Horner's contention that it is only when success becomes salient that the motive to avoid it arises.

As Deaux (1976) concludes, both men and women will avoid success if the consequences of that success seem likely to be unpleasant. Conversely, both men and women will seek success/achievement if the consequences are likely to be pleasant. Thus, if males get more rewards by achieving in academic and competitive situations, they will be more oriented in academic and competitive directions. If females get more rewards for achieving in cooperative, interpersonal situations and in the domestic sphere, they will be more oriented in those directions. If these positive consequences are coupled with negative consequences for deviation, it is quite clear how the above results could be obtained.

As was reviewed in Chapters Seven and Eight, the sexes generally are rewarded differentially during childhood for different behaviors, and they perceive different achievement behaviors in the models presented to them in the media, at home, and at school. Girls, compared to boys, generally receive less encouragement for independence, more parental protectiveness, nurturance, and restrictiveness, and fewer models of female achievement (Donelson & Gullahorn, 1977a; Hoffman, 1972); instead, especially during adolescence, most girls are expected to develop social skills. As a result, many girls continue to be dependent upon others, developing neither confidence nor adequate achievement skills. Many boys, on the other hand, are encouraged to be achievement oriented. They are reinforced for being independent and for conquering challenging tasks. They also perceive many models of male achievement.

By college, a young woman who is intellectually equal or superior to her male peers may suppress her achievement behavior because she has learned to be more interested in affiliation. And affiliation, she has also learned, may be threatened by her achieving (Donelson & Gullahorn, 1977; Komarovsky, 1946). A young man, on the other hand, may feel compelled to achieve and may be afraid to express or act upon tenderer feelings or affiliative needs.

One result of these socialized differences is that low self-esteem seems to be related to low course grades for boys but seems either to be related to high course grades or to show no relationship to grades for girls (Hollender, 1972; Purkey, 1970). It appears that boys with less self-esteem may not behave in sex-appropriate ways. In regard to achievement, this means boys with low self-esteem do not do well in school. Girls with lessened self-esteem also may not behave in sex-appropriate ways, but in their case, this may be unrelated to academic achievement or may mean doing well in school.

From these findings, it can be predicted that the more traditional an individual is in sex-role attitudes, the more his/her achievement behavior would be affected by situational factors. Canter (1979) found that sex-role conceptions in female undergraduates play a central role in mediating the effects of situational factors on achievement-related expectations. Alper (1974) found that, in general, women with traditional female orientations, attitudes, and beliefs scored lower on achievement-motivation measures than did women with nontraditional female orientations. In one study (Major, 1979), a significant negative relationship was found between androgyny and fear of success. In other studies (Olds, 1979; Sadd, Miller, & Zeitz, 1979), a significant negative relationship was found between masculinity and fear of success, especially in women. In general, the more masculine characteristics an individual admits to, the fewer achievement conflicts he or she is likely to have. Somewhat surprisingly, most recent studies have not found a relationship between measures of femininity alone and achievement conflicts (Olds, 1979; Sadd et al., 1979; Savage et al., 1979). This lack of a consistent relationship between femininity and fear of success may mean that the femininity scale measures traits that have little to do with achievement. It should be recalled that it was the masculinity scale, not the femininity scale, that was found to relate strongly to achievement orientation overall (Spence & Helmreich, 1978). It now seems that the masculinity scale relates to achievement conflicts as well.

Peplau (1976) also investigated the relationship between sex-role attitudes and achievement behavior by studying college-aged dating couples in competitive and noncompetitive situations. She found that sex-role attitude had a greater impact than did fear of success on college women's achievement both in the laboratory and in daily life. College women who adhered to traditional sex-role beliefs achieved more in a noncompetitive or team-goal-setting situation than in individual competition. The noncompetitive situations may be viewed as more compatible with traditional femininity than the individual competitive one. Liberal college females, on the other hand, excelled in the more "masculine" individual, competitive conditions. They also had higher educational and career aspirations. Significantly, the two groups of females did not differ in actual grade point average. Glasser (1974) and Lesser et al. (1963) found similar patterns; that is, the more traditional an individual's sex-role attitude, the more affected he/she is by the sex-appropriateness of the task.

Definition of Achievement. Because females who achieve in male-defined areas often do meet with negative consequences, it is no wonder that many females do not demonstrate achievement in such areas but prefer interpersonal situations. Social areas may represent achievement for females, not a way to satisfy affiliation or social approval needs, as previously thought. It is not that females have no need for achievement; this motive is equally present in females and males. It is not that females are blocked by a unique fear of success; this does not differentiate males and females across situations. Rather, it must be concluded that males and females are basically similar in their achievement behavior; only their areas of striving and the consequences of that striving may differ as a result of traditional sex-role socialization. Females who accept achievement behavior as part of the female role respond like males to achievement-instigating conditions (Donelson, 1973).

Thus, the definition of achievement may be different for females and for males. The definition of achievement used for most achievement measures may be tapping achievement only in its traditional, male-oriented sense: vocational aspirations and attainments, competitive games, and so forth (Spence & Helmreich, 1978). Besides being more interested in social achievements than are some males, many females also appear to be more interested than many males in self-directed improvement for the process of mastery rather than for the impact such mastery would bring (Depner & Veroff, 1979; Kipnis, 1974; Veroff, 1977). That is, many females seem more autonomous in their achievement strivings, whereas many males seem to respond more to normative pressures for performance. Indeed, Spence and Helmreich (1978) found in their investigation of the antecedents of achievement motivation that girls are expected to be devoted to hard work for its own sake, whereas boys are expected to work hard in order to be better than others.

More women than men also may try to satisfy their achievement needs through a vicarious achievement ethic. That is, some women may choose indirect achievement satisfaction through the successes of important males in their lives (husbands, sons, fathers, brothers, bosses) rather than direct satisfaction through their own success. Although more women than men seem to have a vicarious achievement motive (Lipman-Blumen & Leavitt, 1976), research has not found related behaviors to be very gratifying (for example, Veroff & Feld, 1970).

A further point needs to be made regarding achievement and male sex-role behavior. Whereas the underemphasis on achievement behavior for females may be counterproductive for effective human functioning, its overemphasis for males may lead to the same result. Analysis of the male sex role reveals that it is primarily defined by success and status gained through working and achieving (Brannon, 1976; Cicone & Ruble, 1978; Fasteau, 1974; Pleck, 1974). All that counts is the material rewards of achieving—money, possessions, power, and "winning" in sexual and athletic areas. In contrast to many women, many men achieve more for the social rewards of achieving than for the personal rewards of mastery. Many men also use social comparison to find a standard with which to compete and to surpass rather than as a way of gaining information (House, 1973). This emphasis on achieving may prevent the development of other human abilities—sensitivity to others, nurturance, emotional expressiveness, and formation of relationships.

As Pleck (1976a) points out, although the area in which men are expected to achieve may be changing (more intellectual and interpersonal skills as compared to physical strength skills are now positively sanctioned), the fundamental stress on achievement remains. The very nature of the male role, both traditional and modern, may be dysfunctional because it contains inherent role strain between role demands and more fundamental personal needs. In addition, in a competitive society like America, only a few can win or come out on top in terms of success or status. Even when success is obtained, it usually lasts for only a limited time, since there is always either something else to achieve or someone else who achieves more. Consequently, many males spend their lives competing endlessly with little possibility of reaching their goal. Furthermore, since masculinity is so tied to working and achievement, when unemployment occurs, some men also may experience damaging losses of self-esteem. All these pressures may give rise to frustration, aggression, and/or depression, among other consequences.

Summary. Achievement behavior for women and men is a function of both achievement motivation and sex-role expectations. Achievement itself may have multiple meanings, referring to both process and impact dimensions. In general, women have been discouraged from achieving in male-defined areas such as medicine and mechanics, and men have been discouraged from achieving in female-defined areas, like nursing and clerical skills.

Flexibility of Behavior

How comfortable and effective do you feel in situations requiring assertiveness? empathy? mechanical skills? nurturance? physical aggression? social skills? leadership? intuition? The wider the range of behaviors, the more flexible one is in one's behaviors. Sex-role stereotypes markedly affect this range through the impact of socialization practices.

In order to examine how the stereotypes affect the range of behaviors in which we feel comfortable engaging, a closer look at the effects of the socialization processes involved in sex typing is warranted. Following the consideration of socialization processes, a review of the original work by Sandra Bem and her associates on sex typing and behavioral flexibility will be undertaken together with some assessment of the current status of their work.

Socialization. As was reviewed in Part Three, males appear to receive more intense socialization than do females. Males are both punished and rewarded more than females, particularly with regard to sex-appropriate behaviors (for example, Fling & Manosevitz, 1972). One result of this intensity of socialization is that such differential pressures lead to differential attachment to sex-role stereotypes and to sex-typed behaviors.

Males, starting at age 3 and continuing into adulthood, are generally found to be more sex typed and to be more reluctant to express a preference for, or engage in, other-sex activities than are females (Bem, 1974; Connor & Serbin, 1978; Donelson, 1977a; Helmreich, Spence, & Holahan, 1979; Hoffman & Fidell, 1979; Lynn, 1959; Maccoby & Jacklin, 1974; McArthur & Eisen, 1976). This strong preference for sex-typed tasks has been found especially in masculine-sex-typed males. Females, on the other hand, generally appear to have greater role flexibility than do males. They frequently prefer and adopt male roles and activities throughout childhood; hence, the common phenomenon of "tomboy" behaviors in girls between ages 6 and 9. These differences may reflect differences in the consequences of sex-role deviation; that is, boys seem to be more punished than are girls for engaging in sex-role-inappropriate behaviors. These differences in role flexibility also may reflect differences in the intrinsic nature of the roles themselves, with the male role and male-identified activities seen as being more desirable and suitable for establishing personal competence (Donelson, 1977a; Hoffman, 1977). Indeed, as some researchers note (for example, McArthur & Eisen, 1976), if girls are to acquire any sense of competence, assertiveness, or achievement behaviors, they must identify, to some extent, with males and male characters in stories. This is so because males appear three times as often as do females in stories, and they are the only ones displaying such behaviors (see Chapter Eight).

From grades 6 through 12, both sexes show increasing consistency with sex-role stereotypes in their self-descriptions (Carlson, 1965; Silvern, 1977). For females, however, this means experiencing greater restrictiveness than previously experienced. This may cause role conflict and strain (Bardwick, 1971; Donelson, 1977b; Katz, 1979; Locksley & Douvan, 1979). Girls now are pressured subtly to give up outside interests (sports, academic achievement, and so on) and to concentrate on finding a mate. It is at this point, in high school and especially in college, that academic performance by females declines. Girls start acting "dumb" to make themselves more desirable (Freeman, 1971; Komarovsky, 1946). Their hours and their personal environment are restricted more than that of their male peers, and this restrictiveness continues into adulthood. Some results of this restrictiveness may be a confused self-identity, lessened self-esteem, and/or high anxiety. In general, strong socialization narrows the options available to women, whereas it increases the options available to men (Block, 1973). Women often must choose between a family and a career. If they choose a career, they are often restricted to a few female-dominated occupations, such as teaching or nursing. Men, on the other hand, can have both a family and a career and have a wider variety of careers from which to choose.

The consequences of socialization for men, however, are not all positive. As mentioned above, males hold to their sex-role identity very rigidly and are punished for deviations. This intense socialization causes a great deal of anxiety over anything vaguely feminine and leads males to deny certain aspects of themselves that have been associated with femininity, particularly feelings of dependence and vulnerability. As Fasteau (1974) notes, this denial sets up a classic scapegoating process whereby what is feared becomes disliked, and those who display the feared behavior become hated and ridiculed. That boys often express dislike and contempt for girls is a common observation ("yech, girls!"), but Fasteau remarks that this early misogyny never really disappears but only becomes more subtle and disguised. This scapegoating obviously will affect relationships between the sexes.

Hartley (1959) describes a similar process. Because boys learn more what they should not do than what they should do, they are caught in a constant striving to find ways to be masculine. Some overstrive with explicit hostility against anything feminine and with marked rigidity concerning sex-role stereotyping. Some overstrive with less hostility but still with marked rigidity. Some give up the struggle and rebel against the expectations. And some few develop a balanced implementation of the role with flexibility and understanding of the female role. These latter males fall into the androgynous category.

Babl (1979) found experimental support for Hartley's compensatory-masculinity hypothesis. In investigating the reactions of college men to a threat to their masculinity (information that American college males are becoming less masculine), he found that masculine-sex-typed males responded anxiously. They subsequently reported exaggerated levels of masculinity and antisocial behavior. In contrast, although androgynous males also reported anxiety, they responded by lowering their level of masculine endorsement and did not increase their endorsement of antisocial behavior. A similar pattern of findings was reported by Watson (1979). Masculine college males were more likely than androgynous men to utilize avoidance defenses to maintain their high self-esteem. College women did not show any relationship between sex typing, self-esteem, and use of avoidance defenses. Sex-typed males, then, seem to adhere in a particularly rigid manner to their sex role.

Although among children more males than females appear strongly sex typed, among adults the proportions are relatively equal. There is approximately the same proportion of masculine men as feminine women, at least among college students (Bem, 1974; Heilbrun, 1976; Spence et al., 1975). There are fewer feminine men than masculine women, however, suggesting that certain restrictions in sex-role behaviors still exist for men more so than for women. Of course, these proportions depend upon how the groups are formed.

There is also evidence that men may be becoming less behaviorally restricted than was once thought. O'Leary and Donoghue (1978) reviewed two studies that demonstrated that nonstereotyped males (those who had nontraditional personality traits and vocational interests or who advocated nontraditional behaviors) were not devalued by high school or college students. O'Leary and Donoghue suggest, however, that this may be so among adults only because childhood adherence to the male role was so strict. In other words, once masculinity is firmly established, then flexibility is allowed. These same authors do acknowledge that there are still limits on the latitudes of acceptable masculine behavior. For example, men are still punished for demonstrating incompetence and for failing (Deaux & Taynor, 1973; Feather & Simon, 1975; Larrance, Pavelich, Storer, Polizzi, Baron, Sloan, Jordan, & Reis, 1979; Spence et al., 1975), for passivity and dependence (Costrich, Feinstein, Kidder, Maracek, & Pascale, 1975), and for sexual difficulties (Polyson, 1978).

How do different degrees of sex typing affect behaviors across a wide range of situations? Based on Sandra Bem's work, a number of researchers have suggested that androgynous people are the most adaptive, flexible, and effective of all sex-typed groupings. Although this simple conclusion has since been challenged, a closer examination of Bem's original research will be instructive.

Bem's Research. Sandra Bem and her colleagues have accumulated an impressive body of evidence demonstrating the effects of sex-role stereotypes on a wide variety of behaviors (1974, 1975a, 1975b, 1976, 1977; Bem & Lenney, 1976). Individuals who hold strongly to sex-role stereotypes—that is, those who rate themselves as strongly sex typed via an adjective check list (the Bem Sex-Role Inventory, or BSRI)—have been found to be markedly less flexible in their behaviors than are individuals who are less strongly sex typed. These latter individuals Bem termed "androgynous."

In a sequence of studies, Bem and associates found that masculine males (those who checked more masculine than feminine characteristics on the BSRI) were highly capable of effective performance when it came to instrumental behaviors, such as independence in a conformity situation, assertiveness in a request situation. But when it came to expressive behaviors, they performed poorly. For example, they were nonnurturant to a human baby, nonplayful with a kitten, and nonempathic to a lonely student. Feminine females (those who checked more feminine than masculine characteristics on the BSRI), on the other hand, were the reverse—high in the expressive domain, except with the kitten, and low in the instrumental domain. Cross-sex-typed individuals (the 10% who scored much higher on the other-sex scale than on the same-sex one) showed the same pattern of behavioral restrictiveness as their other-sex partners; that is, masculine females and feminine males had the same behavioral pattern as masculine males and feminine females, respectively. It was only the androgynous individuals (those who possessed characteristics of both sexes in equal proportions), males and females, who were able to perform well in both domains. Thus, both androgynous males and androgynous females could be nurturant and empathic and independent and assertive. In the study with the kitten, in fact, androgynous individuals were more nurturant than feminine individuals, since the situation required some initiative, which feminine individuals were unable to take. Thus, androgynous individuals are the most flexible behaviorally; strongly sex-typed individuals, the most restricted.

The reason for this restrictiveness in strongly sex-typed individuals seems to be that, for them, engaging in cross-sex behavior is very uncomfortable and anxiety producing. Cross-sex behavior is thus actively resisted. Bem and Lenney (1976) found that sex-typed individuals were more likely than sex-reversed or androgynous individuals to prefer activities that are sex-appropriate and to resist those that are sex-inappropriate, even when those preferences incurred a cost to the individual in terms of loss of offered payment for engaging in sex-inappropriate tasks. For example, if a sex-typed male was asked to choose between being photographed preparing a baby bottle for 4¢ and oiling a hinge for 2¢, he would be more likely to choose the oiling task than would an androgynous or feminine male. Additionally, when sex-typed individuals did engage in cross-sex activity, they experienced discomfort and negative feelings about themselves. If the male subject in the above example did perform the bottle task, he said he felt more uncomfortable and negative doing so than did either the androgynous or feminine males.

These findings extend findings in achievement behavior and fear-of-success studies to other types of behavior. Individuals, females and males, refrain from engaging in cross-sex activities or functions because of the consequences of so doing. This conclusion is further clarified by the concept of androgyny. It is primarily sex-typed individuals who appear concerned about the negative consequences of engaging in sex-role-inappropriate behaviors. Consequently, they are the ones who restrict their behavior accordingly. Androgynous individuals either do not expect such negative consequences or are not concerned about them. They seem the most balanced of all groups, with the most freedom and flexibility of behavior.

Current Findings. Recent investigations of the relationship between sex typing and behavioral flexibility have tempered somewhat the glowing reports about androgynous individuals. There is some suggestion that androgynous men may differ from androgynous women in several ways. In the first place, men appear more likely to characterize themselves as androgynous than do women (Bem, 1974; Ruble & Higgins, 1976; Wiggins & Holzmuller, 1978, in press). Secondly, androgynous males appear more flexible regarding interpersonal behaviors as measured by self-reports than either sex-typed males or androgynous females. Wiggins and Holzmuller (1978) found that androgynous college men have a relatively flat profile when the strength of certain interpersonal variables was charted (dominant/ambitious, aloof/introverted, arrogant/calculating, cold/quarrelsome, unassuming/ingenuous, warm/agreeable, gregarious/extroverted, lazy/submissive); that is, androgynous males appear relatively flexible in interpersonal behavior in contrast to masculine males, who were very high on dominance and low on warmth and submissiveness. Androgynous females, on the other hand, did not show a profile similar to androgynous males. Rather, their profile was as variable as feminine females and, in fact, was the mirror image of it. Whereas feminine females were high on introversion, submissiveness, and ingenuousness, androgynous females were low on these variables and high on dominance, extroversion, and arrogance. Thus. androgynous females may be more inflexible than androgynous males, or they may have a more differentiated self-perception. Of course, these data are from self-reports and not from actual behavior. The data were also collected in 1972. Because consciousness of sex roles has increased dramatically since that time, earlier research no longer may be relevant. Indeed, in a 1977 replication, Wiggins and Holzmuller (in press) no longer found androgynous female college students to be different from their androgynous male peers; that is, both groups of androgynous individuals were significantly more flexible on interpersonal characteristics than were their sex-typed peers.

Another problem with Bem's conceptualizations involves the reason for less behavioral flexibility among sex-typed individuals than among androgynous individuals. In a conceptual replication of Bem and Lenney's (1976) study using the Personal Attributes Questionnaire (PAQ) instead of the BSRI, Helmreich and colleagues (1979) found a similar pattern of results but the relationships were much weaker than those found by Bem and Lenney. Androgynous individuals of both sexes had higher comfort ratings regarding performance of a variety of tasks, independent of the sex typing of the task, than did feminine and undifferentiated subjects. However, masculine individuals also had high comfort ratings, independent of type of task. The findings regarding masculine subjects somewhat contradict Bem and Lenney's (1976) hypothesis regarding why sex-typed individuals are behaviorally restricted. The different results, however, may be due to the different measures of sex typing used. Helmreich et al. (1979) contend that their scale of sex typing, the PAQ, measures only instrumental and expressive personality traits, rather than sex roles (see also Spence & Helmreich, 1978, 1979a). Therefore, only minimal relations should be expected between instrumental and expressive personality characteristics and many sex-role-related behaviors. Helmreich et al. (1979) explain their findings regarding comfort ratings in terms of differences in self-esteem among the sex-typing groups, rather than in terms of differences in sex typing per se.

More disturbing to Bem's conclusions, however, are the results of a comprehensive study by Jones, Chernovetz, and Hansson (1978). These researchers studied more than 1400 college students in five general areas of psychological functioning: feminist ideology and gender identity, personality and adjustment, intellectual competence, helplessness, and sexual maturity and heterosexuality. Within these five areas, 16 specific behaviors were examined. Jones and colleagues hypothesized that, across all situations, androgynous individuals should be the most flexible and adaptable. They found, however, that the androgyny-equals-adaptibility hypothesis does not seem to hold for males and needs to be greatly qualified for females. For both sexes, the more masculine the orientation, the more adaptive the behavior. Masculine males were more competent and confident on numerous dimensions than were either androgynous or feminine males. The group of feminine males was the least adaptive. For females, although androgynous individuals were more flexible and adaptive than feminine ones, masculine females were the most adaptive and competent of all groups. Thus, although androgyny is certainly not the least adaptive response mode, it is not clearly the most adaptive either, as Bem predicts. Rather, the more adaptive, flexible, and competent patterns of responding occurred among more masculine individuals, independent of their gender. What this finding implies is that the instrumental behaviors that comprise the masculine sex role are vitally important for social rewards for both females and males. Similar conclusions were made with regard to self-esteem and self-confidence. It must be noted, however, that Bem's concept of androgyny was meant to apply specifically to flexibility of expressive and instrumental behaviors. The study of Jones et al. extended Bem's predictions considerably by including such areas as attitudes and sexual identity. Wiggins and Holzmuller (in press) argue persuasively that Bem's index of androgyny is specific to the interpersonal domain. In that area, they found support for her predictions. For other domains, such as temperament, interests, and cognitive styles, other indexes of androgyny are needed. Therefore, the extensions made by the Jones group may not be warranted, and their negative findings may not detract from Bem's thesis per se.

Locksley and Colten (1979) question the concept of androgyny on theoretical and methodological grounds. Of relevance to the present discussion regarding behavioral flexibility is their contention that, since the world we live in makes distinctions on the basis of sex, in many situations it is more adaptive to be sex typed than to be androgynous. Indeed, these researchers conclude that the idea of being free entirely from the social effects of sex-related categorizations is impossible and that therefore androgyny is an arbitrary concept. Bem's (1979) response to this critique acknowledges that it is impossible to be free completely from sex-related social effects; however, individuals still differ in the extent to which they believe in sex differences and in their use of gender to code and process information. Androgynous individuals, for Bem, are those who use gender less often than do sex-typed persons in processing information about the world around them. Therefore the behavior of androgynous persons is less a function of the sex typing of a behavior or a situation than is the behavior of sex-typed persons. Other research (such as Deaux & Major, 1977) supports this cognitive interpretation of androgyny.

Another important point is a developmental one. Almost all of these researchers have studied sex typing in college students. Yet, as was pointed out in Chapter Seven, androgyny appears to be a developmental attainment, following a stage of sex typing. It appears logical, then, that many, if not most, college students are still in the process of achieving a stable sexual identity. Therefore, contradictory results at this life stage do not preclude clearer results with adults. Martha White (1979) argues this point well. She has shown that female nurse practitioners, median age 29, show strong differences as a function of sex typing. Women high in both agentic and communion competencies (measured by an original scale) had many advantages over those who were low in both competencies or who were competent in only one area. The high-androgynous-competency group were the most responsible, caring, competent, tolerant, self-controlled, and satisfied, to name just a few of the differentiating characteristics. Whether men or women in other occupations integrate similarly is still unanswered. More research on adults definitely is needed.

In conclusion, then, the adaptibility of androgynous individuals and the comparability of androgynous males and females are still open subjects. It does appear clear, however, that certain masculine qualities are extremely adaptive and that being strongly sex typed may limit one's behaviors in certain areas deemed appropriate for the other sex.

Summary. Because of their more intense socialization, boys appear to hold to the sex-role stereotypes even more rigidly than do girls. The cost of such sex typing is high. Bem demonstrated that many sex-typed males are markedly deficient in the expressive domain, being uninterested or unwilling even to play with a kitten. Furthermore, not only do males limit themselves from engaging in sex-inappropriate activities, they practically demand that others, both females and males, do likewise. Yet certain masculine qualities can be adaptive, especially in instrumental areas.

For many females, sex-role stereotypes have led to a negative self-image and to inhibitions about achieving in male-defined areas. For sex-typed females in particular, the stereotypes appear to restrict their instrumental activities. Consequently, the behavior of sex-typed females is sometimes less adaptive than that of sex-typed males.

In general, across most situations, androgynous individuals appear the most behaviorally flexible of all sex-typing groups. Behavioral restrictiveness, whatever the cause, does not aid one in developing the skills needed to lead a full life—that is, expressive and instrumental skills. Such restrictiveness for many sex-typed males and females affects their emotional and physical well-being as well.

MENTAL HEALTH

In moving from the areas of self-concept and behavior to the area of mental health, it is again striking how strongly and how deeply the sex-role stereotypes affect individuals regarding their feelings of psychological well-being and their evaluation of the psychological well-being of others. Looking at the indexes of anxiety, adjustment, neuroses, psychoses, hospitalization, depression, and drug and alcohol dependence, a common pattern emerges: both those individuals who feel they are not living up to their sex-appropriate stereotypes and those who hold to them most rigidly suffer from the greatest number of psychological problems. We will examine next three areas of mental health and their relation to sex typing—adjustment, mental illness, and depression.

Adjustment

Mental health is often viewed as proper adjustment. There is a strongly prevailing assumption that individuals will be "better off" if they conform to their sex-role stereotype (Bem, 1976). Thus, males who are doctors are considered, a priori, better "adjusted" than males who are nurses. The latter group, even if not considered disturbed, certainly would have their sexual identity questioned ("Is he 'gay'?"). Yet a variety of studies indicate that good adjustment is not related to sex-role conformity. In fact, a high correlation is frequently found between sex typing and psychological and social *maladjustment*, particularly for females.

For females, the picture is relatively clear—the higher the femininity score, the poorer the adjustment; that is, the higher the anxiety, the lower the self-esteem and the lower the social acceptance (Bennett, 1979; Cosentino & Heilbrun, 1964; Gall, 1969; Heilbrun, 1968; Olds & Shaver, 1979; Sears, 1970; Spence & Helmreich, 1978; Webb, 1963). Similarly, Bart (1972) found that it is the excessively feminine woman who encounters problems with middle-age transition. Particular aspects of the feminine sex-role stereotype (verbal passive-aggressiveness and excessive conformity) have been found to be related negatively to self-esteem (Spence, Helmreich, & Holahan, 1979). Furthermore, despite the prevalent belief that women should not work, evidence has accumulated that career women are not worse off psychologically than home-oriented women. In some cases, career women may be even psychologically healthier and happier than non-career women (Bart, 1972; Bernard, 1973; Birnbaum, 1975; Donelson & Gullahorn, 1977b; Hoffman, 1974).

The pattern of strong feminine sex typing going hand in hand with poor adjustment needs some clarification, however. Garnets and Pleck (1979) go one step further. They make a strong case for a sex-role-strain analysis of the relationship between sex-typed personality characteristics and psychological adjustment. Their point is that two variables are important: the amount of *discrepancy* between same-sex ideal and real self, and the amount of sex-role *salience*. It is only for those people for whom sex roles are important that a self-ideal discrepancy would cause stress. Thus, a sex-typed person for whom sex roles are salient is likely to experience role strain only if he or she desires to be androgynous. If the ideal is a sex-typed one, strain may not occur. Sex-role strain should be low, also, whenever sex-role salience is low. This prediction needs testing.

Sex-role strain appears high for boys during childhood, when socialization pressures on them to conform to their sex role are most intense. This may be related to the findings that, throughout childhood, boys consistently have much higher rates than girls of adjustment problems. antisocial disorders, gender-identity disorders, and learning disorders (see Eme, 1979, for an excellent review). Some form of biological or psychological vulnerability may also account for these findings. One's choice of basic life-style is a critical factor. Hoffman and Fidell (1979) found that feminine-sex-typed women, although having lower self-esteem than androgynous and masculine-sex-typed women, did not differ significantly from the other groups on neuroticism. Feminine women also seemed adequately adjusted, perhaps because their life choices (housework, no external employment, child-care responsibilities) were consistent with their sex type. Indeed, Hoffman and Fidell conclude that what is crucial for adjustment may be consistency between attitude and behavior, not attitude or sex typing per se. Some studies find femininity ratings to be unrelated to measures of adjustment (for example, Silvern & Ryan, 1979).

The relationship between masculine sex typing and adjustment is somewhat more confusing. Mussen (1962) found that highly masculine males, although better adjusted in high school, 20 years later were less self-acceptant, were less sociable, and had more need for self-abasement than males who were not so masculine. Similarly, Hartford, Willis, and Deabler (1967) found in their study of 213 males aged 20 to 60 that high masculinity was positively correlated with anxiety, guilt-proneness, neuroticism, and suspectingness. Low masculinity was correlated with warmth, emotional stability, and sensitivity. Eysenck (1971), too, found high masculinity to be directly related to psychoticism.

Yet, in recent years, there has been an increasing body of literature that suggests that masculine instrumental activities are particularly likely to be associated with effective functioning. Spence and Helmreich (1978; Spence et al., 1979) have conducted research showing that, for both sexes, high masculinity is strongly and positively correlated with high self-esteem and social competence. High masculinity is negatively correlated with feelings of anxiety, depression, neuroticism, and dissatisfaction with current life circumstances. Feminine expressive attributes also contribute to high self-esteem in both sexes, but these attributes are not as influential as the instrumental ones. Silvern and Ryan (1979) also found that differences in masculinity, not femininity, were associated with self-rated adjustment differences among sex-typing categories. Olds and Shaver (1979) too found that high masculinity in both sexes was associated with fewer achievement conflicts and stress symptoms. They found high masculinity to be positively associated with feelings of mastery and work satisfaction.

Thus androgynous- and masculine-sex-typed individuals should be the best adjusted groups; feminine-sex-typed individuals, the worst adjusted group. A number of researchers (Bennett, 1979; Silvern & Ryan, 1979) have verified these predictions among college students. However, the previously reported study by Jones and colleagues (1978) only partially supports these predictions. Among males, those who were feminine-sex-typed were the most neurotic, were lowest in self-esteem, and had the most drinking problems. There were no differences for females, however.

Spence and colleagues (1979) caution, however, that not all components of the masculinity scale are socially desirable. Such characteristics as arrogance, cynicism, and egocentrism are strongly and positively correlated with the occurrence of acting-out, sociopathic behaviors. Spence and associates suggest that desirable expressive attributes (on the feminine scale) may moderate some of these negative qualitites. Similarly, Olds and Shaver (1979) found that not all masculine traits are positive. Particularly for college women, competitiveness is associated with mental and physical health problems. For both sexes, the most productive combination seems to be high work motivation and low competitiveness (see also Helmreich, Beane, Lucker, & Spence, 1978; Helmreich, Spence, Beane, Lucker, & Matthews, 1979).

Part of the confusing picture regarding sex typing and adjustment results from the different methods of measuring masculinity and femininity used in the various studies. Since 1974, most studies use either the BSRI or the PAQ. Some, however, use Heilbrun's (1976) adaptation of the Adjective Check List or Berzins et al.'s (1978) PRF Andro scale. Research before 1974 relied upon a variety of measures that did not give androgyny ratings—for example, the California Personality Inventory (Gough, 1957). Although the current scales do bear some relationship to each other, they are not interchangeable (Kelly & Worell, 1977; Spence & Helmreich, 1979b; Worell, 1978), nor are they clearly related to the older means of assessing sex typing.

The prediction of good adjustment for androgynous individuals frequently has been supported. Among college women and men, those who were androgynous (who combined instrumental and expressive behaviors) were found to be either the best or among the best adjusted and to have high self-esteem (Bennett, 1979; Heilbrun, 1968; Silvern & Ryan, 1979; Spence et al., 1975). Androgynous individuals, especially males, endorsed the fewest negative self-statements (Kelly, Caudill, Hathorn, & O'Brien, 1977; Wiggins & Holzmuller, 1978). With middle-class adults, similar results were found. Androgynous subjects had the highest level of psychosocial development, the highest self-esteem and were the most stable—nonneurotic (Hoffman & Fidell, 1979; Waterman & Whitbourne, 1979; M. White, 1979).

Of all groups, the undifferentiated (those low on both masculinity and femininity, appear to be the most poorly adjusted (Bennett, 1979; Hoffman & Fidell, 1979; Spence & Helmreich, 1978). They have the lowest self-esteem and the most external locus of control. They are also the most introverted and the most neurotic. Previous research that found feminine women to have the poorest adjustment may have inadvertently pooled undifferentiated women with those who are feminine sex typed. It is only in the past few years that general agreement has been reached regarding the importance of examining undifferentiated individuals separately from other groups (Bem, 1977; Spence et al., 1975).

An important point needs to be made with regard to androgyny. Current research now suggests that androgyny is not always the most adaptive state (Garnets & Pleck, 1979; Jones et al., 1978; Hoffman & Fidell, 1979; Kaplan, 1979; Kenworthy, 1979; Locksley & Colten, 1979; Olds & Shaver, 1979). Many situations involve different contingencies and norms for females and males. Just having high levels of masculine and feminine characteristics does not mean that these characteristics will, in fact, be integrated. In some cases, they may cause conflict and stress, particularly if the ideal self is sex typed and if sex-role salience is high. Perhaps, as some of the above researchers have suggested (especially Garnets & Pleck, Kaplan, Olds & Shaver), we need to define a mental health ideal independent of notions of femininity and masculinity.

Until such time as a new mental health ideal is defined, however, we can sum up the current research relating sex typing to emotional adjustment. The safest conclusion that seems warranted is that androgyny and masculine sex typing, as currently measured, appear to be correlated with good adjustment; undifferentiated sex typing, with poor adjustment; and feminine sex typing, somewhere between the first and second groups.

Other evidence, reported in previous chapters, has shown that strong sex typing is related to poorer intellectual development (Maccoby, 1966), less creativity (Donelson, 1973), less behavioral flexibility (Bem & Lenney, 1976), and lower levels of cognitive maturity (Haan, Smith, & Block, 1968). Thus, the belief that a high level of sex-appropriate behavior facilitates a person's general psychological or social adjustment is not supported. This is even more strikingly evident when more serious emotional problems are examined.

Mental Illness

Gove and Tudor, in a series of articles (Gove, 1979; Gove & Tudor, 1973, 1977) on the relationship between sex roles and mental illness, have accumulated a vast amount of data indicating that women are generally more mentally disturbed than are men. They base their conclusion on information from community surveys, first admissions to psychiatric hospitals, psychiatric care in general hospitals, psychiatric outpatient care, private outpatient psychiatric care, and psychiatric illnesses in the practice of general physicians. Mental illness was defined as "a disorder which involves personal discomfort . . . and/or mental disorganization . . . that is not caused by an organic or toxic condition" (Gove, 1972a, p. 50). These disorders include neurotic disorders and the functional psychoses (schizophrenia, paranoia, and manic-depression). The greatest sex differences were in the neurotic and depressive disorders (see also Bart & Scully, 1979; Dohrenwend & Dohrenwend, 1976; Schumer, 1979; Weissman & Klerman, 1979). Similar data were also obtained for transient situational personality disorders and psychophysiologic disorders (see also Seiden, 1979).

Chesler (1971, 1972), in her summary of National Institute of Mental Health hospital statistics from 1950 to 1968 and from statistics on private treatment, also concluded that more women than men were likely to be mental patients, to experience nervous breakdowns, to suffer from nervousness, insomnia, and nightmares, and to be in psychotherapy. Sutherland (1978), too, concluded that college women were more likely than college men to suffer from general nervousness and unfocused anxiety. Women are three times more likely than men to attempt suicide, although men are three times more likely than women to actually die from such attempts (Lester, 1979; Seiden, 1974). The 1970 census also indicates that there are more female mental hospital inmates than male inmates, although 1975 data show a trend in the other direction (Brody, 1979b).

There is one type of "mental illness" in which rates for men consistently surpass rates for women—the category of personality disorders (Dohrenwend & Dohrenwend, 1976; Gove, 1979). Gove did not include this category in his definition of mental illness, since it involves neither personal distress or psychotic disorganization. Rather, it is a category of social deviance most commonly characterized by aggressive and impulsive antisocial or asocial behaviors, as in psychopathy. Such behaviors are more integral to the male sex role (Spence et al., 1979), and it is therefore not surprising that men are more likely to exhibit such behaviors and receive the diagnosis than are women. This is true among adolescents as well (Eme, 1979).

When data on mental illness rates are broken down in terms of marital status (Gove, 1972a), an interesting pattern emerges (see Table 9-1 for a typical pattern). The finding of greater mental disturbance in women is limited to married women compared to married men. When single (never married, divorced, widowed) individuals are compared together, it is the single male who is more likely to be disturbed. The pattern for suicide attempts and completions is similar. When single individuals are compared to married ones, it is single men who are most suicidal (Gove, 1972b). Married people of both sexes, however, tend to have lower rates of mental illness than the unmarried. Brody (1979b) reports 1975 data from state and community psychiatric categories showing that rates of admission to mental institutions were highest for those separated and divorced, followed by those who were widowed and those who never married.

Table 9-1
Rate of Residency in Mental Hospitals as a Function of Marital Status (persons per 100,000)

	Men	Women	Men/Women
Married	178.3	227.3	0.78
Widowed	997.7	684.0	1.46
Never married	1,275.0	849.3	1.48
Divorced	2,013.2	1,201.6	1.68

From "The Relationship between Sex Roles, Marital Status, and Mental Illness," by W. R. Gove, *Social Forces*, 1972, *51*(1), 34–44. Copyright 1972 by the University of North Carolina Press. Reprinted by permission.

A number of explanations are possible for why women in general have higher rates of mental illness. The differences may be owing to biological factors, different role definitions, sex biases in diagnosis, or differential role strain. Each explanation will be examined in turn.

Biology. There is no support for the hypothesis that women may be biologically more susceptible to mental problems than men, since it is only married women who have higher rates of emotional disturbance than married men. Perhaps it is that the more biologically susceptible female and the less biologically susceptible male get married, while their "healthier" sisters and "sicker" brothers remain single either out of choice or because of inability to find a mate. Divorced and widowed individuals, then, having once been married, would be expected to have rates of mental illness similar to their married counterparts. This again is not the case. Divorced and widowed women have lower rates of mental illness than divorced and widowed men. Thus, a biological explanation cannot account for these data.

Sex Roles. Another explanation for the mental health statistics centers on the definitions of male- and female-appropriate behavior—

that is, the sex roles. Perhaps more females than males act emotionally disturbed or seek treatment because it is more acceptable that they do so. Perhaps females are more likely to be diagnosed as emotionally disturbed because that is part of our stereotype of femininity. Both these interpretations have received some support. Although they, too, fail to account for the data on marital status, these interpretations merit closer examination.

The idea that females may have higher rates of mental illness than males because of their emotional expressiveness has received some support from Phillips and Segal (1969). They found that, when the number of physical and psychiatric illnesses were held constant, women were more likely than men to seek medical and psychiatric care. They argued that, in community studies, more women may appear mentally ill because it is more socially acceptable for them to talk about their psychological symptoms and to do something about them than it is for men. Other research supports the assertion that women may seek out health-care services more frequently than men do (Scarf, 1979). This pattern develops sometime about puberty, a time when female to male ratios of mental health problems start changing (Gove, 1979).

Although more women than men may seek treatment, this explanation alone cannot account for why females are diagnosed as more mentally disturbed, since such diagnoses presumably are based on more than self-reports. This approach also cannot account for the data on marital status, as it makes the same predictions as does the biological explanation. The data do not bear out either explanation; for example, divorced and widowed women are less likely than married women to seek help for emotional problems. Furthermore, research has indicated that when level of disorder is controlled for, there is no marked sex difference in help-seeking behaviors (Gove & Tudor, 1977). Similarly, response bias has been ruled out as a satisfactory explanation for why women may report more symptoms (Clancy & Gove, 1974; Gove & Geerken, 1977).

The second possibility—that more females may get diagnosed as emotionally disturbed because of the sex-role stereotypes—has received much support. These findings can be grouped together as examples of sex bias in diagnosis.

Sex Bias. A closer look at how psychiatric diagnoses are made reveals a disturbing double standard of mental health operating in this country. Broverman and associates (1970), in their now classic study of 79 male and female psychologists, psychiatrists, and social workers, found that these mental health professionals made clear-cut distinctions between a healthy man and a healthy woman. The healthy woman, according to the subjects of the study, is more emotional, more submissive, more concerned with her appearance, less independent, less aggressive, and less competitive than is the healthy man. Even more disturbing than this negative assessment of females, however, is the finding that the behavior and characteristics judged healthy for an adult, sex unspecified, were similar to those judged healthy for an adult male but not for an adult female. Thus, mental health workers see women as having more negative and less healthy characteristics than a "typical" adult—that is, a man—a clear example of a male-centered bias.

Although there has been some question as to both the validity of, and the conclusions to be drawn from, Broverman et al.'s findings (for example, Abramowitz & Abramowitz, 1977; APA Task Force, 1975; Aslin, 1977; Delk, 1977; Fabrikant, 1974; Franks, 1979; Gilbert, 1977; Maffeo, 1979; Stricker, 1977), the bulk of research does indicate that psychotherapists (male and female) do sex-role stereotype to the disparagement of females. Nontherapists have been found to hold a double standard of mental health as well (Costrich et al., 1975; Zedlow, 1976). These findings, taken together, suggest that such stereotyping is more a cultural standard than a function of therapists' sex. However, some research (for example, Aslin, 1977; Garfinkle & Morin, 1978; Sherman, Koufacos, & Kenworthy, 1978) does suggest that women therapists may be better informed, more liberal, and less stereotyped in their attitudes toward women and in regard to standards of mental health than are male therapists. This nonstereotyped attitude only or primarily may apply to female clients, however. Loeffler (1978) found female therapists to hold more stereotyped views of men than did male therapists.

This double standard of mental health, paralleling as it does societal sex-role stereotypes, is probably a reflection of an "adjustment" standard of mental health. In other words, a woman is seen as healthy if she is more emotional and submissive because that is what society has termed acceptable for females. Using this approach, an independent, assertive woman would be labelled "deviant." Not only do clinicians holding this view foster conformity and restrict the choices open to women and men, but they also may foster emotional problems, since it has been shown that strong sex typing for women is more associated with emotional problems, not less so.

Chesler (1972) and others go even further in their condemnation of such a view of mental health for women. These writers blame psychology and psychotherapists for directly tyrannizing and oppressing women into staying in their (second) place. According to Chesler, more women than men are in psychotherapy because psychotherapy is one of the two institutions socially approved for middle-class women; the other socially approved institution is marriage. Both institutions allow a woman to express and diffuse her feelings by experiencing them as a form of emotional illness. If a woman is married and her husband treats her well and provides for her (and for the children), then any feelings of dissatisfaction may be taken as a sign of some emotional problem on her part ("Why aren't you happy when you have everything a woman should want? There must be something wrong with you."). Both institutions also isolate women from each other and emphasize individual, rather than social, solutions to problems (the problem is in you, rather than in society or your husband). Both views are based on a woman's dependence on a strong male (in most cases) authority figure. Even diagnostic categories may reflect a male bias (see Bart & Scully, 1979, for an analysis of the politics of hysteria).

Using this interpretation, it is no wonder that more females than males have higher rates of emotional disturbance; they are more likely to be diagnosed as disturbed even if they show "healthy adult" behaviors, and they are more likely to fit into male-centered psychotherapy. Yet, although this explanation may account for the larger number of married women in psychotherapy, it does not fully account for the other differences associated with marital status.

Role Conflict.   Another explanation for the mental health statistics, one that Gove and Tudor themselves favor, centers on the concept of role conflict. It is not that women's roles make them more susceptible to mental problems per se but that there is some conflict or strain in the roles they hold that promotes mental illness.

In this view, women's role in modern industrial societies is seen as having a number of characteristics that produce stress. In the first place, women are typically restricted to a single role—housewife—whereas men have two roles—breadwinner and husband/father. This means men have two potential sources of satisfaction, while women, for the most part, have just one. If married women do work, they may have the strain of holding down two jobs (inside and outside the home) and the strain of a less satisfying job (less money, less prestige, fewer job openings, more career roadblocks, and so forth). Although they appear emotionally better off than full-time homemakers (Bernard, 1973), recent studies have found that working wives have very high levels of stress on Fridays and Saturdays. That is the time they must do household chores, tasks that still predominantly rest with them (*New York Times*, August 28, 1977, p. L50). Although performing two jobs may not lead to, by itself, emotional problems, such stress may take its toll, emotionally or physically, over the years.

The critical variables here may be spouse support and commitment to the work role. Holahan and Gilbert (1979) found in their study of 51 employed mothers with equivalent levels of education (college graduates) that it was only those women who thought of their work as a job rather than as a career who experienced role conflict. The conflict arose between parent-self and spouse-self roles. Importantly, the support of a spouse was crucial in reducing such role conflict. Women who defined their work as a career reported no role conflicts. These women also tended to have more spouse support.

Another strain for women comes from the double bind inherent in choosing home and/or career. Pines and Solomon (1978) had college students view a videotape depicting a competent, intelligent woman who had a husband and child. When the woman chose to have a career too, both females and males viewed her as being less feminine and less likeable than if she stayed home. However, the choice of remaining at home led to her being viewed as less competent. The result was a "no win" situation.

If a married woman does not work, she often finds her major instrumental activities, such as raising children and keeping house, to be frustrating and confusing, being often in conflict with her educational and intellectual attainments, having little prestige attached to them, and being virtually invisible. Bernard (1976a) suggests that the lack of emotional support from a husband (because of men's conditioning) and from friends (because of social conditions mitigating against female-female bonds) has contributed to the apparent rise in female depression. A wife also is under strain because of the unclear expectations for her future (husband may change jobs, transfer). This role strain is strongest for married women; hence their higher rates of emotional problems. If women's roles were clearer, were more highly valued, and demanded more time and skill, such strain should not occur. This was true more for women before World War II. Indeed, mental health statistics bear this out—more men than women were hospitalized for mental illness at that time (Gove & Tudor, 1973, 1977). It should be noted, however, as Dohrenwend and Dohrenwend (1976) point out, that the nature of psychiatric diagnosis has changed during that time. Since World War II, diagnoses have become broader and more inclusive, particularly regarding neurotic and depressive symptomatology. Hence, increasing rates of mental illness for women since World War II may reflect such methodological changes.

If mental health statistics are a product of the social system, it also can be predicted that those men who experience role conflict or strain should also have higher rates of emotional problems. Because males are expected to devote themselves single-mindedly to achieving, single males are under more strain than single women and married males because they do not have anyone to take care of their other needs, both physical and emotional. Because of social inhibitions on males expressing their emotions, especially to other men, wives are often the only source of emotional relief for men. Thus, there are higher rates of emotional disturbance in single men than in single women. The latter group has been trained to provide the basics of physical and emotional care for themselves.

Since the major role for males centers on their working ability, in times of economic depression and high unemployment, more men than women should experience problems. Statistics reported in Gove and Tudor (1973) bear this out, as do more recent reports of increases in male depression, suicide, sexual impotence, child abuse, and so on accompanying the high unemployment rates of the 1970s (Drummond, 1977). As was noted previously, 1975 mental hospital statistics show more men than women admitted. One study (cited in Drummond, 1977) found that, after looking at data from 750,000 New York state mental patients during a 127-year period, the only significant factor accounting for the rise and fall in admission to mental hospitals was employment. This is true of women as well as men. In fact, women may be even more affected than men by unemployment. Whereas one out of every four unemployed males was clinically depressed, the proportion for unemployed women was two out of five (Drummond, 1977). This, again, points to the difficulty in dichotomizing the activities of the sexes and the consequences of these activities.

Related to this concept of differential role strain is a proposal by Bernard (1973) of a *shock theory of marriage* for women. When a woman enters into a conventional marriage, she undergoes a number of emotional shocks that could disturb her emotional well-being. She experiences conflict between attachment to her husband and attachment to her parents. She discovers her husband is not super strong, protective, and so forth. She is pressured to reshape her personality and behavior to meet her husband's wishes and needs. And she finds her husband values her domestic behaviors more than her affectional ones (Wills, Weiss, & Patterson, 1974). Thus, marriage, for some women, appears to be an emotional hazard. This, of course, is not to say that marriage is a hazard for all women. Much depends on the woman and the marriage. It should be recalled that rates of emotional disturbance (and, as we shall see, physical disorders) are less for married individuals than for those who are unmarried. And many women handle role combinations without any role strain.

Yet, using role conflict and role strain to explain emotional problems also does help explain certain age patterns. Hartley (1959) and others (Bardwick, 1971; Eme, 1979; Gove & Herb, 1974; Locksley & Douvan, 1979) have concluded that adjustment pressures are different for males and females at different ages. As was discussed previously, males experience the most intense socialization pressures during childhood and early adolescence, and it is then that males have higher rates of neurosis, psychosis, learning problems, behavior problems, gender identity disorders, stuttering, and enuresis than females. Girls experience their most intense socialization pressures during and after adolescence, and it is then that the statistical trends just mentioned start reversing themselves. Girls begin receiving more diagnoses of neurotic and affective psychotic disorders after puberty than males do (Eme, 1979).

It is important to note here that the problems for which males and females are referred to child guidance centers are different. Boys are most often referred for aggressive, antisocial, and competitive behaviors; girls, for personality problems, such as excessive fears, shyness, and feelings of inferiority (Beller & Neubauer, 1963; Chesler, 1971; Gove & Herb, 1974; Locksley & Douvan, 1979). These differences again parallel the stereotypes of males being more active, females more passive, illustrating the negative aspects of both sex-role stereotypes.

There are other age patterns as well. Bird (1979) reports new data on the age group 20–59. Although community surveys taken in the mid-1950s and the 1960s found that impairment rates rose regularly among successive age groups, being higher for women than for men at all ages, follow-ups done in the 1970s showed women in their 40s and older were now less impaired than in the past. In fact, their rates of impairment were now comparable to their male peers (around 8% to 9%). Surprisingly, new data on women in their 30s showed their impairment rate to be about 30%, the highest in the sample. This suggests that stress for this age group is higher now than ever before, perhaps as a function of changing role expectations and conflicts over motherhood and career ambitions. Middle-aged women may be past such conflicts. Troll and Turner (1979) report on significant sex differences in problems associated with aging but find that these differences do not favor either sex.

Thus, although role pressures and conflicts may be partially responsible for emotional problems, how the problems become manifest and how they are viewed by an observer are determined by what is socially acceptable for one's sex. And social acceptability is determined by the sex-role stereotypes. Depression serves as a case in point.

Depression

Statistics show that the incidence of clinical depression is rising, affecting about one in every five Americans and affecting women two to six times as frequently as men (Scarf, 1979; Weissman & Klerman, 1979). Depression is greatest among low-income women with young children, particularly those who are divorced or separated. (The typical depressed person is a woman under age 35.) This can be viewed as a time when pressures (role, economic, social) on them are the strongest. Single women and married men are least likely to suffer from depression, and they also experience the least role strain. Women whose children have left home are also unlikely to suffer from depression, contrary to the myth that menopause and the *empty nest syndrome* are major producers of depression (Barnett & Baruch, 1978; Bird, 1979; Weissman & Klerman, 1979). Bart (1972) reported that it is only those women who defined themselves solely in terms of their maternal role ("the supermothers") who suffered from middle-aged depression.

Yet, the roots of depression are not just in social pressures but rather are in the "uniquely vulnerable role into which women are socialized" (Albin, 1976, p. 27). In this view, American society trains women in helplessness (Bem & Bem, 1970; Dweck et al., 1978; Radloff, 1975). It is this cognitive outlook and its related attitude of dependence that is directly related to depression (Arieti & Bemporad, 1978; Seligman, 1974). This feeling may be particularly strong for married women, especially for those with young children, explaining their higher incidence of depression. Single women may be less indoctrinated with the helplessness stereotype than those who marry; widowed and divorced women may be less helpless than widowed men because they at least usually know how to care for themselves. It is interesting, in this regard, that Baucom and Danker-Brown (1979) found sex-typed college students, in contrast to androgynous and undifferentiated students, to be particularly susceptible to the development of helplessness. The results for feminine-sex-typed persons are understandable, given the previously cited findings of relatively poor adjustment and low self-esteem in feminine-sex-typed persons and the higher incidence of depression in women. The findings regarding masculine-sex-typed persons are slightly more perplexing. As Baucom and Danker-Brown (1979) suggest, it is likely that, because sex-typed persons are less flexible behaviorally than androgynous persons, sex-typed persons react more strongly than androgynous individuals to losing control and failing. Outside laboratory settings, however, masculine-sex-typed persons, because of their agentic qualities, may be able to avoid uncontrollable situations more often than individuals of other sex types. Since more males than females are masculine sex typed, the result may be a sex difference in the incidence of learned helplessness and depression.

Another explanation of the higher rates of female depression invokes the concept of *attachment bonding*. Weissman and Klerman (1979; Klerman, 1979) suggest that women, for reasons either biologically or socially based, are particularly sensitive to certain stressors related to disruption of intimate social relationships. Because modern industrial society is replete with disruptors of such relationships (moves, divorce, separation, diminution of family ties), women are more vulnerable to depression than are men. Supporting this hypothesis is the finding that the most common external *trigger* of depression for women, when one exists, is loss of a love bond (Scarf, 1979). For men, the relationship between depression and loss of a love bond is less strong, although it still exists.

In addition to learning helplessness as part of learning the female role and to acquiring close attachments, females also are more likely than males to learn to turn anger and rage inward and to be self-critical. In contrast, males are more likely than females to turn these feelings outward and to be physically aggressive (Cox, 1976; Mundy, 1975). Thus, statistics on emotional disturbance, reflecting an internal state, are higher for females. Statistics on drug and alcohol dependence, behavior problems, psychopathy, and crimes—more external indices—are higher for males (Davison & Neale, 1978; Gomberg, 1979; Gove, 1979).

In this regard, it is interesting to note that, although male alcoholics outnumber female alcoholics, the number of female alcoholics has risen dramatically since the mid-1960s. This is particularly true for younger age groups (Gomberg, 1979). In the mid-1960s, only one out of every eight reported alcoholics was female; in the mid-1970s, it was one out of every four or five. In a national study of correlates of alcohol use among women, Johnson (1978) found that the group most likely to have drinking problems was employed, married, middle-class women. Possible explanations for this relationship emphasize the stress of dual-role demands plus the exposure to traditional male drinking norms. Again, it is apparent how role stress may increase the likelihood of an emotional problem and how societal norms affect its expression.

Summary

The findings regarding the effect of the sex-role stereotypes on mental health point in one direction—the more instrumental qualities an individual has (as in androgynous- and masculine-sex-typed persons), the better that person's psychological adjustment. One's marital status is also important. As a result of the sex-role stereotypes, more married women than married men and more single men than single women experience role strain and conflicts. Also as a result of the stereotypes, women are more likely than men to experience these strains as resulting from emotional, rather than social, problems, are more likely to talk about them, and are more likely to seek psychotherapeutic help. When they obtain help, women are more likely than men to be viewed as psychologically unhealthy as a result of a double standard of mental health, again based on the differential sex-role stereotypes. These factors explain why more married women than married men are diagnosed and treated as mentally ill. Once again, belief in the sex-role stereotypes bears the brunt of the blame.

PHYSICAL HEALTH

As if the above consequences were not enough, sex-role stereotypes also affect one's physical health. Evidence has been cited that more women than men suffer from psychophysiologic disorders (Gove, 1979; Gove & Tudor, 1973; Seiden, 1979). There are also sex differences in the incidence of specific disorders (Fisher & Greenberg, 1979; Gove, 1979). Women are more likely than men to report headaches, throat and urinary problems, constipation, nervous stomach, weight difficulties, or hypertension. Men are more likely than women to report ulcers, asthma, stomach symptoms, and eye complaints. Some of these differences may involve sex differences in the reporting, not the incidence, of the symptoms.

Other statistics discussed in Chapter Two show that males have a shorter life expectancy, contract more serious illnesses, and have more accidents than do females. Males also use and abuse alcohol and illicit narcotics more than do females (Gomberg, 1979). Many researchers and authors directly connect these statistics to the male sex role (see Harrison, 1978, for a persuasive analysis).

Brannon (1976) has abstracted four themes of the stereotyped male role:

1. No Sissy Stuff: the need to be different from females.
2. The Big Wheel: the need to be superior to others.
3. The Sturdy Oak: the need to be self-reliant and independent.
4. Give 'em Hell: the need to be more powerful than others.

All four themes involve self-evaluation in terms of an external standard, and all four limit the expression of feelings. This combination can be hazardous to one's health. Pleck (1976a) concludes that both the traditional and modern definitions of the male role are inherently stressful, since they require males to shut off certain parts of their emotional functioning for the sake of achieving.

Since, for many men, their sole identity rests on their role as breadwinner, when this role is threatened the stress is sometimes overwhelming. A number of studies have found increased numbers of peptic ulcers, heart attacks, and strokes related to unemployment in middle-aged men (Drummond, 1977). One study (Kasl & Cobb, 1970) found that 100 men who were about to have their job terminated had significant increases in their cholesterol and norepinephrine levels and in their blood pressure in anticipation of their job loss. These changes continued for 24 months afterward. All of the above changes adversely affect the cardiovascular system.

In addition, because many men tend to overestimate their abilities and because of the reality involved in competitive situations, they often do not win and achieve. Slobogin (1977) suggests that executive stress and/or the competition to get ahead may result in greater vulnerability for men. Yet, men have few acceptable ways of releasing feelings of inadequacy and frustration—"real" men do not show their emotions. Figure 9-1 gives an example of this. In fact, as Bem demonstrated, they may not even know *how* to release feelings.

Jourard (1971) suggests that it is a male's typically low self-disclosure, lack of insight and empathy, incompetence at loving, and

Figure 9-1
*A "real" man never
shows his feelings.
(Reprinted by
permission. © 1978
NEA, Inc.)*

general dispiritation that result in his earlier death. These factors certainly add to the stress arising from a male's life situation and make it difficult for some males to release the tension that builds up.

Even when men are ill, their stoic role may make it more difficult for them to seek help. Greenberg and Fisher (1977) found that anxiety about being passive is associated with resistance to becoming a patient. It is not surprising, then, that sixty percent of all medical appointments are made for females (Scarf, 1979). The fact that women go to physicians regularly regarding reproductive functions may inflate these statistics, however. Furthermore, the data on sex differences in medically-related behaviors are somewhat contradictory. Fisher and Greenberg (1979) found negligible sex differences among college students in total symptom frequency, in delay in seeking medical consultation, and in the frequency with which medical treatment is obtained. Fisher and Greenberg also found no relationship between masculinity-femininity and the frequency with which physicians were consulted, although masculinity-femininity was related to the particular symptoms presented (Olds, 1979). If men really are less likely than women to go to doctors with physical problems, minor illnesses may develop into major ones, accounting somewhat for the higher rates of serious physical problems in men than in women.

In looking more closely at the major causes of death (Table 2-1), a number of them are directly attributable to certain behaviors, such as cigarette smoking, drinking, reckless driving, violence, and aggressive-competitive, Type A, or "coronary-prone" behavior. All these behaviors occur more in men than in women and all can be viewed as extreme forms of certain components of masculinity—risk-taking, competition, status, power, and violence. Harrison (1978) suggests that such behaviors may develop as compensation for the anxiety derived from sex-role expectations.

Unfortunately, women seem to be joining men in some of these behaviors, especially in smoking and drinking habits. Consequently, their rates of physical problems, like lung cancer, heart attacks, and alcoholism, are on the rise. As was cited in Chapter Two, in the last 3 decades, deaths from lung cancer among women have quadrupled. One of the most frequently suggested reasons for the increasing percentage of women who smoke is that cigarette smoking may be a symbol of equality with men—"You've come a long way, baby" (Brody, 1979a). This would be a sad testimonial for equality indeed.

Interestingly, some writers have argued that there is, in fact, no increase in female death rates from stress-related diseases (see Ehrenreich, 1979), nor are women who work, as a group, more vulnerable to such stress-related ailments as heart disease. On the contrary, there is evidence that employed women actually have fewer physical ailments and fewer days in bed than housewives. But physical and emotional problems are associated with achievement conflicts and traditionally female jobs, like clerical and sales work, especially for Blacks (Ehrenreich, 1979; Zeitz, 1979). These problems are compounded when a boss is nonsupportive and the worker also has marital and family responsibilities. Thus, Ehrenreich (1979) argues, it is not "liberation" that is dangerous to women's health but the lack thereof.

As with the data on emotional problems, an interesting interaction has been found between longevity and marital status. A number of researchers (Brody, 1979b; Gove, 1973; *Psychology Today*, January 1977, pp. 20–22) report that, although women outlive men by about eight years, the difference is much less for married men and women. In general, married individuals of both sexes live longer than single people, perhaps because close interpersonal ties are important for a sense of well-being. This seems particularly true for men. Gove (1973) found that single men were more likely than their female counterparts to die directly from prolonged diseases (tuberculosis and diabetes) and overt social acts (suicide, homicide, accidents) and to die indirectly from the use of socially approved "narcotics" (cirrhosis of the liver and lung cancer). Gove further found that, based on certain internal patterns within the data (the least vulnerable time for men is when young children are at home), a role explanation of these statistics is most likely. Table 9-2 shows the percentage of higher mortality rates of single people compared to married persons of the same sex.

Unmarried men who live alone have the highest mortality rate, almost double that of their married counterparts. Unmarried males who head a family live the longest. A slightly different pattern emerges for unmarried females. Although they, too, benefit most from being family heads, women are much better off living alone than within a family in which they are not head. The explanation proposed suggests that social ties and status are both related to longevity, the former, perhaps, being most important. Women generally have social ties whether they live alone or not, but they lack status particularly when they live with a family without being its head ("doubly dependent"). Men have status whether they live alone or not (by virtue of their role), but they may lack social ties without a family. This study (reported in *Psychology Today*, January 1977) suggests that certain aspects of the sex-role stereotypes may indeed be "lethal" for certain women and men.

Another similarity with the data on emotional problems is the suggestion that doctors may be biased in favor of male physical complaints (Schmeck, Jr., 1979). A limited survey of medical records done

Table 9-2
Percent Higher Mortality Rates of Single Persons Compared to Married Persons of Same Sex

	Males	Females
Unmarried compared to married, family head	40%	19%
Unmarried compared to married, living with a family, not head	60%	100%
Unmarried compared to married, living alone	94%	27%

Data from "The Life-Giving Properties of Marriage," *Psychology Today*, 1977, 20–22. (Based on a national cross-section of 20,000 individuals by Kobrin and Hendershot.)

on the West Coast found that, when age, geography, socioeconomic status, and type of complaint were controlled for, the only variable that correlated with the extent of the medical workup was the sex of the patient. Men received more extensive workups than women, suggesting that illness in men is taken more seriously. Perhaps that is why doctors prescribe mood-modifying drugs at least twice as often for their female patients as for male patients (Scarf, 1979; Gomberg, 1979)—to mollify their "complaints."

In sum, sex-role stereotypes appear to contribute, in part, to the higher rates in men than in women of serious physical problems. They also seem to account for differences in treatment for men and for women.

SUMMARY

The evidence shows that the sex-role stereotypes have a variety of negative consequences on the individual level, affecting one's self-concept, behavior, and mental and physical health. In regard to self-concept, it has been demonstrated that, for females, strong sex typing is associated with low self-confidence, low expectations, and a generally negative self-image. For males, sex typing is associated with high expectations, low self-acceptance, and a generally positive, albeit unrealistic, self-image. These differences in self-concept, combined with other aspects of the stereotypes, have direct consequences on one's behavior—strongly sex-typed females perform poorly in "masculine" situations and activities requiring competition, independence, or assertiveness, all of which are abilities needed to function effectively in an industrial, competitive society; strongly sex-typed males perform poorly in "feminine" situations and activities requiring empathy, nurturance, or expressiveness, which are needed in relating effectively to other individuals. Thus, to the extent that an individual is strongly sex typed, she or he is restricted from living a full and rewarding life.

Of even greater importance is the effect of the stereotypes on one's mental and physical health. The more strongly sex typed the individual, the more psychologically and socially maladjusted she or he tends to be, this being especially true for females. Married women in particular have the highest incidence of serious emotional problems, a consequence of the strain involved in their roles and the differing standards used to judge mental health in females and in males. Single males and unemployed males also show high rates of emotional disturbance, resulting from the strains of their roles. In addition, males in general are more likely than females to suffer from physical diseases and to die young, a possible result of the strains of their role-defined behaviors and of their limited means of tension release.

This picture of the consequences of sex-role stereotypes would be gloomy indeed if there also did not exist a model of a viable alternative. By examining those individuals who are not strongly sex typed

—that is, the nearly one-third of Americans who are androgynous—a picture emerges of individuals who can function effectively in a variety of situations, who tend to be more intelligent, and, even more importantly, who tend to be more emotionally well adjusted than strongly sex-typed individuals. Thus, these people serve as a reminder of the alternatives to the stereotyping trap. By increasing the variety of behaviors allowed in male and female roles, there is also the likelihood of decreasing emotional tension and enhancing the personal growth for members of both sexes. And, although there may be problems involved in such a changeover, the results of so doing certainly seem worthwhile.

RECOMMENDED READING

American Psychological Association Task Force on Sex Bias and Sex-Role Stereotyping in Psychotherapeutic Practice. Source materials for nonsexist therapy. *JSAS Catalog of Selected Documents in Psychology*, 1978, MS. 1685. Materials intended for use in the education and training of psychotherapists. Includes survey results.

Gomberg, E. S., & Franks, V. (Eds.). *Gender and disordered behavior: Sex differences in psychopathology*. New York: Brunner/Mazel, 1979. Excellent collection of recent research on sex differences in the expression of a wide range of psychopathological behaviors.

Jourard, S. *The transparent self*. Cincinnati, Ohio: Van Nostrand & Reinhold, 1971. A sensitive argument about the importance of self-disclosure for the mental and physical health of human beings.

Spence, J. T., & Helmreich, R. L. *Masculinity & femininity: The psychological dimensions, correlates and antecedents*. Austin: University of Texas Press, 1978. A review of the impressive research done by the authors and their colleagues in this area, particularly with regard to personality and achievement behaviors.

Tresemer, D. W. *Fear of success*. New York: Plenum, 1977. Thorough review of the history and status of the concept of "fear of success."

10 | Relationship Consequences

A couple with their 5-year-old daughter visits some friends who have a 5-year-old son. As the parents become involved in conversation, the boy tells his parents that he and the girl will go upstairs to his bedroom and play. Although the girl's parents do not consider this statement noteworthy, the boy's father remarks with a sly smile "It won't be long before we'd think twice about letting them do that!"

This anecdote, modeled on a true story told by Sandra Bem, demonstrates that we have clear expectations regarding male-female relationships. Young children can have same- and other-sex friends. As children mature, however, we assume mixed-sex friendships will lead to sexual and/or romantic involvements. Such expectations are very much shaped by the sex-role stereotypes of our society.

In the previous chapter, the consequences to the individual of defining self in terms of sex-role stereotypes were examined. In many ways, the most negative consequences (lower self-confidence, higher incidence of emotional disturbances, lower achievement) occurred predominantly in females, although males, as a group, certainly had their share of problems (for example, shorter life expectancy). In this chapter, the consequences for relationships of adherence to the stereotypes will be reviewed. It will become apparent that somewhat more negative consequences occur for males as a group than for females as a group, although, again, females also may suffer significantly.

This difference in area of most impairment (individual level for females; relationship level for males) parallels the differential emphasis on the appropriate sphere of activity for the sexes. Females generally are expected to operate on a relationship, or *communal*, level and are encouraged to develop related skills—interpersonal sensitivity, empathy, emotional expressiveness, nurturance. These skills facilitate females' expected major role, that of mother. Females generally are not expected to be independent or assertive, and many females, in fact, have difficulty demonstrating these qualities. For males, the picture is reversed—they are expected to be agentic, independent, achievement oriented, and aggressive. These qualities facilitate the assumption of their expected major role, that of breadwinner. Males generally are not expected to be relationship oriented, except as it may further their individual goals, such as sexual achievement and professional advancement. Most males are not encouraged to develop relationship skills and are taught, instead, to hide their emotions. Indeed, research has found that men who disclose personal information are liked less than those who do not self-disclose (Chelune, 1976; Derlega & Chaikin, 1976). Such self-disclosing men may be considered poorly adjusted. In contrast, women who disclose themselves are liked more than those who do not self-disclose. Such women are likely to be considered well adjusted. Masking of emotion by males may facilitate competitive strivings, but it may also hinder the development of intimate relationships. Consequently, many men experience great difficulty in the area of relationships, which may be manifested in feelings of emptiness, isolation, and frustration.

For both sexes, the negative effects on relationships of believing in the sex-role stereotypes are far-reaching. In this chapter, the effects on friendships, love relationships, and parental relationships will be examined.

FRIENDSHIPS

The term *friendship* has been used to describe a variety of relationships, from those with casual acquaintances to those with colleagues to those with intimates. In this discussion, *friendship* refers to an intimate, personal, caring relationship with attributes such as reciprocity, mutual choice, trust, loyalty, and openness (Strommen, 1977). As was discussed in Chapter Four, males and females generally have different types of friendships—boys tend to have more numerous and less intimate relationships ("gangs"); girls tend to have two or three close relationships and to use them more for interpersonal exploration. This pattern is by no means universal. Furthermore, individuals of both sexes choose friends who are similar to themselves. Kandel (1978) found in her study of nearly 2000 adolescents that both female and male friendships are characterized by similarity of sex, race, age, school grade, and certain behaviors, such as illicit drug taking. Similarity on personality characteristics is relatively unimportant.

An experimental study with 7- and 8-year-olds (Foot, Chapman, & Smith, 1977) found that, for both sexes, friendships facilitated social responsiveness. Social responsiveness was defined as laughing, smiling, talking, looking at the companion, and touching. Children showed more expressive behaviors when watching a cartoon when paired with a friend than they did when they were paired with a stranger. Intimacy of the interactions was also varied by having the pair of children either sit close together (1 m. apart) and draw pictures of each other (high-intimacy condition) or sit with a screen separating them (low-intimacy condition). Results showed that girls felt more comfortable (smiled more, laughed less) with a higher level of intimacy than did boys. Since the later development of love relationships is facilitated by the capacity for intimacy, which first develops in same-sex friendships (Strommen, 1977), these results may have serious implications. If some males are uncomfortable with intimacy and form less intimate friendships, this situation suggests negative consequences for their future love and marital relationships.

Although adolescence is a time in which friendships are most intense, adults, too, benefit from the support and enrichment of self that close friends can provide. Here, again, research suggests that male friendships may be less intimate than those of females. Crawford (cited by Horn, 1978) studied 306 married couples in their 40s, 50s, and 60s. She found that many more women than men said they had a close friend. Of the women in the study, 63% specifically named someone of the same sex as their best friend. In contrast, 60% of the men named a married couple as their best friends. Furthermore, women defined friendships in terms of trust and confidentiality, whereas men emphasized companionship. Similar sex differences were found in a study of the friendship patterns of noninstitutionalized adults over 70 years old (Powers & Bultena, 1976). A closer look at the nature of female-female, male-male, and male-female friendships of all ages seems warranted.

Female-Female Friendships

As has been noted above, girls as a group are more likely than boys as a group to have close, intimate relationships with a small number of people. The manner in which young girls relate to each other is also quite different from how young boys relate together. Bardwick (1979) describes the typical pattern of friendships between girls as alternating between intimacy and repudiation. Most girls either experience or observe a close relationship between "best friends" that is broken by a third girl, only to have the triad reassemble in a different configuration shortly thereafter. This pattern may arise because more overt forms of aggression and dominance are not sanctioned for girls. Thus, covert aggression takes place. Such aggression can be even more potent than overt aggression (Feshbach & Feshbach, 1973). These experiences may lay the groundwork for girls to develop a core sense of mistrust of other females. This groundwork is established even before boys become the object of female-female competition.

During adolescence, female friendships are particularly intense, with great concern over sensitivity to others and mutual trust (Strommen, 1977). Friends are an important source of emotional support in personal crises. Female adolescents rank interpersonal relationships as third in importance, after identity and sexuality, as an area of concern. For males, autonomy ranks third in importance, the first two concerns being identical to those noted for girls.

Once dating begins, a change in friendship patterns frequently occurs. The capacity for closeness and intimacy developed in same-sex relationships begins to generalize to heterosexual relationships. Friendships become more neutral and playful and, in some cases, competitive. Since, traditionally, a female's identity has been determined by the status of the male to whom she is attached, like, for example, the high school football captain, girls may come to view other girls as competitors for the high-status males, thereby limiting friendships. Or they may view friendships with girls as unimportant, since no status accrues from such relationships. It is not uncommon for girls to break plans with their girl friends if a "date" comes along. The girl friend even is supposed to understand "the way it is." One consequence is that many females feel isolated (Chafetz, 1978; Strommen, 1977).

Once married, if a woman is primarily a homemaker, she has few opportunities to meet other women to form friendships. She is likely therefore to remain isolated. A further inhibiting factor in forming adult friendships is the generally deprecatory view that society has of women and that many women have accepted of each other. Many women believe that other women are gossipy, untrustworthy, and uninteresting. This view affects their interest in forming friendships with other women (Strommen, 1977). This deprecatory view of women may be held particularly by those women who have achieved some measure of success in male-dominated fields. Although such women might be expected to help other women after succeeding in their own struggles against sexist practices and expectations, research reveals that the reverse is more likely to be true. Women who achieve in male-dominated fields tend to identify with their male co-workers and superiors. Consequently, they tend to adopt the view that they have made it because they are different from most women. This attitude and the resulting behaviors have been termed the *Queen Bee syndrome* (Staines, Tavris, & Jayaratne, 1974).

If women manage to overcome the above obstacles, however, the resulting friendships tend to be deep and rewarding. Fortunately, since the rise of the feminist movement, increasing numbers of women have challenged the sex-role stereotypes and traditional patterns of relating to other women. Through consciousness-raising groups, activities, meetings, and so on, women have learned to give and receive support from other women in meaningful ways.

Male-Male Friendships

Despite the popular image of the closeness of male "buddies," in the past few years male writers have acknowledged the poor quality of many male-male relationships (David & Brannon, 1976; Fasteau, 1974; R. Lewis, 1978; Pleck & Sawyer, 1974). Although boys as a group do have some intimate friendships during adolescence, these friendships generally are concerned less with interpersonal intimacy and sensitivity than are those of girls (Strommen, 1977). The "gang" serves as a source of support in case of conflict with adults, rather than as a source of emotional support in personal crises. These generally superficial and often ritualized ways of relating extend into adulthood, when many male friendships tend to focus on shared activities rather than on shared feelings. As a result, many males do not receive maximum benefits from friendships—the relief of being able to release feelings with someone else and receive support, and the opportunity to broaden interests and perspective. In fact, many adult males never have had a close male friend or known what it means to share affection and concern with a male without fear of ridicule (H. Goldberg, 1976; Komarovsky, 1974).

The barriers to emotional intimacy between males stem from the male sex-role stereotype as inculcated through socialization practices—the emphasis on independence and competition, suppression of feelings and self-disclosure, and an instilled fear of homosexuality. These barriers will be examined next.

Competition. Most males are socialized early into believing that actions are more important than feelings and that they must compete in everything they do to "win" or come out on top. This intense male competition may pervade nearly every area of encounter among men, including sports, work, sex, and conversation. It makes intimate relationships among men most unlikely (Fasteau, 1974; Komarovsky, 1974; R. Lewis, 1978; Pleck, 1976b; Townsend, 1977). Because some males always are comparing themselves to other males, some relationships among men tend to be awkward and uncomfortable, sometimes marked by distrust and by an undercurrent of violence. It is difficult to be supportive toward people with whom one is competing.

Self-Disclosure. An even more important factor than competitiveness in inhibiting male friendships is the strong message most boys receive to suppress feelings and, particularly, to suppress the *disclosure* of feelings. Thus, maxims such as "Big boys don't cry," "Keep a stiff upper lip," and "Take it like a man" all pressure boys to keep their feelings hidden. If boys do not hide their emotions, they are likely to suffer marked loss in prestige (such as when Edmund Muskie's public opinion ratings dropped after he shed a few tears during the 1972 Presidential primary), to be liked less (Chelune, 1976), and to have difficulty assuming the competitive role society has set out for them. By sharing feelings, people become vulnerable. In a competitive atmosphere, this means that someone might take advantage of such vulnerability. According to male sex-role prescriptions, showing feelings is "weak" and must be avoided at all costs.

As a consequence of the above stereotyped beliefs, males tend to be low in self-disclosure, beginning to cover up their feelings as early as age 4. Research has found, however, that the quality that most facilitates friendship formation is openness to others (Jourard, 1971; Strommen, 1977). Such openness may arise through willingness to reveal oneself (high self-disclosure) and/or through open-mindedness (low dogmatism). Males who have incorporated the stereotyped male sex-role expectations and are low in self-disclosure are at a marked disadvantage in forming close relationships. Low self-disclosure also explains why many male conversations tend to be monologues rather than give-and-take communications, since responding to another may reveal feelings (Fasteau, 1974; Henley, 1977). Another reason male conversations tend to be monologues may be because both of the men involved may try to dominate and interrupt the conversation.

Homophobia. Related to this fear of expressing feelings is an even more specific fear of expressing *positive* feelings toward other males

—the fear of being thought a homosexual *(homophobia)*. Imagine one man asking another to come over to his place just to talk, not to watch TV, go to a bar, or get together with other men or women. If the first time this happened, the man who was asked did not feel a little uncomfortable about possible implications, he would be unusual (Fasteau, 1974).

This homophobia is so pervasive that intimacy between males often is deliberately suppressed. Fathers stop kissing and hugging sons; boys stop touching each other except in ritualized ways (handshakes, shoulder slaps, and fanny patting in sports). A stigma is attached to anything vaguely feminine (Brannon, 1976; McCandless, 1970). As Lehne (1976) and Morin and Garfinkle (1978) note, homophobia is not rational, since most beliefs about homosexuals are false. The majority of homosexuals are not afraid of women, do not appear effeminate, are not limited to a few occupations, do not molest children, and are not psychologically abnormal or even unusual. Homophobia, then, is not a specifically sexual fear but rather a political one. It is related to a range of personality characteristics typical of prejudiced individuals: authoritarianism, conservative support of the status quo, and rigidity of sex roles. The best single predictor of homophobia is a belief in the traditional family ideology—a dominant father and a subservient mother. Individuals (male and female) with nontraditional sex-role behaviors, attitudes, and personality characteristics are least likely to hold negative attitudes toward homosexuals (Montgomery & Burgoon, 1977; Riddle & Sang, 1978). The real issue, as Lehne and Morin and Garfinkle conclude, is the general maintenance by men of a society in which men control power through the regulation of sex roles. Homophobia serves this purpose by defining and reinforcing sex-role distinctions and the associated distribution of power. It keeps men within the boundaries of traditionally-defined roles.

An experimental study by Karr (1978) exemplifies this social control factor. A group of college men were led to believe that one member of their group was homosexual. The labeled male was perceived by others in the group as being significantly less masculine and less preferred as a fellow participant in a future experiment than when the same individual had not been so labeled in a different group. Furthermore, the man in the group responsible for labeling the targeted individual (both men actually were experimental confederates) was perceived as more masculine and more sociable when he did the labeling than when, in another group, he did not. These results suggest that men are reinforced for publicly identifying homosexual men and that men have good reason to fear being labeled "homosexual." The negative reactions to the labeled male and positive reactions to the labeler were even stronger when the subjects were homophobic men.

The price paid by men for conforming to male role expectations is great, since conforming to the male stereotype seriously impairs both same-sex and heterosexual relationships, causes severe anxiety, and narrows the range of legitimate male emotions, interests, and activities. In conjunction with this interpretation, Fasteau (1974) hypothesizes that the real function of all-male groups is to provide mutual assurance of masculinity, to make personal communication difficult, and to defuse any assumption of intensity of feelings. Lehne (1976) argues that homophobia must be eliminated before a change in sex roles can be brought about. Dispelling homophobia clearly is necessary before close male relationships can occur.

Role Models.   R. Lewis (1978) suggests a fourth barrier to the expression of emotional intimacy between men to be the lack of *role models* for such behaviors. We do not see many examples of affection giving between males, even between fathers and sons. This barrier is both a cause and an effect of sex-role training and has a cyclical effect on succeeding generations. That is, if a young boy grows up without seeing intimate emotions expressed between men, he most likely will inhibit his emotional expressiveness when he becomes an adult. Consequently, he will not be able to serve as a role model for such expressive behaviors for other young men. The pattern thus is likely to continue.

Male-Female Friendships

If male-male friendships are difficult to establish, male-female ones are even more so. The frequent sexual segregation of activities limits opportunities for meeting other-sex peers, and the perceived inequality in status between the sexes also makes other-sex friendships unlikely (Strommen, 1977). The stereotypes themselves play a large part in inhibiting such relationships. Both males and females tend to believe that members of the other sex are significantly different from themselves in attitudes, interests, and personal styles, even though actual sex differences in these areas are small and certainly are not found consistently (Borges, Levine, & Naylor, 1978; H. Freeman, 1979; Strommen, 1977; Unger & Siiter, 1975). Furthermore, in some cases, boys' early socialization to reject anything vaguely feminine may lead to fear and hatred of females (Fasteau, 1974; Korda, 1973). Such feelings are unlikely to facilitate friendship formation between the sexes. During adolescence, the emphasis by females on viewing males as potential mates and by males on viewing females as sex objects further mitigates against the development of male-female friendships (Chafetz, 1978; Townsend, 1977).

As Figure 10-1 indicates, adherence to the sex-role stereotypes may make communication between the sexes difficult. Ickes and Barnes (1978) studied this question by forming mixed-sex dyads of male and female undergraduates on the basis of their sex-role orientation as measured by the BSRI. The dyads were simply left in a room to await further instructions. The researchers found pronounced differences in the nature of the 5-minute interactions that ensued. Specifically, the dyads composed of a sex-typed male and a sex-typed female showed significantly greater interpersonal incompatibility and stress than did dyads in which one or both members were androgynous. For example, sex-typed couples verbalized to each other less and had less positive feelings about the interaction than did

Figure 10-1
How adherence to sex-role stereotypes can affect relationships between the sexes. (Copyright Bülbül, 1973. Reprinted by permission.)

other dyads. Ickes and Barnes account for these findings by assuming that sex-typed males and females adopt highly stereotyped and socially opposed sex roles in such unstructured situations. The authors rule out the possibility that the sex-typed individuals were more socially distant or less physically attractive than the non-sex-typed members of the other dyads. Differences in expressive control (masculine-sex-typed individuals controlling their emotional expressiveness more than feminine-sex-typed individuals) may compound the effects of the sex roles themselves in such situations. The result is that, in situations like the interaction described above, the stereotyped sex roles are dysfunctional in forming relationships. In actual practice, however, such effects may be somewhat mitigated by situational factors such as past history and external cues. For example, in more familiar and typical social situations, stereotyped male verbal dominance and stereotyped female verbal reticence may lead to positive feelings about an interaction.

Another factor that may explain the findings of Ickes and Barnes (1978) is the perceived interpersonal attractiveness of sex-typed persons. Kulik and Harackiewicz (1979) found that male and female high school students, regardless of their sex type, consistently preferred, as friends, androgynous individuals of the other sex, rather than sex-typed individuals of the other sex. Undifferentiated individuals of the other sex were the least popular choices for friends.

The frequently found difference in self-disclosure between the sexes also inhibits friendship formation. Although it appears that women are more likely than men to receive self-disclosures *from* men (Chafetz, 1978; Komarovsky, 1974; Olstad, 1975), communication is not necessarily two-way. Rather, females often provide a listening and support service ("ego boosting") for males without receiving any reciprocal service. Some males may not know how to listen or give support; others may not realize such behaviors are desired (Chafetz, 1978; Pleck, 1976a).

Male-female friendships do occur, but society conspires against them. In fact, the very idea of platonic relationships between the sexes often is scoffed at, as the anecdote beginning this chapter implies. Instead, members of the two sexes are systematically steered into romantic relationships.

ROMANTIC RELATIONSHIPS

If friendship formation is affected by sex-role stereotypes, the establishment of more intimate relationships is affected by them even more. Dating, marriage, and sexual interactions all reflect society's messages about appropriate male-female behavior. Since sexual behavior was discussed in Chapter Five, only dating and marital relationships will be examined here.

Dating

On the average, dating begins shortly after puberty, at about age 14 for girls and age 15 for boys (Strommen, 1977). With it begin many anxieties about sex role and sexual competence. For both sexes, many dating and romantic involvements serve instrumental purposes— peer acceptance and conformity to sex-role expectations—and not necessarily emotional ones. In fact, true intimacy often actually is discouraged between the sexes by the stereotypic emphasis on sexual achievement for males and by the stereotypic emphasis on attracting a mate for females. Being viewed as a status symbol by females may make some males feel superior, but it also may make them unduly attached to status-attaining activities such as athletics. Similarly, being viewed as a sexual object by males may make some females feel denigrated, but it also may cause some females to be overconcerned with their physical appearance. For both males and females, trusting the other sex would be difficult. Intimacy also is discouraged by the highly ritualized nature of most dating situations and by the inequality in the dating relationship itself (Laws & Schwartz, 1977; Strommen, 1977). Traditionally, males do the asking and initiating; females can only refuse or accept. In addition, the training of many males to avoid expressing emotions is an impediment to open communication.

Another factor affecting dating relationships is the traditional emphasis on *male dominance*, especially in intellectual matters. This "ideal" has been modified in recent years and the norm now is more one of equality and intellectual companionship (Komarovsky, 1973; Pleck, 1976b). One consequence of the fact that norms are changing, is that females are less likely to hide their intellectual capabilities than they were previously (Komarovsky, 1946; 1973). Yet, there are indications that many college-aged males actually are ambivalent in this regard. Since about half of all college students are female, the likelihood of female intellectual equality and even superiority occurring in choosing a dating partner is high. Komarovsky (1973, 1976), in her study of male seniors at an Eastern Ivy League college, found that 30% of the men experienced some anxiety about not being intellectually superior to their dating partners. Of the 70% who expressed a desire for intellectual equality with their dating partners, most of the men in the study still felt their future wife should spend at least some of her life being a full-time homemaker, a role they held in low esteem. Olstad (1975) found similar results with a Midwestern college population. The ambivalence that college males have regarding their wife working can lead to conflict and frustration in marital relations if the spouse is truly equal or if the woman has other expectations.

Peplau and colleagues (Peplau, Rubin, & Hill, 1976, 1977), in their two-year study of 231 dating couples in Boston, found college men to be consistently more traditional than women regarding their preferred marriage option. (*Traditional* refers to the preference for the pattern of employed husband and nonemployed wife.) Table 10-1 presents the forced-choice response of Peplau et al.'s couples to a question about their marriage preference in 15 years. Although dual-career marriage is popular among a sizable number of students of both sexes, it is 17% more popular among women than men. And the traditional marriage with the wife not working is preferred by only 5% of the women but by 20% of the men. Such differences in preferences could cause problems in a marriage.

A 1977 national survey of high school seniors by Herzog, Bachman, and Johnston (cited in *ISR Newsletter*, Spring 1979, p. 3) revealed a similar pattern of opinions, although the questions were not as personally relevant as for Peplau et al.'s sample. In the Herzog et al. study, the pattern of both marital partners working full time was opposed by 25% of the males but by only 14% of the females. Three times as many females as males (38% to 13%) completely rejected the traditional pattern of employed husband and nonemployed wife.

Table 10-1
Fifteen-Year Plans of Dating Couples

	Males	Females
Single	6%	6%
Wife not working	20%	5%
Wife working part time	26%	24%
Wife working full time (dual career)	48%	65%

Adapted from Peplau, Rubin, & Hill, 1977.

Thus, although norms may be changing, they are changing more for females than for males.

Another indication that more men than women have traditional expectations of their romantic partners is a finding from Kulik and Harackiewicz's (1979) study of high school students. Although males tended to prefer androgynous females over feminine and undifferentiated females for friendships, males tended to prefer feminine females for romantic relationships. High school girls, however, consistently preferred androgynous males over masculine and undifferentiated males for both types of relationships.

In the Peplau et al. (1976) study, dating couples overwhelmingly favored equality as the norm in their relationships in intellectual and other areas. This ideal contrasted strongly with reality, however— less than half the couples actually felt there was equality in their particular relationship. When individuals perceived an imbalance of power, it was usually in the direction of male dominance.

Equality in relationships was hard to achieve. Three factors worked against it: (1) a belief in sex-role stereotypes (the more traditional, the more male power), (2) the relative involvement of one of the couple (the less the involvement, the greater the power), and (3) the woman's educational career goals (the lower the goals, the greater the male power). Neither sex-role attitude nor the amount of male dominance in the relationship was a good predictor of whether a couple would break up or remain together, however. What was most important was the sharing of attitudes and values. When partners disagreed, the relationship generally was short-lived.

Similarity of ideology may not be important for all couples, however. Grush and Yehl (1979) found that sex and ideology interact when it comes to judgments of interpersonal attractiveness. Female college students with nontraditional attitudes toward sex roles in marriage had distinct preferences for partners who shared their ideology. Traditional college men also had a preference for partners with ideologies similar to theirs. Both groups rated similar other-sex individuals as more likeable and as more desirable as dating and marital partners than they did other-sex individuals who had dissimilar views. For traditional women and nontraditional men, on the other hand, partner similarity was not important for ratings of likeability and desirability. The researchers suggest that this interaction between sex and traditionality is due to the possibility that nontraditional women and traditional men have irreconcilable differences that would make constant conflicts likely. In contrast, traditional women and nontraditional men are more likely to be adaptable to their partner's preferences.

Even when both partners are traditionally stereotyped, however, men and women may not fit together very well. As discussed above, Ickes and Barnes (1978) found sex-typed couples to be more incompatible in their interactions in an unstructured laboratory setting than couples in which at least one member was androgynous. Thus, although some matching of ideology and traits is probably needed for a couple to get together in the first place, the exact mix needed is not clear.

What happens when the sexes do get romantically involved with each other? How do the sex-role stereotypes affect behaviors in romantic relationships?

Although women generally are thought of as emotional and likely to fall in love easily, research suggests that men tend to fall harder. Men rate the *desire to fall in love* as a stronger motive in starting a relationship than do women, and they are more upset when their relationship breaks up than are women (Hill, Rubin, & Peplau, 1976; Seaman, 1972). It may be that, as a result of sex-role socialization, women become more adept at cognitively managing their feelings. Alternatively, since women traditionally have been so dependent on their mate for their own status and economic situation, they may need to be more practical and utilitarian than do men in choosing a mate. In contrast, men traditionally have been freer to "follow their fancy." Perhaps with the economic liberation of women, they, too, will become freer to marry for love or become less likely to marry at all. The recent reports of increased age of both sexes upon entering first marriages (Van Dusen & Sheldon, 1976) may indicate that women no longer have to get married to survive in this culture. It is also possible that the later age at which first marriages occur reflects the changing norms regarding premarital sex. Men no longer have to get married just to get sex. The fact that most people eventually do get married may mean that at least some marriages currently are being based on more than practical necessity. If so, these marriages may be stronger and last longer than those already in existence. A closer look at marital relationships is warranted.

Marriage

From the dating situation, men and women often move into marriage. Such a progression is no longer inevitable, especially in recent years (see J. Ramey, 1976, for an interesting discussion of alternatives). More and more couples are deciding to live together without a marriage ceremony. By the Census Bureau's conservative estimates, 1.1 million mixed-sex couples were estimated to be living together in 1978, more than twice the number that existed in 1970 and three times the number in 1960 (*New York Times*, July 1, 1979). Those under age 25 account for most of the increase. More women also are deciding to remain unattached (Van Dusen & Sheldon, 1976). Still, about 90% of the U.S. population will marry at some point in their lives. Such figures attest to the continued popularity of marriage itself or, at least, to the acceptance of the stereotype that a "normal" adult is a married one.

Traditionally, marriage has been viewed as one of two major goals of a female's life, the other being the bearing of children. Once the marriage goal is attained, a woman has been expected to give up all other interests and devote herself to satisfying her husband's needs and those of her future children. See Figure 10-2 for a tongue-in-cheek look at what a marriage proposal might really mean. Reinforced by marriage laws, customs, and beliefs, this sexist view of a happy mar-

Figure 10-2
What marriage might really mean. (From I'm Training to Be Tall and Blonde, *by Nicole Hollander. Copyright 1979 by Nicole Hollander. Reprinted by permission of St. Martin's Press, Inc.)*

riage has remained the ideal until challenged by the women's liberation movement.

Marriage as a legal contract is based on a legal doctrine known as *coverture*. Although this doctrine has been modified in most states in the past 20 years, before 1960, this doctrine meant that, upon marriage, the wife loses her legal existence and is considered an extension of her husband's will and identity (Women in Transition, 1975). A wife takes on her husband's name and place of residence, gives up her right to accuse her husband of rape (he is legally entitled to her sexual services), and agrees to provide domestic services without financial compensation. The husband agrees to provide shelter, food, and clothing for his wife and children according to his ability. A wife has no legal right to any part of her husband's cash income or any say in how it is spent. Although each state has its own marriage laws and there has been an increasing trend to define marriage partners as equals, in many states the above legal elements still hold. For example, in all but four states (Delaware, Iowa, Oregon, and New Jersey), a wife cannot accuse her husband of rape, even if they are legally separated. Louisiana has a *head-and-master* law that allows a husband to sell the family home without his wife's consent and to cut off her credit even if she has her own salary (from *National NOW Times*, August 1978, p. 2). Few women or men, in contemplating marriage, consider these legal implications. If the relationship does not work out satisfactorily, however, these legalities may become extremely important.

In one type of analysis, marriage can be viewed as a bargaining situation—women trade domestic work and sex for financial support; men get their basic needs satisfied for a price (DeBeauvoir, 1953; Friedan, 1963). Few Americans think of marriage in these terms, however. In our culture, although it has not always been true and certainly is not true in many other cultures, romantic love is idealized as the basis for marriage. Unfortunately, romantic love, involving strong sexual attraction and idealization of the partner, is not a very sound basis for making a supposedly lifelong commitment. The first real test of a relationship is surviving the inevitable process of partial disillusionment. Consequently, the longer a couple have known each other before making a commitment, the better the prognosis for the relationship (Ferguson, 1977).

Some writers suggest that the current extremely high divorce rate (nearly one out of every two marriages ends in divorce) is due to the assumption that romantic love is necessary for a satisfactory marriage. Prince Charming will meet the Princess and they will live happily ever after. Lederer and Jackson (1968) argue that companionability, tolerance, respect, honesty, and a desire to stay together for mutual advantage are the crucial elements in marital success, not a feeling of living for another person. These qualities characterize intimate friendships. As was noted above, the likelihood of such friendships forming between the sexes is small, and males, in particular, prefer a different type of woman for romance than for friendship (Kulik & Harackiewicz, 1979). Yet, tradition and the media have led people, especially women, to believe and expect that finding true love means happiness ever after. A wife's general life happiness and overall well-being are more dependent upon marital happiness than are her husband's, and women consequently experience more dissatisfaction with their marriages than do men (Donelson, 1977b). When the disillusionment comes, many marriages do not survive.

Another factor related to marital happiness is the wife's career. Half of all married women work outside the home (U.S. Dept. of Labor, 1979a). In traditional marriages, a wife's career, if it exists at all, is clearly secondary to that of her husband. If he moves, she must move also, making planning for her own career difficult. More commonly, if a child or children are involved, they traditionally are considered the wife's responsibility. Such responsibility may necessitate her withdrawing from the labor force partially or completely, temporarily or permanently. It is no surprise, then, that women scientists, who may be viewed as having a strong professional commitment, have a much lower marriage rate than male scientists or female nonscientists (Cuca, 1976). For example, in 1975, only 53% of female Ph.D. psychologists were married, compared to 90% of male Ph.D. psychologists and 68% of women in the general population. Psychology seems to foster marriage for men (only 75% of men in the general population were married in 1975). Yet psychology seems to undermine marriage for women, perhaps because of the disproportionate pressures placed upon women professionals. This pattern characterizes other scientific fields as well.

Men's attitudes about working wives are particularly influential in determining a wife's attempt to combine a career and a satisfying marriage. Indeed, such attitudes seem to determine the happiness of the marriage itself (Bailyn, 1970; Horner, 1970). In particular, marriages of career-oriented men to women who want to integrate career and family life are not very happy. This may be because no one is caring for home or family to either parent's satisfaction or because of competition between the partners. A longitudinal study of 51 male college graduates (Winter, Stewart, & McClelland, 1977) found that the greater the male's power motivation, the lower the likelihood of his wife's working and/or the lower the level of his wife's career. The power-motivated man may choose a non-career-oriented wife, or he may use his power to suppress her career goals once married. In the latter case, the marriage itself may be adversely affected (Seidenberg, 1973).

In point of fact, mismatched marriages are unlikely to occur. Peplau and colleagues (1976, 1977) found in their longitudinal study of dating couples that couples mismatched regarding attitudes about dual-career marriages were nearly twice as likely as other couples (41% compared to 26%) to break up in the year following the initial testing. Such couples also were less satisfied with their relationships while they were together.

Dual-career marriages are difficult. The practical problems are many, especially if children are involved. And there is often the added pressure that arises from feeling that one is deviating from the social norm. The fact that there are more exceptions to, than examples of, the norm does not much help. Yet many couples seem to be making such arrangements work, usually to the benefit of all involved. (See Bardwick, 1979, and Rapoport, Rapoport, & Bumstead, 1978, for an interesting discussion of the key processes involved.)

If a couple has bought the romantic expectation of marriage and the traditional marital roles that go with it, a number of consequences are possible. If these expectations are not actualized, a couple might break up, they might try to transcend the stereotypes and grow as individuals and as a couple, or they might ignore the differences and work around them. The last solution is the most common (Chafetz, 1978). However, when differences are ignored, a wife may feel unfulfilled and try to get some compensation from her husband via money, material things, or vicarious achievements. In turn, a husband may feel increasingly resentful that his expectations have not been fulfilled, and he may withdraw defensively from his wife. From this sequence of events comes the nagging-wife/withdrawn-husband pattern of marital interaction that is the butt of so many jokes and appears so often in the offices of marriage counselors.

If the stereotypes are lived up to, the emotional cost for both sexes still may be great. A woman financially and emotionally dependent upon her husband can be an enormous burden. A fully stereotyped male usually is unable to satisfy his wife's emotional needs and may, in fact, find them threatening. In addition, the less similar two people's daily activities are, the more difficult is any form of communication between them. One person spending an entire day doing housework and child care usually is not a very stimulating or interesting partner for someone who spends the entire day working outside the home, as some recent househusbands have learned (for example, Roache, 1972).

As was discussed in Chapter Nine, marriage appears to benefit men more so than women both physically and emotionally. The paradox here is that many men stereotypically view marriage as a trap, yet, statistically speaking, it does them a world of good, and they tend to remarry quickly if divorced or widowed (Bardwick, 1979; Bernard, 1973). Research (P. Brown & Fox, 1979) has shown that divorce appears to have more adverse consequences on the health of the divorced man than it does for the divorced woman. For many women, who stereotypically view marriage as their ultimate goal in life, marriage seems to be somewhat of a health hazard, at least according to statistics. A wife may experience more stress and strain in marriage than her husband, partly because she typically is the one expected to adapt to her husband's life and not vice versa, and partly because she typically receives little emotional support from him or anyone else. There is considerable evidence that employed wives do not show as severe an effect from marriage as do unemployed wives (Birnbaum, 1975; Ferree, 1976; Hoffman, 1979; Shaver & Freedman, 1976). Compared with working wives, homemakers reported feeling more anxious (46% to 28%), more lonely (44% to 26%), more worthless (41% to 24%), and less happy and satisfied with their lives. Welch (1979) found that employed wives, especially professionals, are more androgynous than are homemakers and are less likely to derive their identity from significant others. In another study (Campbell, 1975), however, married homemakers reported feeling equally as happy as working wives. It may be that some "housewives" do accept and enjoy their situation, since they have achieved their "goal in life."

In conclusion, adherence to the sex-role stereotypes has negative consequences for marital satisfaction and stability, especially for women. The fact that many couples are trying to break out of these patterns suggests that change is possible and may be occurring. Some of the positive consequences of changing the sex-role patterns include the following: (1) inexpressive males who manage to alter their behavior often develop very strong marriages (Balswick & Collier, 1974), (2) marriages based on friendships have a good chance of surviving (Shapiro, 1977), and (3) working wives are happier than full-time homemakers (Hoffman, 1979). A truly open, rewarding relationship is only possible among equals. Breaking away from the sex-role stereotypes is thus imperative.

Marital relationships and friendships usually are voluntary relationships; that is, they are usually entered into intentionally and freely. But another powerful relationship that people have is not so intentional—that between parents and their children. Even if a child is planned, parents cannot predict exactly what characteristics their child will have, yet the relationship between a parent and a child may be the most profound relationship that either will ever have. And these relationships are strongly affected by sex-role stereotypes.

226

**Part Four:
Consequences of
Sex-Role
Stereotypes**

PARENTAL RELATIONSHIPS

For both parents, the birth of a child involves great changes—changes much greater than those involved in marriage. The stressfulness of this period is reflected in the findings that child-free couples describe their lives in more positive terms than those with young children and that child-free women experience less stress than comparable women with children (Campbell, 1975).

Parent-child relationships have been undergoing marked changes in recent years, spurred by the women's liberation movement and resulting changes in sex-role stereotypic behavior, population growth, and control of contraception. Van Dusen and Sheldon (1976) have noted some of the changing patterns. More fathers are taking active roles in child care, and more mothers are working. Figure 10-3 shows the percentage of married women from 1950 to 1976 holding outside employment with husband present.

In 1978, 60% of all mothers with school-aged children worked, which was more than double the number in 1950. The number of mothers in the labor force with children under 6 years old has more than tripled in the same period of time (from 11.9% in 1950 to 42% in 1978). Altogether, nearly half of all mothers are now working, which is a figure comparable to the number of married women without children who are in the labor force. By 1990, only 1 in 4 married women is expected to be a full-time homemaker and mother (*N.Y. Times*, September 25, 1979, p. B9).

Childbearing patterns are changing (David & Baldwin, 1979; Van Dusen & Sheldon, 1976). Women are having fewer children than ever before and are having them later in life. In 1976, the birth rate was an

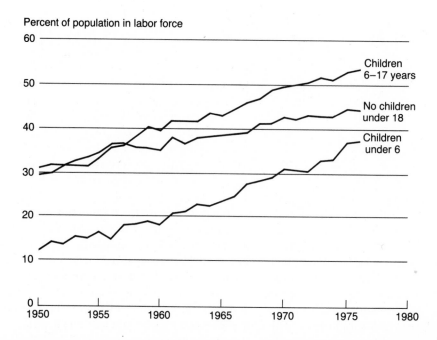

Figure 10-3
Labor force participation rates of married women, husband present, by presence and age of own children, 1950–1976. (From U.S. Dept. of Labor, 1977c.)

average of 1.8 children per family, lower than the level reached during the Depression of the 1930s. The average American family in 1960 had 3.6 children. For women in the 25- to 29-year age range, the increase in the number expecting only two children has been dramatic, from 29% in 1967 to 52% in 1974. Of men aged 18 to 49, in 1978, 58% said they considered two or fewer children to constitute the ideal unit (Brozan, 1979). In addition, more women are deciding to remain child-free. In 1974, 11% of child-free married women under 24 and 27% of child-free married women 25 to 29 years old did not expect to have any children. That's approximately 10% of all married couples. Despite the changes in childbearing, 90% of all couples do have at least one child. Over three-fifths of all college freshmen in 1979 viewed rearing a family as essential or very important (*Chronicle of Higher Education*, January 28, 1980, p. 5), and there has been some suggestion that the declining birth rates are beginning to level off and even reverse themselves (Nordheimer, 1977).

Some of the decline in the birth rate may have been due to a forced-choice situation for some women. Because most career patterns traditionally have ignored childbearing and child-care activities, women who have wanted both a career and a family may have felt forced to choose between the two. To some extent, the women's movement in the 1970s may have contributed to this conflict by emphasizing the importance of work, almost to the exclusion of family life. At the start of the 1980s, the movement has begun to focus on women's desire to have children, as well as on some ways in which family life and work can be better integrated (Friedan, 1979).

Aside from the diminishing size of the family, another type of change in parenting has been the increased interest in the *quality* of parent-child relationships. This interest has focused mainly on mother-daughter and father-daughter relationships, since most of the writers use a feminist perspective (Friday, 1977; D. Lynn, 1979; *Ms.*, June 1979; Stone, 1979). The greatest emphasis has been on the special nature of the mother-daughter bond, with its inherent closeness and consequent challenge for separateness. Unfortunately, the special nature of mother-son and father-son relationships has been neglected.

Sex-role stereotypes significantly affect parent-child relations but in different ways for mothers and for fathers. In fact, father-child relationships, by and large, have been ignored by most researchers —parental behavior has been assumed synonymous with maternal behavior. Therefore, both maternal and paternal relationships will be looked at separately in the following sections.

Mother-Child Relationships

"Why should a man marry a woman who refuses to be a mother to his children? He can get everything else he wants from women at a price much cheaper than marriage" (Schlafly, 1977, p. 51).

As Schlafly's quote illustrates, having children is usually viewed as a justification of female existence. Motherhood is chief among the requirements of female sex typing and has been considered a woman's major goal in life. Some writers (for example, Russo, 1976) go further and assert that, even more than a goal that one theoretically chooses, motherhood is a *mandate* that women are required to fulfill. According to this mandate, every woman should have at least two children and "raise them well"—that is, spend most of her time with them.

Motherhood Mandate.   The Motherhood Mandate is transmitted in numerous ways. One means of transmittal is via restrictions on a woman's ability to control reproduction by limiting contraceptive information and availability of, and access to, abortions. Another way the mandate is transmitted is through the impact of sex-role socialization on the sexual behavior of young people. Although sex is emphasized in our culture, it is rarely connected with pregnancy. (Think of one case in the movies in which the man asks his sex partner if she is using contraception before they have sex.) Hence come the skyrocketing rates of teenage pregnancies. One in every ten girls between the ages of 15 and 19 gets pregnant. Of these pregnant teenagers, 60% actually give birth, accounting for one-fifth of all births in the country today (Fosburgh, 1977).

A third way the Motherhood Mandate gets conveyed is through the psychological restraints brought on by sex-role socialization. Women who fear success in the business world may use family size as a form of achievement. White women with high fear of success have been found to produce larger families than those with low fear of success (Russo, 1976). Two other factors in the transmittal of the mandate are lack of alternative role models and the very real limitations of options.

The effects of such a mandate are quite serious for women. The responsibility of a child limits a mother's access to life options, such as higher education or work. This is especially true for young women who have children, which is particularly disturbing in the face of the soaring rate of teenage pregnancies. The Motherhood Mandate supports job discrimination against women because it maintains that women are likely to get pregnant and quit their jobs. It also produces role conflict in those women who also want careers, since society provides little support for working mothers—few part-time jobs, few day-care centers.

It should be noted that it is not motherhood itself that is under attack but rather the mandate that *all* women should experience motherhood. When motherhood becomes a choice, not a requirement, the quality of the mother-child relationship should improve, as should the happiness of individual women. Some changes are already occurring, as noted above—the birth rate is decreasing, more women are having fewer children at a later age, more women are deciding to remain child-free or have just one child, and more mothers are working. These changes seem to be related to sex-role stereotypes. Clarkson and associates (1970) found that women who viewed themselves as stereotypically feminine tended to have larger families than did women who did not have such a stereotypic self-concept.

Yet, for most mothers, motherhood follows traditional lines prescribed by sex-role standards. Although many women always have expected to be mothers, many find with a jolt that mothering is learned, not innate (Wilborn, 1978). Many mothers undergo a difficult period of postpartum adjustment that is made more difficult by a mother's inability to share her feelings about motherhood. Support for the mother is also important at this time (Boston Women's Health Book Collective, 1976; Ferguson, 1977). Unfortunately, in a typical nuclear family, a mother may receive little support. Her husband may be unable or unwilling to give it, her own mother and other relatives may live at a distance, friends may not be that close, societal supports, like day-care, often are unavailable.

If a mother accepts the Motherhood Mandate and devotes all her time to nurturing her children and her husband, she is likely to lose touch with her own identity and needs and to live her life through others. She also is likely to lose touch with the world outside her domestic circle and have little intellectual stimulation. She is likely to spend a minimum of 80 hours a week in child care and homemaking activities, plus being constantly "on call" for sickcare, entertaining, and so on (Polatnick, 1973). This pattern of activity produces a heavy burden on the woman and on her family. Such mothers are more likely than others to interfere with their children's struggle for autonomy and privacy, to dominate their husbands and children, and to make their family feel guilty continually because they (the mothers) do "so much" (Bart, 1972; Dinkmeyer & McKay, 1973; Ferguson, 1977; Hoffman, 1979; Rossi, 1964; Wilborn, 1978). As was noted previously, a certain amount of pressure on the child towards independence, which is realistically timed, and moderate levels of maternal warmth and protectiveness, facilitate achievement behaviors in children. Thus, overprotective, overnurturing mothers may interfere with the development of achievement behaviors in their children.

Despite the strong belief that mothers should be home with their children, studies of other cultures have found that nowhere do mothers spend as much time with their children as do mid-20th century American mothers. In less complex societies, the job of mothering is shared by other members of an extended family, including husbands, or by institutional supports, such as day-care facilities and children's houses. More importantly, research has shown that it is not in the interest of either the mother or her children for the mother to be kept dependent and housebound. Bronfenbrenner (1974), after reviewing the literature on child development, concludes that "to function effectively as a parent, a mother must also have the opportunity of being a total person" (p. 4). The best arrangement for the development of a young child is one in which the mother is free to work part-time and in which the child is exposed to other caretakers, especially to the father (Bronfenbrenner, 1974; Hoffman, 1979; Mead, 1954).

The factors important for healthy infant and child development include consistent and sensitive care in a stable environment with physical and intellectual stimulation, love, and affection (Ainsworth, 1979; Wortis, 1971). While children need love and attention, they do not need it constantly from their biological mothers. Children respond as well (or better) to multiple mothering, to paternal attachment, or to any other regular caretaker (Beit-Hallahmi & Rabin, 1977; Belsky & Sternberg, 1978; Hoffman, 1974; Mead, 1954; Rubenstein & Howes, 1979). The fear that children will be harmed if mothers do not stay home is a myth that some argue is perpetuated by men because it serves their needs (someone takes care of all domestic responsibilities for them), because it eliminates women from competing with them in the labor force, and because it maintains their superior power position in relation to women (Polatnick, 1973; Seaman, 1972).

Employed Mothers. Perhaps one of the best-kept secrets from the American woman is that maternal employment is not harmful for children. In fact, it may be beneficial. Since, as Figure 10-3 shows, 60% of all mothers with children aged 6 to 18 and more than 40% of all mothers with preschool children are in the labor force, such findings are tremendously important in reducing the guilt working mothers often feel because of the Motherhood Mandate (Hoffman, 1974, 1979). Thomopoulos and Huyck (1976) found that, although employed mothers of preschool children had the same amount of personal and marital happiness as matched unemployed homemakers did, the working mothers felt less satisfied with the job they were doing as mothers. They felt they "should" be spending more time at home. Research (see Hoffman, 1979) has found that employed mothers often compensate for their absence by increasing the amount of direct interaction with the child when they are at home.

In surveying a broad range of studies, Lois Wladis Hoffman (1974, 1977, 1979; Hoffman & Nye, 1974) and others (for example, Etaugh, 1974) found that there is absolutely no evidence that children of employed mothers are neglected or affected adversely on the whole. These children, compared to children of full-time housewives, tend to receive more independence training, have generally higher career goals and somewhat higher achievement motivation, tend to have less traditional conceptions of the sex roles and a more positive evaluation of female competence. These results are particularly true for daughters, perhaps because employed mothers present a positive model of female achievement and because girls, under traditional child rearing, usually do not receive independence training. Sons of middle-class employed mothers do not fare quite as well as do daughters in a few studies involving academic performance, although this finding has not been a consistent one (Hoffman, 1979). A more consistent finding is that middle-class sons of employed mothers tend to be less stereotyped in their conceptions of sex roles and to be better adjusted socially than middle-class sons of nonemployed mothers. Sons of lower-class employed mothers appear to do as well as their sisters in terms of cognitive ability and social adjustment, although the sons tend to be somewhat stereotyped regarding sex roles. The only somewhat negative effect of maternal employment on children has been the attempt by some mothers to overcompensate for their absence. As a result of the fear that they are harming their children by working outside the home, some mothers may give their children fewer limits and responsibilities than they would if they were not working. This is especially true of mothers who enjoy their work (Hoffman, 1974), perhaps because they feel the most guilty. Thus, overcompensation is the result not of the mother's working but of the stereotyped expectation (Motherhood Mandate) that she should not be working.

A nationwide survey taken in October 1977 by a *New York Times*/CBS News poll (Meislin, 1977) indicates that nearly 40% of those interviewed (45% of the men, 36% of the women) believed employed women were worse mothers than those who devote all their time to the home. As Figure 10-4 shows, many (one out of four) employed women felt the same way. No wonder mothers who are engaged in outside employment feel concerned about whether they are doing the right thing—nearly half of the general public feel they are poor mothers!

Such negative attitudes about employed mothers are particularly unfortunate, since more than half of all mothers work. A somewhat optimistic note might result from the finding that about 10% fewer people in 1977 thought employed mothers made poor mothers than did in 1970. Perhaps, then, some change is occurring.

Even so, acceptance of employed women still has a way to go. Of those interviewed in 1977, 60% balked at the idea of uprooting a family in which both spouses worked to advance the woman's career. Only 11% were in favor of such a move.

Other research has shown that children, at least, tend to be more supportive. Three-fourths of the 6- to 12-year-olds thought it was all right for their mother to work if she wanted (reported in *Do It NOW*, October 1977).

The effect of maternal employment on the mother is also important. Numerous studies have found that employed mothers tend to have higher morale, higher self-esteem, stronger feelings of competence, and fewer feelings of loneliness or of being unattractive than nonworking mothers. Employed mothers also tend to see child rearing more in terms of self-fulfillment than self-sacrifice (Birnbaum, 1975; Ferree, 1976; Hoffman, 1974, 1979; Paloma, 1972; Shaver & Freedman, 1976). This increased happiness and self-esteem in employed mothers compared to unemployed homemakers is particular-

"Do working women make better or worse mothers than nonworking women?"

	Better	Equal	Worse
Men	Better 21%	Equal 20%	Worse 45%
Nonworking Women	Better 14%	Equal 29%	Worse 44%
Working Women	Better 43%		Equal 27%	Worse 24%

Figure 10-4
Opinions on mothers and wives who hold outside employment (Adapted from Meislin, 1977. Poll taken by New York Times-CBS News, *October 1977.)*

ly true after a woman's children start school. When a woman first marries and has children, her self-esteem tends to be higher than that of the career-oriented woman, perhaps because her (stereotypic) life's ambition has been fulfilled (Rossi, 1965). A few years later, however, when her children are in school, the homemaker's life has less focus, while the career woman is just getting involved in her career. Thus, Birnbaum (1975) found, while interviewing women in their 30s, that homemakers had lower self-esteem, felt less competent, and were more unhappy than either married or single professionals.

Working does produce a considerable amount of strain for some mothers, whether employment is a necessity or a personal desire. Two important variables in the amount of strain experienced by employed mothers are work commitment and spouse support. Employed mothers who view their work as a career rather than as a job and who have spouse support report little role conflict (Holahan & Gilbert, 1979). However, mothers who view their work as a job and who lack spouse support report conflict in their parent-self roles and in their spouse-self roles.

In addition to their outside jobs, employed mothers generally still are expected to take care of the home and to take care of the children too, giving these women three full-time jobs. Vanek (1974) found that employed wives have about 10 fewer hours of free time each week than do employed men and unemployed homemakers. Although husbands of employed wives are more likely to help with the housework, the wife still maintains the larger share of the household chores (Hoffman, 1977). If the mothers are financially fortunate, they may be able to hire help, but, because of the ingrained belief that such jobs are their responsibility, they usually do not take advantage of this opportunity. Vanek (1974) found that employed wives are no more likely than homemakers to have paid help. Even if a woman wants to hire help, qualified people are hard to find. A study by the American Medical Women's Association in 1970 found that one-third of women physicians not then practicing would return to medicine if competent substitutes could be found to take over their child-care and housekeeping duties (*N.Y. Times*, October 11, 1976).

How do employed mothers handle such a load of responsibilities? Paloma (1972) found that professional women used one of four tension-management techniques: (1) they looked primarily at the benefits of combining career and family, (2) they decided in advance which role to emphasize in case of conflicting demands (almost always the family), (3) they compartmentalized the two roles as much as possible, or (4) they compromised their career to fit into family commitments. The compromised career is a frequent solution and accounts for the fact that many women are underemployed, underpaid, and undercommitted. The majority of traditionally female jobs, such as, for example, teaching and secretarial work, are least in conflict with a primary commitment to home and family. Unfortunately, such compromising also reinforces the stereotype that women are not really serious about their work.

It should be noted, however, that, for some women, activities associated with child care and homemaking are truly productive and satisfying. Such activities seem to engage their interests and talents, at least for part of their lives (Barnett & Baruch, cited in *APA Monitor*, September–October 1978, p. 29). However, for other women, the lack of economically productive work is associated with problems of self-esteem, dignity, and life satisfaction. A 1977 Yankelovich Monitor study found that one-third of all full-time housewives planned to enter the salaried work force at some time in the future (reported in *Ms.*, August 1977, p. 43).

If a mother stays home for a number of years while her children are young, it is often difficult for her to enter the labor force in her late 30s (or later) and still achieve a significant degree of success (Bernard, 1971; Suelzle, 1970; M. S. White, 1970). She may never have acquired job-related skills and therefore must settle for very low-level jobs. Her training may be outdated. She may be without the crucial informal contacts for professional success. She may have lost self-confidence through years of subverting her needs to those of her family. She may have lost her ambition. Yet, despite these inhibiting factors, increasing numbers of middle-aged women are joining the labor force. In October 1979, 66% of women aged 35–44 were in the labor force, compared to 59% in May 1977 and 50% in 1970 (U.S. Dept. of Labor, 1976c, 1977a, 1979b). Older women also are returning to school. The number of women aged 25–34 attending college rose 187% from 1970 to 1978 (*N.Y. Times*, November 13, 1979, p. A27). These numbers reflect women's growing recognition of the rewards of outside employment and the realities of our economic system and of our 50% divorce rate.

Change. More than consciousness raising is needed, however, to ameliorate some of the negative effects of the Motherhood Mandate. The negative effects of motherhood for both mothers and children probably will continue unless a number of changes occur. Fathers need to be more willing to share household and child-care functions. Society and employers need to provide some supports for working mothers—day-care centers, good part-time jobs, flexible-hour jobs, paternity leave, equitable tax deductions. The Motherhood Mandate needs to be eliminated. These suggested changes would go a long way toward making motherhood predominantly rewarding—a choice, not an obligation; an opportunity for growth, not a burden.

From another perspective, of course, it can be argued that, rather than adjust the lives of women to the Establishment, it might be more appropriate to adjust the Establishment to the lives of women (Bernard, 1971). That is, the concept of a career itself is a masculine concept, entailing full devotion to a job at the price of other interests. Perhaps the goal should be to reduce the emphasis on having a career for everyone, males especially, and to encourage more interpersonal activities (including child care) for both sexes. Such a change would liberate men as well as women. Many men, in fact, are finding the strains of ambition and the breadwinner role to be excessive. These men are finding alternatives, including more time in their family relationships. In 1978, 84% of a national sample of men aged 18–49 said they considered family life to be "very important" to their life satisfaction (Brozan, 1979). A national survey of college freshmen conducted in the Fall of 1979 found that an equal number of men and women (65%) said that raising a family was something they considered either "essential" or "highly important" to them (*Chronicle of Higher Education*, January 28, 1980, p. 5). This percentage was an increase of 3% over the year before.

The problem with motherhood is not that it is a worthless activity. It can be argued quite convincingly that such activity is the most important thing anyone can do, if it is done well, since society's future depends on it. Rather, the problem is that motherhood is held in such low esteem by everyone, including many women, and that the strains involved in being a mother are magnified by the lack of alternatives and supports for women in that role. As the Motherhood Mandate recedes, as institutional supports increase, and as people speak of parental, not specifically maternal, behavior, we can expect to find happier and better adjusted parents and children.

Father-Child Relationships

Although there is no mandate for fatherhood comparable to that of motherhood, sex-role stereotypes still strongly affect father-child relationships. The belief in a maternal "instinct" has been so strong that little research has been done directly on paternal relationships. Yet evidence has accumulated indicating the importance of paternal relationships to both children and fathers. Future fathers in equally high proportion to future mothers report strong desires for children and anticipate their children being important in their life (Association of American Colleges, Fall 1978; Donelson & Gullahorn, 1977b; Rabin, 1965). Yet these college men also believe children are more important to women in general than to men and that women want children to fulfill a basic need or purpose in life. Thus, many men consider their desire for children unusual, even though it is not. Furthermore, in a 1977 survey, 35.5% of the male freshmen and 19.8% of the female freshmen thought women's activities should be confined to the home (Association of American Colleges, Fall 1978). Thus, although men may want families, many still see women as the primary caretakers.

Immediately after their child is born, fathers often become completely engrossed in their child, showing immediate, strong affective responses (Collins, 1979; M. Greenberg & Morris, 1974; Parke & Sawin, 1977). This is especially true if fathers are allowed to interact with the baby immediately after birth. Early contact with infants may be as important for the development of father-child bonds as it is for the development of mother-child bonds (Parke & O'Leary, 1976). Traditionally, however, a father is not encouraged, or even allowed, in some hospitals, to see his newborn. His interaction with his child soon wanes, and both are deprived of continuing, meaningful intimacy. When fathers do interact, they tend to be more attentive and physically playful than mothers but are less active in feeding and care-taking activities (Collins, 1979; Parke & Sawin, 1977). Nonetheless, when fathers do undertake these traditionally female tasks of child care, they do very well. Recent findings suggest that fathers are more likely to do these tasks if they are specifically instructed in these aspects of child care and if the child is a boy (Parke, cited in *Psychology Today*, February 1979, p. 23). In fact, regardless of instruction, fathers are more likely to touch and vocalize to first-born sons than to first-born daughters or to later-born children (Collins, 1979).

In a cross-cultural study of the time mothers and fathers spend in child care, they do very well. Recent findings suggest that fathers are more likely to do these tasks if they are specifically instructed in these aspects of child care and if the child is a boy (Parke, cited in *Psycholo*-Western fathers. An astounding finding was that the average American father spends only 12 minutes a day with his children. Considering that children spend, on the average, 6 hours a day watching television, it is not surprising that a 1975 survey found that 44% of children preferred watching TV to spending time with their father (only 20% preferred TV to their mother) (in *Stars & Stripes*, December 1975). A 1977 Gallup Youth Survey (Gallup, 1977) found that three times more teenagers of both sexes reported getting along better with their mother than with their father (twice as many boys; more than three times as many girls). Only 18% thought their relationship with their father was better; one-third thought their relationships with both parents were the same. This is a sad commentary on the father-child relationship, especially in light of the studies, reviewed in Chapter Seven, that fathers are important figures in the lives of their children from infancy on (Collins, 1979; Fein, 1978; Ferguson, 1977; Hoffman, 1977; Lamb & Lamb, 1976; Parke & Sawin, 1977).

A number of factors account for the generally inadequate father-child relationship typically found. Among them are belief in the motherhood myth, the existence of strong sex typing, the power differences between the sexes, and the traditional pattern of divorce and custody arrangements.

Motherhood Myth.   The motherhood Myth states that only mothers can establish an intimate relationship with their children because of the maternal "instinct." As was discussed in Chapter 4, there is no such thing as a maternal instinct. Nurturing behavior is learned, and fathers are equally capable of acquiring such behaviors, especially if they have early contact with the child. In addition, although mothers are biologically equipped to bear and nurse children, there is no biologically decreed responsibility to rear and care for them (just as there is no biological prerequisite for doing housework, often seen as part of a mother's "natural" work). In fact, Harlow (1958) found with his studies of monkeys that the critical aspect of mothering is not the provision of food but the provision of warm, comforting physical contact. Fathers are equally as capable as mothers of providing this.

Yet the father role for males is usually consistently ignored during a boy's socialization or is specifically deemphasized. Boys generally do not have any early experience with parental behaviors, such as dolls and babysitting (Brenton, 1966; Chafetz, 1978; Fasteau, 1974; Fein, 1974). They often see in their own homes and in the media that fatherhood is either irrelevant or very narrow. They usually are taught that fatherhood is only a minor part of the masculine role, that achieving comes first. In addition, there is no clear role for fathers. They used to be the benevolent disciplinarians and mentors ("Father knows best"), but such a role is no longer viable in our current egalitarian family ideal. Besides, mothers are now the family disciplinarian (*Do It NOW*, October 1977). As a result, fathers often feel like outsiders, not knowing what role to play, often opting simply to avoid the situation completely.

Sex Typing. A major obstacle in father-child relationships is the masculine personality itself. Men who are uncomfortable with expressing their emotions may be inhibited from establishing closeness and intimacy with their children. Small children cannot be dealt with using reason alone, and they need more direct expressions of affection than roughhousing, slaps on the back, or material rewards (Fasteau, 1974; Pleck & Sawyer, 1974). In addition, the pressure of the male sex role to achieve concrete things (money, status, top grades, and so on) makes it difficult for many men to appreciate the much subtler rewards of feelings and relationships. Consequently, if fathers do spend any time with their children, which is often difficult if they are the primary breadwinner, they may displace their achievement strivings onto their children and engage in competition with them. Some fathers also may make their children feel they must earn their father's love in mechanical ways (Chafetz, 1978; Fasteau, 1974; Pleck & Sawyer, 1974). As a result, paternal relationships tend not to be close, as the Gallup Youth Survey noted above illustrates.

Power Differences. Another reason that men, as a group, do not rear children may be that it is to their advantage, in a power sense, not to be the caretakers. Polatnick (1973) analyzes the advantages of avoiding child-rearing responsibilities and the advantages of breadwinning responsibilities. Full-time child rearing limits the opportunities one has to engage in other activities, whereas the breadwinning role earns money, status, and power in society as well as in the family. Consequently, many men have an interest in defining child rearing as exclusively a woman's role—it limits women's occupational activities and thus their competition, and it enables men to have children without limiting their own occupational activities. As Ross Wetzsteon (1977) has noted, "The real difficulty men have in becoming feminists . . . lies in the fact that American capitalism . . . still gives a strong competitive edge to men with traditional masculine values" (p. 59). Having a wife who cares for home and children is a strong advantage to men in the professional and business worlds. Although it is true that breadwinners must shoulder the financial burden involved in raising children, many men at least have the possibility of selecting work suited to their interests, and they can take time off from such work. In contrast, many women are arbitrarily assigned to child rearing on a 24-hour-a-day, 365-day-a-year basis.

Although there are many disadvantages to full-time child rearing, these disadvantages could be alleviated by changed societal conceptions of the parent role and by the sharing of responsibilities among both parents and society. Many fathers now are beginning to find the rewards of child rearing from which they previously have been excluded (and have excluded themselves). The joys of nurturance and the pleasures of exchanging love with children are allowing some fathers to get in touch with the emotional aspects of themselves that they previously had shut off (Brenton, 1966; Fasteau, 1974; Fein, 1974, 1978). The emotional rewards are high—emotional honesty, simplicity, and directness—and many fathers are deciding that they want to be more involved with their children, even if that means changing their career plans and/or their ambitions.

The *emergent* perspective on fathering (Fein, 1978), one that characterizes current research, is based on the premise that men have the capacity to be effective nurturers of their children and that such behaviors would be beneficial to both children and parents. This perspective contrasts with the traditional one of the aloof and distant father. It also contrasts with the "modern" perspective of the 1960s, which concentrated on certain child-outcome variables, such as sex-role development, but ignored the positive effects of parenting on fathers and ignored men's capabilities in this area.

Increasing numbers of fathers are participating in childbirth classes and the birth process itself and are finding it rewarding. More men are sharing child-care responsibilities with their wives, using a variety of patterns—househusband, two part-time jobs, morning-evening shifts, weekly shifts, dual careers, and more. And more men are becoming involved in early childhood activities as child-care workers, elementary and nursery school teachers, and so on (Boston Women's Health Book Collective, 1976; Fein, 1974, 1978; Levine, 1973; Parke & Sawin, 1977). But the numbers participating in these child-care activities, in general, are still small. And the numbers of men participating in the truly critical aspect of parenting—the sense of emotional *responsibility*—are smaller still (Collins, 1979).

Divorce. There is still another factor that has contributed to the difficulties of the father-child relationship: the typical pattern of child custody has been to award custody of children to the mother if a couple divorces. This tradition is, of course, both a result and a cause of distance in father-child relationships. The traditional awarding of children to the mother has been a result of the 20th century's emphasis on maternal care of children and the diminution of the father's role in child rearing. However, because children in Western society are generally considered to "belong" to the mother, fathers often keep their distance from their offspring.

It is an indication of changing father-child relationships that increasing numbers of divorced fathers are requesting and, in many cases, obtaining custody of their children after divorce. Other fathers are getting joint custody in some kind of cooperative, co-parenting arrangement. In a society in which two out of every five children born in this decade will spend part of their childhood in a single-parent household, it is becoming more and more a possibility that that household will be the father's (Molinoff, 1977; *Time*, 1980). In 1976, 6.8% of all American households were single-parent families (U.S. Bureau of the Census, 1977). Over 90% of these one-parent units were female headed. Yet, close to 800,000 children under 18 lived with their fathers, and at least an equal number shared their fathers through joint custody (Roman & Haddad, 1978). Between 1970 and 1978, the number of children under age 18 residing with divorced fathers increased by 136%. This number is likely to increase as courts begin reflecting society's changing attitudes toward sex roles. The media are reflecting some of this change in attitudes toward the male role. The end of 1979 saw a number of TV shows on divorced men as well as the release of "Kramer v. Kramer," a movie about a father's awakening to parenthood, which received an Academy Award as the best movie of the year.

Many divorce lawyers and judges still are reluctant to recommend and grant custody to fathers for two reasons: (1) the stereotyped belief that mothers are "naturally" the better parent, and (2) the more than a century of mother-oriented custodial rules and traditions (Molinoff, 1977; Roman & Haddad, 1978). Yet, changes have begun. Part of the pressure has come from men's rights organizations, which have active memberships in more than 30 states (Molinoff, 1977). Another pocket of pressure has come from men who have come to terms with their own nurturing capabilities and with what they view as the best interest of their children. With increasing numbers of mothers pursuing careers, women are no longer automatically considered the best parent.

A key factor in determining whether a father will seek custody of his children is not his sex-role orientation, but his own experiences with his family when he was a child. Gersick (in Albin, 1977) found that male custody seekers described their childhood family experience in terms of distance from their fathers, along with ambivalent but intense relationships with their mothers. They may thus be trying to make up for the lack of closeness they experienced with their own father in their relationship with their children. In any case, fathers awarded custody were similar to divorced mothers in coping patterns and adjustment (DeFrain & Eirick, 1979; *Time*, 1980). They had little difficulty managing the care of their children and fared much better psychologically than did divorced fathers without custody (Albin, 1977). Of course, fathers who seek child custody may be quite different, as a group, from fathers who do not seek custody. Many of these fathers who sought custody became more sensitive and expressive and did not experience the marked depression and feelings of incompetence characteristic of other groups of divorced fathers (Hetherington, Cox, & Cox, 1977; *Time*, February 4, 1980, p. 40).

Divorced fathers not given custody often withdraw from their children as a function of the strain of dealing with their ex-wives, geographical distance, financial status, their own discomfort or pain in relating to their children, and/or the nature of the marriage itself (Albin, 1977; Brown & Fox, 1979; Hetherington et al., 1977; Muenchow, 1977). If fathers have little contact with their children before the divorce, they are less likely to have contact with them afterward than are fathers who had much contact with them prior to the divorce. Such limited contact is especially true in working-class families. Yet, many fathers spend more time or have qualitatively more meaningful interactions with their children after the divorce than they had previously. Often such parent-child experiences lead to personal change for the father. Many fathers report increased personal growth, more expressiveness, greater sensitivity to others, and less concern about work as a consequence of their parenting involvement (Albin, 1977; *Time*, February 4, 1980, p. 40). Such changes suggest some of the rewards men are likely to obtain from increased parenting.

In examining the effects of divorce on children, more researchers are beginning to acknowledge that single-parent families are an alternative to two-parent families and that they are not necessarily pathological (Albin, 1977; D. Lynn, 1979). When divorce produces negative outcomes in a child, such as insecurity, depression, and poor academic performance, the cause is likely to be unclear communication between parents and the child, or the guilt a child may feel in missing the absent parent (Albin, 1977; Muenchow, 1977). The negative consequences are not the result of the divorce per se and are not inevitable. Since many fathers, when married, interact minimally with their children (12 minutes a day, on the average), it is not surprising that the father's absence after divorce may not be severely detrimental. An examination of families practicing joint custody (Roman & Haddad, 1978) indicates that the children involved are thriving, not just "adjusting." Contrary to popular opinion, children in such families are not "torn" between two parents. Although such arrangements may necessitate a great deal of planning and negotiation, they certainly seem a viable alternative, if desired, to a battle of custody.

In sum, many fathers are beginning to realize how much they have missed by not sharing child-care responsibilities. The lessons learned in parenting—relating to someone weaker and dependent in a socially responsive way—may carry over into men's relations with the rest of the world and may lead to a more caring, humane society. At the very least, greater involvement in child care would permit men to both work and love, to touch the parts of their emotional lives they have kept hidden. And because men would be *sharing* child-care responsibilities, it would free more women to develop their competencies in other areas. The end result may be the development of fully functioning, androgynous individuals—mothers, fathers, and children (Stockard & Johnson, 1979).

SUMMARY

In this chapter, the effects of the sex-role stereotypes on relationships have been examined. As friends, males as a group tend to have a large number of casual relationships with other males. Females as a group tend to have intimate relationships with a few females. (These and all differences noted for males and females are group differences and are not necessarily true of all individuals of the group.) The superficiality of many male friendships is due to the emphasis of the male role on competition, suppression of emotions, fear of homosexuality, and the lack of adequate role models. Male-female friendships are also difficult to form because of the behaviors associated with sex roles themselves and because of the difficulty males have in establishing any form of intimate relationship.

Romantic relationships also show the effects of the sex-role stereotypes. Dating relationships often are characterized by much game playing and manipulation. Although equality in relationships has become more the norm among college students, in practice there is still ambivalence on the part of many males. Despite prevailing opinion, males as a group tend to be more emotionally involved in such relationships than do females. Once married, men generally flourish, but many women experience great strain. Employed wives generally are happier than homemakers.

Parental relationships suffer from adherence to sex-role stereotypes as well. Sex-role expectations force women to believe they should be mothers and stay home with their children. The same expectations neglect the important role fathers play with their children. If women live up to the Motherhood Mandate, they may feel frustrated and take out their feelings on their families. If they work, they are generally happier but tend to feel guilty, despite there being no evidence of any negative effect of maternal employment on children. Paternal relationships have been ignored because of men's lack of training, the characteristics of the stereotyped masculine personality, and the career disadvantages of parenting. However, this pattern appears to be changing.

Thus, nearly all relationships, particularly men's, suffer from adherence to the sex-role stereotypes. Men and women both would benefit if they could develop the emotional and agentic parts of their personalities. Such an androgynous development would facilitate all the relationships of women and men.

More than the stereotypes need to be changed in order to liberate males and females in their relationships, however. Societal support in the form of job flexibility, child-care facilities, and changed institutional practices are also needed. These will be examined in succeeding chapters.

Hoffman, L. W., & Nye, F. I. *Working mothers*. San Francisco: Jossey-Bass, 1974. A summary of the myth-dispelling research done by these authors over the previous decade. A must for all women who plan to have both children and a career.

Komarovsky, M. *Dilemmas of masculinity*. New York: Norton, 1976. A thoughtful presentation of how the changing norms regarding masculinity and relationships affect young men.

Levine, J. *Who will raise the children? New options for fathers (and mothers)*. New York: Lippincott, 1976. An interesting discussion of alternatives to traditional child-care options.

Ramey, J. *Intimate friendships*. Englewood Cliffs, N.J.: Prentice-Hall, 1976. A provocative presentation of alternatives to the traditional marital relationship.

Rapoport, R. N., Rapoport, R., & Bumstead, J. (Eds.). *Working couples*. New York: Harper & Row, 1978. A topical collection of articles directly addressing issues most couples must face if they both want to work.

11

Societal Consequences: Prejudice and Work

As discussed in the last two chapters, sex-role stereotypes seriously affect nearly all aspects of personal and interpersonal functioning. The stereotypes also affect our interactions with society at large. As shown in Table 11-1, one effect is on paychecks. Women consistently earn less than men and the salary gap has been steadily increasing, from a difference of 36% less in 1955 to one of 41% less in 1977. These salary figures are examples of two major social areas affected by the sex-role stereotypes—interpersonal prejudice and the world of work. Figure 11-1 gives a "humorous" look at how these two areas overlap. However, this overlap does not account for all the data on work force sex differences and for that reason we will deal separately with the areas of prejudice and work.

Because societal effects are so pervasive, this book can, of necessity, only examine a few areas. This chapter will focus on prejudice and work; the next, on power and aggression.

PREJUDICE

Numerous studies and personal experiences have documented that men and women are prejudiced against women solely on the basis of their sex. In P. Goldberg's (1968) classic study, female college students were asked to evaluate journal articles for their value, persuasive-

Table 11-1
Median Annual Earnings of Year-Round Full-Time Workers 14 Years and More by Sex, 1955–1977

| | Annual Earnings | | Women's Earnings as |
Year	Women	Men	Percentage of Men's
1955	$2,719	$4,252	63.9
1960	$3,292	$5,417	60.8
1965	$3,823	$6,375	60.0
1970	$5,323	$8,966	59.4
1975	$7,504	$12,758	58.8
1977	$8,618	$14,626	58.9

Source: U.S. Dept. of Labor, 1977c, 1978.

Figure 11-1
Example of how sex-role stereotypes affect us on a societal level: prejudice against women and salary inequities. (Copyright 1977 by G. B. Trudeau/distributed by Universal Press Syndicate. All rights reserved.)

ness, and profundity. They also evaluated the authors for their writing style, professional competence, status, and ability to persuade the reader. The articles were from predominantly "masculine" fields (such as law and city planning), predominantly "feminine" fields (elementary school teaching and dietetics), and "neutral" ones (linguistics and art history). They differed only in that the author was presented as male in half of the articles and as female in the other half. The results showed that college women consistently found an article more valuable and its author more competent when the article bore a male rather than a female name. These differences in evaluation as a function of author sex were significant only in the traditionally masculine fields and the "neutral" field of linguistics. The importance of the sex typing of the field has been overlooked frequently by later researchers.

Further study of this phenomenon, using different procedures, has lent clarification to Goldberg's findings. Prejudice against women is most likely to occur toward those women who are seen as violating sex-role stereotypes. Bias has been found against women who aspire to status or power equal to that of men (as in fields or behavior typically associated with men—Denmark, 1979; Etaugh & Rose, 1975; Mischel, 1974; Unger, Raymond, & Levine, 1974). For example, Denmark (1979) found that college women more negatively evaluated outspoken female professors than they did male professors who demonstrated identical behavior. Interestingly, male college students did not devalue outspoken female professors, although all subjects tended to rate female professors less favorably than they rated male professors. Bias is also found against aspiring women, rather than against women who have already achieved some measure of success (Kaschak, 1978b; Pheterson, Kiesler, & Goldberg, 1971; Starer & Denmark, 1974; Taynor & Deaux, 1973). This bias may be due to the competitive image of aspiring women and may be mitigated by some formal recognition of achievement, such as for award-winning pictures or teaching performance.

Interestingly, with respect to articles on subjects that are traditionally "neutral" or "female related," more recent studies have found that females are judged to be equal or better writers than males, at least by female critics (Etaugh & Rose, 1975; Levenson, Burford, Bonno, & Davis, 1975; H. Mischel, 1974; Pheterson, Kiesler, & Goldberg, 1969). This latter finding suggests that discrimination can work both ways. A study by this author and a colleague (Basow & Howe, 1979b) illustrates this pattern. Female college students found a non-sex-typed career that was presented and explained by a female to be more interesting and of more importance than the identical career presented in the identical way by a male. There were no differences in the ratings on competence required, status and prestige, or salary. Thus some prejudice against women may be abating, at least in non-sex-typed fields. Brichta and Inn (1978) also found no sex-contingent differences in the evaluation of individual performance. The Basow and Howe findings suggest, however, that at least in some dimensions, women may view a field more positively when they see a woman in it. Other researchers suggest that in real-life settings, each sex may be biased in favor of itself (as in book reviews—Moore, 1978—and ratings of instructors—Kaschak, 1978a, 1978b).

Ellyn Kaschak (1978a, 1978b) examined the dynamics involved in such biases. In a series of studies, she investigated how college students evaluate professors' teaching methods. When students evaluated written descriptions attributed to either a male or a female professor, female students showed no bias. (See Figure 11-2.) That is, female students rated female and male professors equally as effective, concerned, likeable, and excellent, regardless of teaching field. They did, however, rate female professors as less powerful. This may have been realistic assessment. And they were more willing to take a course from the female rather than the male professor. In contrast, male students showed consistent bias against female professors and/or in favor of male professors.

In a second study by Kaschak (1978b), the professors were described as award-winning teachers. Under this condition, some of the sex bias disappeared. Male and female professors were seen as equally excellent and male and female students were equally desirous of enrolling in their courses. Yet all evaluations were not equal. Female and male professors were seen as achieving their award-winning status in different and stereotypic ways: female professors in traditionally "feminine" fields were rated as more concerned and likeable than male professors in those fields. Male professors in all fields were rated as more powerful and effective than female professors. Again we see an affective/instrumental split in attributing success to females and males. One implication of this study is that when female accomplishments are "legitimized" through awards, prejudice against them by males is minimized.

In fact, in some situations where women behave outside of a stereotypical role but in a laudable or superior manner, they may be evaluated even higher than men in the same situations. Such results have been found by numerous researchers (Abramson et al., 1977;

245

Chapter 11:
Societal
Consequences:
Prejudice and
Work

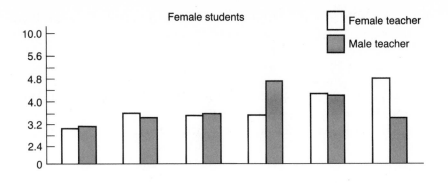

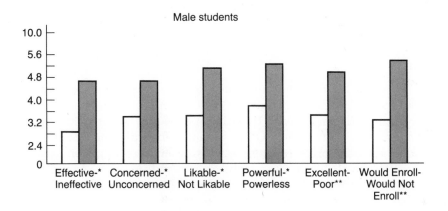

* Effects for sex of student, sex of professor, and the interaction between the two
(*p* < .05).
** Effects of sex of professor and interaction with student sex (*p* < .01).

Figure 11-2
Mean ratings of the teaching methods of male and female college professors by male and female college students. (Adapted from Kaschak, 1978a.)

Brichta & Inn, 1978; Gruber & Gaebelein, 1979; Taynor & Deaux, 1973, 1975). For example, Taynor and Deaux (1973) found that a woman who behaved in an exemplary manner in a civic emergency was perceived as being more deserving of a reward, as performing better, and as trying harder than a man. Abramson and colleagues (1977) have termed this pattern of results *the talking platypus phenomenon*. That is, when an individual achieves an unanticipated level of success, the achievement becomes magnified because "After all, it matters little what the platypus says, the wonder is that it can say anything at all" (p. 123).

In sum, although prejudice in evaluations may be minimized for successful individuals, differential sexist attributions regarding the reasons for the success remain. And, more to the point, most people, whether males or females, are not award-winners or superior performers. Sexist prejudice against these "everyday" people is still prevalent.

Even children show this sex bias. As mentioned in previous chapters, boys show much more negativity toward traditionally female-related qualities and activities than do girls toward male-related qualities and activities. Connor and Serbin (1978) conducted a study of fourth-, sixth-, and eighth-graders' reactions to male and female story characters. In this study, the stories were identical except for the sex of the main character. Thus there were four stories—a boy or girl engaged in either boy-related or girl-related activities. Connor and Serbin found that boys' negativism toward stories about girls and girl-related activities increased with age. Girls, to a lesser degree, tended to prefer same-sex story characters as friends and to like same-sex stories better. However, both girls and boys preferred to be the male character and to do the things the male character did when the story's main character was male. For girls, positive same-sex feelings were opposed by a bias in favor of male activities and roles. Thus, explanations invoking some greater intrinsic value to the activities usually associated with males do not hold. Here, the value was clearly attached to being male, in and of itself.

Sex-role attitudes may affect such perceptions. Spence and Helmreich (1972) found that, at least among college students, it is predominantly males with traditional attitudes toward women who dislike competent women. Other groups (moderate and liberal males and all females) preferred competent women to incompetent women, regardless of the stimulus person's sex-typed interests. Nonetheless, all subjects liked competent "masculine" females most of all, showing a bias in favor of "masculine" interests. In this study, "masculine interests" meant being a physics major who was also interested in competitive sports, history, and biography. A somewhat later study by these researchers (Kristal, Sanders, Spence, & Helmreich, 1975) revealed that when sex-typed *interests* were paired with sex-typed *qualities*, the woman liked best by both male and female subjects was one who had "masculine interests" but "feminine qualities" (considered to be, for example, sensitivity and sincerity). Thus, competent women are liked as long as they do not lose completely their "femininity." More recent studies (Pines, 1979; Vaughn & Wittig, 1979) generally confirm the findings above. Competent women are not devalued consistently by college students, but their evaluations are a complex function of the rater's sex and sex typing, the ratee's description, and the specific attributes rated.

As suggested above, prejudice also operates against men. Studies have found that males who talk about their emotional problems, who are passive in group discussions, or who express sexual concerns are liked much less and are viewed as more in need of professional help than are females who do so (for example, Costrich et al., 1975; Polyson, 1978). In fact, prejudice against males may be even greater than prejudice against females when one's behavior is considered sex-inappropriate. For example, data cited in Chapter Nine about female and male achievement behavior indicate that males who succeed in sex-inappropriate activities more often have negative consequences predicted for them (by both females and males) than do females who succeed in sex-inappropriate activities. Similarly, men who are in

247

**Chapter 11:
Societal
Consequences:
Prejudice and
Work**

sex-inappropriate occupations are generally perceived less favorably than are women who are in either sex-appropriate or sex-inappropriate occupations, at least by male and female undergraduates (Shinar, 1978). In sex-inappropriate occupations, men are perceived as significantly less likeable, less well adjusted, and less physically attractive than are women in sex-inappropriate occupations. These men are also perceived as being even less active and having even fewer leadership attributes than are women in the same occupations. Shinar explains these findings by suggesting that the emergence of women's liberation has resulted in increasing acceptance of women in formerly "male" occupations. The lack of a parallel men's movement, however, has left men with less social sanction for crossing sex boundaries. Alternatively, the results may be explained by the differential evaluation of masculinity and femininity. Since male-related things have high value, women who begin doing them benefit from the positive assessment. In contrast, since female-related things have low value, men who do them are rated even more negatively than women, since there is no "acceptable" reason for them to want such a change. We saw a similar process at work in the differential reactions people have toward male and female homosexuality (Chapter Five).

Other research supports the differential evaluation hypothesis. Carol Shreiber (1979), in a study of 50 employees who took on nontraditional jobs, found that the pressures on the men and women involved were different. The nontraditional women wanted to be regarded as like the men with whom they worked; the nontraditional men wanted to be viewed as different from and superior to their female co-workers.

Ratings of competence also show signs of differential evaluation. Deaux and Taynor (1973) asked male and female college students to evaluate applicants for a study-abroad scholarship. Competent males were rated more highly than competent females, but males of low competence were rated *lower* than females of low competence. Larrance and colleagues (1979) obtained similar results in a field study using male used-car salespeople as subjects. Male confederates showing little knowledgeability about automobiles (the low-competence group) were given higher price estimates than were low-competence female confederates or competent confederates of both sexes. Again, conformity to sex-role expectations may explain these findings. When men conform to role expectations by being competent and in control of their emotional lives, they benefit by being perceived favorably. When they do not conform to these expectations, they receive even lower ratings than females.

Still, most achievement situations are sex typed as masculine. In these, prejudice seems to operate against women. The consequences of such prejudice can be seen in educational settings and media portrayals of the sexes (see Chapter Eight), in the treatment of children by parents and others (see Chapter Seven), and in the worlds of work, politics, and law. These last two areas will be discussed in Chapter 12. It is to the world of work that we now turn.

WORK

Volumes of data have been accumulated regarding women and men in the labor force. Because of the wealth of data, only a cursory survey will be attempted here. The interested reader is encouraged to read Kreps (1976), Sweet (1973), and the additional sources cited within this chapter for more detail.

In general, women in the labor force have been underemployed, underpaid, and discriminated against. Figure 11-3 gives a simplified view of how the sex-role stereotypes influence our work lives. Occupational tracking and salary inequities are just two of the major consequences.

In this section we will review the data on participation rates, salaries, barriers to equal employment opportunities, and men's role in the work force.

Participation Rates

As Figure 11-4 indicates, the participation of women in the labor force has been steadily increasing since 1950, whereas participation by men has been slowly declining. Slightly over half of all women currently work, compared to somewhat less than 80% of all men. In October 1979, 51.3% of all women over age 16 were in the labor market, compared to 78.2% of all men. The participation of women is

Figure 11-3
For this you went to college? One example of how the sex-role stereotypes influence our work lives. (Copyright 1973, Bülbül. Reprinted with permission.)

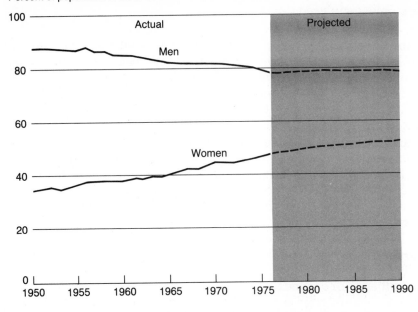

Percent of population in labor force

249

Chapter 11:
Societal
Consequences:
Prejudice and
Work

Figure 11-4
*Labor force
participation rates of
women and men,
annual averages,
1950–1976, and
projected rates for
1980, 1985, and 1990.
(From the U.S. Dept. of
Labor, 1977c.)*

expected to continue to increase through 1990 to between 54% and 60%. The greatest increase in labor force participation has been by women between 25 and 34 years old. Between 1970 and 1979, their participation rate advanced 20 percentage points, from 45% to 65% (U.S. Dept. of Labor, 1979b). These are the women who historically remained at home to rear children.

Despite the strong belief that a breadwinning husband, home-making wife, and at least one child constitute the typical family in the United States, only 15.9% of all households actually conformed to this pattern in 1976 (U.S. Bureau of the Census, 1977). A more common pattern (18.5%) is one where both father and mother are wage earners.[1] Only 7% of all husband-wife families conform to the stereotypic working husband, nonworking wife, and two children pattern. More than half of all mothers (about 55%), and nearly half of all wives without children, work. Of all single women (either never married or presently separated, divorced, or widowed), three out of five (60%) were employed in 1979 (U.S. Dept. of Labor, 1979b).

In 1979, more than two-fifths of the labor force (42%) was composed of women. Nine out of every ten women work for pay at some point during their lives. In 1977, only 3% of 17-year-old females in a national survey picked "housewife" as their first career choice (Association of American Colleges, June 1978, p. 3). Given the large labor force participation of women, relatively little preparation is given them for later employment.

The reasons for the increasing participation of women in the labor force are numerous. Among them are economic necessity, rising

---

[1] Most households comprise married couples without children (30.5%) or single persons (20.6%) (U.S. Bureau of the Census, 1977).

educational attainments, changing demographic trends, and changing employment needs.

Economic Necessity.   Like men, most women work out of economic necessity (Cook, 1978; Crowley, Levitin, & Quinn, 1973). In March 1976, nearly half (43%) of all working women were single, separated, divorced, or widowed. Another 41% had husbands earning less than $15,000 a year; 15% had husbands earning less than $7,000 a year (U.S. Dept. of Labor, 1977a). High unemployment, high inflation, and changing notions of what constitutes a decent standard of living all contribute to the need for married women (and men) to work outside the home. Because of inflation alone, many families now need two paychecks simply to maintain their former standard of living.

Many people think that most divorced women are financially secure because of alimony. However, in 1974, for example, only 14% of all divorced women even were awarded alimony, and fewer than 7% of these received regular payments (*Do It NOW*, February 1977, p. 2). The financial situation is particularly acute for the rising number of families with dependent children that are headed by a woman. In 1979, for example, fewer than 25% of divorced mothers received child support (*N.Y. Times*, July 2, 1979, p. A14).

In June 1978, a record 8.2 million families (one out of seven) were headed by women. This represents an increase since 1960 of 10% of such families headed by White females and 35% headed by Black females (U.S. Dept. of Labor, 1978; Van Dusen & Sheldon, 1976). Nearly three-fifths of these women were in the labor force, but about one out of every three of these families was living at or below poverty level in 1976. The comparable rate for families headed by men only is 1 out of 18 (U.S. Dept. of Labor, 1978).

Rising Educational Attainments.   Another reason more women are working is that more women are obtaining college and advanced degrees, giving them access to jobs for which they were previously unqualified. Table 11-2 illustrates this trend. Nearly half of all bachelor's and master's degrees are now awarded to women. In fact, in 1977–78, the number of men and the number of women in the starting classes of undergraduate and master's level programs were equal for the first time (Association of American Colleges, March 1978). On the highest education levels, the increased percentage of women has been dramatic. Women received only 3.5% of the first professional degrees in 1965 but are expected to receive 26% of them in 1983. Women in 1977 received one-quarter of all Ph.D.'s compared to only 10.8% in 1965.

Postsecondary education increases the likelihood of women working (Pifer, 1976). In all income brackets, wives who had completed college were more likely to work than were wives with less education (U.S. Dept. of Labor, 1976a). Also, because college-educated women are more likely to have worked for a longer period of time both before marriage and before childbearing, they are accustomed to employment outside the home and therefore less likely to

Table 11-2
Percent of Educational Degrees Awarded to Women in 1965, 1971, 1977, and (projected) 1983

251

Chapter 11:
Societal
Consequences:
Prejudice and
Work

	1964–1965	1970–1971	1976–1977	1982–1983 (projected)
B.A.'s	42.4	43.4	45.7	46.3
M.A.'s	33.8	40.1	47.0	50.5
Ph.D.'s	10.8	14.2	24.0	28.5
First Professional (e.g., law, M.D.)	3.5	6.3	18.6	26.2

From *Chronicle of Higher Education*, 10/23/78, p. 11; 11/13/78, p. 13, and the National Center for Education Statistics, "Projections of Education Statistics to 1986–87."

drop out of the paid labor force (Sweet, 1973; Van Dusen & Sheldon, 1976).

Changing Demographic Trends. Women's marital and family status are changing and these changes affect their labor force participation. Young persons in the 1970s are remaining single longer than in previous decades. The number of women in their early 20s who have not married rose from 36% in 1970 to 45% by 1977 (U.S. Bureau of the Census, 1977). In addition, there are fewer married women in the population at any one time than ever before. Only 59% of all women were married in 1976, compared to 65.6% in 1960 (U.S. Dept. of Labor, 1977c). Too, families are decreasing in size and are being started at later ages than was true in previous decades (Van Dusen & Sheldon, 1976). Consequently, more women are experiencing longer periods of time during which they may advance their careers.

Changing Employment Needs. Another factor contributing to women's entry into the paid labor force has been the growth of those industries that have primarily employed women. The post-World War II baby boom created the need for more services—educational, medical, governmental, and recreational. These services, especially the professional ones, have been traditional employers of women. Consequently, the demand for female workers has increased significantly since the 1940s. For example, in 1950, 62% of all clerical workers and 45% of all service workers (other than household workers) were women. In October 1979, the numbers were 80% and 60%, respectively (U.S. Dept. of Labor, 1979b). The labor demand for women should intensify in the future, since women outnumber men in the population by 7 million, population expansion has been halted, and the participation rate of males in the labor force has been declining due to earlier retirement (Pifer, 1976).

Other Factors. Another factor that may contribute to the increasing participation of women in the labor force is diminishing social prejudice against the idea of women working. A Fall 1978 survey by the American Council on Education found that only 27.3% of all college freshmen believed "women's activities are best confined to the home"

(*Chronicle of Higher Education*, January 22, 1979, p. 15). New legislation promoting equality in employment and education, and advances in household technologies, have also aided women's entry into the world of paid work.

It should be noted that the reasons women work are virtually identical to the reasons men work: economic necessity, work as part of their identity, a desire for achievement, and the satisfaction from meaningful, rewarded activity (Crowley et al., 1973; Renwick & Lawler, 1978).

Women's compensation for employment, however, has consistently been below that of men. Salary inequities between the sexes are as pervasive as they are long-standing.

Salary

What is a woman worth? In terms of employment compensation, only about three-fifths of the worth of a man (see Table 11-1). When part-time workers are included, the median earned income of women in 1975 was only two-fifths (40%) that of men (Pifer, 1976). Despite the fact that more women are working and most are working out of economic necessity, the salary differential between men's median income and that of women has been increasing. Women belonging to minority groups are especially at a disadvantage. In 1977, they earned only 52% of the salary earned by White men and 73% of that earned by men belonging to minority groups (U.S. Dept. of Labor, 1978).

Table 11-3 shows the salary differential for several occupational and industry groups in May 1976. The salary differential is greatest for sales workers and managers/administrators and least for farm workers. Full-time female workers constituted well over half (57%) of those individuals earning less than $7000 a year in 1974 and they constituted only 5% of those earning $15,000 or more a year (U.S. Dept. of Labor, 1976b). A case in point is college faculty salaries, as depicted in Figure 11-5. At every level, males earn more than their female counterparts. This is especially marked at the highest levels. In 1978–79, female professors averaged only 82.5% of the average salary of male professors.

A number of factors contribute to this salary differential. One is occupational segregation. Women are concentrated in less-skilled, low-paying jobs. Another factor is the increased numbers of women in the labor force in entry-level positions. A third factor is the differences in education, training, and counseling between the sexes that direct women into lower-paying jobs. A fourth factor is the greater likelihood of men to work overtime and earn extra income—men are three times more likely than women to do so (U.S. Dept. of Labor, 1976b). Yet even these factors do not sufficiently account for the large difference in salaries. It has been estimated that from one-half to two-thirds of the differential is due to outright discrimination (Gunderson, 1978; Institute for Social Research, 1978).

These five factors all serve as barriers to equal female income achievement in the world of work. There are many others. For exam-

253

Chapter 11:
Societal
Consequences:
Prejudice and
Work

Table 11-3
Median Usual Weekly Earnings of Full-Time Wage and Salary Workers by Sex,
Occupation, and Industry Group, May 1976

Occupation and Industry Group	Usual Weekly Earnings		Women's Earnings as Percent of Men's
	Women	Men	
OCCUPATION			
Professional-technical	$218	$299	73
Managerial-administrative, except farm	187	320	58
Sales	111	244	45
Clerical	147	228	64
Craft	149	243	61
Operatives, except transport	121	202	60
Transport equipment operatives	([1])	216	—
Nonfarm laborers	121	166	73
Service	109	170	64
Farm	107	122	88
INDUSTRY			
Agriculture	$113	$129	88
Construction	167	244	68
Mining	([1])	280	—
Manufacturing	137	231	59
Durable goods	148	235	63
Nondurable goods	127	222	57
Transportation and public utilities	190	270	70
Wholesale trade	148	240	62
Retail trade	113	188	60
Finance, insurance, and real estate	144	270	53
Private household	66	([1])	—
Miscellaneous services	160	224	71
Public administration	173	269	64

[1] Median not shown where base is less than 75,000.
From U.S. Dept. of Labor, 1977c.

ple, research by Mahoney and Blake (1979) has indicated that there is
a negative relationship between perceived femininity of an occupation and judgments of monetary compensation, independent of other
occupational characteristics. All these factors affect female occupational achievement in ways other than monetary reward. A closer look
at some of these barriers, both internal and external, will illustrate
the complexity of the problem. Of the barriers, the external ones are
most important and most serious, yet people often deliberately ignore
them to focus on internal ones. It is easier to "blame the victim" than
to institute social change, and psychologists have been as responsible
as anyone else for this misdirected emphasis. Therefore, after briefly
noting some of the internal barriers, we will focus at length on some
of the external ones.

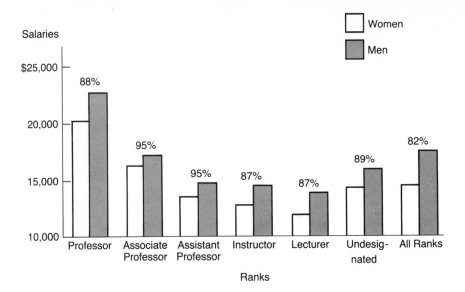

Salaries

Figure 11-5
*The 1978–1979
faculty salary gap.
Salaries of male and
female college
professors.*
(Chronicle of Higher
Education, *March
12, 1979, p. 12.)*

Internal Barriers to Female Achievement

There are many internal barriers to female achievement—a traditional female life plan, sex-typing and sex-role attitudes, fear of success, attribution patterns, and a mate's attitude.

Of them all, the most critical internalized factor barring women from achievement is the different *life plans* for the sexes to which children are socialized (see Part Three). Despite the fact that nine out of every ten women will work at some point in their lives, many women work their entire adult lives, and more than half of all mothers work, most girls grow up unprepared psychologically and professionally to assume a career. Girls grow up expecting to be mothers; boys grow up expecting to have careers.

Sex typing and *sex-role* attitudes also affect career planning. Vincent Harren and colleagues (Harren, Kass, Tinsley, & Moreland, 1978, 1979; Kass, Tinsley, Harren, & Moreland, 1978) have found that among college students, feminine sex typing is associated with female-dominated majors and occupations. A liberal attitude toward women is associated with more male-dominated majors and occupations. The causal sequence here is not clear, however. Sex-role attitudes and sex typing seem to lead some individuals to choose certain career paths, whereas for others, the choice of a career itself leads to certain attitudes and attributions. Canter (1979) suggests that sex-role conceptions play a central role in career aspirations and mediate the effects of all other career-related variables.

Some of the other internal barriers to female achievement were discussed in Chapter Nine. For example, many women experience anxiety ("fear of success") with regard to achieving in male-related activities. Since most jobs are male dominated and having a primary career focus is itself seen as masculine, many women steer away from such fields and such a focus.

Women's typical *attribution pattern* also may serve as a barrier to occupational achievement (see Frieze, 1978, and Chapter Nine). By attributing their successes to luck rather than skill, women's level of aspiration remains low. A 1978 survey of women at six of the country's most prestigious colleges found that women underestimate their academic ability by overpreparing for exams and they underaspire in their career goals (reported in *New York Times*, December 10, 1978, p. 85). Therefore, many women never establish any occupational life plan or prepare themselves for a career. When they do enter the labor force, it is usually at low-level jobs. Even among women who serve on national boards of directors of major U.S. corporations (a small but growing number), "luck" is the reason they cite most often to explain their success (Klemesrud, 1979). But, in their case, other attributions such as "hard work" and "sacrifice" are also given. Similar results were obtained in Deaux's (1979) study of female and male first-level managers. The men were significantly more likely to attribute their success to their ability than were the women.

Another important factor is the *attitude of the man* with whom a woman may be romantically involved. Since attracting and keeping a mate have been viewed traditionally as a woman's major goal in life, if the man involved views working women unfavorably, she is unlikely to work (Bailyn, 1970; Horner, 1972). College women who perceive traditional sex-role expectations in their male friends expect more negative outcomes from success and have lower career aspirations than do women who do not perceive such expectations in their male friends (Canter, 1979). Since more men believe women's activities are best confined to the home than do women (35.5% of the male college freshmen in 1977 compared to 20% of the female—Association of American Colleges, Fall 1978), such attitudes serve as another barrier to women's occupational aspirations and achievement.

External Barriers to Female Achievement

Of greater importance than any internal barrier, however, are the many external barriers to female achievement in the labor force. These are both social, as in socialization and discrimination, and institutional, as in occupational segregation, restricted access to education, business, and the professions, and trade unions and laws.

Socialization. Primary among the social factors are those associated with socialization. As discussed in Chapter Eight, the media, school environment, and vocational and counseling programs all virtually ignore the concept of women working and, instead, promulgate the "feminine mystique"—that complex of beliefs and attitudes assuming that women's primary focus should be domestic. Whereas males must choose their careers, most females first have to choose whether to have a career at all. That decision is often difficult and is affected by a variety of factors. (See Almquist, 1977; Brown, Aldrich, & Hall, 1978; Canter, 1979; Frieze, 1978; Marini, 1978; O'Neil, Meeker, & Bor-

255

Chapter 11:
Societal
Consequences:
Prejudice and
Work

gers, 1978; Weitz, 1977, for more detail.) Among the important factors are:

1. Parental encouragement, particularly by fathers.

2. Role models of successful women, especially mothers and college professors (see also Almquist & Angrist, 1971; Basow & Howe, 1979a; Goldstein, 1979).

3. Expectations of women held by others. Greenstein, Miller, and Weldon (1979) found this factor to be a better predictor of college women's occupational choice than the women's own attitudes toward work or toward achieving women.

4. Number of siblings. The more siblings, the lower the career and educational aspirations, particularly for boys.

5. Supportive peer group, male and female. Especially important for nontraditional career choices (see also Canter, 1979; Holahan, 1979).

6. Social class. Careers are more an ideal of the middle- and upper-class woman, although lower-middle-class women whose husbands earn between $7,000 and $10,000 a year are the ones most apt to be working (U.S. Dept. of Labor, 1976a). However, socioeconomic background is a much stronger indication of a boy's educational and occupational aspirations than it is of a girl's (see Marini, 1978).

7. Academic ability and academic performance. More strongly related to boys' educational and occupational aspirations than to girls'.

8. Dating behavior. An orientation toward activities leading to early marriage are negatively related to girls' educational and occupational aspirations.

9. Residence. Those women more likely to work outside the home come from urban as opposed to rural settings and from the Northeast and Far West as opposed to the South.

10. Supply of and demand for jobs. In World War II, when the demand for labor was high and the supply low, 38% of all U.S. women were in the labor force, compared to 29% and 34% for the non-war years of 1940 and 1950, respectively. The current increasing number of service sector jobs traditionally employing women has presented a similar picture of high demand and low labor supply.

11. Availability of solutions to the real problems of dual-career marriages and of combining motherhood and a career (Berger, Wallston, Foster, & Wright, 1977). Women's work force participation tends to be broken. Many drop out for a few years to rear children, then re-enter the work force either full- or part-time (U.S. Dept. of Labor, 1976a). About 32% of all female workers work only part-time (U.S. Dept. of Labor, 1979b). Women with children also tend to limit their professional involvement. For example, such women are three times less likely to work overtime or to engage in extra-professional activities than are men or women without children (Epstein, 1970; U.S. Dept. of Labor, 1976b). Furthermore, mamy women may experience geographic constraints on their career opportunities. In two-career families, the woman is usually the one to accommodate her own job location to her husband's job location. This factor of geographic constraint has been found to be a major one in explaining the status difference between men and women in academia (Marwell, Rosenfelt, & Spilerman, 1979).

257

**Chapter 11:
Societal
Consequences:
Prejudice and
Work**

These patterns handicap women in occupational achieving. Because of geographic constraints and child-care demands, some competent women may be underemployed or even unemployed. The jobs currently available for part-time workers are usually limited to low-paying, low-skilled jobs. Occupationally, the years from the late 20s to the early 30s, when many women are out of the labor force, are the most important for laying a foundation for one's future career path and for creativity (Rossi, 1964). Limitations on the time available to women for professional involvement can seriously limit professional advancement (Epstein, 1970). If more professional jobs were available on a part-time basis, if more jobs had flexible hours, and if more women postponed child rearing until their 30s, more women could achieve occupationally. Having day-care centers, after-school care, child care, and household help available and reasonably priced would also help, as would greater cooperation by husbands in housework and child-care activities and in employment flexibility.

Discrimination.   Of general societal factors, perhaps the most dramatic is outright discrimination against women. As discussed at the beginning of this chapter, many men and women believe that men are more competent and more interesting and their contributions more valuable than those of equally qualified females. Fidell (1976) found that psychology department chairpersons (all male) tended to place male applicants in higher positions than similarly qualified female applicants. (Written profiles were used with only the names and pronouns changed.) Likewise, male college graduates receive four times as many job offers as do female college graduates (Association of American Colleges, June 1977). The unemployment rates also show the effects of discrimination, women's rates being higher than men's for all classifications of workers (7.0% and 5.2%, respectively, in October 1979—U.S. Dept. of Labor, 1979b). However, at least one study by Cole (cited in Robertson, 1979) reports that there is little discrimination in the upper levels of American science, except in the area of promotions. Cole's study has been strongly attacked by other researchers on the basis of sample size and data interpretation.

Of course, men trying to enter feminine sex-typed jobs may also suffer from discrimination. In the beginning of this chapter, we reviewed evidence of prejudice against men in female-related occupations. R. Levinson (1976) found that male applicants met with more discrimination than did females in applying for jobs associated with the other sex, perhaps because desiring less highly valued "feminine" jobs throws doubts on a male's masculinity, mental stability, or intelligence. Yet a pro-male bias was still evident. Many males deemed inappropriate for "women's work" were encouraged to apply for other, more prestigious positions within the company, whereas females were more often encouraged to take lower status jobs.

As noted above, a major index of discrimination is the salary differential between women and men. In 1976, female college graduates earned 73% as much as men with an eighth-grade education and only 59% of the salary earned by male college graduates (J. W.

Brown, Aldrich, & Hall, 1978; U.S. Dept. of Labor, 1976b). Even when female and male workers are matched for skill, education, tenure on the job, and so on, the salary gap still remains (Levitin, Quinn, & Staines, 1973; Suter & Miller, 1973; U.S. Dept. of Labor, 1976b).

Levitin and colleagues (1973) studied salaries of 351 women and 695 men drawn from a national sample of workers in 1969. They estimated that fully 95% of the women they studied earned less than they deserved. This 95% figure should be contrasted with 50%, the figure predicted if only random errors were operating. Yet, when these women were questioned, only 8% were aware of this inequity!

Awareness of discrimination has increased dramatically since that time, but the salary gap remains and is widening. A more recent study (Calder & Ross, 1977) found that many women who have a male supervisor or who work on a male-sex-typed task expect to be discriminated against. They also feel such discrimination is "socially appropriate"—that is, that a man *should* earn more than a woman. This is a sad commentary on the internalization of the sex-role stereotypes.

Chesler and Goodman (1976) contend that, because of socialization, women see a different relationship between work and money than do men. Where men see work primarily as a way of earning a living and as being central to their identity, many women see work as tangential to their major socioemotional role. (Some of these differences regarding the meaning of work and achievement were discussed in Chapter Nine.) Support for this contention comes from research on self-pay behavior conducted by Lawrence Messé and colleagues (Callahan-Levy & Messé, 1979; Messé & Watts, 1979; Watts, Messé, & Vallacher, 1979).

Females from first grade through college paid themselves less for work performed than did males. They also paid themselves less than other people (males and females) paid them. Females were less certain than males of the connection between their work and monetary pay and consequently relied more on external cues than did males. Females also felt less comfortable about paying themselves than did males. However, the more "masculine" the occupational orientation of these females (that is, the greater the number of male-dominated occupations preferred), and the more agentic the characteristics they possessed, the more their allocation pattern resembled that of the males. Perhaps, then, as women become more androgynous and move out of "female" occupations, they will be less willing to tolerate economic discrimination directed against themselves.

Much of this discrimination is due to a variety of myths people hold regarding women workers:

Myth 1. Women work just for "pin money." *Fact:* As discussed above, most women work out of economic necessity.

Myth 2. Women don't really want to work or to have a "career." *Fact:* Most studies have found that the majority of women still would work even if they did not have to. Women and men are equally concerned about getting ahead when they have a realistic chance of being promoted and are equally concerned that work be self-actualizing

(Crowley et al., 1973; Kanter, 1976; Renwick & Lawler, 1978). A study of 123 workers (Rosenbach, Dailey, & Morgan, 1979) found that, when organizational job level was held constant, male and female workers viewed job dimensions and work outcomes in similar ways.

Myth 3. Women are less reliable employees. *Fact:* Although the sex difference in absence because of illness is small, most reports do indicate that women are more likely than men to be absent from work—5.1 days a year for women, 4.8 days a year for men (U.S. Bureau of the Census, 1977; U.S. Dept. of Labor, 1977c). Women are out more often for shorter periods of time on account of acute illnesses; men are out for longer periods of time because of chronic illnesses. These official causes for sick leave may be misleading. A recent study of personnel sick-leave records and self-reports found that women were more likely to be absent due to child-care activities and to officially report these activities as personal illnesses than were men (Englander-Golden & Barton, 1979). Women and men without children did not differ significantly in sick-leave hours. Furthermore, a survey by the University of Michigan's Survey Research Center (reported by the Association of American Colleges, June 1978, p. 3) found that women workers actually waste less time on the job than do men, as measured by coffee breaks and personal activities.

Myth 4. Women have a higher job turnover rate than men and thus their training and education often are wasted. *Fact:* Although some studies show that turnover rates are higher for women than for men, when skill level, education level, age of worker, and length of service are controlled variables, there is no significant difference between the sexes in job turnover (U.S. Dept. of Labor, 1975). For example, 90% of all female Ph.D.s were employed ten years after receiving their degree, the same percentage as male Ph.D.s (Chafetz, 1978). However, a 1978 survey of 321 U.S. graduate departments of psychology (Stapp, 1979) found that women and minority faculty members were more likely to leave their university before a tenure decision was made than were White male faculty members. The reasons for such early leavetaking by women are unclear. The women may receive better job offers elsewhere, may be discouraged by their departments from remaining, or may have conflicting career demands from a two-career household. In terms of occupational mobility, 9% of all working men in 1973 had changed jobs during the previous year compared to 8% for women. In occupations where there were large numbers of both males and females employed, mobility rates were higher for men (U.S. Dept. of Labor, 1975).

It is true that the average female's work life is shorter than the average male's, which is 43 years, since most women do take some time off for child-rearing. Yet one-tenth of all women never marry and they average a 45-year work life, 2 years longer than the male average because women live longer; one-tenth more marry but don't have children, and they average a 35-year work life. Of those who do marry and have children, most still work for between 24 and 28 years (Suelzle, 1970). Thus job training and preparation are not "wasted." If day care were more available, even more mothers would work. Fur-

259
Chapter 11:
Societal
Consequences:
Prejudice and
Work

thermore, child bearing appears to have no negative effects on work productivity, at least among female scientists (Robertson, 1979).

Myth 5. Women have different aptitudes than do men and therefore should stick to "women's jobs." *Fact:* There are very few group differences between males and females in aptitudes, intelligence, or behavior, and what differences exist are not all-or-none (for example, some females are better at mathematics than some males). In addition, most jobs are sexless—tradition and status, not aptitudes, have labeled jobs as more appropriate for one sex than another.

Myth 6. Women take jobs away from men. *Fact:* Women and men have not competed traditionally for the same jobs (for example, jobs as a secretary or a nurse). More significantly, since women make up over 40% of the work force, if they all quit, the economy would collapse. However, as more women enter the work force and apply for nontraditional jobs, they *will* be competing with men. In times of high unemployment it may, in fact, be true that some women will take some jobs away from men. In a society that prides itself on equal opportunity, this situation will have to be accepted.

Myth 7. Mixing the sexes in the work environment disrupts concentration. *Fact:* Most studies show that initially mixed-sex groups are more self-conscious than single-sex groups, but that they tend to adjust with time (Aries, 1977; Kanter, 1977; Suelzle, 1970). Women may suffer more than men in a mixed-sex group, especially if the women are greatly outnumbered. Studies of "token women" show that such individuals have a hard time being accepted as full members of the work group and feel isolated and invisible (Epstein, 1970; Hennig & Jardim, 1977; Kanter, 1976, 1977; Wolman & Frank, 1975). However, given time, increased numbers of women in mixed-sex groups, and institutional supports, such problems should be reduced.

Myth 8. Women cannot handle positions of power and men would not want to work under them. *Fact:* A few studies (Inderlied & Powell, 1979; Massengill & DiMarco, 1979; Powell & Butterfield, 1977) have shown that individuals do prefer a masculine manager but this refers to sex-role identity, not to actual sex. Thus masculine-sex-typed female managers were preferred over feminine- or androgynous-sex-typed managers. Interestingly, the majority of business school graduates, male and female, are masculine-sex-typed.

Much field research has demonstrated that sex does not seem to affect leadership style or ability, although it does seem to affect co-workers' expectations (Bartol & Wortman, 1979; S. M. Brown, 1979; P. Johnson, 1976, 1979; Kanter, 1977). In 1965, over two-thirds of male and one-fifth of female executives said they would not feel comfortable working for a woman (Bowman, Worthy, & Greyser, 1965). However, when people who actually had a female supervisor were questioned, most evaluated her favorably (Kanter, 1976). A favorable evaluation is particularly likely to come from female subordinates who have female supervisors. Feild and Caldwell (1979) found that female subordinates supervised by men were less satisfied with their supervisor and with their co-workers than were female subordinates

261

**Chapter 11:
Societal
Consequences:
Prejudice and
Work**

supervised by women. In experimental situations, also, people are usually equally satisfied with male and female leaders, although some studies (for example, Fallon & Hollander, 1976) have found male leaders to be more influential than female leaders. A major factor is the individual group member's attitudes toward women. In general, however, workers of both sexes want a boss who is competent, directive, and dominant.

If someone is given a supervisory position without real system power, he or she is likely to become petty and punitive (Kanter, 1976). Hence the image of the "bitchy boss," although this effect is true for both females and males. Because women have so rarely been given legitimate power (power that comes from occupying a particular role), they may need some time to adjust to it and learn how to use it effectively. Recent studies of female executives and programs to help them adapt show that some adjustment is already occurring (Bunker & Seashore, 1977; Foster & Kolinko, 1979; Hennig & Jardim, 1977; Powell & Butterfield, 1977; Tung, 1979).

Myth 9. Women have come a long way already. *Fact:* Women's relative status has been declining or remaining the same in recent years. The salary differential has been increasing, even among Ph.D.s. The percentage of doctorates in science awarded to women is just now matching the rate during the 1920s (nearly 30%) (J. W. Brown, Aldrich, & Hall, 1978). The all-time low was during the 1950s when fewer than 15% of all such degrees were awarded to women. Furthermore, women's unemployment rate has always been higher than men's, even among Ph.D.s.

These nine myths all serve to perpetuate job discrimination against women. When combined with *institutional barriers*, their effect is overwhelmingly negative on the career aspirations of women.

There are a number of institutional barriers to women's career aspirations, most reflecting a lack of understanding of and/or a lack of consideration for women's unique career patterns. That is, institutions do not take into account that most women have children for whom they are primarily responsible and thus women may need or want to take some time out from full-time careers for child rearing or to work or go to school part-time. By having only one career pattern in mind—full-time, uninterrupted work—institutions shut many women out of many jobs.

The primary institutional barrier is the sex typing of occupations. If women are steered into and hired for jobs in only a few low-paying, low-status job fields, it is no wonder that there is where most end up.

Occupational Segregation. Figure 11-6 illustrates the occupational distribution of women in the labor force in 1979. The demand for female workers is restricted to a small number of sexually segregated occupations. The principal employer of women in 1979 is the service industry, as it was in 1940 (Waldman & McEaddy, 1974). As Figure 11-6 shows, women are underrepresented as craft workers, laborers, nonretail sales workers, and managers, and are overrepresented as private household and clerical workers. Of all women who work outside the home, 80% are concentrated in light industry, clerical, and so-called service jobs (U.S. Dept. of Labor, 1978). Of the 441 occupations listed by the U.S. census bureau, women are primarily concentrated in the 20 lowest-paid job classifications. In fact, 60% of the women working in 1976 were in just four job fields (clerks, sales people, waitresses, or hairdressers)(Women Employed, 1977).

Oppenheimer (1970, 1975) argues that there are really two labor markets—one male, one female—and that the two groups rarely compete for the same jobs. Practically all (93% to 98%) of the craft workers, transport equipment operatives, farmers, and workers earning over $15,000 are men, whereas practically all of the stenographers, typists, receptionists, secretaries, telephone operators, and private household workers are women (Kanter, 1977; U.S. Dept. of Labor, 1979b). Segregation of jobs by sex is even more severe than segregation of jobs by race (Blau, 1975).

Not only are many women limited in terms of which jobs they may hold, but even within the same occupations men and women are often assigned different tasks. Females are usually assigned the lowest-paying ones. For example, most female sales workers sell items costing under $70, whereas most male sales workers sell items costing over $100. Thus, males make more money in commissions and, as a result, earn two and one-half times what female sales workers earn (Blau, 1975).

This pattern of males holding the highest-paid and highest-status jobs is found in other societies as well. For all occupations in all societies, as the salary and status of an occupation increase, the proportion of women in that occupation decreases (Epstein, 1970). In

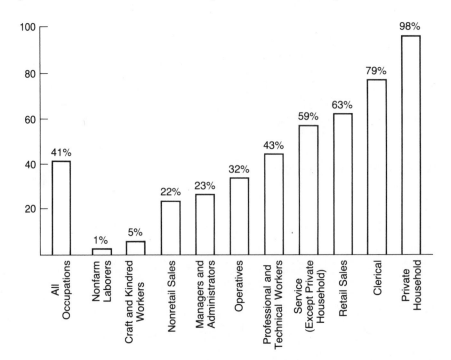

Figure 11-6
Occupational distribution of employed women, October 1979. (From U.S. Department of Labor, Bureau of Labor Statistics, Employment & Earnings, *November 1979.)*

fact, as discussed in Chapter Six, the status of an occupation can be manipulated by varying the proportion of women in it—the more women, the lower the status.

263

Chapter 11:
Societal
Consequences:
Prejudice and
Work

Underlying the sex labeling of jobs are factors that have traditionally influenced female participation in the labor force but that no longer are valid for many female workers. Most traditional "women's jobs" do not require long-term commitment. The hours are flexible, the jobs exist all over the country, and the jobs do not necessitate employer investment in training. Hence, women can drop in and out of these jobs according to family needs and personal desires. These jobs are also viewed as an extension of "natural female functions"—nurturing, servicing others, housework, and so on (Van Dusen & Sheldon, 1976). The fact that women are limited to a few jobs and may have limited mobility (they usually live where their husbands work) means that many constitute a reserve pool of qualified women outside the paid labor market (Blau, 1975). This, in turn, allows salaries to be kept low.

Interestingly, the small decrease in job segregation from 1960 to 1970 has been due to the increase in less sex-segregated occupations, such as computer specialties, and to men entering traditionally feminine jobs, not vice versa (Van Dusen & Sheldon, 1976). And once men enter "women's jobs," the salary and status of the occupations increase. For example, the number of male secretaries increased from 17,000 in 1965 to 29,000 in 1975. Their average weekly salary was $179 compared to women's $145 (*E-R Monitor*, January–February 1977, p. 5).

Access to Education. Occupational segregation is just one institutional factor of the many that act as barriers to female achievement in the labor force. Another is access to education.

The lack of equal access to higher education also seriously handicaps many women in their career plans. As Roby (1972) and others (J. W. Brown et al., 1978; Freeman, 1975; O'Connell, 1977) have noted, structural barriers to women in higher education abound. There are stricter admission policies, less financial aid, active discouragement or disregard of women's career aspirations by counselors and faculty, inflexible residency and full-time study requirements, lack of maternity and paternity leaves, and lack of child-care facilities. There are also few female faculty members as role models, especially in the higher ranks (only 9.5% of full professors were female in 1977–78). Although the number of women in higher education has been increasing during the past 15 years (see Table 11-2), women received less than one-quarter of the doctorates and less than one-fifth of first professional degrees awarded in 1977.

The chance of obtaining a job commensurate with her advanced training may also discourage a woman from pursuing further education. Solmon (1978) found that the inability of many female Ph.D. psychologists to obtain jobs as good as those of men was a prime factor in dissuading women from pursuing a career in psychology. Thus restricted access to business and professional opportunities may limit female educational achievement.

Access to Business and the Professions.   In the professions and business, a number of characteristics serve as barriers to women (J. W. Brown et al., 1978; Bunker & Seashore, 1977; Epstein, 1970; Fidell, 1976; Helmreich, Spence, Beane, Lucker, & Matthews, 1979; Hennig & Jardim, 1977; Kanter, 1976; O'Connell, 1977; Rossi, 1965; M. White, 1970). In sex-typed male occupations (that is, most professions, such as science, engineering, medicine, mathematics, and law), women are frequently excluded from "socialization into a profession" by not being "adopted" by a sponsor or mentor. The "old boy network" is strong. In a survey of academic administrators, only 24% of the positions were filled by individuals without any prior connections with the institution or with the individuals doing the hiring (Association of American Colleges, Fall 1978, p. 1).

The colleague system is also important for professional advancement. Women tend not to become as involved as men in the system, since women's contributions and performance are less visible, partly because of discrimination. Women tend to be cited in professional publications less frequently than are men, which may contribute to their work being under-recognized and under-supported (Helmreich, Spence, Beane, Lucker, & Matthews, 1979; Miller & Zeitz, 1978). Women belong to fewer professional organizations, limit their own professional interactions, and generally put in fewer hours (often because they have family responsibilities). In addition, women are usually excluded (and exclude themselves) from informal channels of communication, like lunches, in which they may stand out and feel uncomfortable. Women also are more likely than men to be given leadership positions without real power.

To counteract the "old boy network," scores of new professional women's groups have arisen in the last few years; for example, The Women's Forum, Women in Business, and the Assocation for Women in Psychology (Nemy, 1979a). Most of these groups were formed deliberately "to make the buddy system work for women."

There is also the issue of sexual harassment and sexual intimacy, to which women are particularly vulnerable, although one study (Gutek & Nakamura, 1979) found no sex difference in self-reports of such behaviors. About 10% of all respondents in the Gutek and Nakamura study reported some sexual harassment on their current job. However, a nationwide survey of clinical psychologists in 1978 (Pope, Levenson, & Schover, 1979) found strong sex differences in the frequency of sexual contact between teachers and students. When the respondents were students, 16.5% of the women and 3% of the men reported that they had had sexual contact with their educators. A striking finding was that, of the female respondents who graduated in the last 6 years, 25% had had such sexual contact. As psychology educators, 19% of the men—compared with 8% of the women—reported sexual contact with their students. Other research has found that some men may try to use their power to get sexual favors, to test the woman, or simply to enact sex rituals because it is their most familiar mode of interacting with women (Bralove, 1976; Bunker & Seashore, 1977; Hennig & Jardim, 1977; Kelber, 1977; Lindsey,

·265

**Chapter 11:
Societal
Consequences:
Prejudice and
Work**

1977). Many women are thus put in awkward positions, face a risk to their job and to a superior's good will, and have the focus shifted from their job ability to their physical attributes. Similar negative effects appear to be true for some men.

Overall, women must learn the informal rules of business and professional behavior with which most men are brought up. (See Chapter Eight on the importance of sports and teamwork for success in business.)

There are some factors that help professional women (Epstein, 1970; Heilbrun, 1976; O'Connell, 1977; M. White, 1970). Among them are part-time training and work opportunities, flexibility of role playing, and awareness on the part of male colleagues of women's particular problems. Structuring the work situation also aids women. They benefit by formality in the professional context, defined standards of performance, and supervision of the professional interaction. Professional women also fare better as a function of the length of their career and professional relationships, and as a function of the rank of their institution. A major aid to such women is active support by men with power and by female peers.

Trade Unions. Trade unions often pose another barrier to female occupational aspirations (Falk, 1975). In 1976, only 11.3% of all women workers belonged to a labor union (U.S. Dept. of Labor, 1978). Occupations dominated by women are usually not unionized (household workers, nurses, secretaries), although some attempt currently is being made toward unionization. It is more difficult for women to get into a union and especially into apprenticeship programs in which a sponsor is needed and sons of union members are preferred. Women are discriminated against in seniority systems and are underrepresented in union leadership. It is no wonder, then, that women made up only 6% of all craft and kindred workers in 1979. Union membership is valuable. Research has shown that the salary differential between the sexes is much less for union workers than it is for nonunion workers (Levitin et al., 1973).

Laws. Legally, women face barriers also, although the 1972 amendments to the Civil Rights Act of 1954 and the Equal Pay Act of 1963 make job and salary discrimination illegal. Complaints often take years to be resolved, and many employees simply do not bother. Changes in the law in recent years have certainly helped, however. Before 1972, many states had "protective" laws prohibiting women, for example, from working overtime and from engaging in "dangerous" high-paying work. The federal minimum wage law still does not apply to household workers, 98% of whom are women. Part-time workers, most of whom are women, also are denied major benefits from employers. The 1978 Pregnancy Disability Bill finally makes discrimination on the basis of pregnancy illegal. Previously it was common practice to exempt pregnancy-related disability from coverage under temporary disability or health benefit programs while allowing men to get benefits for vasectomies and hair transplants. In fact, such exemptions had been ruled legal under the 1976 *Gilbert* versus *General Electric* decision by the U.S. Supreme Court. Even the new law, however, has its limitations. It only applies to those employers covered by the federal antidiscrimination law in Title VII of the Civil Rights Act.

Until now, we have mainly been examining women's role in the labor force. As has been shown, the sex-role stereotypes markedly affect what kinds of jobs a woman might have as well as the salary she might earn. But the stereotypes also affect men's role in the labor force. And, contrary to prevailing opinion, not all effects are beneficial. We will now examine some of these effects.

Men and the Labor Force

Whereas many women have had to struggle to enter the labor force, such participation usually is required of men by virtue of the male sex role. A woman's identity traditionally has been defined by her relationships; a man's, primarily by his job. As Pleck and Sawyer (1974) note, "work is the institution that most defines the majority of males" (p. 94). Although work can provide a sense of satisfaction and self-worth and is usually necessary for satisfying one's material needs, the overexaggeration of the work role for men has as serious consequences for them as does the overexaggeration of the homemaker role for women.

In the first place, as was discussed in Chapters Nine and Ten, the emphasis on most males to participate in the work force encourages males to develop a high achievement and competitive orientation. Success and status become the bedrock of the male sex role, and masculinity is often measured by the amount of money a man earns or by his material possessions (David & Brannon, 1976; Gould, 1973; Pleck & Sawyer, 1974). This goal orientation and competition often obliterate other rewards of working, such as mastery of a skill. They may also lead to finding substitute ways of gaining status—one-upsmanship, athletic prowess, emphasis on sexual performance—especially if one's job is *not* intrinsically rewarding (David & Brannon, 1976; Fasteau, 1974; Korda, 1973; Shostak, 1969; Tolson, 1977; Van den Berghe, 1970; Williams, 1970). Such intense competition and stress to achieve also may make many men more vulnerable to stress-related diseases.

As a result of such an achievement and competitive focus, some men's relationships may suffer. As was discussed in Chapter Ten, because they are usually trained to develop these qualities and neglect their emotional side, it is difficult for many men to trust other men and form close relationships with them, with women, and especially with their children. When work becomes a primary focus in one's life, other things and people are excluded (Brenton, 1966). Many jobs actually require such exclusion. Men often are expected to work overtime, to put in many hours in work-related activities (for example, cocktail parties, golf), to travel, and so forth, Research has shown the business executive and the blue collar worker to be particularly

267

Chapter 11:
Societal
Consequences:
Prejudice and
Work

caught in the masculine stereotype, the former because he believes he can "make it" (Bartolome, 1972; Maccoby, 1976); the latter, because he realizes he cannot (Shostak, 1969, 1972; Tolson, 1977). In any case, many families rarely see their "breadwinner," causing serious damage to the marital and the parent-child relationships.

In addition, when an individual's identity is solely defined by one thing, when that one thing ends, emotional problems may result. Thus women who are identified solely as mothers may experience marked depression and marked loss of self-esteem when their children leave home. Similarly, many men who are unemployed or retired also may experience marked depression and loss of self-esteem, often leading to alcoholism, suicide, heart attacks, and other ailments (see Chapter Nine).

As many women have rejected their sex typing, many men, especially the younger ones, also are doing so. Both as a result of the questioning of sex roles prompted by the women's movement and the fact that most paid work no longer provides the sense of self-worth that it is supposed to, many men are also beginning to question the responsibility and expectations placed on them (Appley, 1977; Bardwick, 1979; Friedan, 1979; Tolson, 1977). Like women, many men want more options and more satisfaction. Some retire early. Others drop out of the work force because of health problems, lack of education, or because they are economically able to do so. Still others are becoming less willing to transfer from one location to another. Many men now show a preference for shorter or more flexible work hours, and some are increasing their participation in household maintenance and child-care functions (Appley, 1977; Pifer, 1976). Many men also are rejecting the whole notion of a career as being the sole means of male identity. They want a richer, fuller life, one that makes use of their full range of human potentialities. Instead of adjusting to the "Establishment," many are expecting the Establishment to become more androgynous and to adjust to them (Bernard, 1971).

Some organizations are, in fact, changing (Shepard, 1977). Many jobs now require more emphasis on human relations and less on simple hierarchical relationships. In some cases, competition is becoming less important and, in fact, dysfunctional. Authority and obedience are no longer always the foundation of an organization. Many modern businesses are requiring nonstereotyped, multifaceted functioning for maximum effectiveness. Androgyny as an ideal for occupational and individual functioning is supplanting the traditional ideology of strictly sex-typed functioning in a number of places.

Summary

In sum, women are a vital part of the work force, yet their importance often is not acknowledged, materially or otherwise. They often are discriminated against, steered into a few low-paying, low-status job fields, and barred from advancement and alternatives. Yet change is occurring and women are continuing to enter the labor force in record numbers, currently constituting 42% of all workers.

Men also often are steered into certain jobs, but their choice of jobs tends to be broader and their pay and status higher. Many suffer from the pressure on them to achieve, to be "a success," and some men are rejecting their stereotyped identity as "breadwinner" for a more human one. Recent trends to decrease occupational sex typing and to temper the "work ethic" will help humanize both the work world and the workers.

Change is needed in five major areas in order to allow women full entry into the labor force (Pifer, 1976): (1) Vigorous new measures are needed to reduce unemployment, such as by jobsharing and flextime opportunities (whereby individuals work 40 hours a week but not necessarily from 9 to 5). New measures are also needed to press for compliance with laws that prohibit discrimination against women, increase the advance of women (such as by vigorous recruitment and training), and build in recognition of parental child-rearing responsibilities (such as by leave policies, child-care facilities). (2) A comprehensive family support system is needed with adequate day-care and after-school care arrangements for all who need them. (3) Continuing attack on sex discrimination and sexist practices in education must be made. (4) Traditional assumptions of female dependence will have to disappear. (5) Greater flexibility in the traditional life-cycle patterns is needed, allowing males and females to alternate periods of study, employment, and work in the home. All these changes entail a reordering of American priorities with greater choice for the individual and improved quality of life in contrast to the traditional concern for productivity. Whether or not we, as a society, will embrace this new goal remains to be seen.

SUMMARY

In this chapter we have reviewed some of the societal consequences of the sex-role stereotypes. One of the most basic is the widespread prejudice against women on the part of both males and females. This prejudice is particularly manifested in the world of work, where women as a group are underpaid and are channeled into only a few, low-status positions. The barriers against women achieving in the area of employment are both internal, as a result of sex-role socialization, and external, in the form of societal and institutional obstacles.

Men, too, may be penalized by their sex role in the world of work. They stereotypically are expected to be aggressive, competitive breadwinners and are defined predominantly by their job. This role restricts the development of men's full human potential and may affect their relationships with others and their own health.

The sex-role stereotypes have other societal consequences as well, particularly in the areas of power and aggression. These areas will be explored in the next chapter.

RECOMMENDED READING

269

**Chapter 11:
Societal
Consequences:
Prejudice and
Work**

Bernard, J. *Women and the public interest*. Chicago: Aldine, 1971. An interesting argument for adjusting the Establishment to the lives of women rather than vice versa.

Hennig, M., & Jardim, A. *The managerial woman*. New York: Doubleday, 1977. Interviews with and analysis of the women who have "made it" into management: how to get and stay there.

Kreps, J. (Ed.). *Women and the American economy: A look to the 1980s*. Englewood Cliffs, N.J.: Prentice-Hall, 1976. The role women have played and are likely to play in our economy.

U.S. Department of Labor, Bureau of Labor Statistics. U.S. Government Printing Office. Monthly and yearly compilation of employment and earnings statistics, broken down by numerous variables.

12 Societal Consequences: Power and Aggression

Sex-role stereotypes affect society not only on a specific, tangible level, as in discrimination and employment concerns, but also on a more abstract and global level, as in the use of power and aggression. This chapter will focus on these hard-to-quantify effects.

POWER

In terms of power in American society (the ability to influence another, to get done what you want to get done), women are generally at a marked disadvantage. This is true personally, economically, politically, legally, and militarily. Power in America is predominantly in the hands of the "White male club," from which women and minorities traditionally and deliberately have been excluded. *U.S. News and World Report* magazine runs an annual survey on "Who runs America." Their 1978 results, which appeared as the cover story of their April 17, 1978, edition, pictured 12 White males, including Jimmy Carter, Cyrus Vance, and George Meany. Table 12-1 shows further evidence of this club. In every public office, particularly the most powerful, men predominate. This is true around the world (Lipman-Blumen & Bernard, 1979). The world mean for the proportion of female to male administrators is only about 10%.

Power is important since, as a number of writers have noted (for example, Blumberg, 1979), it is differential power that underlies all inequality. Therefore, it will be instructive to examine the five forms of power (personal, economic, political, legal, and military) and the sexes' relationship to them in more detail.

Personal Power

Goodchilds (1979) discusses three different aspects of personal power—the ability to get one's way, the ability to get along with others, and the ability to get things done. Traditionally, men have been associated with getting one's way, and this aspect has been the most emphasized of the three. Getting along with others is an aspect of power traditionally associated with women, and this aspect has been viewed as conflicting with the first. Men and women perceive the sexes as handling power differently, even if they don't. Goodchild's

271

**Chapter 12:
Societal
Consequences:
Power and
Aggression**

Table 12-1
Men Run America, 1979.

	% Men	% Women
U.S. Population	48.7	51.3
U.S. Senate	99	1
U.S. House	96	4
U.S. Supreme Court	100	0
Federal Judges	95	5
Governors	96	4
State Representatives	89	11
State Senators	95	5
Statewide Elective/Appointive Offices	89	11
County Governing Boards	97	3
Mayors and Councilors	92	8
School Board Members	75	25

Data compiled by the National Women's Education Fund and the Center for American Women in Politics. Used by permission.

point is that we should be concerned about the third aspect of power, getting things done. Power should be conceived in terms of accomplishments, rather than relationships. In this way, conflict between "masculine" and "feminine" power styles would be reduced and such distinctions, in fact, might be irrelevant.

When interpersonal relationships are examined, women have been found traditionally to use indirect, emotional, helpless strategies to get their way. P. Johnson and Goodchilds (1976) found these strategies to be markedly ineffective in the long run and found that the use of such strategies decreases the user's self-esteem and increases others' personal dislike. Ironically, when women use more direct messages that rely on their expertise, they tend to be rated as more aggressive than men who use such messages.

Within a romantic relationship, such differences in power strategies are less likely to occur. Peplau and colleagues (1976) found in their study of dating couples (see Chapter 10) that men were as likely as women to use emotional appeals or to ask questions. Of 12 different power strategies, the sexes differed in the use of only two: men gave information more often and women were more likely to disagree with or contradict information given by their boyfriends. Yet, in most relationships, men were viewed as dominant, and this is certainly true in traditional marital relationships. As Gillespie (1971) notes, most husbands obtain power in marriage not because of individual resources or personal competence but simply because they are male and men in our society have all the institutionalized power. For a wife to gain even a little power, she usually must obtain it from external sources—she must work, have an education superior to her husband's, or participate in organizations more than he. As discussed previously, access to these sources of power has traditionally been blocked for women.

Times are changing somewhat. The U.S. census bureau announced that in 1980 it will no longer view husbands as the only legitimate head of a household. The Bureau will now interview the owner or renter of the house or, failing such a person, any adult household member.

The fact that economic power generally translates into family power should not be surprising given the fact that traditional marriages have been based on female financial dependence. The more money a woman brings in, the more power in the family she tends to have and the more egalitarian the marriage arrangement tends to become. Because a woman does not generally earn as much as her husband, the husband's dominance is still somewhat assured. This fact may work directly or indirectly to keep the salary differential wide. It should be recalled from Chapter Six that, throughout history and across cultures, the more women work in the main productive activity of a society, the greater their societal status (Blumberg, 1977). Although productive labor does not lead women directly to freedom and equality, it can lead them to economic power, which, in turn, seems to be the strongest influence on women's relative equality and freedom. Such power can aid women in controlling their personal destiny—marriage, divorce, sex, children, free movement, education, and household power (Blumberg, 1977, 1979; Youssef & Hartley, 1979).

Economic Power

Even though more women are in the work force than ever before, they are still predominantly in the low-salary, low-status jobs. Very few women are in the upper ranks of corporate management in the United States. Although in 1974 they made up 42% of the total labor force, women accounted for only 5% of all those earning $15,000 or more and only 2.4% of those earning more than $25,000 (U.S. Dept. of Labor, 1976b). Women hold fewer than 2% of the directorships of top U.S. corporations, fewer than 1% of top management posts, and only about 6% of all middle-management positions in this country (Crittendon, 1977). They have made little headway in the hierarchies of heavy industry, insurance, many high technology fields, and retailing. The reasons for the slow pace of women's progress have been attributed to the ambivalent attitudes of many male managers, a reluctance to take a chance and relax the requirement for extensive experience, and the need for women to prove their competence repeatedly (Crittendon, 1977).

The consequences of male dominance of the economy are manifest not only in the power men exert but also in the way the economy, especially business, is run. The way business is run, in turn, affects all members of the society, workers and nonworkers alike. Because business executives succeed on their ability to make decisions that maximize corporate profit, and because such executives usually epitomize the rational, nonemotional, insensitive, competitive male (Bartolome, 1972), these decisions often are contrary to human needs (Platt, 1976; Pleck & Sawyer, 1974; Tolson, 1977). Thus we live in a country of enormous wealth, natural resources, and productivity, yet many children suffer from malnutrition, our air and water have become increasingly polluted, and our safety standards for motor vehicles and consumer products are low. The hierarchy that is dominant in the business world (as well as in the political and military worlds) implies control of many by a few. This hierarchical structure then becomes the primary mode in which many men operate—being dominated and oppressed at work and going home to dominate their wives and children (Pleck & Sawyer, 1974; Tolson, 1977). Institutions may use and perpetuate the masculine stereotype because it serves their purpose. Through the emphasis on getting ahead and "staying cool," many men fit right into institutions "whose function is not to increase general human welfare but to enhance the profit, power and prestige of the few who control them" (Pleck & Sawyer, 1974, pp. 126–127).

The fact that many women are now trying to enter these bastions of male power may mean that they will need to adopt similar ways of dealing with situations—competitively, hierarchically, and unfeelingly. Whether this is a desirable state of affairs is, of course, a value judgment. It is the opinion of the author that androgynous functioning should be an ideal of institutional as well as individual functioning, that the masculine stereotype of achievement should be used in conjunction with the feminine stereotype of concern for people. Some companies are beginning to realize such a shift is necessary. As some specialists who work in women's management-training programs note, corporations will profit most by learning how to use the abilities that have been encouraged in most women—their talent for teamwork, their tenacity, and their human relations skills (Cravens, 1977). Society will certainly benefit as a result. Thus humanization of institutions is as much a goal of the women's liberation movement as is human liberation.

Political Power

Salaries, a small part of economic power, are an even smaller part of political power. But political power can and does influence salaries and the work situation in general. And, politically, women have consistently had negligible power. Women won the right to vote in the United States in 1920 and currently make up 53% of the nation's registered voters. Yet they have never used this voting power to their advantage—for example, by voting as a bloc (Bernard, 1979a). Although women currently vote with nearly as much frequency as do men (education is the most important factor in voter participation), and have similar party affiliations (N. Lynn, 1975), they are underrepresented in the party hierarchies and in elected and appointed offices. They are, however, overrepresented in volunteer (unpaid and nonpowerful) positions.

On the political party level, women have served as indispensable volunteers, but rarely in positions of responsibility or decision making. Only 18% of the top jobs of the 1976 major presidential campaign organizations are estimated to have been held by women (*Stars & Stripes*, January 27, 1976). Since 1972 and the efforts of the McGovern-Frasier Committee of the Democratic Party and women's

273
Chapter 12:
Societal
Consequences:
Power and
Aggression

rights organizations, more women have served as party delegates than ever before (38% of Democrats, 30% of Republicans in 1972). For the 1980 convention, Democrats voted to require that half their delegates must be women. Republicans have promised to aim for similar representation. Although delegates are visible and this is certainly an improvement, these are not the most powerful party positions.

Women still occupy less than 10% of all elected offices in the United States, with women officeholders concentrated in a few offices at the state and local level (see Table 12-1). At these lower levels, there have been impressive gains. In 1979, the number of women elected to state legislatures increased two and a half times from what it was in 1969 (from 305, or 4.1%, to 767, or 10.3%). Even more gains have been made in local government, but primarily in positions traditionally reserved for women, such as on library boards or in part-time, poorly-paid elective offices. Few women are state governors (2 out of 50 in 1979), mainly because women are more readily accepted as a representative than as a leader.

On a federal level, the number of women in Congress is still minimal, as shown in Table 12-2. The proportion has fluctuated at around 2% of total members during the last 20 years. Representation in the Senate has been strikingly low. Until 1978, no women had been elected there since Margaret Chase Smith was defeated in 1972. In the 1979–80 Congress, there was only one woman in the Senate, and only 16 in the House. Few women who have served in Congress have been able to build up enough seniority to be powerful, and none has been elected to any of the party leadership roles.

In other positions on the federal level, women also have little power. In 1975, women held only 11% of the 22,256 positions on

Table 12-2
Number of Women in Congress, 1947–1980

Congress	Year	Senate	House
80th	1947–1948	0	8
81st	1949–1950	1	9
82nd	1951–1952	1	10
83rd	1953–1954	2	11
84th	1955–1956	1	16
85th	1957–1958	1	15
86th	1959–1960	1	16
87th	1961–1962	2	17
88th	1963–1964	2	11
89th	1965–1966	2	10
90th	1967–1968	1	11
91st	1969–1970	1	10
92nd	1971–1972	1	12[a]
93rd	1973–1974	0	16[b]
94th	1975–1976	0	19
95th	1977–1978	2[c]	18
96th	1979–1980	1	16

[a] Charlotte Reid left Congress to accept a presidential appointment.
[b] Lindy Boggs and Cardiff Collins were elected in special elections in 1973 to succeed their late husbands.
[c] Muriel Humphrey and Maryon Allen were appointed in 1978 to succeed their late husbands.

275

Chapter 12:
Societal
Consequences:
Power and
Aggression

federal advisory committees and commissions, predominantly appointed positions (*N.Y. Times*, September 19, 1976), and fewer than 2% of the highest paying federal jobs (N. Lynn, 1975). Despite the Carter administration's pledge to significantly increase the number of women in top government jobs, as of February 1979, women's representation was only about 18% (Ford's record was 14%). Again, women's greatest representation has been at the lower levels, although Carter did appoint three of the nation's six women cabinet officers (Roberts, 1979). Interestingly, in Federal agencies headed by women, nearly 50% of the appointed positions have been filled by women. Such appointments suggest that qualified women are available. Certain appointive posts have rarely been held by a woman, most noticeably in the judiciary. Among nations, the United States still has one of the worst records for the holding by women of national public office (N. Lynn, 1975).

The barriers to women in politics are numerous and are similar to those present for women in the work force. One set of barriers arises from sex-role socialization. Many people (women and men) still think politics is "masculine" and are concerned that political participation would somehow "coarsen" women (Bernard, 1979a). Consequently, women have a difficult time developing the self-confidence needed to run for public office. They also tend to believe that family responsibilities should come first. The major barriers, however, are external; for example, prejudice and discrimination against female candidates. In 1970, the Gallup Poll found that 13% of males and females would not vote for a *qualified* woman for Congress (N. Lynn, 1975). In 1978, 10% still said that they would not vote for a woman "under any circumstances" (Broder, 1978). Preconceptions about female candidates, such as "she can't take time away from her family," "she's too emotionally unstable due to her menstrual cycle," and so on, also serve as barriers. Jobs women hold often make office-seeking difficult. Family responsibilities, a major obstacle, have traditionally fallen on women. Most women who have been elected to office are older and they are usually widowed or divorced (N. Lynn, 1975). Women also have a great deal of trouble raising funds. They suffer from a loser's image and frequently shoulder the burden of mistakes and reputations built by other women in public life. In addition, political clubs and social activities usually exclude women formally and informally (the "smoke-filled back rooms"). Party leaders may force women into a no-win position by encouraging them when a nomination seems worthless and ignoring them when it looks valuable.

Even when a woman has some political power, she may not be able to wield it as effectively as a man in the same situation because of sex-role stereotypes. Female politicians may be reproached for assuming male prerogatives (Jaquette, 1974). Outspoken women, in particular, may be negatively evaluated, at least by women (Denmark, 1979). An interesting example of the difficulties facing women in politics occurred in February 1979 when Queen Elizabeth II of England visited the Persian Gulf countries. In order to be received by her Moslem male hosts and be accorded the honors generally bestowed upon a visiting chief of state, Queen Elizabeth had to become an "honorary man" and cover herself with veils and wrist-to-ankle clothes. Women in most of these countries generally are not even allowed to speak in front of men.

The outlook is improving, however, and the traditional attitudes and barriers to women's involvement in politics can be broken down. A 1975 Gallup poll found that 73% of Americans would support a qualified woman for President (*Time*, January 27, 1976, p. 18), up from 66% in 1971 and 54% in 1969 (N. Lynn, 1975). A 1976 Gallup poll found that seven out of ten Americans said the nation would be governed as well or better than it is now if more women held political office (WEAL, December 1976), probably reflecting a reaction to the Watergate episode. A study by Schneider and Rall (1976) found that males and females are beginning to show same-sex loyalty in their preference for political candidates, a marked change from the previous findings of prejudice against women by males and females.

With increased numbers of women in the labor force and in higher education, their political activity should also increase. More women than ever before are running for office and this means they are gaining valuable political experience for future races as well as serving as role models for other women. Two national groups have been organized to help women raise funds—the National Women's Political Caucus and the Women's Campaign Fund. All women incumbents who sought re-election to statewide posts in 1978 won their races. These factors combined may help women attain some measure of political power. Women also appear to be gaining power during election campaigns as an important interest group (Roberts, 1979).

The consequences of male dominance of the political system are far-reaching. The stereotypic male preoccupations with power and status and the need to prove masculinity by being "tough" and unemotional have had tremendous impact on both domestic and foreign policy. George Romney (1968 presidential primary candidate), Edmund Muskie (1972 presidential primary candidate), and Thomas Eagleton (1972 first-choice running mate of McGovern) each had their political careers seriously damaged after an admission of "weakness"—having been "brainwashed," tearfully upset over slander, or having had previous treatment for emotional problems, respectively (Farrell, 1974). A number of writers (Farrell, 1974; Fasteau, 1974; Steinem, 1972; Stone, 1974) have argued persuasively that the United States' reactions to the Cuban missile crisis and, particularly, the Vietnam war, were significantly colored by the needs of Presidents Kennedy, Johnson, and Nixon to prove their "toughness." As I. F. Stone (1974) notes, "The first rule of this small boy statecraft is that the leader of a gang, like the leader of a tribe, horde, or nation, dare not appear 'chicken'" (p. 131). Not only must a leader prove his toughness to other leaders but he must be at least as tough as his predecessors. Thus President Johnson was concerned that he would be thought "less of a man" than Kennedy if he did not follow through with Vietnam (Fasteau, 1974; Steinem, 1972). Nixon was particularly obsessed with "winning," "saving face," and being "tough," as the Pentagon papers and the White House tapes all too clearly show

277
Chapter 12:
Societal
Consequences:
Power and
Aggression

(Farrell, 1974; Fasteau, 1974; Steinem, 1972). The "cult of toughness" during the Vietnam years extended to political advisors as well, whom some considered intellectuals and unmasculine (Fasteau, 1974). From this perspective, some advisors might have had a double reason to prove their masculinity. All this is not to say that standing firm, threatening, or using force is never valid. Clearly, certain situations require such responses, as President Carter learned during the Iranian and Afghanistan crises of 1979 and 1980. What is being questioned is the use of such responses to satisfy a psychological or political need, rather than as a clearly thought out and appropriate humanitarian foreign policy. Thus the Pentagon papers revealed that in March 1965, the U.S. aims in South Vietnam were only 20% to keep South Vietnam out of Chinese hands, only 10% to allow the South Vietnamese a freer, better way of life, but 70% to avoid a "humiliating defeat" (in Fasteau, 1974).

As is true with business institutions, if women want to achieve positions of political power, they often must prove themselves even "tougher" than men. Yet women, for the most part, are not obsessed with proving their strength, saving face, or prestige. Polls (Gallup, 1965, 1967, 1975, 1976) consistently show women to be generally against specific wars and against military solutions to international problems. Women are also more often against capital punishment. Analysis of the voting patterns in the House of Representatives in 1977 (*National NOW Times*, January 1978, p. 11) suggests that women do vote differently than men on some issues although the small number of women in the House makes meaningful comparisons difficult. Whereas 56.5% of the men voted in favor of the Hyde Amendment banning federal funds for abortions for poor women, 68.7% of the women voted against the ban. Whereas 55.4% of the full House voted against a ban on loans to nations violating fundamental human rights, 52.9% of the women favored the ban. Other studies of the voting patterns of women in Congress from 1917 through 1976 and of women voters also show them to be more humanistic and altruistic than are men (see Bernard, 1979a).

Women are not biologically more humane than men, but many learn to be so due to sex-role socialization. Yet political institutions, by their very structure, tend to operate on "masculine" aggressive, nonhumanitarian, competitive principles, and women who "make it" to the top often have adopted those values. To expect more humane politics just because women are in power is a sexist as well as a false notion, as Indira Gandhi in India demonstrated. The "system" itself must change and become more concerned with human values. Again, an androgynous political system seems most beneficial to individuals, the country, and even the world.

Legal Power

Few women serve in the judiciary of the United States, especially in the higher courts, and few serve in the political offices responsible for making and enforcing laws. There has never been a woman on the U.S. Supreme Court. As of September 1978, women held only one of the 97 Federal Courts of Appeal judgeships, only 11 of the 399 judgeships in the U.S. District Courts, and only 12 of the 932 judgeships in state courts of appeal or state supreme courts (*ER-Monitor*, January–February 1977, p. 6; NOW Legal Defense and Education Fund, 1978). The 1978 Omnibus Judgeship Act created 152 new judgeships and was partially intended to "open up the system" to qualified women and minority members. If the 79 nominations for judgeships made by President Carter in 1979 all are approved, the percentage of women on the federal bench will increase from approximately 3% to approximately 5% (Segal, 1979). However, reviews of the nominating and selection process reveal that although more women and minority members are being recommended, the process is slow, discriminatory, and generally indicative of "politics as usual" (that is, federal judgeships being used as political patronage) (Snow, 1979; Tolchin, 1979). Thus, women currently have very little legal power and are unlikely to make significant gains in the near future.

In addition, very few attorneys are women (9% in 1977). This soon will change, however, since nearly one-third of those entering law school now are women (U.S. Dept. of Labor, 1977c). Even the current small number of women lawyers is an important increase from the past. In fact, in 1873 U.S. Supreme Court Justice Bradley allowed Illinois to bar Myra Bradwell from practicing law since women "naturally" belonged in the domestic sphere (Agate & Meacham, 1977). Since law is the route to power, particularly political power (one-third of President Carter's female appointees are lawyers), we can expect to see some changes in male dominance of this area in the future (Lipson, 1977).

Partly as a result of male dominance of the legal system and partly due to sex-role stereotypes themselves, women are frequently at a marked disadvantage under the law. Unfair treatment still exists despite significant changes in the laws and their enforcement over the past ten years toward the reduction of discrimination against women in employment, salaries, education, family planning, and credit (for example, the Pregnancy Disability Bill of 1978; the Equal Employment Opportunity Act of 1972; the Equal Pay Act of 1963 as amended by the Education Amendments of 1972; Title IX of the Education Amendments of 1972 as amended by the Bayh Amendment of 1974 and the Education Amendments of 1976; and the Equal Credit Opportunity Act of 1975). These are statutory laws, however; judicial decisions (common law) are made by legislators and judges, who are usually men, some of whom may not be able to transcend their own socialized belief that women and men are meant to have distinct and different roles in life.

Until 1971, sex was always held to be a difference that warranted different legal treatment (Agate & Meacham, 1977). In the case Reed versus Reed, a woman was prevented from becoming a bartender due to a state law excluding women from that occupation. The Supreme Court, for the first time, held a state statute to be unconstitutional because it discriminated against women. However, in 1974, the Supreme Court upheld a Florida law (Kahn versus Shevin) which granted widows a property tax exemption but did not extend the benefit to widowers (Agate & Meacham, 1977). More recently (1976), the Supreme Court's Gilbert versus General Electric decision allowed employers to exempt pregnancy-related disability from coverage under temporary disability or health benefit programs while allowing vasectomies and hair transplants to be covered. (The 1978 Pregnancy Disability Bill has changed the law for certain employers.) Thus, sex has still not been given the status of a suspect classification (as has race). Discriminatory laws still abound.

In property law especially, women are discriminated against. Only eight states have community property laws which theoretically recognize the contribution of housework to a marriage and consider that each spouse owns half of the earnings of the couple. In the 42 other states, the husband has sole control over his earnings and the right to support his wife in the manner *he* chooses. In several states (Alabama, Florida, Indiana, North Carolina), a wife cannot even sell her own property without her husband's consent.

Social Security laws also discriminate against women (Porter, 1979; Roberts, 1978). Especially disadvantaged are those women who take time out of the labor force to rear children, a job that offers no retirement benefits. Displaced homemakers (those who are widowed, divorced or separated) who have no other options for their own support must fend for themselves. If eligible, they may elect to take Social Security benefits early, at age 60 instead of 65, but must do so at a lower rate. Some homemakers do not qualify at all—women married less than 10 years are not entitled to any of their former husband's benefits. (Before 1979, the law required 20 years of marriage before benefits could be collected.) Working women, if their husbands also pay into the system, generally receive no benefit for their own contributions since their salary was usually less than their husband's. And, of course, since women earn less than men, fewer women receive maximum benefits. The plight of many elderly women is tragic—among women 65 and older who live alone, 30% of the White and 68% of the minority women are living in poverty (U.S. Dept. of Labor, 1976c). Amendments and new laws to alleviate these inequities have been proposed each year (for example, the Householders Benefit Act; the Displaced Homemakers Act), but have yet to be passed by a predominantly male Congress.

There are other laws that discriminate on the basis of sex. For instance, in many states it is illegal for males to use obscene language in the presence of females and children. In some states, statutory rape is only possible for males. Women are allowed to marry younger than are males in most states. A woman is generally assumed to be the person best qualified to care for her children and the husband to be the person best qualified to financially support them. Unwed fathers have no rights in many states. Some "protective" labor laws in some states still establish a maximum number of hours a woman may work. As can be seen from this sampling, men, as well as women, are often discriminated against by law (see Hayman, 1976).

The Equal Rights Amendment, introduced into every Congress since 1923 and still unratified, would equalize men's and women's rights in almost all instances. The amendment provides that "equality of rights under the law shall not be denied or abridged by the United States or by any State on account of sex." It would finally eliminate legislative inertia that keeps discriminatory laws on the books. It would provide clear constitutional recognition of equal rights and responsibilities for men and women. And it would serve as a clear statement of the nation's moral and legal commitment to full sexual equality (Agate & Meacham, 1977). Although seemingly clear-cut and favored by a majority of the populace (*N.Y. Times*, July 16, 1978, p. 24), the ERA has met significant roadblocks all along the way. Even with an extension for ratification to June 30, 1982, it is not certain that it will be ratified. (The ERA controversy will be discussed at greater length in Chapter 13.)

Military Power

Women traditionally have been excluded from gaining military power. They traditionally have not been subject to the draft in the United States and it has only been since the draft ended in the early 1970s that women have entered the services in significant numbers. They now constitute 6% of all military personnel, more than double the number during the Vietnam war (*N.Y. Times*, September 2, 1977). Because of the present volunteer nature of U.S. military service, a decrease in the number of available males due to the lower birth rate, and competition from the civilian job market, the armed forces have had a difficult time filling their quotas with males. Thus they have been taking in more females, but discriminatory regulations and practices abound.

By federal statute, women are prohibited from combat duty and from jobs that are labeled combat-related in the U.S. Navy, Marines, and Air Force. The U.S. Air Force classification of its aircraft as combat-related keeps women from working on maintenance crews of planes and out of jobs on missile sites. The Navy barred women completely from sea duty even on support vessels, except hospital ships and transports, neither of which were in use until July 1978, when a U.S. District Court judge struck down the 30-year-old congressional decision that barred women from serving on U.S. Navy ships. Women still are restricted from permanent assignment to combat vessels, however, and from even temporary assignment if the ships are headed for actual battle (*N.Y. Times*, September 2, 1977, p. A17). While there is no law against combat duty for U.S. Army women, it is current Army policy to exclude them from the infantry, armor, field artillery, and air force artillery. Since 1978, however, women have been allowed to join combat-support units, such as helicopter outfits.

In all branches of the service, as in civilian life, women are restricted to the less prestigious, lower-paying jobs. And, as in civilian life also, women seem to prefer traditional specialties, such as those in offices and hospitals and in communications (*N.Y. Times*, April 22, 1979, p. 48). It is difficult to break free of traditional roles, although there is evidence that some change is occurring. From 1973 to 1975, the percentage of enlisted female soldiers in traditional jobs declined by 14% while the percentage in nontraditional jobs rose by 11% (Savell, Woelfel, Collins, & Bentler, 1979). Other signs of change were evident during the 1979 hearings by the House Military Personnel Subcommittee (*N.Y. Times*, November 18, 1979, p. 28). At that time, both Congress and the Carter administration were trying to open up more combat-support jobs for women without actually clearing women for combat. Officer training for women also is becoming more available. The Army's Reserve Officers Training Program (ROTC) first admitted women in the 1973–1974 academic year. In the 1977–1978 academic year, women made up 21% of the total enrollment (Association of American Colleges, June 1978). The service academies opened their doors to women in 1976 only after being ordered to do so by federal legislation.

A 1977 report by the Brookings Institute (in the *Asbury Park Press*, August 5, 1977, p. A17) urged the armed forces to move toward less restrictive personnel policies so that more women can enter the services by 1982. The Pentagon's projection for that year was 147,000 women, or 7% of the forces; the Brookings report recommended a projection of 400,000 women, or 22% of the forces, as the most conservative estimate. This goal could be met even if women were still excluded from front-line combat jobs. Easing job restrictions could allow women to fill one-third of all military jobs by 1982. Without such participation, the Pentagon may be forced to reduce the size of the armed forces, increase military pay (and thus the defense budget), or bring back the draft. New Pentagon projections for 1984 target the number of enlisted women in the armed services at 208,000, somewhat higher than the original Pentagon projections but still only half of the Brookings Institute's recommendations (*N.Y. Times*, April 22, 1979, p. 48).

There is no rational basis for denying women an equal role in the military. Studies have shown that women as soldiers prove less expensive than men and have a rate of lost time for illnesses and absenteeism (including time lost for pregnancy) only half that of men (*Newark Star Ledger*, July 25, 1977, p. 7). They learn fast, perform well, and stay in service longer than many male volunteers (*N.Y. Times*, November 6, 1977). Studies of women army recruits given regular male basic training found "little difference in relative performance" when these women were compared to an equal number of men, using scientifically-based standards (WEAL, 1977). Most women at the service academies passed the difficult first year with flying colors (Lichtenstein, 1977; WEAL, 1977). Studies are currently being made to determine the impact of women in front-line combat units. So far, little overall difference in company performance has been found (Toth, 1977). Within the military, the majority of men and women now favor the concept of assigning women to traditionally male jobs, including assignments to combat units or aboard naval vessels (*Asbury Park Press*, August 5, 1977; Savell et al., 1979).

Some people feel that having women in the military who are not prepared for combat is "a can of worms" (Revell, 1976). Others are concerned about what would happen if women *were* prepared for combat. Gilder (1979) argues that "the hard evidence is overwhelming that men are more aggressive, competitive, risk-taking, indeed more combative, than women" (p. 44). Greater aggressiveness and physical strength are seen as imperative in a combat situation. Furthermore, such writers hold that every society must protect its women for its own survival. Societies do this by ensuring that male physical strength and aggressiveness are not directed against women. Thus, if women are allowed to engage in combat, the result may be "nothing more nor less than a move toward barbarism" (Gilder, 1979, p. 46).

It is important to note that only 10% to 15% of our defensive force consists of front-line troops. Technology has displaced brute strength in conventional combat situations. And if women were eligible for combat service, it is most likely that only women with the same minimum skills as men would be allowed in a combat situation. As Senator William Proxmire remarked in the October 4, 1978, Senate debate on the Scott amendment to the ERA (which would have exempted women from combat duty), "Are you any less dead if killed by a woman than a man? . . . War has become so impersonal that distinctions of gender are no longer relevant."

With the number of military volunteers (male and female) at an all-time low, talk about reviving the military draft has increased. In his 1980 State of the Union address, President Carter called for registration for a draft of both women and men. Interestingly, the public is fairly evenly divided on whether women should be registered for possible future drafting—50% favored registration of women, 41% were against it (1979 Gallup poll, reported in *National NOW Times*, June 1979, p. 2). However, this poll was taken before the Iranian or Afghanistan crises of 1979 and 1980.

The critical issue seems to be whether to allow women to be killed in a war-time situation. As of November 1979, neither Congress nor the Carter administration was ready to put women into military combat (*N.Y. Times*, 1979, p. 28). It is indeed a terrible thing to have to decide whose life to risk, but if defending one's country is a duty of citizenship and men and women are supposedly equal citizens, it is difficult for many people to justify sparing one sex over the other as a general rule (*N.Y. Times*, January 27, 1980, p. E18).

One consequence of current military policy is that men do risk their lives as combat troops during war and women do not. The military has been viewed by some writers as the last bastion of masculinity, where men can prove their "toughness" physically through aggressiveness, risk-taking, and violence (Arkin & Dobrofsky, 1978; Pleck & Sawyer, 1974; Stouffer et al., 1949). And the military has fostered this image of masculinity in order to train men to kill and to risk their lives. "Be a real man," the ads say. The U.S. Marines want "a few good men." This masculine image of the military may account for some of the marked resistance against allowing women to participate equally.

One of the consequences of "macho" military training is that military men often engage in unnecessary violence and wanton acts of killing and destruction. Seymour Hersh (1970) analyzed the My Lai massacre in Vietnam as a predictable outcome of military exaggerations of the male sex-role stereotypes. These occur in every war by every army, and sex-role stereotypes may have much to do with it.

The effect of women on the military remains to be seen. Since so much training goes into the making of a soldier, it seems clear that women recruits can be trained to be equally as cold, aggressive, and deadly as male recruits. A 1979 study of cadets at West Point found that the female cadets tended to adopt traditional masculine qualities, such as roughness and competitiveness, in order to win acceptance (*N.Y. Times*, October 10, 1979, p. C17). Given the tendency, because of socialization, for more women than men to be against war in general, and to be humanistic, it is possible that not many women will desire such a role. The increase in the number of women enlistees makes this assumption questionable, although statistics do show that the Army's, Navy's, and Air Force's goals for recruitment of women were not met during the first half of fiscal year 1979 (*N.Y. Times*, April 22, 1979, p. 48). Perhaps the Services' projections of the number of women wishing to serve have been too optimistic. But it only seems fair to let those who do desire that role, to have access to it. An important point is the fact that in peace time, the military is a job with excellent educational and training opportunities, excellent fringe benefits, and good chance for advancement. It is the kind of job from which women have traditionally been barred. In addition, all individuals who have served in the military—in the past, predominantly men—receive five points' preference on federal Civil Service exams. In some states (for example, Massachusetts) veterans receive an absolute preference. This procedure was recently upheld by the Supreme Court (May 1979). Historically, veteran's preference points have hurt women's job chances. Consequently, although women make up 41% of those who pass the Civil Service Professional and Administrative Career Exam, they are only 27% of those who are hired (*National NOW Times*, August 1978, p. 15). Allowing women full equality in the military will go a long way toward allowing them an equal role in society. It will also alleviate the burden now placed on men.

AGGRESSION AND VIOLENCE

Inherent in the above discussion regarding military activities is a questioning of the commonly held belief that because men are "naturally" more aggressive, they should, of course, be the soldiers and fighters. Although males, in general, do seem to have a greater predisposition toward aggression, aggressive behavior is definitely learned and is responsive to a wide range of situational conditions. In our culture, far more than in most others, male aggressiveness appears to be viewed ambivalently. While violence and its social effects (crime, rapes, wars) are overtly condemned, aggression and violence are covertly glorified in the media (films, books, and, especially, TV) and in daily interactions (Komisar, 1970; Millet, 1970). For example, an advertising campaign for a Rolling Stones record album entitled

"Black and Blue" showed a scantily clad, bound and beaten female saying "I'm 'Black and Blue' from the Rolling Stones and I love it."

Aggressiveness and violence are definite parts of the "masculine mystique" in America, and probably Western society as a whole. In fact, males with traditional attitudes toward women have been found to be more aggressive than males with nontraditional attitudes toward women (Nirenberg & Gaebelein, 1979; Taylor & Smith, 1974). These attitudes were not related to female aggressiveness. Boys generally are encouraged to "fight for their rights." Those who avoid fights are considered "sissies"—something feminine and, by implication, inferior (David & Brannon, 1976; Komisar, 1970). One way to "prove" one's masculinity is by some form of aggression or act of daring. This may manifest itself in criminal activity, aggression against women and children, risk-taking acts, obsession with sports, and war.

Crime

The National Commission on the Causes and Prevention of Violence found that this country is "the clear leader among modern, stable, democratic nations in its rates of homicide, assault, rape and robbery, and at least among the highest in incidence of group violence and assassination" (quoted in Komisar, 1970). Significantly, most of these violent crimes are committed by men between the ages of 15 and 24, mostly poor.

In this section, criminal activity for the two sexes will only be examined as a function of the sex-role stereotypes. The crime of rape will receive special attention since it is so closely associated with the theme of this chapter—sex-role socialization and aggression.

Men and Crime. The National Commission concluded that violence is often a way for a young man to prove his masculinity and become a "successful" member of ghetto society. David and Brannon (1976; also Tolson, 1977) suggest that when a man is not receiving the conventional status rewards of a society, he may try to maintain a "masculine" image by being considered aggressive and violent. This may certainly be true for many young Black men whose unemployment rate often runs as high as 40%. (During the summer of 1977 in New York City, the rate was as high as 75%.)

The problem of youth gangs and their violence is a direct function of the fact that many members of gangs are cut off from the mainstream status system due to age, class, or race. Their status then becomes based on public aggressiveness and their willingness to fight (David & Brannon, 1976; Short & Strodtbeck, 1976; Tolson, 1977).

Although the rate of reported crime in the United States continued to drop during the first six months of 1978 compared with the same period in 1977, violent crime increased by 1% during that period. The sharpest rise was in the category of forcible rape, which rose 5% over the first half of 1977 (*National NOW Times*, October 1978, p. 6). A closer examination of this particular crime appears warranted.

285

Chapter 12:
Societal
Consequences:
Power and
Aggression

Rape.   Rape is a crime that can be viewed as being directly related to sex roles (see Brownmiller, 1975, for an excellent discussion of this subject). As Fasteau (1974) notes, violence, to some degree, is equated with both masculinity and sexuality in America. The words we use for sex demonstrate this connection with violence: sexual "conquest," "screw," "bang," and so forth. Such an equation makes rape the "perfect" combination to prove masculinity: it is aggressive, it is sexual, and it involves dominance over a woman (Brownmiller, 1975; Griffin, 1975). The masculine stereotype, the sexual double standard in which women supposedly want to be dominated and have no sexual feelings themselves, and the traditional female role (helpless, passive, dependent), all help serve to make rape part of traditional male-female relationships in a patriarchal society.

A series of studies by Seymour Feshbach and Neal Malamuth and colleagues elucidate the connections among sex, aggression, and violence toward women (Feshbach, 1978; Feshbach & Malamuth, 1978; Malamuth, Feshbach, & Jaffe, 1977; Malamuth, Haber, & Feshbach, in press). Sex and aggression seem to be reciprocally related for American men and women in that loosening inhibitions in one area also loosens inhibitions in the other. However, when aggression is extreme (that is, painful and violent) and is connected to sexual activity (as in forcible rape), the direct relationship no longer holds, at least for most women and some men. In one study, male and female college students were presented with stories of a rape containing either high or low pain cues and either a positive or negative victim reaction. For women, high pain cues resulted in low sexual arousal regardless of depicted outcome. In contrast, for men, high pain cues were associated with sexual arousal when the outcome was depicted as pleasurable, the typical pornographic rape-story outcome. Thus, sex and violence may be more closely connected to the male sex role than is usually admitted (Feshbach, 1978). Support for this connection comes from a study by Donnerstein and Hallam (1978). They found that, when college men were exposed to highly erotic films, they tended to give more nonsexual aggressive responses (as measured by electric shock settings) to college women than did college men who had not viewed such films.

An individual's level of arousal and subjective reaction to erotic material may be critical variables. A number of researchers (Baron, 1979; Baron & Bell, 1977; L. White, 1979) have found evidence for a curvilinear relationship between sexual arousal and aggression for both male and female college students. When individuals are mildly or pleasantly aroused, aggressive retaliatory behavior is reduced. In contrast, when erotic material is highly arousing or perceived negatively (as disgusting or unpleasant), retaliatory aggression is increased. Although these findings are important in understanding the effects of pornography, all these studies examined aggression against same-sex persons. It is not clear if the same relationships hold for male sexual arousal and aggression against women.

In the Feshbach and Malamuth studies, it is striking to note that both sexes estimated that nearly half of all men would engage in acts of sexual violence if assured they would not be caught (Malamuth et al., in press). See Table 12-3. Both sexes also estimated that a substantial percentage of women (about 30%) would enjoy being victimized if no one knew. However, when asked to estimate their own reactions to such situations, very few women believed they themselves would derive pleasure from such an experience. In contrast, more than half of the males indicated some likelihood that they would engage in such behaviors under the circumstances described. Furthermore, this self-reported tendency was correlated with a pattern of attitudes toward rape that were similar to the callous attitudes often held by convicted rapists (for example, agreeing that women enjoy being raped). These findings support the interpretation of rape as a part of the traditional masculine sex role and traditional attitudes toward women (Brownmiller, 1975; Marolla & Scully, 1979). Feild (1978) also found that people who view women in traditional roles are likely to see rape as being a woman's fault and as motivated by the rapist's need for sex.

The myths that have been perpetuated about rape illustrate masculine prejudice.

Myth 1. Women provoke rape by their appearance or actions. *Fact:* As many as 90% of rapes are premeditated—for example, a decision is made to rape the next unaccompanied female who enters an elevator. Thus, what a victim does or wears cannot be considered relevant. In fact, less than 4% of all rapes are provoked by the victim (Griffin, 1975; Lester, 1976).

Myth 2. Rape is a sex crime committed by sexually abnormal males. *Fact:* Men who commit rape are psychologically indistinguishable from other men (Lester, 1976; Marolla & Scully, 1979). About one-third of all rape victims know their attacker (Amir, 1971). Rape is a crime of violence, a form of assault, not a crime of passion (Lester, 1976).

Myth 3. Many reports of rape are unfounded. *Fact:* Fewer than 10% of rape complaints are unfounded, about the same as for other violent crimes. In some areas, the percentage of false reports may be as low as 2% (Lester, 1976).

Table 12-3
Estimating the Likelihood of Rape

	Projections		Self-Report (number indicating at least some likelihood)
	Males	Females	
Percent of men likely to commit rape if they would not be caught	45	42	51
Percent of women likely to enjoy rape if no one would know	32	27	2

Adapted from N. M. Malamuth, S. Huber, and S. Fesbach, "Testing Hypotheses Regarding Rape: Exposure and Sexual Violence, Sex Differences and the 'Normality' of Rapists," *Journal of Research in Personality,* in press.

Myth 4. Rape has no lasting effects. *Fact:* Nearly all victims suffer severe aftereffects, both emotionally and in their relationships with others (Lester, 1976).

Myth 5. Most rapes are performed by Black men on White women. This myth reflects both sexism and racism—the White woman viewed as valuable property of the White man. *Fact:* Over 90% of reported rapes are *intra*racial, with Black women being the most vulnerable victims (Amir, 1971; Lester, 1976).

287

Chapter 12:
Societal
Consequences:
Power and
Aggression

The preposterousness of such myths is illustrated in the following story using a robbery as an analogy for rape.

> A man was testifying regarding his having been robbed while walking down a street.
>
> *Prosecutor:* Can you tell the jury what time the alleged crime occurred?
> *Victim:* About 11:30 P.M.
> *Prosecutor:* And what exactly were you doing?
> *Victim:* Just walking down the street.
> *Prosecutor:* Alone?
> *Victim:* Yes.
> *Prosecutor:* And what were you wearing?
> *Victim:* Oh, a three-piece suit.
> *Prosecutor:* An expensive suit?
> *Victim:* Well, I do like to dress well.
> *Prosecutor:* Let me ask you this. Have you ever given money away?
> *Victim:* Why, of course . . .
> *Prosecutor:* In fact, Mr. D., you have quite a reputation for philanthropy. So here you are, a well-dressed man, with a history of giving money away, walking alone late at night, practically advertising yourself as a mark. Why, if we didn't know better, Mr. D., we might even say that you were asking for it!

Because of these myths, rape victims often are treated insensitively and antagonistically by the police, medical personnel, and the courts. Krulewitz (1978) has found that there are strong sex differences in the perception of victims of sexual assault. Both men and women were more certain of rape and evaluated the victim more positively when she responded aggressively, although women were more favorable than men toward the victim in all cases, regardless of her reaction. It is important to recall that most police, doctors, and judges are men and this fact may affect their treatment of rape victims. For example, in a June 1977 rape trial in Michigan, a judge released a convicted 15-year-old boy, remarking that he had reacted only "normally" in a community known to be "permissive." In that situation, the community mobilized and successfully sought to repeal the judge. Such consequences are not frequent. A judge in Connecticut only was "privately censured" for remarking during a trial for attempted rape that "You can't blame somebody for trying" (*N.Y. Times*, March 29, 1979, p. B4). And in Indiana, a judge was cleared of a judicial misconduct for dismissing a similar case and saying that "a woman visiting bars to meet a man is like a fisherman baiting a hook" (reported in *National NOW Times*, April 1979, p. 4).

Only one complaint of rape in four results in an arrest, and only one in 60 ends with a conviction, according to a two-year research project by the Law Enforcement Assistance Administration (LEAA) released in August 1978 (cited in *N.Y. Times*, August 26, 1978). Consequently, prosecutors often are reluctant to pursue rape cases since a low percentage of convictions is "not good for one's career." Due to judicial treatment and the fact that courts frequently do not make convictions, many women fail to report the crime in order to spare themselves additional trauma.

Reporting the crime may itself be traumatic because of police treatment. Field research and personal reports have indicated that police officers often treat the victim as if she were the guilty party. In fact, Feild (1978) found that the attitudes of police officers toward rape did not differ from those of convicted rapists on four out of seven dimensions. As a consequence of all this, the LEAA estimates that four out of five rapes never even are reported.

Laws against rape originated to protect the rights of males, not the rights of women (Brownmiller, 1975; Griffin, 1975). Since a woman was viewed as her father's property, to be bartered in marriage, virginity was important to ensure exclusive "ownership" for the prospective husband. Hence, the assumption that raping a virgin is more serious than raping a nonvirgin since the virgin is more highly valued by men. After marriage, a woman "belongs" to her husband, and this is the reason a man cannot be accused of raping his wife in most states—she already is his "property."

The publicity over such sexist notions regarding rape has begun to bring a change in some people's attitudes, especially those of women. But another crime, also an extension of the glorification of aggression, violence, and dominance of the male sex role, is just coming to society's attention—wife beating.

Wife Beating.   It has been estimated that the cases of battered wives outnumber rape cases by three to one (*National NOW Times*, December 1977, p. 5). (See Martin, 1976; Moore, 1979; Roy, 1977, for more thorough accounts of this crime.)

Whether the incidence of such assaults is increasing or whether just the reporting of them is, the numbers are startling and serious. Many women's groups currently are trying to set up shelters for battered wives and are pressuring the police and the courts to be more responsive to their problems. Researchers are just beginning to probe the reasons for both the behavior of the husband and that of the wife (see Frieze & Washburn, 1979; and Moore, 1979, for recent findings). In general, sex-role stereotypes and expectations, marital roles, and traditional attribution patterns appear to have much to do with the problem.

The crimes discussed so far have been committed by men. However, sex-role stereotypes, in relation to criminal behavior, can affect women as well.

Women and Crime.   While most crimes are committed by males, the rate of female crime is increasing rapidly. Between 1960 and 1973, the incidence of all violent crime increased 278% for women but only

88% for men. During the same period, all crime, violent and nonviolent, rose 316% for women and 77% for men. In all cases, the highest rates were for juvenile females (Sarri, 1979). The crimes that increased the most for females were embezzlement, larceny, forgery, and fraud—all property crimes. Like her male counterpart, the female criminal usually is interested more in improving her financial circumstances than in violence (Adler, 1975). Women no longer are limiting themselves to the so-called traditionally feminine crimes of shoplifting and prostitution.

Although some people have tried to blame the rise in female crime directly on the women's movement, studies of female offenders show that they have extremely traditional sex-role views, more so than females of comparable age and socioeconomic level (Adler, 1975; Widom, 1977). Furthermore, their crimes rarely are an assertion of equal rights. In fact, some female criminals may be operating to gain male approval or operating in auxiliary roles (Harrentsian, 1973). Still, the trend toward more equality for males and females does seem to underlie some of these statistics. As more women seek and obtain jobs, they probably experience stresses and frustrations similar to those that men experience. Some women, therefore, may attempt similar solutions. For example, with more women working in banks, embezzlement by women becomes more possible. Even old frustrations may be alleviated in new ways (that is, by crime) as women stop blaming themselves for their situation and start blaming society, as many men have done. And guns, more prevalent than ever in crimes, are a great equalizer of strength. Freda Adler (1975), an expert on female crime, predicts that "as the social status of women approaches that of men, so . . . will the frequency and nature of their crimes" (p. 42).

Yet male crime, especially violent crime, still greatly exceeds that of females. And some writers (for example, Michaud, 1977; Sarri, 1979; Simon, 1975) question whether there has been a true increase in crimes committed by females at all, especially because differences in the sizes of the cohorts being compared have rarely been controlled for. Furthermore, some research (Michaud, 1977; Simon, 1975) shows that the most frequent offenses for which women are brought into court are drunk driving, disorderly conduct, illegal lotteries, prostitution, and narcotics violations. Thus, it may be that women are turning to alcohol and drugs more than even property crime as a way to deal with their frustrations. Certainly the incidence of female alcoholism has skyrocketed in recent years (see Chapter Nine).

One difficulty in evaluating criminal statistics correctly is that so many biases operate in the penal and judicial systems. In general, adult women traditionally are less likely to be arrested and often are treated more leniently by the courts than are their male counterparts, part of a paternalistic pattern of discrimination (Harrentsian, 1973; Nagel & Weitzman, 1972; Sarri, 1979). However, they are more likely to be picked up for certain offenses than are their male counterparts; for example, prostitution. This differential treatment by sex is even more the case with adolescents. Female adolescents are generally

289

Chapter 12:
Societal
Consequences:
Power and
Aggression

dealt with more punitively by the criminal justice system than are male youths (Sarri, 1979). For example, nearly 75% of underage females arrested, as opposed to fewer than 30% of the boys, are charged with a noncriminal "status offense" such as promiscuity, running away from home, or "bad behavior" (Milton, Pierce, & Lyons, 1977). Such girls also are more likely to be detained and held longer than boys accused of criminal offenses. Sentencing disparities also are determined by the geographic area in which a criminal lives, local politics being the most important influence (Michaud, 1977). Until recently, in some states, women who were 18 were treated as minors while their male peers were tried as adults. Another disparity is that in some jurisdictions some crimes, especially sex-related ones (for example, statutory rape and homosexuality), are exclusively male offenses.

In sum, crime statistics are frequently influenced by the sex-role stereotypes. Many crimes, especially those committed by men (by far the majority of crimes), can be viewed as an extension of the masculine mystique of violence and aggression.

Sports

Another area in which the male mystique of violence and aggression can be seen is in sports. Although defined as "good clean fun," many sports (the contact ones—football, hockey, boxing, wrestling, basketball, soccer) involve often serious and violent confrontations. The frequent injuries to the participating athletes demonstrate the violent nature of these sports. The greater the danger of injury and the more combative the activities, the more the sport and its players are likely to be viewed as "masculine" (David & Brannon, 1976; Farrell, 1974; Fasteau, 1974). Sports such as golf or swimming, which are neither combative nor extremely competitive, generally do not earn the "masculine" label. Perhaps not coincidentally, there is considerable evidence that athletes as a group, especially those in the contact, "masculine" sports, tend to be more violent in their attitudes and behaviors than are comparable groups of nonathletes, at least on college campuses (J. M. Brown & Davies, 1978).

Watching contact sports may give vicarious satisfaction of aggressive impulses and affirm one's masculinity (Fasteau, 1974). The increasing popularity of watching such sports relative to watching noncontact sports suggests that there may be fewer outlets for aggressive impulses than there were previously (Fasteau, 1974; Gagnon, 1971). Physical strength can no longer be taken as the measure of manhood in the modern world. Yet many men still are learning aggressive behaviors as part of their sex role. Sports, being one of the few areas where strength still counts, may be one of the few remaining socially acceptable outlets for aggression. So aggression in sports may continue, and some players may endure physical pain and injury to prove they are "men" (Hyland, 1978; Simpson, 1978).

As was discussed in Chapter Eight, one result of this connection between sports and aggression may be that many young boys (and girls) develop a distorted view of sports and athletics (Pleck, 1976b).

Rather than viewing athletics as a way to develop and enjoy one's body and have fun, athletics may become equated with combat and aggression. As a result, some adolescents may reject athletic activity completely and may lose touch with their bodies as well. The recent interest in physical fitness, such as in jogging and yoga, for females and males may reflect a move away from the equating of sports with aggression and toward a more balanced view of body activities.

War

In many ways, war may be viewed as similar to violent athletic contests (Fasteau, 1974). In both situations, one side is pitted against the other, both trying to win. In both, the allowable level of violence is not always clear or clearly adhered to. Some writers (Fasteau, 1974; Gagnon, 1971; Gilder, 1979) view the military, and contact sports as well, as the last bastion of "masculinity"—where some men can act out, to the utmost, the aggressive, competitive, unfeeling sex role they have been socialized into. This may explain, in part, the strong resistance to allowing women to join in these particular activities.

SUMMARY

This chapter has examined two global consequences of the sex-role stereotypes. In a variety of areas, women consistently have little power. Although they may have some personal power in a relationship, even there males tend to dominate. Institutionally, power remains in the hands of White males—economically, politically, legally, and militarily. Although women are gaining in the employment area, their progress in the power area is extraordinarily slow and difficult. Women's lack of power means men virtually run our society. Consequently, society generally functions using the standards of the male sex-role stereotype: competition, achievement, aggression, hierarchical relationships, and insensitivity to feelings. Thus, our society, in general, has been run for profit and the good of a few, those at the top of the status hierarchy, rather than for the benefit of the many.

Major aspects of the male sex role that are strongly emphasized by our society are aggression and "toughness." This emphasis may be associated with the skyrocketing crime rates, especially violent, aggressive crimes by men (often teenagers) who may be "proving" their masculinity. The values of the male sex role also indirectly may foster crimes of rape and wife beating, both on the rise. Greater equality for males and females in the general society seems to be related to a rise in female crime, which has become more similar in nature to male crime. But male crime still is far more frequent. The masculine emphasis on violence and aggression also is evident in the traditional "masculine" sports and in war—two areas compatible with the "male mystique." Changes here may mean less emphasis on contact sports compared to noncontact sports, fewer injuries, and perhaps less chance of war or fewer acts of meaningless violence in a war situation.

291
Chapter 12:
Societal
Consequences:
Power and
Aggression

RECOMMENDED READING

Arkin, W., & Dobrofsky, L. Military socialization and masculinity. *Journal of Social Issues*, 1978, *34*(1), 151–168. An interesting overview of how the military ethic shapes our definition of masculinity.

Brownmiller, S. *Against our will: Men, women and rape.* New York: Simon & Schuster, 1975. A powerful feminist analysis of rape as a "natural" product of our sex-role stereotypes.

Johnson, P. B. Women and power: Towards a theory of effectiveness. *Journal of Social Issues*, 1976, *32*(3), 99–110. A research report on how women use power.

Lynn, N. Women in American politics: An overview. In J. Freeman (Ed.), *Women: A feminist perspective.* Palo Alto, Calif.: Mayfield, 1975, pp. 364–385. Although somewhat dated, an informative overview of women in politics.

Martin, D. *Battered wives.* San Francisco: Glide Publ., 1976. A frightening account of the incidence and history behind wife beating today.

PART FOUR: SUMMARY

In the preceding four chapters, the effects of sex-role stereotypes on individuals and their relationships and on society in general have been examined. The evidence is persuasive that the stereotypes negatively affect nearly all aspects of human and societal functioning for men as well as women.

On a personal level, many women experience a negative self-concept, particularly low self-confidence and self-blame for failures, constricted achievement behavior and fear of success in masculine-defined activities, and serious problems in adjustment and mental health, particularly depression. Many men suffer from physical health problems as well as from overconfidence and fear of success in feminine-defined activities. Both sexes, if strongly sex typed, suffer from behavioral constriction and inflexibility, especially those who are feminine sex typed. All these consequences can be traced to the sex-role stereotypes.

On a relationship level, both sexes experience difficulty in forming close relationships with members of the same sex and of the other sex. This is especially true for males, and may account for the sometimes superficial quality of their relationships with friends, lovers, spouses, and children. Women, who more often are trained for and steered into interpersonal relationships, frequently experience marked disappointment in their relationships with men, and marriage often is a great stress for them. Due to the Motherhood Mandate, many women become trapped in that role. Negative effects then may occur for the woman, her husband, and the children. Fathers may become trapped in the breadwinner role, resulting in minimal interactions with their children and with negative effects on the entire family.

On a societal level, the sex-role stereotypes have led to marked prejudice against women by both men and women; underutilization and discrimination against women in the world of work in terms of hiring, status, and salary; a dramatic lack of power by women vis-a-vis men in the areas of economics, politics, law, and military affairs; and high rates of male aggression and violence as revealed in crime rates, sports, and war.

The effects of these stereotypes may be seen in the priorities of American society—profit, concrete rewards, competitiveness, dominance, unemotional functioning, aggression—that is, the masculine stereotype. This is in contrast to a society in which human life and human qualities are valued above profits, a less hierarchical and authoritarian mode of operation, greater concern with the quality of life, cooperative efforts—that is, the feminine stereotype. Evidence was presented to argue that androgynous functioning, the incorpora-

tion of positive masculine and feminine stereotyped characteristics
—the agentic with the expressive, as in an action-oriented concern
about the environment—would improve not only individual functioning and adjustment but societal functioning as well.

The next section will explore the implications of such changes
and ways to achieve them. Problems that might arise also will be
discussed.

ALTERNATIVES TO SEX-ROLE STEREOTYPES

In the preceding chapters, the traditional sex-role stereotypes, their underpinnings, origins, and consequences have been examined in some detail. A study of the material leads to the conclusion that such stereotypes have little basis in facts and, in today's world, are dysfunctional for individuals, their relationships, and society in general. This section will address itself to some alternatives to rigid sex typing, ways to achieve such changes, and the implications of such changes for our society.

13 | Toward Androgyny and Beyond

Instead of a society where females attempt to be "feminine" (nurturant, emotional, vain) and fear being called "mannish," and males attempt to be "masculine" (aggressive, logical, strong) and fear being called "effeminate," imagine a society where each individual can develop in her or his own unique way. This chapter will examine one alternative—androgyny—and problems associated with the concept. Models and modes of change, problems, and some of the implications for individuals, society, and institutions also will be considered.

ANDROGYNY

As described by Bem (1976) and refined by A. Kaplan (1979; Kaplan & Bean, 1976), androgyny refers to flexibility of sex role, the integration of strong masculine (agentic) and feminine (expressive) traits in unique ways, influenced by individual differences across situations and over the span of one's life. Individuals who alternate between masculine and feminine behavior in inflexible ways are not androgynous, according to our definition. Thus a woman who is always very competitive and aggressive at work but very passive and dependent at home (or vice versa) and who is unable to adjust her behavior to what the situation requires is neither integrated nor flexible and is therefore not androgynous. Uniqueness refers to the fact that because androgynous individuals would no longer be restricted by stereotyped behavior, it is impossible to predict their behavior across situations. For example, an individual may be nurturant in one situation, assertive in another, sensitive in a third, and rational in a fourth. Thus, each individual will have the opportunity to develop his or her potential to its fullest, without the restriction that only sex-role-appropriate behaviors be allowed. Clearly that means each individual will be different from others, since each individual has different capabilities and interests. Conceptions of a completely unisexual society with no sex differences (for example, Winick, 1968) are not models of androgyny and, as we'll see in the next paragraph, they are more scare tactics than they are realistic alternatives.

Winick suggests that without sex-role stereotypes, a society of neuters would develop, with males and females indistinguishable from each other in behavior and appearance. According to him, a likely consequence of such a society would be the lack of sexual attraction between the sexes and the eventual extinction of the species. Besides the obviously alarmist conjecturing involved (sexual attraction is learned and is not contingent on certain hair styles or behavior), an androgynous society would not be "neuter" or regulated in its conformity at all. Individual differences abound and are much greater than sex differences for nearly all measurable behaviors and attributes. Such differences would remain, but the negative consequences now experienced by individuals who do not conform to current sex-role norms would be eliminated.

Implicit in this definition of androgyny is the concept of transcending traditional sex-role polarities to reach a new level of synthesis. Androgyny is not just a question of combining what have been considered opposite qualities, but is rather a third dimension. There appear to be at least three stages in reaching sex-role transcendence, as described by Rebecca and colleagues (1976) and Berzins (1979). First is the stage of the thesis or initial proposition. This first stage represents an undifferentiated conception of sex roles. Such a conception exists in preschool children who have not yet learned the sex dichotomy. From this stage stems the antithesis, the opposite of the initial proposition. Stage II is a polarized either/or conception of sex roles. Here, males and females are seen as opposite and distinct from each other in nearly all behaviors. This stage is cognitively necessary in order for a young child to organize her or his world. Everything is classified absolutely into black/white; good/bad; masculine/feminine; and so on. But the antithesis too is one-sided and generates its own countervailing force. The third stage thus combines or synthesizes these propositions into a new and more balanced whole. Stage III is a transcendence of sex roles. Here, an individual is able to move and behave freely and adaptively as a function of the situation. In this stage, a person might act tenderly with a child, forcefully with subordinates, and sympathetically with a friend. The world, in this stage, is not divided into polarities of masculinity and femininity. Rather, it is composed of unique individuals with different aptitudes and potentials.

A majority of individuals and institutions of the Western world appear to be fixed at the Stage II level of polarities. Yet Stage III functioning is possible. It evolves over a long period of time, is facilitated by societal supports, and is a dynamic, not a final, process. As was discussed in Chapter Seven, Block (1973; Haan, Smith, & Block, 1968) and others (for example, Waterman & Whitbourne, 1979) have found evidence that an androgynous sex-role definition is a component of the most advanced levels of ego development and moral reasoning. There is suggestive evidence that, given present socialization practices, differentiation of the masculine and feminine might well be a precondition of the integration of the two (Suziedelis, 1977; M. White, 1979). Other studies (Constantinople, 1973; Donelson, 1977a) find that from the middle twenties on, males score increasingly "feminine" on traditional "masculine-feminine" scales. Middle-aged people, especially, admit to and display traits usually considered appropriate only for the other sex (Lowenthal et al., 1975; Neugarten & Gutmann, 1968; Sheehy, 1976). In fact, such an integration is considered part of the healthy adult by some personality theorists, such as Erikson (1963), Jung (1956), and Maslow (1962).

As discussed above, androgyny does have certain limitations. A closer examination of these problems is needed in order for us to move beyond them.

Problems

Androgyny as a concept does have its problems. The first is that of built-in obsolescence (Bem, 1979; Locksley & Colton, 1979). Androgyny presupposes separate masculine and feminine stereotypic characteristics. If people stop adhering to such characteristics, and if the two sex-role stereotypes become modified and less distinct from each other, androgyny in its current sense no longer would be meaningful. This problem can be circumvented by speaking of agentic and expressive attributes, instead of sex-role attributes, as Spence and Helmreich (1979a) suggest. Thus, androgyny would mean a flexible integration of agentic and expressive qualities; sex typing of these qualities could be ignored.

A second problem with androgyny relates to the use of this concept in research. There is increasing evidence that the different instruments used to measure androgyny may not be measuring identical concepts (Locksley & Colton, 1979; Wilson, 1979). Furthermore, different scoring methods yield different results and imply different definitions of androgyny (Lenney, 1979b; Locksley & Colton, 1979; Pedhazur & Tetenbaum, 1979; Spence & Helmreich, 1979b). Another research problem is that the concepts measured are factorially more complex than some researchers have acknowledged (Bem, 1979; Gross, Batlis, Small, & Erdwins, 1979; Pedhazur & Tetenbaum, 1979; Powell, 1979; Richardson, Merrifield, & Jacobson, 1979). Factor analytic studies have shown that current scales may involve up to two masculinity factors—assertiveness, dominance, or instrumentality, and independence—and up to two femininity factors—interpersonal sensitivity, or caring, and immaturity. Ellen Lenney (1979a, 1979b) identifies three additional research problems: too rigidly-held values about what androgyny and sex typing mean, too many atheoretical research projects, and too little integration of androgyny research with more traditional personality and social psychology research. All these problems can be resolved and may be viewed as reflecting the increasing maturity of androgyny research. Lenney (1979b) makes some excellent suggestions to facilitate the productive development of such research.

A third problem with androgyny is that the concept may become the new standard of mental health, replacing sex-typed behavior. Everyone then would be expected to acquire thoroughly both agentic and expressive characteristics in equal amounts. This new standard essentially would double the pressure people already are under. Instead of acquiring thoroughly one set of characteristics (their own sex role), they now must acquire two sets of characteristics. Thus a little boy might be pressured to play with dolls and with trucks and to be aggressive and sociable. The main point about androgyny is that any standard of behavior, if it is prescribed rigidly, is restrictive and inimical to effective functioning. People need to be allowed to develop their natural qualities and aptitudes without the restrictions of any stereotypes. If that means some people are more expressive and others more agentic, so be it. But, and this is the major point, these distinctions are unlikely to divide solely on the basis of physical sexual characteristics. That is, most males are unlikely to be purely agentic and most females are unlikely to be purely expressive. The differences will be individual ones, not sex-linked ones.

Furthermore, we simply do not know enough about androgynous individuals to assert that androgyny is always superior to sex typing. Related to this problem are the findings discussed in Chapter Nine indicating that high "masculinity" scores, as measured by the Bem Sex-Role Inventory and the Personal Attributes Questionnaire, may be related more to effective personal functioning and self-esteem than high androgyny scores per se (for example, Jones et al., 1978). These findings reinforce the view that there are serious hazards in using androgyny as a new criterion of mental health. What we need is to define healthy human functioning independent of sex-role related characteristics (Olds & Shaver, 1979; Vogel, 1979). That is, we need to construct an ideal of adult behavior without reliance on traditional concepts of femininity and masculinity. We need also to pay more attention to situational factors. We need to determine those situations in which androgyny is more functional than sex typing, those in which sex typing is more functional than androgyny, and those in which sex typing per se is irrelevant (Lenney, 1979b; Locksley & Colton, 1979).

A fourth difficulty with the concept of androgyny is that it does not, in fact, eliminate sex differences. Males and females can be androgynous in different ways—that is, by having different combinations of agentic and expressive qualities. For example, males may be androgynous by being strongly athletic, aggressive, dominant, warm, affectionate, and unpredictable. Females may be androgynous by being strongly self-reliant, assertive, ambitious, compassionate, soft-spoken, and loving of children. (These are hypothetical combinations.) Although there have been some recent suggestions that androgynous females and males may differ from each other behaviorally (Jones et al., 1978; Wiggins & Holzmuller, 1978), studies have not examined yet whether there are different components of androgyny in females and males. One study that examined this question by separately factor analyzing the response of male and female graduate students to the BSRI did find different factor structures for the sexes (Pedhazur & Tetenbaum, 1979). To the extent that the sexes still might be socialized into developing different attributes as a function of their sex, androgyny itself would not eliminate that problem.

Alexandra Kaplan (1979) proposes that there really are two stages of androgyny. The first is the *dualistic* stage where masculine and feminine characteristics coexist but are not necessarily integrated. The second, more advanced level, is the *hybrid* stage where each group of characteristics truly becomes integrated and tempered by the other. Indeed, in this advanced stage, speaking of androgyny at all would be misleading since such a term implies two differing sets of sex-role-related characteristics. As Garnets and Pleck (1979) suggest, we need to go beyond merely broadening the sex-role norms. Rather, we need to transcend the norms themselves and help make sex roles less salient. When that occurs, people can be just people —individuals in their own right, accepted and evaluated on their own terms. Bem's (1979) most recent writing also reflects this point of view. Androgynous persons are thought to use gender distinctions less frequently than sex-typed persons in perceiving and structuring their environment. Whereas a sex-typed person might describe a social situation by first noting the number or proportion of males and females present, an androgynous individual might describe the same situation without making any note of gender factors.

Thus, the major thrust of change should be on transcending sex-role stereotypes. Androgyny simply is one way that may be done, at least in this transition period. It certainly is not the only nor necessarily the best way and it may not be the endpoint of change.

With these cautions in mind, we now will examine three different ways of conceptualizing social change.

MODELS OF SOCIAL CHANGE

There are three basic models that can be used in conceptualizing social change for equality: a pluralist model, an assimilation model, and a pluralist-hybrid model (Agassi, 1979; Bernard, 1971, 1974; Kaplan & Bean, 1976; Rossi, 1969; Yates, 1975). One model, in particular, seems well suited to moving society in an androgynous direction—the pluralistic-hybrid model.

Pluralist

In a pluralist society, males and females are viewed as being, "by nature," different. Therefore, the best a society could do would be to retain these differences and value them equally. Bernard (1974) refers to this as the "moderate-equivalent" school of thought. Yates (1975) refers to this model as the "women's liberationist" viewpoint, in which segregation rather than unity is sought.

In contemporary society, the assumed sex differences are valued differently. On the whole, masculine attributes are valued more highly than feminine attributes. In a pluralistic society, such value differences theoretically would be eliminated. As Rossi (1969) points out (and as Blacks have found), however, separate does not mean equal. The traditional roles for males and females are themselves imbalanced. Man is the producer, the breadwinner, the aggressor; woman is the consumer, the homemaker, the nurturer. Maintaining the current distinct sex roles will not lead to equal evaluation of them as long as society values money and power above feelings. The pluralist goal is essentially a conservative one that accepts the status quo as good and desirable. Barring women from colleges and universities because their place was in the home can be viewed as an example of pluralism, as can the existence of single-sex institutions (Adler, 1978). Books and programs such as *The Total Woman* (Morgan, 1975) and *Fascinating Womanhood* (Andelin, 1975) are more recent examples of a pluralistic approach. These approaches preach that the way for a woman to be happy is to ensure her husband's happiness by submitting totally to his absolute authority ("accept, admire, adapt, adjust") (Maynard, 1975). Through various connivances (for example, acting out her husband's sexual fantasies) and self-denials, a wife will get her husband to value her. He will then want to be with her more and make her happy by bringing home more money and presents.

The women's liberationist aspect of this model (Yates, 1975) is much more pro-woman than the other pluralistic versions described above. Still, its emphasis on segregation and women as quite distinct from men would do little to change the stereotypes themselves.

Assimilation

The second model of social change is an assimilation model. In contrast to the pluralist model where the sexes supposedly are separate but equal, the assimilation model describes a society in which women assume the lifestyle and characteristics of the mainstream male culture. Women, in this model, are viewed as equal to men, rather than women and men viewed as equal to each other. It assumes that the current institutional structure of United States society is the best possible, and that women should want to be like men. Until recently, higher education could be characterized by this model. Graduate school, in particular, required students to adapt to competitive, entrepreneurial modes (Adler, 1978). This model perhaps accounts for the much higher attrition rate of women than men. As was discussed previously, the assumption underlying this model creates problems. Institutions run by masculine values (that is, most institutions) are goal- (that is, profit-) oriented, competitive, aggressive, and insensitive to human values. Furthermore, women are unlikely to be assimilated into high-paying jobs where competition with men would be the strongest. Since many higher positions require an unpaid wife to fulfill social obligations and take care of domestic functioning, women would still be at a disadvantage even if they obtained such positions (Gullahorn, 1977b). Adjusting women's lives to the standards of the Establishment (Bernard, 1971) would do little to alleviate the negative consequences of such institutional practices. Women would just learn to be as competitive, aggressive, and insensitive as are many men (Bernard, 1974). Since the uninterrupted work pattern would continue to be the norm, women and men interested in child-rearing would continue to be at a disadvantage. This assimilation model is the goal of some feminist ideology and has sometimes been called the liberal or feminist view. As noted, however, it would still maintain the institutional status quo, although women would have more opportunities than they now have to dominate others.

Pluralist-Hybrid

The third model, the pluralistic-hybrid model (Kaplan & Bean, 1976; referred to as "hybrid" by Rossi, 1969, as "progressive-equal" by Bernard, 1974, and as "androgynous" by Yates, 1975) necessitates institutional change as well as changes in the roles of males and females. As stated above, women and men would be seen as equal to each other. In such a society, values themselves would be different. For example, family, community, and play may be valued as highly as politics and work for both sexes, all races, and all social classes. Academic tenure and promotion might be based on community service, quality of teaching, and colleagueship, not just number of publications (Rossi, 1969). More flexible institutional arrangements would exist to allow both sexes to combine work and study and family. Greater cooperation in teaching and research would also be likely (Adler, 1978).

The pluralistic-hybrid model involves a radical reconceptualization of society, one in which individual differences are acknowledged (pluralism) but are integrated into a third, hybrid form—what we have called *androgyny*. This model, then, provides support for a person to move beyond sex roles and for the Establishment to adjust to the lives of human beings, females and males. Androgynous changes in society probably would mean a move toward a social-welfare economy, since capitalism is based on the competitive, achievement-oriented values of the male model (Kaplan & Bean, 1976). Judith Buber Agassi (1979) urges women to seek a way of restructuring the basic system of production so that disagreeable low-level jobs can be eliminated and so that women and men of all classes can work for a fair share of high-level jobs. Block (1973), in examining sex-role stereotypes across six cultures (Norway, Sweden, Denmark, Finland, England, and the United States), found that the countries with the longest and most well-established commitment to social welfare (Sweden and Denmark) were also the countries with fewest sex differences.

Because individual behavior is affected by a wide range of factors, change must be instituted simultaneously on a number of levels for real change to occur on any one level. Such changes already have begun, spurred by the resurgence of the women's liberation movement in the mid-1960s. Although the cry for women's liberation has been at the heart of the movement, it is important to recognize that what is really being proposed is human liberation: freeing both women and men from the restrictiveness of their sex roles so that each individual can realize her/his full human potential. The men's liberation movement, begun in the early 1970s, reflects this broader perspective. Before turning to an examination of the various modes of change, a brief look at the rise of the liberation movements will be instructive.

LIBERATION MOVEMENTS

Women's Liberation

During the 20th century, the United States has twice been confronted with demands for sexual equality. From the turn of the century to the 1940s, the women's rights movement gained momentum—the right of women to vote was passed in 1920; the Equal Rights Amendment was introduced in 1923. After World War II, however, many women who had been urged to join the labor force during the war were urged to leave to make room for the returning male soldiers (Chafetz, 1978). Of course, many others willingly quit to have families. During the 1950s, the "feminine mystique" was promoted: women should be mothers, housewives, and consumers, roles very profitable to an industrialized capitalistic society changing over from peak war-time production to peace-time production (Chafetz, 1978). During the early 1960s, society itself began to change: the "baby-boom" children rediscovered a social conscience and became active in civil rights, the New Left, and the antiwar movement. Some males began rejecting the masculine mystique and the goals of blind patriotism and productivity. Some also began rediscovering sensuality and emotionality. Hence, the occurrence of "hippies," draft resistance, and concern about ecology. On another level, career women were also becoming mobilized. In 1961, the federal Commission on the Status of Women was formed and documented women's second-class status. State commissions followed, and the federal Equal Employment Opportunity Commission (EEOC) was established on the basis of, among other things, complaints on discrimination.

Two forces—younger New Left women and older career women—became welded together into a movement in the late 1960s as a result of a series of crises (J. Freeman, 1973, 1975). Their orientations and values, however, remained different. The older group became dissatisfied with the refusal of EEOC to take "sex discrimination" complaints seriously and they formed their own political and professional organizations. The National Organization for Women (NOW) was founded in 1966 by Betty Friedan, followed by the Women's Equity Action League, Federally Employed Women, and many professional women's caucuses.

At the same time, women from New Left and civil rights organizations became dissatisfied with the traditional roles they were being forced to take in the movements (making coffee, typing, and so forth). They spontaneously formed their own groups in 1967 and 1968, focusing on personal revolution through grass-roots organizing and consciousness-raising groups (Freeman, 1975).

These two groups remained separate, the older branch functioning as a pressure group, focusing on political, legal, and economic changes, the younger branch focusing on consciousness-raising and individual changes (Freeman, 1975). Yet they agreed on two theoretical concerns: criticism of the sex-role-stereotyped division in our society, and the view that sexism exists as institutionalized discrimination, sometimes beyond conscious awareness. The two core concepts of sexism are that men are more important than women and that women exist to please and serve men (Freeman, 1975). The goal of the women's movement, then, is to eradicate sexism and replace it with the concepts of equality and liberation. The former means that the sexes are equal and therefore differential sex roles must go; the latter means that the sex roles themselves must be changed since they are restrictive. Thus, the goal of the women's movement is really human liberation. Despite popular misconceptions, "feminism" does not mean dominance by women, but the equality of women's political and social rights with those of men. As argued throughout this book, such equality and liberation will be beneficial to all members of society.

Men's Liberation

As a result of the changes women were making and the questions they were asking, and also as a result of the inherent strain of the male role, many men began reevaluating their roles and raising their own consciousness. To this end, the men's liberation movement arose in the early 1970s and has been slowly growing, especially in urban areas (Berkeley Men's Center, 1973; David & Brannon, 1976; Sawyer, 1970; Tolson, 1977). The focus is on the changes men want in their lives and how best to achieve them. So far, the most common activity of this movement has been consciousness-raising groups, and many of the men in them do not consider themselves part of a "movement." Other activities are growing as well: conferences, books, magazine articles, research, men's studies courses, and organizations to fight for men's legal and social rights, such as Boston Fathers for Equal Justice (B. Katz, 1973). In 1978, a nonprofit organization called the Society for the Study of Male Psychology and Physiology was started by a group of faculty members at Bowling Green State University.

Both men's and women's liberation movements appear to be expanding slowly and infiltrating our cultural consciousness. Where ten years ago women who wanted both to work and to have a family might have their mothering abilities questioned, this is much less true today. Similarly, ten years ago few men could talk about cooking, doing the laundry, or child care without having their masculinity questioned; this too is much less true today.

How does change come about? How can we help move individuals and society toward androgyny? The following section suggests some alternatives.

MODES OF CHANGE

Change needs to occur on individual, social, and institutional levels. No one tactic or orientation will accomplish the entire task. People choose their tactics based on personal preferences and their diagnoses of the problem. Their approach will be influenced by whether they view women's oppression as due, for example, to sex-role socialization, value differences between masculine and feminine culture, the power inequality between women and men, or capitalism itself, with its view that women are property and cheap labor (Polk, 1976).

Personal Level

Regardless of perspective, self-change is an important part of any alteration in the social order. Ways to achieve such changes are numerous and include consciousness-raising groups, personal psychotherapy, experiential groups, general education, explicit training, and experimenting with new behaviors. Each of these ways is discussed below.

Consciousness-Raising Groups. Perhaps the most prevalent and valuable contribution of the women's movement has been the consciousness-raising (CR) group as a way to achieve personal and social change. CR groups generally consist of 7 to 15 same-sex individuals who meet together, usually weekly, to focus on members' common values, attitudes, and experiences. Many personal problems are seen as having a social cause and a political solution. Through sharing of experiences, members increase their awareness of sex-role stereotypes and their consequences, receive support, explore new ways of behaving and relating, and learn to trust and respect other members of their sex (Brodsky, 1973; J. Freeman, 1975; Kravetz, 1978; Kravetz & Sargent, 1977; Nassi & Abramowitz, 1978; Tolson, 1977).

A key aspect of CR groups is the alteration of traditional (that is, masculine) hierarchical leadership norms. Most groups are run democratically with no fixed leader and each member is regarded as an expert. This new norm applies to the women's liberation movement itself and partially explains why many observers view the movement as disorganized and fragmented. With no recognizable leader or spokesperson, the media have a difficult time focusing on an organization—the male norm expectation here is evident.

Research has documented many changes that appear to occur as a result of CR groups: an altered world view and greater understanding of social, political, and economic factors; a clearer sense of identity and job-career orientation; a greater sense of self-acceptance and higher self-esteem and self-confidence; more egalitarian relationships with other-sex members and increased trust and respect for same-sex members; and a feeling of group solidarity (Cherniss, 1972; Eastman, 1972; Farrell, 1974; J. Freeman, 1975; B. Katz, 1973; Kravetz & Sargent, 1977; Kravetz, 1978; Levine, 1973; Weiss, 1974). The strongest findings have been with regard to the development of profeminist attitudes. The most equivocal data have been with regard to the promotion of self-esteem and personal growth. Although self-reports verify such psychological changes, results from various psychometric measures have been conflicting and few in number (Nassi & Abramowitz, 1978). All researchers agree, however, that CR groups are potent vehicles for resocialization. For men, especially, CR groups appear to be extremely powerful. By their egalitarian structure and their concern with talking about feelings and doubts, these groups challenge male sex-role stereotypes. For this reason, men's CR groups are more difficult to start and to continue than women's CR groups, but the experience itself is often profound (Farrell, 1974; Levine, 1973; Pleck & Sawyer, 1974; Tolson, 1977; Weiss, 1974).

A question arises as to whether these changes are brought about by CR groups themselves or because only certain predisposed individuals join such groups. The answer seems to be, both. Studies of individuals who joined women's CR groups in the late 1960s showed that members—when compared with nonmembers of similar ages, education levels, and socioeconomic levels—were more active, independent, creative, and achievement-oriented, as measured by questionnaires. More members than nonmembers had strong mothers from whom they were often estranged during adolescence. Members as a group also were less authoritarian than nonmembers, were more tolerant of ambiguity, and felt more control over their environment as measured by standardized tests (Cherniss, 1972; Joesting, 1971; Pawlicki & Almquist, 1973). The goals and composition of CR groups during the 1970s seem somewhat different from those described for CR groups in the 1960s. Personal change and support have been emphasized more in the recent groups, and most women who joined the 1970s groups were already members of the women's movement. Yet, in nearly every case studied, involvement in the groups intensified the individual's ideological commitment and also produced real personal change (Kravetz, 1978).

Psychotherapy. A second and more traditional way of achieving personal change has been through psychotherapy. Despite popular misconception, psychotherapy is not reserved for individuals who are severely emotionally disturbed. Rather, it is a way to increase self-awareness and effect behavioral and emotional changes. This method is likely to be beneficial to most people since most of us can benefit from learning more about ourselves and our behaviors. But, as was discussed in Chapter Nine, traditional psychotherapy may discriminate against women in a number of ways. It may incorporate a double standard of mental health. It may "blame the victim" by looking for personal solutions to social problems. And it may reinforce powerlessness by the hierarchical nature of the therapist/client relationship itself. Awareness of these problems has brought changes in therapeutic techniques and has given rise to what A. Kaplan (1976) refers to as a "therapy of *resocialization*." Others have termed this new approach *feminist* or *nonsexist* therapy (Brodsky, 1973; Franks, 1979; A. Kaplan, 1979; Lerman, 1976. See Brodsky et al., 1978, for a review of source materials for nonsexist therapy.).

In a therapy of resocialization, characteristics that have been distorted during initial socialization, such as anger and dependence in many women, are reexamined. These characteristics are then given the opportunity to develop, through expression or modulation, without external restraints (A. Kaplan, 1976). In this way, individuals can move from stereotypic to more androgynous styles of being. In feminist therapy, anger and dependence are dealt with, sex-role stereotypes are discussed, and traditional assumptions regarding appropriate behavior are discarded. Clients are helped to appreciate the social/political context of their behavior and self-nurturance is encouraged. The therapist-client relationship is non-authoritarian and the therapist serves as a model of androgyny (Brodsky, 1973; Lerman, 1976).

Since feminism refers to equality between the sexes, men as well as women can be feminist therapists or clients of feminist therapists. Some people (for example, Chesler, 1971) do argue that only women should be therapists for other women since the therapist's role as a model can be one of the most powerful aspects of therapy. Orlinsky and Howard (1976) found that of 118 women receiving outpatient psychotherapy, those being treated by men were more uncomfortable and self-critical and felt they were getting less encouragement than did women with female therapists. This was especially true of single women 18 to 28 years old. In a similar vein, Shafran (1979) found that women who requested psychotherapy were more likely to prefer a female therapist to a male one. Yet a women is not a better therapist simply by virtue of her sex. Counselors' reactions to female clients vary according to client age, problem type, and counselor sex (Hill, Tanney, Leonard, & Reiss, 1977). The key seems to be sensitivity and awareness of issues particularly relevant to women. Certainly men can become aware and sensitive. It may be, however, at this point in time, that feminist female therapists have more to offer other women than do feminist male therapists, who perhaps would be better working with men.

The question of using psychotherapy for males who are trying to adopt nontraditional sex roles only recently has received some consideration (Bear, Berger, & Wright, 1979; Nikelly, 1979). Problems with such therapy could arise from the fact that many therapists may not be sensitive to the negative effects of the sex-role stereotypes on males: some therapists may have difficulty accepting non-sex-typed behavior in men, and different psychotherapeutic techniques may be needed with men than are needed with women. Interestingly, Shafran (1979) found that men awaiting psychotherapy did not prefer to work with a male therapist and, in fact, viewed their ideal therapist as more similar to a stereotypic female than to a stereotypic male.

Most recently, feminist psychotherapists have been concerned about some of the problems discussed earlier in this chapter related to using androgyny as a standard of mental health. One concern focuses on the importance of helping clients deal with the problems an androgynous sex-role orientation in a sex-typed society might involve (Berzins, 1979; Franks, 1979; Kelly & Worell, 1977; Kenworthy, 1979). Another problem is helping clients move beyond the first stage of androgyny to a level of true integration and sex-role transcendence (Garnets & Pleck, 1979; A. Kaplan, 1979).

Another form of therapy particularly applicable to resocialization is *transactional analysis (TA)*. As we have discussed, traditional sex-role socialization encourages the development of different ego states in men and women and different life scripts. The TA approach is to focus on the neglected ego states, analyze and rewrite the scripts by which many women and men presently live, and analyze and change the games they play, thus altering personal attitudes and behaviors (Jongeward & Scott, 1976; Wyckoff, 1974).

Experiential Groups. A third vehicle for personal change are experiential groups or T-groups ("Training groups"). These groups have been particularly helpful in opening men up to their feelings and in improving their listening skills and interpersonal sensitivity. For this reason, some businesses have instituted such programs to improve the effectiveness of their staff. Interestingly, it is in precisely these areas that most women already are competent due to sex-role socialization. Putting more women who are otherwise qualified in influential positions also might achieve the business objectives, although anything that helps more men increase their interpersonal sensitivity should be encouraged.

Robert Lewis (1978) reports that an increasing number of men have been attending his intimacy workshops conducted at men's conferences around the United States and Canada since 1975. These workshops focus on developing self-disclosure communication skills and the ability to extend affection. The reported experiences have been powerful:

> I have never even told my wife about that feeling I have often had. Now, I cannot wait to get home and tell her. What a relief this is for me (p. 117).

Education. Education, both general and specific, is a fourth way to promote individual change. Women's studies, men's studies, courses on sex roles, and so on have proliferated in the last few years on the college and, in a few cases, the high school level. The American Psychological Association (APA) officially accepted the Psychology of Women as a legitimate field of study by establishing a separate Association division in 1973. By 1979, this division had nearly 2000 female and male members and published its own journal. That work in the field is growing is indicated by the increasing number of papers presented at meetings, books, journal articles, and dissertations (Denmark, 1977). The National Women's Studies Association was founded in 1976, and the third edition of the *Men's Studies Bibliography* came out in February 1977 with 58 pages of references. In 1978, a Task Force on the Male Sex Role and the Psychology of Women was formed. At the same time, a new APA division was proposed, the division of the Psychology and Physiology of Men. This type of focus encourages people to challenge traditional sex-role stereotypes and assumptions and to consider seriously the consequences of such sex typing. Research on the effects of women's studies courses has just begun, but preliminary results suggest that the effects duplicate some of the results of CR groups; that is, after such courses women tend to feel better about themselves and about other women and sometimes change their future plans (Brush, Gold, & White, 1978; M. Johnson, 1979; Scott, Richards, & Wade, 1977). Not all studies have found such changes, however, and the effects of such courses on men have not been examined yet.

Another method of achieving personal change is through explicit training for women in problem solving (Sherman, 1976), mathematics (Tobias, 1978), career planning (O'Neil, Ohlde, Barke, Prosser-Gelwick, & Garfield, 1979), management and leadership skills (Evers

& Bellucci, 1978; Hennig & Jardim, 1977), and self defense. Both sexes need training in assertiveness (Alberti & Emmons, 1970; Franks, 1979; Jakubowski-Spector, 1973; Phelps & Austin, 1975; Richardson, 1977). In assertiveness training, individuals are taught to discriminate among passive responses (letting others violate your rights, particularly common among women), aggressive responses (infringing upon the rights of others, particularly common among men), and assertive responses (respecting your own rights and those of others). Through role-playing and homework assignments, stereotypic sex-role behaviors can be changed. A group treatment program incorporating principles of both assertiveness training and consciousness raising was found to increase the assertiveness and androgyny and masculinity scores of participating feminine sex-typed college women when these women were compared one year after participation with a matched control group who had been placed on a waiting list (Gulanick, Howard, & Moreland, 1979). The success of such a 6-week program in promoting androgyny is encouraging to those who want to eliminate the negative consequences of feminine sex typing. It would be interesting to assess the consequences of a similar program on males.

Changing Behavior. A fifth way of achieving individual attitude change is through focusing on changing behaviors. As was discussed in Chapter Ten, increasing numbers of men are trying out the role of househusband and are learning much about themselves in the process (McGrady, 1976; Roache, 1972). Women executives are learning how to deal with situations they had never before encountered and many wind up reevaluating previously-held beliefs (Hennig & Jardim, 1977). Other changes are occurring on a smaller, more personal scale—a wife going out to work, a husband doing the laundry, a woman asking a man for a date, a man refusing a sexual overture, and so on. Since behaviors and attitudes interact (Bernard, 1976), such behavioral changes often increase the individual's level of awareness.

All these changes, by their very nature, occur on the individual level and thus touch only one part of the problem. They often are slow and limited to a few, highly motivated people. In addition, individual change itself is not always linear. As Kaplan and Bean (1976) suggest, we seem to follow the pendulum principle: at the beginning, there may be a move from one extreme to another, as in a move from passive to aggressive behavior. With time, however, modifications are made and a middle ground is gradually attained, as in the development of assertive behavior. Such a middle position is never static however; an external force is able to start the swing again at any time. The point to remember is that in order to reject an old, extreme behavior or attitude, a new, equally extreme behavior or attitude may temporarily be needed. It's the dialectical process again: first the thesis, then the antithesis, and finally, the synthesis. Although this process may be difficult for those dealing with someone at the time of antithesis, knowledge of its necessity and temporary nature might help.

Social Level

Changes in individual consciousness only go so far. To be effective, individuals must join together to urge changes at social and institutional levels. On a social level, changes are needed in our basic ideology, socialization practices, and relationships with others.

Ideology. The liberation movements have gone a long way toward changing the ideology of our culture. Equality and freedom of choice are becoming more the norm in personal relationships and individual functioning, although they are not always practiced. Standards of mental health, intelligence, creativity, achievement, and child-rearing are all changing in an androgynous direction although progress is slow and by no means continuous. Such changes are imperative, however, especially for succeeding generations.

Socialization. Since we learn our sex roles through socialization, radical changes need to be made in this area. Parents need to be made aware of the potentially maladaptive consequences of rigid sex typing. Child-rearing practices deliberately need to foster androgynous functioning, such as by encouraging independence in girls and emotional sensitivity and expressiveness in boys. Since males very likely would continue to display higher levels of aggression due to hormonal differences, they may need greater reinforcement of gentleness than girls (Gullahorn, 1977b). Language needs to become less discriminatory (for example, *Ms.* and *Mr.*, not *Miss, Mrs.,* and *Mr.*) and more egalitarian (for example, chair*person*, not chair*man*). The media need to give a more accurate and liberated picture of the roles available for women and men. To these ends, pressure groups have formed that are having some effect. For example, Women on Words and Images, an outgrowth of the Princeton NOW chapter, studied sex typing in children's books. Their recommendations have begun to be incorporated by publishers and adopted by school systems (see Chapter Eight). Women Against Violence Against Women, an activist organization based in Los Angeles, has protested media violence against women by joining with various NOW chapters in 1977 and instituting boycotts against socially irresponsible record companies. Companies that use images of violence against women as an advertising gimmick are targeted. The U.S. Commission on Civil Rights finally recommended in August 1977 that Congress give the Federal Communications Commission power to regulate network TV employment practices and write rules to end sexual and racial stereotyping in commercials and dramatic programs.

Changing sex typing in schools is also imperative. As was discussed in Chapter Eight, present school practices and organization, textbooks, curricula, and counseling all perpetuate sex typing. Recent laws banning any form of sex discrimination in any educational institution receiving public funds will go a long way toward remedying the situation, but enforcement is sometimes spotty and suits often take years to be resolved. Additionally, the changing of regulations does not necessarily change attitudes or behavior. As Guttentag and Bray (1977) found when they tried to institute curriculum changes to counteract sexism in kindergarten, fifth, and ninth grades, the teachers' own attitudes and the age and sex of the children were the most important factors: teachers who cared about the issue of sexism could change the attitudes of their students, and kindergarteners and females were especially affected by the six-week program. Thus, change *can* be effected in the schools, but it also can be thwarted by teachers' attitudes and practices. Perhaps specific training in sexism for our nation's teachers is needed (as well as training in racism, which many schools already have instituted). Parents' groups might be particularly effective in monitoring teacher behavior and school compliance with federal regulations.

Relationships. It is very important that sex-role changes be applied to relationships, however difficult such applications may be. Safilios-Rothschild (1979) argues that social change in the United States must occur on both relationship and institutional levels and must involve *conflict confrontations* between the sexes. Such conflicts already have been occurring on the institutional level and they are needed to move beyond the status quo and break out of paternalistic structures. Conflict confrontations also are needed on a more personal level in order to prevent the substitution of subtle, informal discrimination for structural, institutional discrimination. It is in relationships that have a strong degree of affective and esteem feelings (such as friendships, love, and marital relationships) that such confrontations can lead to personal change and eventually to a gradual diminution of interpersonal conflict.

Alternative Life-Styles. A fourth way to effect change on the social level might be to provide for living situations other than the nuclear family. In a nuclear family, a strict division of labor often is encouraged and family members often feel isolated. Popularization of communes, living complexes with communal cooking and child-care arrangements, increased acceptance of single women living alone, unmarried couples living together, and single-parent families, all represent ways of providing more alternatives for more people and they facilitate breaking away from traditional sex-typed behaviors and patterns.

Institutional Level

Even though change has been progressing on the individual level and some change is beginning on the social level, the institutional level has been markedly resistant to change—although many confrontations have occurred. This level represents "the incorporation of ideology into legally required or generally expected actions" (Kaplan & Bean, 1976, p. 386). Laws, organization of work and family, direct action, and alternative institutions come under this heading and will be examined in succeeding paragraphs. The master variable on the institutional level is *power*. As was discussed previously, power in our society rests predominantly in White male hands; significant change is impossible without a reallocation of society's resources, including power. This is difficult since those in control of societal power administer it in ways that work to their continuing advantage and privilege (Worden, Chesler, & Levin, 1977; also see Lipman-Blumen & Bernard, 1979, for an excellent collection of articles on the interface between sex roles and social policy). Further, even when laws change, socialized beliefs take time to follow.

Laws. There has been a tentative thrust toward enacting legislation prohibiting discrimination on the basis of sex. Yet, despite Affirmative Action guidelines, Title IX of the Higher Education Act of 1972, and other legislation, enforcement still is a problem. "Reverse discrimination" suits are increasing, especially since the 1978 *Bakke* decision. The Equal Employment Opportunity Commission and the U.S. Department of Health, Education and Welfare (HEW) are more than two years behind in hearing sex discrimination cases, and actual prosecution has been minimal. (See Figure 13-1 for an example of grounds for a successful lawsuit.) Many requirements of existing legislation are neither comprehensive nor mandatory. And some regulatory agencies still do not enforce the legal statutes already on the books (Kaplan & Bean, 1976; Polk, 1974).

Perhaps most discouraging has been the failure of the Equal Rights Amendment (ERA) to be ratified and the equivocation regarding abortion. The ERA, proposed yearly since 1923, finally was passed by Congress in 1972. It requires ratification by 38 states to become law. The deadline was extended in 1978 from March 22, 1979, to June 30, 1982. As of May 1980 ratification by three more states was needed.

The amendment states that "Equality of rights under the law shall not be denied or abridged by the United States or any State on account of sex." It also gives Congress the power to pass appropriate legislation to enforce its provisions. The amendment calls for nothing less than equal sharing by all citizens of those rights, freedoms, privileges, and responsibilities already spelled out by the U.S. Constitution and our laws. Society would not be drastically changed, since

Reporting on the Chase Manhattan Bank $2 million job-bias settlement with female workers, *The Wall Street Journal (11/3/78)* wrote: "One named plaintiff, Irene LoRe, said she applied for a job as a credit manager with Chase in 1972 under the name I. S. LoRe. When her application went unanswered for several weeks, she filed a second, identical resume. She said she subsequently received two replies—one addressed to Mr. I. S. LoRe and one addressed to Miss I. S. LoRe. 'The one addressed to Mr. LoRe said I had a wonderful background, please call for an interview,' she said, 'The one addressed to Miss LoRe said I had a good background, but no positions are available.' "

Figure 13-1
*Grounds for a
successful lawsuit.*

some states (12) already have their own Equal Rights Amendments, and many laws that prohibit discrimination already exist (Solomon & Jassin, 1977). Passage of the ERA would make such laws uniform, stop the piecemeal approach to enforcement, express a further commitment to equality, and provide a clear basis that all discrimination, even "benign," is unconstitutional.

Despite its seeming reiteration of the American value that all "men" are created equal and the fact that 58% of the American public supports ratification (compared to 31% in opposition) (*N.Y. Times*, 1978, p. 24), passage of the ERA is by no means assured, for five main reasons.

1. The states that are left to ratify (mostly Deep South and Sunbelt) have a politically conservative tradition. As Florida State Senator Lori Wilson notes, "Good Ole Boys . . . do not consider people issues, like ERA on their merit. They consider only what it might do to their own manpower—their manliness, or their money-ness" (*ER Monitor*, May–June 1977, p. 12). Despite findings from opinion polls that a majority of voters in these states do favor passage of the ERA (*ER Monitor*, May–June 1977), the legislators (mainly White males) continue to vote it down.

2. The ratification of state ERAs has confused the issue. Leo Kanowitz, Hastings Law School professor, argues that we need both state and federal ERAs as safeguards for equal rights. One does not substitute for the other (Kanowitz, 1976).

3. Some of the issues involved, such as the draft for women and the support obligation of marital partners, are highly emotional. People's fears can be, and have been, appealed to and manipulated.

4. Pro-ERA groups are not a homogeneous movement but are a number of diverse ideological groups that cut across party and class lines. Until recently (1977–78), they have not presented a unified approach to winning the most friends and influencing the most people. That disunity has begun to change. In 1977, NOW spearheaded an economic boycott of states that have not ratified the ERA. As of October 1978, 318 organizations, unions, and local governments have joined the boycott, costing the targeted states millions of dollars in lost convention and travel business. Three states (Missouri, Louisiana, and Nevada) sued NOW over the boycott; one (Missouri) lost; the other two suits were still in the courts as of July 1979.

5. Many of those in opposition to the ERA have been organized effectively. The anti-ERA movement consists of both men and women and is shaped and directed nationally by Phyllis Schlafly. One writer (Komisar, 1977) has argued that the national campaign to defeat the ERA is not a spontaneous movement by homemakers but is "a movement aimed at organizing women into a political machine to elect conservatives to office and support right-wing views" (p. 1). Funding and support do appear to come predominantly from such politically conservative organizations as the Conservative Caucus, the John Birch Society, the American Conservative Union, and fundamentalist and Mormon churches (Komisar, 1977).

Some of the myths surrounding the ERA are the following (from Porter, 1977; Solomon & Jassin, 1977). Figure 13-2 is a tongue-in-cheek depiction of one myth.

Figure 13-2
*The "threat" of the
ERA. (From* I'm in
Training to Be Tall
and Blonde, *by
Nicole Hollander.
Copyright 1979 by
Nicole Hollander.
Reprinted by
permission of St.
Martin's Press, Inc.)*

Myth 1. The ERA would not require a husband to support his wife and would require a wife to provide "half the income." *Fact:* What the amendment actually would require would be contributions by both members of the marriage to the marriage, but this contribution may be monetary or in terms of services. Thus, a wife who stays home and cares for house and children would be seen as making as equal a contribution to the marriage as is a husband who earns money. Thus a wife's status would increase, not decrease. This equal contribution requirement already exists in states with community property laws. Financial support would be required from the spouse able to give it to the spouse who needs it. In most cases this would be from the husband to the wife. In some divorce cases, husbands might receive alimony. This already is the case in some states. The U.S. Supreme Court in 1979 found that Alabama's law providing for alimony only for wives is unconstitutional (*Orr* versus *Orr*). Similar sexist laws still exist in a number of other states. Child custody would be awarded according to the best interests of the child, which is the current court practice.

Myth 2. The ERA would mean that having bathrooms and living quarters, such as in dormitories, segregated by sex would be illegal. *Fact:* This is blatantly false. The ERA deals only with public legal relationships. The constitutional right to privacy protects private behaviors such as elimination and sleeping. Even in the legal area, sex classification based on physical or functional differences would continue.

Myth 3. Women would be drafted and assigned to combat duty. *Fact:* Young women would be subject to any military draft but would not be required to perform military duties for which they were not qualified. Congress already has the power to draft women and to exempt people because of family responsibilities.

Myth 4. Husbands will have to pay Social Security taxes twice, once on their own earnings and again on the value of their wives' services as homemakers. *Fact:* This charge has no foundation. The ERA would have no impact on the establishment of Social Security benefits for homemaking activities. The concept of homemaker credit, an excellent idea, would require enactment of a separate law.

Myth 5. ERA is anti-male. *Fact:* The ERA guarantees equality for both sexes. Laws that discriminate against men (for example, alimony and child-custody laws) would also be eliminated. Interestingly, as columnist Ellen Goodman (1979) noted, following the Supreme Court's 1979 decision ruling that alimony is not for women only, it was the *anti*-ERA forces who came across as anti-male. They are the ones who protested against extending equal parenthood and alimony rights to men, demonstrating a deep-seated reluctance to "let men off the hook."

Other myths abound regarding the ERA and, in some cases, have been fostered by anti-ERA groups. Because of their sensationalism, they receive press coverage and stick in people's minds despite factual refutations.

As a result of these factors, the passage of the ERA is uncertain, though the success of the effort to extend the deadline until June 1982 suggests that ratification is still possible.

Another legal battle has centered on abortions. In July 1977, Congress passed an amendment that prevented Medicaid funds from being used for abortions. This, in effect, denied low-income women the right to a legal and safe abortion, despite the 1973 U.S. Supreme Court ruling that restrictions on abortions are unconstitutional. The congressional amendment itself was declared unconstitutional in January 1980. However, "right-to-life" groups still are pressuring Congress to ban legal abortions through a constitutional amendment. The call for such an amendment has been passed by 14 states as of July 1979. The right of women to control their own bodies is an integral part of the women's movement. The issue is a complex one, involving religious, philosophic, political, economic, and other factors. Being against abortion does not necessarily mean being against women. However, a distinction needs to be made between a personal decision and a legal option. Although someone may be personally against abortions, he or she still can support a woman's legal right to choose. Without such a legal right, some women would be forced to find "home remedies" or have unsafe illegal abortions (see *Ms.*, December 1978). Other women would be forced to bear unwanted children who, studies indicate, are twice as likely as wanted children to end up abused, delinquent, on welfare, or with serious emotional problems (for example, David & Baldwin, 1979). Furthermore, unwanted pregnancies would force some women to abandon their jobs or education and/or enter pregnancy-related marriages that might have little chance of success.

Legal action is needed in at least seven areas to guarantee equal rights and opportunities to all. (1) Support of the ERA is imperative. (2) Legislation to assure equal opportunity in employment and salaries must be supported. This involves the effective enforcement of all laws, recognition of the necessity of affirmative action programs, and close monitoring of the 1976 Vocational Education Act. It also involves the passage of displaced homemakers legislation and legislation increasing part-time and flex-time work opportunities. (Some first steps were taken in regard to these last two programs by the 95th Congress.) Legislation is needed to reduce veterans' preference, and to expand the opportunities and benefits of women in the military. (3) Legislation is needed to assure economic equity, especially for married couples. This involves the reform of Social Security regulations and federal and military pensions to give both spouses equity and benefits. Legislation regulating Individual Retirement Accounts (IRAs) must be amended to include unpensioned spouses. Appropriation of adequate funds is needed to enforce the Equal Credit Opportunity Act. Legislation barring sex discrimination in insurance and pension coverage must be passed. (4) The enforcement of Title IX (education provisions) must be monitored. As a result of a suit by the Women's Equity Action League (1978), the U.S. Department of Health, Education and Welfare must hire 895 additional employees to eliminate its backlog of complaints and oversee enforcement. (5) Guarantees for women's health care must be obtained. Any national health insurance legislation must provide adequate and equitable coverage for women. Development and enforcement of health and safety standards are also needed. (6) Welfare reform is important, including opportunities for non-stereotyped job training and child-care and family-planning services. (7) Tax reform is needed to ensure that families with two wage earners would not be penalized.

In sum, with equal treatment under the law, protection from discrimination based on sex, and the right to physical self-determination, political and economic power for women as a class should increase (Eastwood, 1975).

Organization of Work and Family. In contrast to changing laws, a second way to effect institutional change is by changing our way of compartmentalizing work and family functions. For an androgynous society, women need to be truly integrated into the occupational world and men need to be truly integrated into the domestic sphere. Although a number of nations have attempted the former, very few have attempted the latter. The result has been that everywhere in industrialized societies, many women must bear the burden of two jobs—one in the work force and one at home (Bernard, 1979b). This lack of inclusion of men in domestic and child-care responsibilities and the work overload for the employed woman partially account for the redifferentiation of sex roles occurring on many an Israeli kibbutz, contrary to the inhabitants' professed ideology (Beit-Hallahmi & Rabin, 1977; Blumberg, 1977). When both women and men share domestic as well as subsistence activities, sex roles tend to be relatively egalitarian, since men develop a more communal orientation and no longer can be paternalistic and distant (Gullahorn, 1977b). This can be seen in primitive hunting and gathering and horticultural societies (see Chapter Six) and currently in Sweden, "the only example to date of a comprehensive, long-range policy for increasing women's and men's active participation in both parenthood and gainful employment" (Gullahorn, 1977b, p. 278). China also has made tremendous advances in the status of women, where 90% work outside the home (Curtin, 1975).

While Swedish society in practice is not completely egalitarian, Sweden has come further than any other country in egalitarian ideology and national policy except China (Baude, 1979; Haavio-Mannila, 1975; Safilios-Rothschild, 1975, 1979). Perhaps the most important aspect of the Swedish model is that the government has strongly emphasized *men's* role changes. To accomplish this, the Swedes have reformed textbooks, changed school curricula, and developed nonsexist parent education. Nearly all boys learn homemaking and child-care skills, and preference usually is given to male applicants for pre-school teacher training. The government has offered a system of incentives to employers to combat traditional sex typing of occupations, provided occupational counseling, grants-in-aid for education, and training for women, and taken care of child-care costs. Either mother or father can take child-care leave, or work part-time and receive the child-care allowance paid to parents of children under 16. Each adult is considered economically independent and pays individual income taxes.

Some elements of the Swedish model can be incorporated here more easily than elements from the Chinese model. Our country needs a national policy, not just piecemeal efforts toward equality. Important changes would be increasing child-care options, such as leaves of absence for either parent and community-controlled day-care centers, and modifying work schedules, such as by providing more part-time opportunities, flex-time opportunities, and work module systems (Friedan, 1979; Kahn, 1973). And most importantly, there must be an emphasis on changing men's roles as well as women's roles. Such changes would help in creating a pluralistic-hybrid (androgynous) society.

Direct Action.   While legal action is one of the most powerful tactics to employ in trying to change male dominance of institutions, other tactics also can be effective, such as direct action and conflict confrontations (Polk, 1976; Safilios-Rothschild, 1979). Through a variety of actions, women increasingly not only are being heard but heeded. Some organizations, like Women Against Violence Against Women and NOW, are engaging in sit-ins and economic boycotts against products, companies, and states that disparage or discriminate against women. Other women have utilized moral pressure by publicizing reports of sex discrimination or sex typing. Still others are organizing and unionizing groups of secretaries, nurses, and household workers. Women often need help in learning such tactics, and skill-building is an important part of many feminist projects (Polk, 1976).

Safilios-Rothschild (1979) urges women to become actively involved in crucial issues and protest movements other than those specifically related to women in order to achieve maximum sex-role change. She argues that because some changes are occurring on the personal and social levels, confrontations on an institutional level are currently being eroded. By joining with other groups and issues, confrontations can continue. This may speed up the acceptance of nonsexist legislation and social policies as well.

Alternative Institutions.   A fourth approach to accomplishing institutional change is by building alternative institutions (Polk, 1976). The women's movement itself represents an alternative to masculine hierarchical authoritarian organizations, and many groups have begun to use the nonhierarchical model—feminist therapy, Association for Women in Psychology, women's studies courses, and so forth. Numerous self-help organizations have challenged the traditional male monopoly of medical, legal, and psychotherapeutic information, and have helped large numbers of people whom the professional institutions had turned off, put down, and overcharged (Polk, 1976). Collective living situations, as discussed under Alternative Lifestyles, also provide couples and single individuals with an alternative to the nuclear family. Such an alternative may facilitate sex-role change.

PROBLEMS

The difficulties of instituting such a total change in society are enormous. There is the problem of integrating changes occurring on three levels, and there are also the problems posed by minority groups and the general resistance to change.

Integration of Changes

Unless changes occur on all levels—personal (attitudes), societal (ideology), and institutional (power)—the likelihood of achieving a truly androgynous society where each individual can develop according to his or her potential and society itself can be run in an effective and humanistic way is small. Legislation without comparable changes in people's attitudes will raise unrealistic hopes and increase resentments. Changes in attitudes without changes in socialization forces and institutions will lead to frustration and hostility. As social psychologists and sociologists have learned, the relationship between attitudes and behavior change is complex (see Bernard, 1976). Changing behaviors sometimes can lead to changes in attitudes and of the social norm. For example, female premarital virginity no longer is the norm it once was. It is also possible that the norm may change and behavior will follow. For example, equality in relationships now is the norm and behavior is slowly changing. On the other hand, the norm may change and behavior may not follow. For example, the Civil Rights Bill of 1964 legislated racial and sexual equality but equality has yet to be achieved. Or behavior may change but the norm may not. For example, most mothers work outside the home, but the norm is that they do not. Clearly, the relation is a complex one and difficult to predict. Time and persistence are undoubtedly crucial variables.

Further evidence of problems that occur when the three levels of change are not integrated currently can be seen in communist countries, especially those of eastern Europe (Jancar, 1978; Scott, 1979). In their initial stages of development, communist societies generally facilitate progress toward sexual equality, especially when such countries first are moving toward industrialization. Labor is scarce at that time, and women are needed in the labor force. Their participation thus is encouraged through emphasis on equality. But once such advances begin to pose a threat to the male political hierarchy or to lead to greatly reduced fertility, sexist policies reappear. Change never really had taken place on the individual or relationship level. Incorporating women into the work force had meant only that women were called on to perform two roles while men still performed one. When other policy matters became more important, the interest in "equality" abated.

Integration of changes also is important to avoid the "super-woman effect." With changing sex-role ideologies, many women now feel they can, and should, do everything—have a stimulating career, establish intimate relationships, rear children, engage in recreational activities, and so on. Without social support from family and friends —and institutional support, such as child-care assistance and flexible work schedules—many women find themselves subject to seemingly endless demands for their time and energies (see Friedan, 1979, for an interesting discussion of this problem).

Minority Groups

Problems also arise in trying to reach all segments of society. Most of the research and literature reported in this book have been on White, middle-class, usually college-educated individuals, primarily because this is the group that most researchers and writers have studied. Yet this sample is clearly only one part of the whole population, and other groups have somewhat different definitions of, problems with, and reactions to sex-role stereotypes. For example, Black women particularly have been denigrated by White society. They have been cast into the stereotyped image of "non-feminist"—not interested in equality between women and men—"deprecated sex object," or "loser," or else they simply have been ignored (King, 1973).

Where White women suffer the effects of sexism, Third World women suffer from sexism and also from racism, and often from poverty as well. Because of this dual, sometimes triple, oppression, many minority women have had difficulty identifying with the women's movement, which has been primarily a product of the White middle class. Because of the oppression of racism and poverty, many minority men have been only too glad to join with White males in manipulating the power structure to their advantage. As Table 13-1 shows, minority men earn about 70% of a White male's salary, but minority women, especially Chicanas, are the lowest paid of all workers.

Each ethnic group has unique problems and its own diversity. Allen (1978) found that Mexican-American, Black, and Caucasian

Table 13-1
Median Annual Income for Men and Women by Race, 1977

	Income	Percent of White Males' Income
White males	$15,378	100.0
Spanish-origin males	$10,935	71.1
Black males	$10,602	68.8
White females	$ 8,870	57.6
Black females	$ 8,290	53.9
Spanish-origin females	$ 7,599	49.4

Source: U.S. Dept. of Labor, 1978.

women each had consistent ethnic group patterns in regard to sex roles, as measured by the Bem Sex Role Inventory. Caucasians were highest in self-reliance and least likely to be masculine or androgynous. Mexican-Americans were highest in forceful characteristics, lowest in self-reliance, and most likely to be androgynous. Black women had strong personalities and leadership abilities, were the most tender and "feminine," and were the least likely to be undifferentiated.

Despite ethnic group differences, certain similarities emerge among Third World women—Blacks, Asians, Chicanas, and Native Americans (Burciaga, Gonzalez, & Hepburn, 1977; Fujitomi & Wong, 1973; Jones, 1971; King, 1973; LaRue, 1976; Nieto-Gomez, 1976; Norton, 1972; O'Leary, 1977; Rhodes, 1971; Wallace, 1978; Witt, 1976). As a group, they are a minority in a White culture. They tend to hold the lowest-status, lowest-paying jobs. They generally have been made to feel inadequate as women regarding their physical appearance and behavior. They may have difficulty establishing their own identity. And they often disagree with the (White) women's movement on a number of issues. They are likely to define racial oppression as the top priority item rather than sexual oppression. They are also likely to favor the traditional structure of the family and to be against birth control and abortion, which may be viewed by them as genocidal and racist and are particularly problems for Catholic Chicanas (Cox, 1976).

Yet certain similarities exist among Third World and White women, since sexism is a part of all cultures, particularly those from which Third World women come. The sexual double standard exists in all the cultures, and their employment and educational opportunities are limited by sex as well as by race. Above all, the oppression of all women, especially Third World women, is intimately tied to maintaining the political and economic equilibrium of our society. Increasingly, Third World women and men are viewing sex roles as part of a "sick" White society that they do not want to imitate, and they are rejecting the current assimilation model (Cox, 1976). Blacks, for example, already have role integration to a certain degree since circumstances have required Black women to work and be strong (Cox, 1976; Steinman & Fox, 1970; Wallace, 1979). Hopefully, the current division between minority and White women can be minimized through understanding of the perspective of Third World women.

The pluralist-hybrid model of society that has been proposed would mean respect for and tolerance of racial and ethnic as well as sexual diversity, would change the values of the dominant society so that it no longer would reflect only White male values, and would involve equality for all citizens.

Resistance

A third major problem in instituting change is the resistance of many men and women and of institutions. Some resistance may stem from a general fear of the unknown, and some from confusion about the sexual and nonsexual aspects of gender role. Since men typically have been the dominant sex with most of the power, it will be much more difficult for them to give some up than it will be for those without power to acquire some (David & Brannon, 1976; Nikelly, 1979). This especially will be true as long as power remains the criterion by which status is determined. Secondly, as children, most males defined themselves by avoiding anything even vaguely feminine. To now alter their self-definition to include "feminine" behavior may mean a perceived loss of status and self-esteem for some men. Thirdly, the unemotional nature of the male sex role mitigates against some men recognizing problems they may have as a result of their sex role, and certainly mitigates against their expressing such problems.

Yet, as we have seen throughout this book, negative consequences of the male sex role are numerous and are becoming increasingly recognized, especially by men involved in alternate life styles. Increasing numbers of men are rejecting the quest for status and success. They are striving to reduce their competitiveness and increase their sensitivity to themselves and to others (David & Brannon, 1976; Friedan, 1979). Major stimuli for change have been the recent changes in women's definitions of themselves and their place in society as well as the restrictiveness some men have felt regarding acceptable behavior (Pleck, 1976a; Tolson, 1977). Although some men have felt threatened and have become entrenched further in traditional roles, men's liberation has been spreading.

Warren Farrell (1974) describes 21 ways in which women's liberation could function as men's liberation. Essentially, Farrell notes that if a man were no longer the primary breadwinner, he probably would experience less fear about losing his job and probably would feel greater freedom to choose an interesting, low-paying one over an unfulfilling, high-paying one. He might feel less need to compete and less pressure to be the sole source of his partner's happiness. He might be able to devote more time to his children, to the pursuit of nonvocational goals, and to alternative household arrangements. His relationships might be based more on feelings than on security. Sexual interest might increase, and his relationships probably would be more rewarding. Men most likely would experience a reduction of anxiety about their sex role and about homosexuality, an increase in autonomy and intellectual achievement, and might develop a new set of values that accompany true listening and a more balanced ego.

Poor men would benefit from the additional income of a working wife and from "homemaker payments," if needed. Men also would become free of many legal burdens that currently fall on them.

Of course, men are not the only group resistant to sex-role change; many women are resistant as well. Women's resistance may stem partly from misunderstanding the goals of the liberation movements. This misunderstanding is perpetuated by myths, such as those about the ERA. Women's resistance also may stem from a resistance to any change and from women's own prejudice against women (see Chapter Eleven). Many women have accepted male sex-role standards as the norm and as the way it "should" be. Some women may have religious or philosophical reasons for preferring present sex-role standards. Greater publicity about the social, political, and economic factors involved in the current role of women and more accurate portrayals of the women's movement and its goals by the media may change the views of some of these women. A direct effort may be needed to reach women feeling alienated from the women's movement because they cannot identify with some of the extreme positions taken. The International Women's Year Conference at Houston (November 1977), which involved representatives from all the states and which captured the heterogeneity of women in the United States today, may have been an important first step in reaching women who have been resistant to change. Another step may have been the November 1979 National Assembly on the Future of the Family, sponsored by NOW's Legal Defense and Education Fund. Some writers (Friedan, 1979; Nemy, 1979b) view the women's movement as entering a new stage with its new concern about the family. Such a concern may appeal to many of the men and women who previously had felt alienated from the women's movement.

Institutional resistance has been more difficult to overcome. Part of the problem involves the inertia of institutions in general to respond to any type of change. Another part of the problem involves the paternalistic nature of institutional discrimination against women. This form of discrimination encourages women to maintain their dependence on men and fragments the position of women as a group while strengthening the position of men as a group (Safilios-Rothschild, 1979). A third part of the problem involves the lack of a clear image of what a more sex-egalitarian future society would look like (Boulding, 1979). This unknown is frightening since it may involve undesirable as well as desirable changes and certainly would involve a redistribution of power. It thus is interesting to consider what such a future society might be like if sex-role changes did become real. We turn now to such speculations.

IMPLICATIONS

If the changes considered above come to pass, their effect on our society, as we have discussed previously, would occur on three levels —the personal, the social, and the institutional. Figure 13-3 gives a satiric view of one possible future.

Figure 13-3
*A glimpse of the
future? (Copyright
1978 by National
Lampoon, Inc.
Reprinted by
permission.)*

Personal

Although androgynous males and females probably would not be
differentiable by activities, interests, or personality patterns, they
still would maintain their separate sex identities. Sex identity is
basically one's sense of maleness or femaleness (see Chapter Two). It
involves appreciating and valuing one's genitals and, later, one's
secondary sex characteristics and their potentialities. As Gullahorn
(1977b) predicts, "androgynous people would value their sex identity,
and would learn that they have choices about how to use their bodies"
(p. 276). Although some writers (for example, Winick, 1968) have
predicted that the perpetuation of the species might be threatened by
eliminating stereotyped sex roles, further consideration of the question shows this prediction to be unfounded. On the contrary, sexual

experiences should be more gratifying than they are presently since good sex requires openness, trust, vulnerability, assertiveness, and activity—all part of an androgynous individual but only partially represented in sex-typed individuals (see Chapter Five). The sexual double standard should no longer exist.

Many people have expressed a concern that increased androgyny will result in increased homosexuality. Many of these individuals fail to distinguish between sex role and sexuality. Additionally, this fear often demonstrates homophobia (see Chapter Ten). Yet there may be some basis to such a fear, because as inability to express feelings to same-sex members decreases, particularly for males, some homosexual experimentation might increase. However, the number of persons who are exclusively homosexual should decrease since an either/or choice no longer would be necessary, the male and female sex roles being sufficiently flexible to incorporate both homosexual and heterosexual behavior.

The institution of marriage probably would change. Since women no longer would need to look for economic security in a mate, both men and women could choose mates on the basis of companionability, understanding, tenderness, physical attractiveness, or sexual ability. Because a woman would no longer have to marry to fulfill herself, there might be fewer marriages and they probably would occur at a later age—a trend that has already begun. The resulting marriages, however, might be stronger, more emotionally satisfying, and less likely to end in divorce because they would be based on free choice, not economic survival. Because marriage would be an equal partnership, wives would be less like parasites and husbands would be less like exploiters (see Chapter Ten).

In reply to those who argue that such equality would destroy the family, it is hard to imagine a more destructive situation than currently exists. About two out of every five couples now marrying will eventually divorce. In the past, the family provided a legitimate outlet for sexual activity and served as a shelter for dependent offspring. It was a unit of production and a source of status, identity, and personal worth. None of these functions is currently the exclusive province of the family. As marriage becomes more an emotional bond, families will assume a new purpose; they will become a refuge from an intensely complex and frustrating world (Hudzinski, 1977).

Since marriages might come later and divorces no longer would be viewed as a sign of failure (Hudzinski, 1977), there would be more single people in the population at a given time than currently exist. Thus there should be an increase in single-person households, a trend already begun, and in alternative living situations, such as single parents and communes. These alternatives probably no longer would be considered deviant.

The effects on children of alternative family structures probably would differ very little from the effects of traditional family structures. A study by Jerome Cohen (cited in *APA Monitor*, 1977, *8*(6), p. 9) found that children of single mothers (pre-planned) and of couples living in a communal setting and in social contract marriages differed very little in terms of behavior and emotional adjustment from those brought up in standard two-parent marriages. This was predominantly because child-rearing practices differed very little. In an androgynous society, parents probably would serve as androgynous models, sharing responsibility for work and family. Through their own example and their own values, such parents should produce androgynous children (see Chapter Seven and Hoffman, 1979).

In an androgynous society, females most likely would be less frustrated, and maybe mentally healthier—better adjusted, with higher self-esteem. Males probably would be under less strain and maybe physically healthier. Other negative consequences of sex-role stereotypes discussed in Chapters Nine and Ten also should be eliminated, leading to better feelings about oneself and better relationships with same- and other-sex individuals and with children.

Social

On a social level, the work situation probably would show the most changes. More women would be in the labor force and perhaps fewer men. Job competition would mean that the best person would be in any specified position. Greater job flexibility would mean that both women and men would be freer to quit, take leaves, work part-time, and make career changes. There might be more emphasis on psychic as opposed to financial rewards.

If a parent decided to stay home, she or he might receive a percent of the spouse's pay and be entitled to pension fund and/or Social Security benefits and a job training allowance if divorced.

A man's mobility would be affected by his wife's job and ambitions, a situation that currently exists in reverse for many married women. It even might be viewed as a form of downward mobility to have a nonworking wife. Women, in the same numbers as men, would probably take over and run the family business or follow in the profession of their physician, lawyer, or dentist father or mother.

Sex typing of occupations would be vastly reduced and although a 50–50 sex composition probably would not occur in all jobs, motivation and talent not being equally distributed, the status and salary differences between jobs in which women primarily work and those in which men do should be eliminated.

Given that people's life spans are increasing, if more people entered the labor force they probably could not all work 40-hour weeks until age 70. This means that there might be more leisure time for all. More activities and hobbies could be pursued by women and men. Such people may fill the gap left by women who used to be available for traditional community voluntary activities. Since a man's identity would no longer be based solely on his role as worker and breadwinner, much of the emotional and physical stress now experienced by men who retire or who are laid off would be reduced or eliminated.

Child care would be restructured. More day and after-school care would be available, sponsored by government, business, or the community. More job flexibility would be possible—shorter hours, flexible hours, shared jobs, and equal leave policies. Housework might become professionalized and greater status (pay and benefits) for child care might be given. Major alterations in life-cycle stages, such as alternate periods of study, employment, and work in the home, probably also would occur.

It might be argued that many of the possible changes depend on society being affluent. However, even in economically depressed times, androgynous functioning still should lead to change. Although employment might be difficult to obtain, layoffs and limited hiring practices should affect both sexes equally. Child care still could be shared by parents and helped by institutional support. Housework too could be shared, since one sex is not more likely than the other to be employed outside the home.

Institutional

In an androgynous society, industry as well as politics might become more humane and socially oriented. There should be a move away from power, competition, and dominance and toward democracy and group decision-making. More women would be in managerial and top political posts and in other positions of power. Such restructuring of society might lead to more humane domestic and foreign policies. Health care might improve, malnutrition and poverty-related illnesses should decrease, ecological implications of policies should be weighed more strongly, and inhumane work practices should be reduced. In this respect, Borden and Powell (1978) found that androgynous and cross-sex-typed individuals had a significantly higher degree of verbal and actual commitment to the solution of environmental problems than had either traditionally sex-typed or undifferentiated individuals. Our support of corrupt inhumane foreign dictatorships for economic reasons also might be reduced.

If violence became less tied to the masculine sex role, we would expect less violent behavior by men as manifested in violent crimes and war-time atrocities. We also might expect more interest in non-violent sports (see Chapter Eleven).

An androgynous society will not come about automatically, even if people become more androgynous individually. Institutions run on a different dynamic than do individuals and a concerted, deliberate, and persistent effort would be needed before social change became a reality.

SUMMARY

In this chapter, a review of alternatives to sex-role stereotyping has been made. Androgyny presents a desirable goal: a maximization of individual potential and a flexible integration of agentic and expressive behaviors. Individual differences would still exist; it is their differential evaluation that would be altered. Moving toward androgynous functioning on an individual as well as a societal level implies the use of a pluralist-hybrid model of social change. In this model, individual differences are recognized and appreciated and are integrated into a new mode of functioning, an androgynous one, which transcends our current dualities. This means institutional as well as individual change.

Because sex-role stereotypes have implications for all levels of functioning—personal, social, and institutional—change will be required on all levels before real change can occur on any one. The liberation movements have created and reflected the impetus for change and have begun the process. On a personal level, consciousness-raising groups, psychotherapy, experiential groups, education, and alterations in behavior all can lead to change. Changes in ideology, socialization practices, and attitudes toward alternate lifestyles can lead to change on the social level. Changes in the law, organization of work and family, direct action, and alternative institutions can lead to changes on an institutional level. Such changes will not come easily. Firstly, there needs to be an integration of the changes occurring on the three levels, institutional change being the most difficult to achieve. Secondly, minority groups and their special needs need to be specifically addressed. Thirdly, resistance by both women and men needs to be expected and handled constructively.

If such changes occur, and our society and the individuals it contains become more androgynous, the ramifications will be widespread, occurring on personal, social, and institutional levels. Some changes already have begun; others will be more difficult to implement. The future, however, is open. What is at stake is no less than the happiness and effectiveness of our entire country. Eliminating sex-role stereotypes does not mean simply liberating women but liberating men and our society as well. What we have been talking about is allowing people to be more fully human and creating a society that will reflect that humanity. Surely that is a goal worth striving for.

RECOMMENDED READING

Freeman, J. The women's liberation movement: Its origins, structures, impact and ideas. In J. Freeman (Ed.), *Women: A feminist perspective*. Palo Alto, Calif.: Mayfield Publishing, 1975, pp. 448–460. A concise overview of the history of the women's movement.

Lipman-Blumen, J., & Bernard, J. (Eds.). *Sex roles and social policy: A complex social science equation*. Beverly Hills, Calif.: Sage Publishing, 1979. An excellent compilation of international articles on the relation among social policy, social research, and sex roles.

McGrady, M. *The kitchen sink papers*. New York: Doubleday & Co., 1976. A humorous account of one man's experience with role reversal.

Men's studies bibliography (3rd ed.). Human Studies Collection, Humanities Library. Cambridge, Mass.: M.I.T., 1977. A thorough listing of materials related to men.

Wallace, M. *Black macho and the myth of the superwoman*. New York: Dial Press, 1979. A thoughtful and provocative discussion of the sex roles Black men and women have played.

REFERENCES

Abramowitz, S. J., & Abramowitz, C. U. Sex-biased researchers of sex bias in psychotherapy and impartial reviewers (Letters to the Editor). *American Psychologist*, 1977, *32*, 893–894.

Abramson, P. P., Goldberg, P. A., Greenberg, J. H., & Abramson, L. M. The talking platypus phenomenon: Competency ratings as a function of sex and professional status. *Psychology of Women Quarterly*, 1977, *2*, 114–124.

Adams, D. B., Gold, A. R., & Burt, A. D. Cycles of sexual desire. *New England Journal of Medicine*, 1978, *299*(21).

Adler, E. *Sisters in crime.* New York: McGraw-Hill, 1975.

Adler, N. E. Women and higher education: Some speculations on the future. *Signs*, 1978, *3*, 912–915.

Agassi, J. B. Beyond equality. In J. Lipman-Blumen & J. Bernard (Eds.), *Sex roles and social policy: A complex social science equation.* Beverly Hills, Calif.: Sage, 1979. Pp. 355–361.

Agate, C., & Meacham, C. Women's equality: Implications of the law. In A. Sargent (Ed.), *Beyond sex roles.* St. Paul: West, 1977. Pp. 434–450.

Ainsworth, M. D. S. Infant-mother attachment. *American Psychologist*, 1979, *34*, 932–937.

Alberti, R., & Emmons, M. D. *Your perfect right.* San Luis Obispo, Calif.: Impact Press, 1970.

Albin, R. New look at single parenting: Focus on fathers. *APA Monitor*, 1977, *8*(6), 7–8.

Albin, R. Depression in women: A feminist perspective. *APA Monitor*, September–October, 1976, p. 27.

Aliotti, N. C. *Sex differences in reading: A biological explanation.* Paper presented at the Western Psychological Association convention, San Francisco, April 1978.

Allen, M. J. *Ethnic group differences in female sex roles.* Paper presented at the Western Psychological Association convention, San Francisco, April 1978.

Allen, M. J., & Hogeland, R. Spatial problem solving strategies as a function of sex. *Perceptual and Motor Skills*, in press.

Almquist, E. M. Women in the labor force. *Signs*, 1977, *2*(4).

Almquist, E. M., & Angrist, S. S. Role model influence on college women's career expectations. *Merrill-Palmer Quarterly*, 1971, *17*, 263–279.

Alper, T. G. Achievement motivation in college women: A now-you-see-it-now-you-don't phenomenon. *American Psychologist*, 1974, *29*, 194–203.

American Education, 1976, *12*(9).

Amir, M. Forcible rape. *Sexual Behavior*, November 1971, 26–36.

Andelin, H. *Fascinating womanhood.* New York: Revelle Books, 1975.

Andreas, C. *Sex and caste in America.* Englewood Cliffs, N.J.: Prentice-Hall, 1971.

Antill, J. K., & Cunningham, J. D. Self-esteem as a function of masculinity in both sexes. *Journal of Consulting and Clinical Psychology*, 1979, *47*, 783–785.

APA Monitor. Adult years. September–October, 1978, pp. 7, 29, 34.

APA Monitor. Alternative families: So what's new? 1977, *8*(6), 9.

APA Monitor. TV influence revisited: Not exactly kid stuff. June 1977, p. 6.

APA Task Force on Sex Bias and Sex Role Stereotyping. Source materials for non-sexist therapy. *JSAS Catalog of Selected Documents in Psychology*, 1978, *8*(2), 40. (Ms. No. 1685)

APA Task Force on Sex Bias and Sex Role Stereotyping in Psychotherapeutic Practice. Report. *American Psychologist*, 1975, *30*, 1169–1175.

Appley, D. G. The changing place of work for women and men. In A. Sargent (Ed.), *Beyond sex roles.* St. Paul: West, 1977. Pp. 300–318.

Aries, E. Male-female interpersonal styles in all male, all female and mixed groups. In A. Sargent (Ed.), *Beyond sex roles.* St. Paul: West, 1977. Pp. 292–299.

Arieti, S., & Bemporad, J. *Severe and mild depression*. New York: Basic Books, 1978.

Arkin, W., & Dobrofsky, L. Military socialization and masculinity. *Journal of Social Issues*, 1978, *34*(1), 131–168.

Asbury Park Press. Brookings report calls for more women in the military. August 5, 1977, p. A17.

Asch, S. E. Studies of independence and conformity: A minority of one against a unanimous majority. *Psychology Monographs*, 1956, *70*(9, Whole No. 416).

Ashmore, R. D., & DelBoca, F. K. Sex stereotypes and implicit personality theory: Toward a cognitive-social psychological conceptualization. *Sex Roles*, 1979, *5*, 219–248.

Ashton, N. L. *Perceptions of successful and unsuccessful females and males*. Paper presented at the Eastern Psychological Association convention, Philadelphia, April 1979.

Aslin, A. J. Feminist and community mental health therapists' expectations of mental health for women. *Sex Roles*, 1977, *3*, 537–544.

Association of American Colleges. *On campus with women*. June 1977, *17*; March 1978, *19*; June 1978, *20*; Fall 1978, *21*, 3–4; Winter 1979, *22*; June 1979, *23*.

Astin, H. S., & Harway, M. Research on sex discrimination in education. *APA Division 35 Newsletter*, 1976, *3*(4), pp. 12–14.

Athanasiou, R., Shaver, P., & Tavris, C. Sex. *Psychology Today*, 1970, *4*(July), 37–52.

Atkinson, J. W., & Feather, N. T. *A theory of achievement motivation*. New York: Wiley, 1966.

Babl, J. D. Compensatory masculine responding as a function of sex role. *Journal of Consulting and Clinical Psychology*, 1979, *47*, 252–257.

Bailyn, L. Career and family orientations of husbands and wives in relation to marital happiness. *Human Relationships*, 1970, *23*(2), 97–144.

Bakan, D. *The duality of human existence*. Chicago: Rand McNally, 1966.

Baker, S. W., & Ehrhardt, A. A. Parental androgen, intelligence and cognitive sex differences. In R. C. Friedman et al. (Eds.), *Sex differences in behavior*. New York: Krieger, 1979. Pp. 53–76.

Balswick, J. O., & Collier, J. L. Why husbands can't say "I Love You." In D. David & R. Brannon (Eds.), *The forty-nine percent majority*. Reading, Mass.: Addison-Wesley, 1976. Pp. 58–59.

Bandura, A. *Aggression: A social learning analysis*. Englewood Cliffs, N.J.: Prentice-Hall, 1973.

Bandura, A. *Principles of behavior modification*. Stanford, Calif.: Stanford University Press, 1969.

Bandura, A. Influence of the model's reinforcement contingencies on the acquisition of imitative responses. *Journal of Personality and Social Psychology*, 1965, *1*, 589–595.

Bandura, A., & Walters, R. H. *Social learning and personality development*. New York: Holt, Rinehart & Winston, 1963.

Banner, L. Women in the college curriculum. Princeton, N.J.: Princeton Project on Women in College Curriculum, 1977.

Bardwick, J. M. *In transition*. New York: Holt, Rinehart & Winston, 1979.

Bardwick, J. M. *The psychology of women: A study of biocultural conflicts*. New York: Harper & Row, 1971.

Barfield, A. Biological influence on sex differences in behavior. In M. S. Teitelbaum (Ed.), *Sex differences: Social and biological perspectives*. New York: Anchor Books, 1976. Pp. 62–121.

Barnett, R., & Baruch, G. K. Women in middle years: A critique of research and theory. *Psychology of Women Quarterly*, 1978, *3*, 187–197.

Baron, R. A. Heightened sexual arousal and physical aggression: An extension to females. *Journal of Research in Personality*, 1979, *13*, 91–102.

Baron, R. A., & Bell, P. A. Sexual arousal and aggression by males: Effects of type of erotic stimuli and prior provocation. *Journal of Personality and Social Psychology*, 1977, *35*, 79–87.

Barry, H., Bacon, M. R., & Child, I. J. A cross-cultural survey of some sex differences in socialization. *Journal of Abnormal and Social Psychology*, 1957, *55*, 327–332.

Bart, P. Depression in middle aged women. In V. Gornick & B. K. Moran (Eds.), *Women in sexist society*. New York: Basic Books, 1972. Pp. 162–186.

Bart, P. B., & Scully, D. H. The politics of hysteria: The case of the wandering womb. In E. S. Gomberg & V. Franks (Eds.), *Gender and disordered behavior: Sex differences in psychopathology.* New York: Brunner/Mazel, 1979. Pp. 354–380.

Bartol, K. M., & Wortman, M. S., Jr. Sex of leader and subordinate role stress: A field study. *Sex Roles*, 1979, *5*, 513–518.

Bartolme, F. Executives as human beings. *Harvard Business Review*, November–December 1972, 62–69ff.

Basow, S. A. *Women's attributions for success.* Unpublished manuscript, 1980.

Basow, S. A., & Howe, K. G. Model influence on career choices of college students. *The Vocational Guidance Quarterly*, 1979, *27*, 239–243. (a)

Basow, S. A., & Howe, K. G. Sex bias and career evaluations. *Perceptual and Motor Skills*, 1979, *49*, 705–706. (b)

Baucom, D. H., & Danker-Brown, P. Influence of sex roles on the development of learned helplessness. *Journal of Consulting and Clinical Psychology*, 1979, *47*, 928–936.

Baude, A. Public policy and changing family patterns in Sweden 1930–1977. In J. Lipman-Blumen & J. Bernard (Eds.), *Sex roles and social policy: A complex social science equation.* Beverly Hills, Calif.: Sage, 1979. Pp. 145–175.

Bear, S., Berger, M., & Wright, L. Even cowboys sing the blues: Difficulties experienced by men trying to adopt nontraditional sex roles and how clinicians can be helpful to them. *Sex Roles*, 1979, *5*, 191–198.

Bearison, D. J. Sex-linked patterns of socialization. *Sex Roles*, 1979, *5*, 11–18.

Beck, J. Sexist math: Why women don't count in classroom. *Chicago Tribune.* Reported in *ER-Monitor*, 1977, *3*(2), 12.

Beit-Hallahmi, B., & Rabin, A. I. The Kibbutz as a social experiment and as a child-rearing laboratory. *American Psychologist*, 1977, *32*, 534–551.

Bell, A., & Weinberg, M. *Homosexualities.* New York: Simon & Schuster, 1978.

Bell, R. Female sexual satisfaction as related to levels of education. *Sexual Behavior*, 1971, *1*(8), 8–14.

Bell, R. Q. A. A reinterpretation of the direction of effects in studies of society. *Psychological Review*, 1968, *75*, 81–95.

Beller, E. K., & Neubauer, P. B. Sex differences and symptom patterns in early childhood. *Journal of Child Psychiatry*, 1963, *2*, 417–433.

Belsky, J., & Sternberg, J. L. The effects of day care: A critical review. *Child Development*, 1978, *49*, 920–949.

Bem, D., & Allen, A. On predicting some of the people some of the time: The search for cross-situational consistencies in behavior. *Psychological Review*, 1974, *81*, 506–520.

Bem, S. L. Theory and measurement of androgyny: A reply to the Pedhazur-Tetenbaum and Locksley-Colton critiques. *Journal of Personality and Social Psychology*, 1979, *37*, 1047–1054.

Bem, S. L. On the utility of alternative procedures for assessing psychological androgyny. *Journal of Consulting and Clinical Psychology*, 1977, *45*, 196–205.

Bem, S. L. Probing the promise of androgyny. In A. Kaplan & J. Bean (Eds.), *Beyond sex-role stereotypes: Readings toward a psychology of androgyny.* Boston: Little, Brown, 1976. Pp. 47–62.

Bem, S. L. Androgyny versus the tight little lives of fluffy women and chesty men. *Psychology Today*, 1975, *9*, 58–59ff. (a)

Bem, S. L. Sex role adaptibility: One consequence of psychological androgyny. *Journal of Personality and Social Psychology*, 1975, *31*, 634–643. (b)

Bem, S. L. The measurement of psychological androgyny. *Journal of Consulting and Clinical Psychology*, 1974, *42*, 155–162

Bem, S. L., & Bem, D. J. Case study of a nonconscious ideology: Teaching the woman to know her place. In D. J. Bem (Ed.), *Beliefs, attitudes and human affairs.* Belmont, Calif.: Brooks/Cole, 1970.

Bem, S. L., & Lenney, E. Sex-typing and the avoidance of cross-sex behavior. *Journal of Personality and Social Psychology*, 1976, *33*, 48–54.

Bem, S., Martyna, W., & Watson, C. Sex-typing and androgyny: Further exploration of the expressive domain. *Journal of Personality and Social Psychology*, 1976, *34*, 1016–1023.

Bennett, S. M. *Further implications of masculinity and femininity for psychological well-being in women and men.* Paper presented at the meeting of the American Psychological Association, New York, September 1979.

Berger, C., & Gold, D. Do sex differences in problem solving still exist? *Personality and Social Psychology Bulletin*, 1979, *5*, 109–113.

Berger, M., Wallston, B. S., Foster, M., & Wright, L. You and me against the world: Dual career couples and joint job seeking. *Journal of Research and Development in Education*, 1977, *10*(4), 30–37.

Bergman, J. Are little girls being harmed by Sesame Street? In J. Stacey, S. Bereaud, & J. Daniels (Eds.), *And Jill came tumbling after: Sexism in American education*. New York: Dell, 1974.

Berkeley Men's Center Manifesto, 1973. In J. Pleck & J. Sawyer (Eds.), *Men and masculinity*. Englewood Cliffs, N.J.: Prentice-Hall, 1974. Pp. 173–174.

Berman, P. W. *Attraction to infants: Are sex differences innate and invariant?* Paper presented at the American Psychological Association convention, Chicago, 1975.

Bernard, J. Women as voters: From redemptive to futurist role. In J. Lipman-Blumen & J. Bernard (Eds.), *Sex roles and social policy: A complex social science equation*. Beverly Hills, Calif.: Sage, 1979. Pp. 279–286. (a)

Bernard, J. Policy and women's time. In J. Lipman-Blumen & J. Bernard (Eds.), *Sex roles and social policy: A complex social science equation*. Beverly Hills, Calif.: Sage, 1979. Pp. 303–333. (b)

Bernard, J. Homosexuality and female depression. *Journal of Social Issues*, 1976, *32*(4). (a)

Bernard, J. Change and stability in sex-role and behavior. *Journal of Social Issues*, 1976, *32*(3), 207–223. (b)

Bernard, J. *Sex differences: An overview*. New York: MSS Modular Publications, Module 26, 1974, 1–18.

Bernard, J. *The future of marriage*. New York: Bantam, 1973.

Bernard, J. *Woman and the public interest*. Chicago: Aldine, 1971.

Berry, J. W. Temne and Eskimo perceptual skills. *International Journal of Psychology*, 1966, *1*, 207–229.

Berzins, J. I. Discussion: Androgyny, personality theory, and psychotherapy. *Psychology of Women Quarterly*, 1979, *3*, 248–254.

Berzins, J. I., Welling, M. A., & Wetter, R. E. A new measure of psychological androgyny based on the Personality Re-search Form. *Journal of Consulting and Clinical Psychology*, 1978, *46*, 126–138.

Bettelheim, B. *Symbolic wounds*. New York: Collier, 1962.

Biller, H. B. The father and personality development: Paternal deprivation and sex-role development. In M. E. Lamb (Ed.), *The role of the father in child development*. New York: Wiley, 1976. Pp. 89–156.

Biller, H. B. *Paternal deprivation: Family, school, sexuality and society*. Lexington, Mass.: D. C. Heath, 1974.

Bird, C. The best years of a woman's life. *Psychology Today*, June 1979, *13*(1), 20–26.

Birnbaum, J. Life patterns and self-esteem in gifted family-oriented and career-committed women. In T. S. Mednick, S. Tangri, & L. W. Hoffman (Eds.), *Women and achievement*. Washington, D.C.: Hemisphere, 1975.

Bishop, J. D. *The motive to avoid success in women and men: An assessment of sex-role identity and situational factors*. Unpublished doctoral dissertation, Cornell University, 1974.

Blau, F. D. Women in the labor force: An overview. In J. Freeman (Ed.), *Women: A feminist perspective*. Palo Alto, Calif.: Mayfield, 1975. Pp. 211–226.

Blaubergs, M. S. Changing the sexist language: The theory behind the practice. *Psychology of Women Quarterly*, 1978, *2*, 244–261.

Block, J. H. Conceptions of sex-roles: Some cross-cultural and longitudinal perspectives. *American Psychologist*, 1973, *28*, 512–526.

Blumberg, R. L. A paradigm for predicting the position of women: Policy implications and problems. In J. Lipman-Blumen & J. Bernard (Eds.), *Sex roles and social policy: A complex social science equation*. Beverly Hills, Calif.: Sage, 1979. Pp. 113–142.

Blumberg, R. L. Women and work around the world: A cross-cultural examination of sex division of labor and sex status. In A. Sargent (Ed.), *Beyond sex roles*. St. Paul: West, 1977. Pp. 412–433.

Blumstein, P. W., & Schwartz, P. Bisexuality: Some social psychological issues. *Journal of Social Issues*, 1977, *33*(2), 30–45.

Boocock, S. S. *An introduction to the sociology of learning*. New York: Houghton Mifflin, 1972.

Booth, A. Sex and social participation. *American Sociological Review*, 1972, *37*, 183–193.

Borden, R. J., & Powell, P. H. *Androgyny and environmental responsibility: Individual differences in concern and commitment.* Paper presented at the American Psychological Association convention, Toronto, August 1978.

Borges, M. A., Levine, J. R., & Naylor, P. A. *Self-ratings and projected ratings of sex-role attitudes.* Paper presented at the Western Psychological Association convention, San Francisco, April 1978.

Boserup, E. *Women's role in economic development.* London, England: Allen & Unwin, 1970.

Boston Women's Health Book Collective. *Our bodies, ourselves.* New York: Simon & Schuster, 1976.

Bouchard, T. J., & McGee, M. G. Sex differences in human spatial ability: Not an X-linked recessive gene effect. *Social Biology*, 1977, *24*, 332–335.

Boulding, E. Introduction. In J. Lipman-Blumen and J. Bernard (Eds.), *Sex roles and social policy: A complex social science equation.* Beverly Hills, Calif.: Sage, 1979. Pp. 7–14.

Bowman, G. W., Worthy, N. B., & Greyser, S. A. Are women executives people? *Harvard Business Review*, 1965, *43*, 14–17ff.

Bralove, M. Career women decry sexual harassment by bosses and clients. *Wall Street Journal*, January 29, 1976, pp. 1ff.

Brannon, R. Measuring attitudes toward women (and otherwise): A methodological critique. In J. Sherman & F. Denmark (Eds.), *The future of women: Issues in psychology.* New York: Psychological Dimensions, in press.

Brannon, R. The male sex-role: Our culture's blueprint of manhood and what it's done for us lately. In D. David & R. Brannon (Eds.), *The forty-nine percent majority.* Reading, Mass.: Addison-Wesley, 1976.

Bremer, T. H., & Wittig, M. A. Fear of success: A personal trait or a response to occupational deviance and role overload? *Sex roles*, in press.

Brenton, M. *The American male.* New York: Coward, McCann & Geoghegan, 1966.

Brewer, M. B., & Blum, M. W. Sex-role androgyny and patterns of causal attribu-

tion for academic achievement. *Sex Roles*, 1979, *5*, 783–796.

Brichta, H., & Inn, A. *Is female leadership perceived as a disadvantage?* Paper presented at Midwest Psychological Association convention, Chicago, 1978.

Brimer, M. A. Sex differences in listening comprehension. *Journal of Research and Development in Education*, 1969, *3*, 72–79.

Broder, D. Women candidates face formidable obstacles. *Courier-News*, October 18, 1978, p. A9.

Brodsky, A. M. The consciousness-raising group as a model for therapy with women. *Psychotherapy: Theory, Research and Practice*, 1973, *10*(1).

Brodsky, A. M., Holroyd, J., Payton, C. R., Rubenstein, E. A., Rosenkrantz, P., Sherman, J., Zell, F., Cummings, T., & Suber, C. J. Source materials for nonsexist therapy. *JSAS catalog of selected documents in psychology*, 1978, *8*(2), 40. (Ms. No. 1685)

Brody, J. E. Marriage is good for health and longevity, studies say. *New York Times*, May 8, 1979, p. C1. (a)

Brody, J. E. Women and smoking—newest research shows the health toll is mounting. *New York Times*, February 3, 1979. (b)

Bronfenbrenner, U. Toward an experimental ecology of human development. *American Psychologist*, 1977, *32*, 513–531.

Bronfenbrenner, U. Developmental research, public policy and the ecology of childhood. *Child Development*, 1974, *45*, 1–5.

Broverman, I., Broverman, D. M., Clarkson, Rosenkrantz, P. S., & Vogel, S. R. Sex-role stereotypes and clinical judgments of mental health. *Journal of Consulting and Clinical Psychology*, 1970, *34*, 1–7.

Broverman, I., Broverman, D. M., Clarkson, F. E., Rosenkrantz, P. S., & Vogel, S. R. Sex-role stereotypes and clinical judgments of mental health. *Journal of Consulting and Clinical Psychology*, 1970, *34*, 1–7.

Broverman, I., Vogel, S. R., Broverman, D. M., Clarkson, F. E., & Rosenkrantz, P. S. Sex role stereotypes: A current appraisal. *Journal of Social Issues*, 1972, *28*, 59–78.

Brown, C. H. Women's sports gaining acceptance, but ignorance shows progress. *Lafayette Alumni Quarterly*, 1977, *48*(4), 11–15.

Brown, D. G. Sex role preference in young children. *Psychological Monographs*, 1956, *70*(14, Whole No. 42).

Brown, J. K. An anthropological perspective on sex roles and subsistence. In M. Teitelbaum (Ed.), *Sex differences: Social and biological perspectives*. New York: Anchor Press, 1976. Pp. 122–137.

Brown, J. K. Economic organization and position of women among the Iroquois. *Ethnohistory*, 1970, *17*, 151–167.

Brown, J. M., & Davies, N. Attitude towards violence among college athletes. *Psychology Today*, 1978, *11*(9), 34–36.

Brown, J. W., Aldrich, M. L., & Hall, P. Q. *The participation of women in scientific research*. Washington, D.C.: National Science Foundation, 1978.

Brown, L. Study finds stereotyping in TV casts. *New York Times*, October 30, 1979, p. 15.

Brown, P., & Fox, H. Sex differences in divorce. In E. S. Gomberg & V. Franks (Eds.), *Gender and disordered behavior: Sex differences in psychopathology*. New York: Brunner/Mazel, 1979. Pp. 101–123.

Brown, S. M. Male versus female leaders: A comparison of empirical studies. *Sex Roles*, 1979, *5*, 597–611.

Brown, S. M. Sexism in western art. In J. Freeman (Ed.), *Women: A feminist perspective*. Palo Alto, Calif.: Mayfield, 1975. Pp. 309–322.

Brownmiller, S. *Against our will: Men, women and rape*. New York: Simon & Schuster, 1975.

Brozan, N. A study of the American man. *New York Times*, January 19, 1979, p. 47.

Brush, L., Gold, A., & White, M. The paradox of intention and effect: A women's studies course. *Signs*, 1978, *3*, 870–883.

Bryden, M. P. Evidence for sex-related differences in cerebral organization. In M. A. Wittig & A. C. Petersen (Eds.), *Sex-related differences in cognitive functioning: Developmental issues*. New York: Academic Press, 1979. Pp. 121–143.

Buck, R. Nonverbal communication of affect in preschool children. Relationships with personality and skin conductance. *Journal of Personality and Social Psychology*, 1977, *35*, 225–236.

Bunker, B. B., & Seashore, E. W. Power; collusion; intimacy-sexuality; support. In A. G. Sargent (Ed.), *Beyond sex roles*. St. Paul: West, 1977. Pp. 356–370.

Burciaga, C. P., Gonzalez, V., & Hepburn, R. The Chicana as feminist. In A. Sargent (Ed.), *Beyond sex roles*. St. Paul: West, 1977. Pp. 266–274.

Byrne, D. Social psychology and the study of sexual behavior. *Personality and Social Psychology Bulletin*, 1977, *3*, 3–30.

Byrne, D., & Lamberth, J. The effect of erotic stimuli on sex arousal, evaluative responses, and subsequent behavior. *Technical Reports of the Commission on Obscenity and Pornography* (Vol. VIII). Washington, D.C.: U.S. Government Printing Office, 1971, 41–67.

Cacioppo, J. T., & Petty, R. E. *Sex differences in influenceability: Toward specifying the underlying process*. Paper presented at the American Psychological Association convention, New York, September 1979.

Calder, B. G., & Ross, M. Sexual discrimination and work performance. *Personality and Social Psychology Bulletin*, 1977, *13*, 429–433.

Callahan-Levy, C. M., & Messé, L. A. Sex differences in the allocation of pay. *Journal of Personality and Social Psychology*, 1979, *37*, 433–446.

Campbell, A. The American way of mating. Marriage sí, children only maybe. *Psychology Today*, May 1975, 37–43.

Canter, R. J. Achievement-related expectations and aspirations in college women. *Sex Roles*, 1979, *5*, 453–470.

Carlson, J. E. The sexual role. In F. I. Nye (Ed.), *Role structure and analysis of the family*. Beverly Hills, Calif.: Sage, 1976.

Carlson, R. Stability and change in the adolescent's self-image. *Child Development*, 1965, *36*, 659–666.

Carter, C. S., & Greenough, W. T. Sending the right sex messages. *Psychology Today*, September 1979, *13*(4), 112.

Carter-Saltzman, L. Patterns of cognitive functioning in relation to handedness and sex-related differences. In M. A. Wittig & A. C. Petersen (Eds.), *Sex-related differences in cognitive functioning: Developmental issues*. New York: Academic Press, 1979. Pp. 97–118.

Chafetz, J. S. *Masculine/feminine or human?* (2nd ed.). Itasca, Ill.: Peacock, 1978.

Chelune, G. J. Reactions to male and female disclosure at two levels. *Journal of*

Personality and Social Psychology, 1976, *34*, 1000–1003.

Cherniss, C. Personality and ideology: A personological study of women's liberation. *Psychiatry*, 1972, *35*(2), 109–125.

Cherry, F., & Deaux, K. Fear of success versus fear of gender-inappropriate behavior. *Sex Roles*, 1978, *4*, 97–101.

Cherry, L. Teacher-child verbal interaction: An approach to the study of sex differences. In B. Thorne & N. Henley (Eds.), *Language and sex: Differences and dominance*. Rowley, Mass.: Newbury House, 1975. Pp. 172–183.

Cherry, L., & Lewis, M. Mothers and two-year-olds: A study of sex-differentiated aspects of verbal interaction. *Developmental Psychology*, 1976, *12*, 278–282.

Cherulnik, P. D. Sex differences in the expression of emotion in a structured social encounter. *Sex Roles*, 1979, *5*, 413–424.

Chesler, P. *About men*. New York: Simon & Schuster, 1978.

Chesler, P. *Women and madness*. New York: Doubleday, 1972.

Chesler, P. Women psychiatric and psychotherapeutic patients. *Journal of Marriage and the Family*, 1971, *33*, 746–795. (a)

Chesler, P. Patient and patriarch: Women in the psychotherapeutic relationship. In V. Gornick & B. Moran (Eds.), *Women in sexist society: Studies in power and powerlessness*. New York: Basic Books, 1971. Pp. 251–275. (b)

Chesler, P., & Goodman, E. J. *Women, money and power*. New York: Morrow, 1976.

Child, I. L., Potter, E. H., & Levine, E. M. Children's textbooks and personality development: An explanation of the social psychology of education. *Psychological Monographs*, 1946, *60*(3), 1–64.

Chronicle of Higher Education. Characteristics and attitudes of first-year college students. January 22, 1979, p. 15; January 28, 1980, p. 5.

Chronicle of Higher Education. Proportion of degrees awarded to women. October 23, 1978, p. 11; November 13, 1978, p. 13.

Cicone, M. N., & Ruble, D. N. Beliefs about males. *Journal of Social Issues*, 1978, *34*(1), 5–16.

Clancy, K., & Gove, W. Sex differences in mental illness: An analysis of response bias in self reports. *American Journal of Sociology*, 1974, *80*, 205–216.

Clarke, A. E., & Ruble, D. N. Young adolescents' beliefs concerning menstruation. *Child Development*, 1978, *49*, 231–234.

Clarkson, F. E., Vogel, S. R., Broverman, I., Broverman, D., & Rosenkrantz, P. Family size and sex-role stereotypes. *Science*, 1970, *167*, 390–392.

Coates, S. Sex differences in field independence among preschool children. In R. C. Friedman et al. (Eds.), *Sex differences in behavior*. New York: Wiley, 1974. Pp. 259–274.

Cohen, D., & Wilkie, F. Sex-related differences in cognition among the elderly. In M. A. Wittig & A. C. Petersen (Eds.), *Sex-related differences in cognitive functioning: Developmental issues*. New York: Academic Press, 1979. Pp. 145–159.

Coleman, J. S. *The adolescent society*. Glencoe, Ill.: Free Press, 1961.

Collins, G. A new look at life with Father. *The New York Times Magazine*, June 17, 1979, pp. 30–31ff.

Condry, J., & Dyer, S. Fear of success: Attribution of cause to the victim. *Journal of Social Issues*, 1976, *32*(3), 63–83.

Connell, D. M., & Johnson, J. E. Relationship between sex-role identification and self-esteem in early adolescence. *Developmental Psychology*, 1970, *3*, 268.

Connor, J. M., & Serbin, L. A. Children's responses to stories with male and female characters. *Sex Roles*, 1978, *4*, 637–645.

Connor, J. M., Serbin, L. A., & Ender, R. A. Responses of boys and girls to aggressive, assertive, and passive behaviors of male and female characters. *Journal of Genetic Psychology*, in press.

Constantinople, A. Sex-role acquisition: In search of the elephant. *Sex Roles*, 1979, *5*, 121–133.

Constantinople, A. Masculinity—femininity: An exception to a famous dictum? *Psychological Bulletin*, 1973, *80*, 389–407.

Cook, L. Working mothers like their jobs. Associated Press release, in *Hunterdon Democrat*, October 19, 1978, p. 39.

Cooper, H. M. Statistically combining independent studies: A meta-analysis of sex differences in conformity research. *Jour-*

nal of Personality and Social Psychology, 1979, *37*, 131–146.

Cosentino, F., & Heilbrun, A. B. Anxiety correlates of sex-role identity in college students. *Psychological Reports*, 1964, *14*, 729–730.

Costrich, N., Feinstein, J., Kidder, L., Maracek, J., & Pascale, L. When stereotypes hurt: Three studies of penalties for sex-role reversals. *Journal of Experimental Social Psychology*, 1975, *11*, 520–530.

Cox, S. Ethnic diversity of female experience. In S. Cox (Ed.), *Female psychology: The emerging self*. Chicago: SRA, 1976. Pp. 212–215.

Crandall, V. C. Sex differences in expectancy of intellectual and academic reinforcement. In C. Smith (Ed.), *Achievement related motives in children*. New York: Russell Sage Foundation, 1969.

Cravens, G. How Ma Bell is training women in management. *The New York Times Magazine*, May 29, 1977, pp. 12–20.

Crawley, D., & Basow, S. *Helping behavior: Does sex make a difference?* Paper presented at Eastern Psychological Association convention, Philadelphia, April 1979.

Crittendon, A. Is the corporate world more talk than progress? *New York Times*, May 1, 1977, S3, p. 1ff.

Crowley, J. E., Levitin, E., & Quinn, R. P. Seven deadly half-truths about women. *Psychology Today*, March 1973, pp. 94–96.

Cuca, J. Women psychologists and marriage: A bad match? *American Psychologist*, March 1976, p. 3.

Curtin, K. *Women in China*. New York and Toronto: Pathfinder Press, 1975.

Dalton, K. *The menstrual cycle*. New York: Pantheon, 1969.

Dan, A. J. The menstrual cycle and sex-related differences in cognitive variability. In M. A. Wittig & A. C. Petersen (Eds.), *Sex-related differences in cognitive functioning: Developmental issues*. New York: Academic Press, 1979. Pp. 241–260.

Dan, A. J. *Behavioral variability and the menstrual cycle*. Paper presented at the American Psychological Association convention, Washington, D.C., September 1976.

David, D. S., & Brannon, R. (Eds.). *The forty-nine percent majority: The male sex role*. Reading, Mass.: Addison-Wesley, 1976.

David, H. P., & Baldwin, W. P. Childbearing and child development. *American Psychologist*, 1979, *34*, 866–871.

Davidson, R. J., Schwartz, G. E., Pugash, E., & Bromfield, E. Sex differences in patterns of EEG asymmetry. *Biological Psychology*, 1976, *4*, 119–138.

Davison, G., & Neale, J. M. *Abnormal psychology* (2nd. ed.). New York: Wiley, 1978.

Dawson, J. L. M. Cultural and physiological influence upon spatial-perceptual processes in West Africa (Parts I and II). *International Journal of Psychology*, 1967, *2*, 115–128; 171–185.

Deaux, K. Self-evaluations of male and female managers. *Sex Roles*, 1979, *5*, 571–580.

Deaux, K. *The behavior of women and men*. Monterey, Calif.: Brooks/Cole, 1976.

Deaux, K., & Emswiller, T. Explanations of successful performance on sex-linked tasks: What's skill for the male is luck for the female. *Journal of Personality and Social Psychology*, 1974, *29*, 80–85.

Deaux, K., & Major, B. Sex-related patterns in the unit of perception. *Personality and Social Psychology Bulletin*, 1977, *3*, 297–300.

Deaux, K., & Taynor, J. Evaluation of male and female ability; Bias works two ways. *Psychological Reports*, 1973, *32*, 261–262.

Deaux, K., White, L. J., & Farris, E. Skill or luck: Field and lab studies of male and female preferences. *Journal of Personality and Social Psychology*, 1975, *32*, 629–636.

DeBeauvoir, S. *The second sex*. Translated by H. M. Parshey. New York: Knopf, 1953.

DeFrain, J., & Eirick, R. *Coping as divorced single parents: A comparative study of fathers and mothers*. Paper presented at the meeting of the American Psychological Association, New York, September 1979.

Delk, J. L. Differentiating sexist from nonsexist therapists or my analogue can beat your analogue. Letter to the Editor. *American Psychologist*, 1977, *32*, 890–893.

Delora, J. S., & Warren, C. A. B. *Understanding sexual interaction*. Boston: Houghton Mifflin, 1977.

Denier, C. A., & Serbin, L. A. *Play with

male-preferred toys: Effects on visual-spatial performance. Paper presented at the American Psychological Association convention, Toronto, August 1978.

Denmark, F. The outspoken woman: Can she win? Paper presented at the meeting of the New York Academy of Sciences, 1979.

Denmark, F. The psychology of women: An overview of an emerging field. Personality and Social Psychology Bulletin, 1977, 3, 356–367.

Depner, C. E., & Veroff, J. Varieties of achievement motivation. Journal of Social Psychology, 1979, 107, 283–284.

Derlega, V. J., & Chaikin, A. L. Norms affecting self-disclosure in men and women. Journal of Consulting and Clinical Psychology, 1976, 44, 376–380.

Devereaux, G. Institutionalized homosexuality of the Mohave Indians. Human Biology, 1937, 9.

Dinkmeyer, D., & McKay, G. Raising a responsible child. New York: Simon & Schuster, 1973.

Doering, C. H., Brodie, H. K. H., Kramer, H. C., Becker, H. B., & Hamburg, D. A. Plasma testosterone levels and psychological measures in men over a 2-month period. In R. C. Friedman, R. M. Richart, & R. L. Vande Wiele (Eds.), Sex differences in behavior. New York: Wiley, 1974. Pp. 413–421.

Doherty, P. A., & Schmidt, M. R. Sex-typing and self-concept in college women. Journal of College Student Personnel, November 1978, 493–497.

Dohrenwend, B. P., & Dohrenwend, B. S. Sex differences and psychiatric disorders. American Journal of Sociology, 1976, 81, 1447–1454.

Do It NOW. October 1977.

Do It NOW. April 1977, p. 2.

Do It NOW. February 1977, p. 2.

Dominick, J. R. The portrayal of women in prime time, 1953–1977. Sex Roles, 1979, 5, 405–411.

Donelson, E. Development of sex-typed behavior and self-concept. In E. Donelson & J. Gullahorn (Eds.), Women: A psychological perspective. New York: Wiley, 1977. Pp. 119–139. (a)

Donelson, E. Social responsiveness and separateness. In E. Donelson & J. Gullahorn (Eds.), Women: A psychological per-

spective. New York: Wiley, 1977. Pp. 140–153. (b)

Donelson, E. Personality: A scientific approach. New York: Appleton-Century-Crofts, 1973.

Donelson, E., & Gullahorn, J. E. Individual and interpersonal achievement. In E. Donelson & J. Gullahorn (Eds.), Women: A psychological perspective. New York: Wiley, 1977. Pp. 168–184. (a)

Donelson, E., & Gullahorn, J. Social influences on the development of sex-typed behavior. In E. Donelson & J. Gullahorn (Eds.), Women: A psychological perspective. New York: Wiley, 1977. Pp. 140–153. (b)

Donnerstein, E., & Hallam, J. Facilitating effects of erotica on aggression against women. Journal of Personality and Social Psychology, 1978, 36, 1270–1277.

Drummond, H. The epidemics nobody tries to treat. Mother Jones, September-October 1977, pp. 11–12.

Dubbert, J. L. A man's place: Masculinity in transition. New York: Prentice-Hall, 1979.

Dullea, G. Female academics find progress slow. New York Times, November 13, 1977, p. 13.

Dweck, C. S. The role of expectations and attributions in the alleviation of learned helplessness. Journal of Personality and Social Psychology, 1975, 31, 674–685.

Dweck, C. S., & Bush, E. S. Sex differences in learned helplessness: I. Differential debilitation with peer and adult evaluators. Developmental Psychology, 1976, 12, 147–156.

Dweck, C. S., Davidson, W., Nelson, S., & Enna, B. Sex differences in learned helplessness. II. The contingencies of evaluative feedback in the classroom. III. An experimental analysis. Developmental Psychology, 1978, 14, 268–276.

Dweck, C. S., & Repucci, N. D. Learned helplessness and reinforcement responsibility in children. Journal of Personality and Social Psychology, 1973, 25, 109–116.

Dwyer, C. A. The role of tests and their construction in producing apparent sex-related differences. In M. A. Wittig & A. C. Petersen (Eds.), Sex-related differences in cognitive functioning: Developmental issues. New York: Academic Press, 1979. Pp. 335–353.

Eagly, A. Sex differences in influenceability. *Psychological Bulletin*, 1978, *85*, 86–116.

Eastman, P. C. Consciousness-raising: The etiology and examination of the small group process in the Women's Liberation Movement. *Smith College Studies in Social Work*, 1972, *43*(1), 72–73.

Eastwood, M. Feminism and the law. In J. Freeman (Ed.), *Women: A feminist perspective*. Palo Alto, Calif.: Mayfield, 1975. Pp. 325–334.

Ehrenreich, B. Is success dangerous to your health? *Ms.*, May 1979, 7(11), 51–54, 97–101.

Ehrhardt, A. *Biological sex differences—A developmental perspective*. Master lecture presented at the American Psychological Association convention, New York, September 1979.

Eme, R. F. Sex differences in childhood psychopathology: A review. *Psychological Bulletin*, 1979, *86*, 574–595.

Emmerich, W., Goldman, K. L., Kirsh, B., & Sharabary, R. Evidence for a transitional phase in the development of gender constancy. *Child Development*, 1977, *48*, 930–936.

Englander-Golden, P., & Barton, G. *Sex differences in work absenteeism: A reinterpretation*. Paper presented at the meeting of the American Psychological Association, New York, September 1979.

Entwisle, D. To dispel fantasies about fantasy-based measures of achievement motivation. *Psychological Bulletin*, 1972, *77*, 377–391.

Epstein, C. F. Encountering the male establishment: Sex-status limits on women's careers in the professions. *American Journal of Sociology*, 1970, *75*, 965–982.

Erikson, E. *Childhood and society*. (2nd. ed.). New York: Norton, 1963.

ER-Monitor. May-June 1977, p. 12.

ER-Monitor. March-April 1977.

ER-Monitor. January-February 1977, pp. 5–6.

Etaugh, C. Effect of maternal employment on children: A view of recent research. *Merrill-Palmer Quarterly*, 1974, *20*, 71–98.

Etaugh, C., & Harlow, H. Behaviors of male and female teachers as related to behaviors and attitudes of elementary school children. *Journal of Genetic Psychology*, 1975, *127*, 163–170.

Etaugh, C., & Rose, S. Adolescent's sex bias in the evaluation of performance. *Developmental Psychology*, 1975, *11*, 663–664.

Etaugh, C., & Whittler, T. E. *Social memory of preschool girls and boys*. Paper presented at the American Psychological Association convention, New York, September 1979.

Evers, N. A., & Bellucci, J. B. Developing interpersonal competencies in educational leadership (DICEL) project. U.S. Office of Education, Women's Educational Equity Act, 1978.

Eysenck, H. J. Masculinity-femininity personality and sexual attitude. *Journal of Sex Roles*, 1971, *1*(2), 83–88.

Eysenck, H. J., & Nias, D. K. B. *Sex, violence and the media*. New York: Harper Colophon, 1978.

Fabrikant, B. The therapist and the female patient: Perceptions and change. In V. Franks & U. Burtle (Eds.), *Women in therapy*. New York: Brunner/Mazel, 1974.

Fagot, B. I. *Sex-determined parental reinforcing contingencies in toddler children*. Paper presented at the Biennial Meeting of the Society for Research in Child Development, New Orleans, March 1977. (a)

Fagot, B. I. *The consequences of same-sex, cross-sex, and androgynous preferences in early childhood*. Paper presented at the Western Psychological Association convention, San Francisco, April 1978. (b)

Fagot, B. I. *Sex-determined parental reinforcing contingencies in toddler children*. Paper presented at the Biennial Meeting of the Society for Research in Child Development, New Orleans, March 1977. (a)

Fagot, B. I. Consequences of moderate cross gender behavior in preschool children. *Child Development*, 1977, *48*, 902–907. (b)

Fagot, B. I., & Patterson, G. R. An *in Vivo* analysis of reinforcing contingencies for sex-role behaviors in the preschool child. *Developmental Psychology*, 1969, *1*, 563–568.

Falk, G. Sex discrimination in the trade unions: Legal resources for change. In J. Freeman (Ed.), *Women: A feminist perspective*. Palo Alto, Calif.: Mayfield, 1975. Pp. 259–276.

Fallon, B. J., & Hollander, E. P. *Sex-role stereotyping in leadership: A study of undergraduate discussion groups.* Paper presented at the American Psychological Association convention, Washington, D.C., August 1976.

Farrell, W. *The liberated man.* New York: Random House, 1974.

Fasteau, M. F. *The male machine.* New York: McGraw-Hill, 1974.

Feather, N. T. Attributes of responsibility and valence of success and failure in relation to initial confidence and task performance. *Journal of Personality and Social Psychology*, 1969, *13*, 129–144.

Feather, N. T., & Raphaelson, A. C. Fear of success in Australian and American student groups: Motive or sex-role stereotype? *Journal of Personality and Social Psychology*, 1974, *42*, 190–201.

Feather, N. T., & Simon, J. C. Reactions to male and female success and failure in sex-linked occupations: Impressions of personality, causal attributions and perceived likelihood of different consequences. *Journal of Personality and Social Psychology*, 1975, *31*, 20–31.

Feild, H. S. Attitudes toward rape: A comparative analysis of police, rapists, crisis counselors, and citizens. *Journal of Personality and Social Psychology*, 1978, *36*, 156–178.

Feild, H. S., & Caldwell, B. E. Sex of supervisor, sex of subordinate, and subordinate job satisfaction. *Psychology of Women Quarterly*, 1979, *3*, 391–399.

Fein, G., Johnson, D., Kosson, N., Stork, L., & Wasserman, L. Sex stereotypes and preferences in the toy choices of 20-month-old boys and girls. *Developmental Psychology*, 1975, *11*, 527–528.

Fein, R. Research on fathering: Social policy, and an emergent perspective. *Journal of Social Issues*, 1978, *34*(1), 122–135.

Fein, R. Men and young children. In J. Pleck & J. Sawyer (Eds.), *Men and masculinity.* Englewood Cliffs, N.J.: Prentice-Hall, 1974. Pp. 54–62.

Fennema, E., & Sherman, J. Factors predicting girls' enrollment in college preparatory mathematics. *Psychology of Women Quarterly*, in press.

Fennema, E., & Sherman, J. Sex-related differences in mathematics achievement, spatial visualization and affective factors. *American Educational Research Journal*, 1977, *14*, 51–71.

Fennema, E., & Sherman, J. *Sex-related differences in mathematic learning: Myths, realities and related factors.* Paper presented at the American Association for the Advancement of Science Symposium on "Women and Math," Boston, 1976.

Ferguson, L. R. The woman in the family. In E. Donelson & J. Gullahorn (Eds.), *Women: A psychological perspective.* New York: Wiley, 1977. Pp. 214–227.

Ferguson, M. Imagery and ideology: The cover photographs of traditional women's magazines. In G. Tuchman, A. K. Daniels, & J. Benét (Eds.), *Hearth and home: Images of women in the mass media.* New York: Oxford University Press, 1978. Pp. 97–115.

Ferree, M. M. The confused American housewife. *Psychology Today*, September 1976, pp. 76–80.

Feshbach, S. *Sex, aggression and violence toward women.* Invited address at the American Psychological Association convention, Toronto, August 1978.

Feshbach, S., & Feshbach, N. The young aggressors. *Psychology Today*, April 1973, pp. 90–96.

Feshbach, S., & Malamuth, N. Sex and aggression: Proving the link. *Psychology Today*, 1978, *12*(6), 110–117ff.

Fidell, L. S. Empirical verification of sex discrimination in hiring practices in psychology. In R. Unger & F. Denmark (Eds.), *Woman: Dependent or independent variable?* New York: Psychological Dimensions, 1976. Pp. 779–782.

Fields, C. M. What colleges must do to avoid sex bias in sports. *Chronicle of Higher Education*, December 10, 1979, p. 1ff.

Finney, J. C., Brandsma, J. M., Tondoro, M., & Lemaistre, G. A study of transsexuals seeking gender reassignment. *American Journal of Psychology*, 1975, *132*, 962–967.

Finz, S. D., & Waters, J. *An analysis of sex-role stereotyping in daytime television serials.* Paper presented at the American Psychological Association convention, Washington, D.C., 1976.

Fischer, K. I., & Grande, L. M. *The relationship of gender and sex-role orientation to accuracy in nonverbal assessment and to interpersonal needs.* Paper presented at the Eastern Psychological Association convention, Washington, D.C.,

March 1978.

Fisher, S., & Greenberg, R. P. Masculinity-femininity and response to somatic discomfort. *Sex Roles*, 1979, *5*, 483–493.

Fisher, W. R., & Byrne, D. Sex differences in response to erotica? Love versus lust. *Journal of Personality and Social Psychology*, 1978, *36*, 117–125.

Fitzgerald, H. E. Infants and caregivers: Sex differences as determinants of socialization. In E. Donelson & J. Gullahorn (Eds.), *Women: A psychological perspective*. New York: Wiley, 1977. Pp. 101–118.

Flanders, J. P. A review of research on imitative behavior. *Psychological Bulletin*, 1968, *69*, 316–337.

Fleck, J. R., Coffey, C. A., Malin, S. Z., & Miller, D. H. *Father's psychological absence and heterosexual behavior, sextyping, and personality adjustment in adolescent girls*. Paper presented at the Western Psychological Association convention, San Francisco, April 1978.

Fleming, J. Comment on "Do Women Fear Success" by D. Tresemer. *Signs*, 1977, *2*, 706–717.

Fling, S., & Manosevitz, M. Sex typing in nursery school children's play interests. *Developmental Psychology*, 1972, *7*, 146–152.

Foot, H. C., Chapman, A. J., & Smith, J. R. Friendship and social responsiveness in boys and girls. *Journal of Personality and Social Psychology*, 1977, *35*, 401–411.

Fosburgh, L. The make-believe world of teenage maternity. *New York Times Magazine*, August 7, 1977, pp. 29–34.

Foster, L. W., & Kolinko, T. Choosing to be a managerial woman: An examination of individual variables and career choice. *Sex Roles*, 1979, *5*, 627–634.

Foushee, H. C., Helmreich, R. L., & Spence, J. T. Implicit theories of masculinity and femininity: Dualistic or bipolar? *Psychology of Women Quarterly*, 1979, *3*, 259–269.

Fox, L. H., Tobin, D., & Brody, L. Sex role socialization and achievement in mathematics. In M. A. Wittig & A. C. Petersen (Eds.), *Sex-related differences in cognitive functioning: Developmental issues*. New York: Academic Press, 1979. Pp. 303–332.

Frances, S. J. Sex differences in nonverbal behavior. *Sex Roles*, 1979, *5*, 519–535.

Franks, V. Gender and psychotherapy. In E. S. Gomberg & V. Franks (Eds.), *Gender and disordered behavior: Sex differences in psychopathology*. New York: Brunner/Mazel, 1979. Pp. 453–485.

Franzwa, H. H. Female roles in women's magazine fiction, 1940–1970. In R. Unger & F. Denmark (Eds.), *Woman: Dependent or independent variable?* New York: Psychological Dimensions, 1975. Pp. 42–53.

Freedman, M. Homosexuals may be healthier than straights. *Psychology Today*, March 1975, pp. 28–32.

Freeman, H. R. Sex-role stereotypes, self-concepts, and measured personality characteristics in college women and men. *Sex Roles*, 1979, *5*, 99–103.

Freeman, J. How to discriminate against women without really trying. In J. Freeman (Ed.), *Women: A feminist perspective*. Palo Alto, Calif.: Mayfield, 1975. Pp. 194–208. (a)

Freeman, J. The Women's Liberation Movement: Its origins, structures, impact and ideas. In J. Freeman (Ed.), *Women: A feminist perspective*. Palo Alto, Calif.: Mayfield, 1975. Pp. 460–484. (b)

Freeman, J. The origins of the Women's Liberation Movement. In J. Huber (Ed.), *Changing women in a changing society*. Chicago: University of Chicago Press, 1973. Pp. 30–49.

Freeman, J. The social construction of the second sex. In M. Garskof (Ed.), *Roles women play*. Monterey, Calif.: Brooks/Cole, 1971. Pp. 123–141.

Freeman, J. Growing up girlish. *Trans-Action*, 1970, *8*, 36–43.

Freud, S. Three essays on the theory of sexuality. 1905. In I. Struckey (Rev. and Ed.), *The standard edition of the complete works of Sigmund Freud*, Vol. VII. London, England: Hogarth Press and the Institute of Psycho-Analysis, 1964.

Freud, S. The dissolution of the Oedipus Complex. 1924. (a) In I. Struckey (Rev. and Ed.), *The standard edition of the complete works of Sigmund Freud*, Vol. XIX. London, England: Hogarth Press, 1964.

Freud, S. Some psychological consequences of the anatomy. Distinction between the sexes. 1924. (b) In I. Struckey (Rev. and Ed.), *The standard edition of the complete works of Sigmund Freud*, Vol. XIX. London, England: Hogarth Press, 1964.

Friday, N. *My mother/my self.* New York: Dell, 1977.

Friedan, B. Feminism takes a new turn. *New York Times Magazine*, November 18, 1979, p. 40ff.

Friedan, B. *The feminine mystique.* New York: Dell, 1963.

Friedl, E. *Women and men: An anthropologist's view.* New York: Holt, Rinehart & Winston, 1975.

Frieze, I. H. Internal and external psychological barriers for women in science. In J. A. Ramaley (Ed.), *Covert discrimination and women in the sciences.* AAAS Selected Symposia Series, (#14), 1978.

Frieze, I. H. Women's expectations for and causal attributions of success and failure. In M. Mednick, S. S. Tangri, & L. Hoffman (Eds.), *Women and achievement: Social and motivational analyses.* Washington, D.C.: Hemisphere, 1977.

Frieze, I. H., McHugh, M., & Duquin, M. *Causal attributes for women and men and sports participants.* Paper presented at the American Psychological Association convention, Washington, D.C., 1976.

Frieze, I. H., & Ramsey, S. J. Nonverbal maintenance of traditional sex roles. *Journal of Social Issues*, 1976, *32*(3), 133–141.

Frieze, I. H., & Washburn, C. *Battered women's responses to battering.* Paper presented at the Association for Women in Psychology conference, Dallas, 1979.

Frisch, H. L. Sex stereotypes in adult-infant play. *Child Development*, 1977, *48*, 1671–1675.

Frodi, A., Macaulay, J., & Thome, P. R. Are women always less aggressive than men? A review of the experimental literature. *Psychological Bulletin*, 1977, *84*, 634–660.

Frueh, T., & McGhee, P. E. Traditional sex role development and amount of time spent watching TV. *Developmental Psychology*, 1975, *11*, 109.

Fuchs, M., & Weissbrod, C. S. *Math anxiety: Not for women only.* Paper presented at the Eastern Psychological Association convention, Washington, D.C., March 1978.

Fujitomi, I., & Wong, D. The new Asian-American woman. In S. Sue & N. Wagner (Eds.), *Asian-American: Psychological perspectives.* Palo Alto, Calif.: Science & Behavior Books, 1973.

Gagnon, J. H. Physical strength, once of significance. *Impact of Science on Society*, 1971, *21*(1), 31–42.

Gagnon, J. H., & Simon, W. *Sexual conduct: The social sources of human sexuality.* Chicago: Aldine, 1973.

Gall, M. D. The relationship between masculinity-femininity and manifest anxiety. *Journal of Clinical Psychology*, 1969, *25*, 294–295.

Gallup, G. Majority of teenagers assert family ties good. *Asbury Park Press*, July 13, 1977, p. D9.

Garai, J. E., & Scheinfeld, A. Sex differences in mental and behavioral traits. *Genetic Psychology Monographs*, 1968, *77*, 169–299.

Garfinkle, E., & Morin, S. Psychologists' attitudes toward homosexual psychotherapeutic clients. *Journal of Social Issues*, 1978, *34*(3), 101–112.

Garnets, L., & Pleck, J. H. Sex role identity, androgyny, and sex role transcendence: A sex role strain analysis. *Psychology of Women Quarterly*, 1979, *3*, 270–283.

Garrett, C. D., Ein, P. L., & Tremaine, L. The development of gender-stereotyping of adult occupations in elementary school children. *Child Development*, 1977, *48*, 507–517.

Geis, F., Jennings, J. W., Corrado-Taylor, D., & Brown, V. *Sex-role stereotypes in TV commercials: An experimental separation of sex and role.* Paper presented at the meeting of the American Psychological Association, New York, September 1979.

Geis, F., Jennings, J. W., & Porter, N. *Do stereotyped TV commercials depress women's achievement aspirations?* Paper presented at the meeting of the American Psychological Association, New York, September 1979.

Geise, L. A. The female role in middle class women's magazines from 1955 to 1976: A content analysis of nonfiction selections. *Sex Roles*, 1979, *5*, 51–62.

Geller, S. E., Geller, M. I., & Scheirer, C. J. *The development of sex attitudes and selective attention to same-sex models in young children.* Paper presented at the Eastern Psychological Association convention, Philadelphia, April 1979.

Gerbner, G., & Gross, L. The scary world of TV's heavy viewer. *Psychology Today*, April 1976, pp. 41–45ff.

Gilbert, L. A. The sexist psychotherapist: An ephemeral species. Letter to the Editor. *American Psychologist*, 1977, *33*, 888–889.

Gilbert, L. A., Deutsch, C. J., & Strahan, R. F. Feminine and masculine dimensions of the typical, desirable, and ideal woman and man. *Sex Roles*, 1978, *4*, 767–778.

Gilder, G. The case against women in combat. *New York Times Magazine*, January 28, 1979, pp. 29–30ff.

Gillespie, D. L. Who has the power? The marital struggle. *Journal of Marriage and Family*, August 1971, pp. 445–458.

Glasser, K. *Sex-role orientation of the tasks and expectancy of success as variables affecting the achievement behavior of male and female college students.* Unpublished doctoral dissertation, Princeton University, 1974.

Glenn, N. D., & Weaver, C. N. Attitudes toward premarital, extramarital and homosexual relations in the U.S. in the 1970s. *Journal of Sex Research*, May 1979.

Glueck, G. The woman as artist. *New York Times Magazine*, September 25, 1977.

Goffman, E. Genderisms. *Psychology Today*, August 1977, pp. 60–63.

Gold, D., & Berger, C. Problem-solving performance of young boys and girls as a function of task appropriateness and sex-identity. *Sex Roles*, 1978, *4*, 183–193.

Goldberg, H. *The hazards of being male: Surviving the myth of masculine privilege.* New York: Nash, 1976.

Goldberg, P. Are women prejudiced against women? *Trans-Action*, 1968, *5*(5), 28–30.

Goldberg, S., & Lewis, M. Play behavior in the year old infant: Early sex differences. *Child Development*, 1969, *40*, 21–31.

Goldenberg, N. R. *Changing of the gods: Feminism and the end of traditional religions.* Boston: Beacon Press, 1979.

Goldstein, E. Effect of same-sex and cross-sex role models on the subsequent academic productivity of scholars. *American Psychologist*, 1979, *34*, 407–410.

Goleman, D. Special abilities of the sexes: Do they begin in the brain? *Psychology Today*, 1978, *12*(6), pp. 48–59ff.

Golub, S. The effect of premenstrual anxiety and depression on cognitive function. *Journal of Personality and Social Psychology*, 1976, *34*, 99–104.

Golub, S., & Canty, E. *Sex role expectations and the assumption of leadership by college women.* Paper presented at the Eastern Psychological Association convention, Philadelphia, April 1979.

Gomberg, E. S. Problems with alcohol and other drugs. In E. S. Gomberg & V. Franks (Eds.), *Gender and disordered behavior: Sex differences in psychopathology.* New York: Brunner/Mazel, 1979. Pp. 204–240.

Goodchilds, J. D. Power: A matter of mechanics? *SASP Newsletter*, 1979, *5*(3), 3.

Goodman, E. Who says feminists are anti-male? Boston, 1979.

Gough, H. G. *Manual for the California Psychological Inventory.* Palo Alto, Calif.: Consulting Psychologists Press, 1957.

Gough, K. The origin of the family. In J. Freeman (Ed.), *Women: A feminist perspective.* Palo Alto, Calif.: Mayfield, 1975.

Gould, R. E. Measuring masculinity by the size of a paycheck. *Ms.*, June 1973, p. 18ff.

Gove, W. Sex differences in the epidemiology of mental disorder: Evidence and explanations. In E. S. Gomberg & V. Franks (Eds.), *Gender and disordered behavior: Sex differences in psychopathology.* New York: Brunner/Mazel, 1979. Pp. 23–68.

Gove, W. Sex, marital status and mortality. *American Journal of Sociology*, 1973, *79*, 45–67.

Gove, W. The relationship between sex roles, marital status, and mental illness. *Social Forces*, 1972, *51*, 34–44. (a)

Gove, W. Sex roles, marital status and suicide. *Journal of Health and Social Behavior*, 1972, *13*, 204–213. (b)

Gove, W., & Geerken, M. Response bias in community surveys: An empirical investigation. *American Journal of Sociology*, 1977, *82*, 1289–1317.

Gove, W., & Herb, T. R. Stress and mental illness among the young: A comparison of the sexes. *Social Forces*, 1974, *53*, 256–265.

Gove, W., & Tudor, J. Sex differences in mental illness: A comment on Dohrenwend and Dohrenwend. *American Journal of Sociology*, 1977, *82*, 1327–1336.

Gove, W., & Tudor, J. F. Adult sex roles and mental illness. In J. Huber (Ed.), *Changing women in a changing society.*

Chicago: University of Chicago Press, 1973.

Goy, R. W. Early hormonal differences on the development of sexual and sex-related behavior. In F. O. Schmitt (Ed.), *The neurosciences: Second study program*. New York: Rockefeller University Press, 1970.

Greenberg, M., & Morris, N. Engrossment: The newborn's impact upon the father. *American Journal of Orthopsychiatry*, 1974, *44*, 520–531.

Greenberg, R. P., & Fisher, S. The relationship between willingness to adopt the sick role and attitudes toward women. *Journal of Chronic Diseases*, 1977, *30*, 29–37.

Greenstein, M., Miller, R. H., & Weldon, D. E. Attitudinal and normative beliefs as antecedents of female occupational choice. *Personality and Social Psychology Bulletin*, 1979, *5*, 356–362.

Griffin, S. Rape: The All-American crime. In J. Freeman (Ed.), *Women: A feminist perspective*. Palo Alto, Calif.: Mayfield, 1975. Pp. 25–40.

Gross, A. E. The male role and heterosexual behavior. *Journal of Social Issues*, 1978, *34*(1), 87–107.

Gross, L., & Jeffries-Fox, S. "What do you want to be when you grow up, little girl?" In G. Tuchman, A. K. Daniels, & J. Benét (Eds.), *Hearth and home: Images of women in the mass media*. New York: Oxford University Press, 1978. Pp. 240–265.

Gross, R., Batlis, N., Small, A., & Erdwins, C. Factor structure of the Bem Sex Role Inventory and the Personal Attributes Questionnaire. *Journal of Consulting and Clinical Psychology*, 1979, *47*, 1122–1124.

Gruber, K. J., & Gaebelein, J. Sex differences in listening comprehension. *Sex Roles*, 1979, *5*, 299–310.

Grusec, J. E., & Brinker, D. B., Jr. Reinforcement for initiation as a social learning determinant with implications for sex-role development. *Journal of Personality and Social Psychology*, 1972, *21*, 149–158.

Grush, J. E., & Yehl, J. G. Marital roles, sex differences, and interpersonal attraction. *Journal of Personality and Social Psychology*, 1979, *37*, 116–123.

Gulanick, N. A., Howard, G. S., & Moreland, J. Evaluation of a group program designed to increase androgyny in feminine women. *Sex Roles*, 1979, *5*, 811–827.

Gullahorn, J. E. Sex roles and sexuality. In E. Donelson & J. Gullahorn (Eds.), *Women: A psychological perspective*. New York: Wiley, 1977. Pp. 189–213. (a)

Gullahorn, J. E. Equality and social structure. In E. Donelson and J. Gullahorn (Eds.), *Women: A psychological perspective*. New York: Wiley, 1977. Pp. 266–281. (b)

Gunderson, M. The influence of the status and sex composition of occupations on the male-female earnings gap. *Industrial & Labor Relations Review*, January 1978.

Gurwitz, S. B., & Dodge, K. A. Adults' evaluation of a child as a function of sex of adult and sex of child. *Journal of Personality and Social Psychology*, 1975, *33*, 822–828.

Gutek, B. A., & Nakamura, C. Y. *Sexuality and the workplace*. Paper presented at the meeting of the American Psychological Association, New York, September 1979.

Guttentag, M., & Bray, H. Teachers as mediators of sex-role standards. In A. Sargent (Ed.), *Beyond sex roles*. St. Paul: West, 1977. Pp. 395–411.

Guttentag, M., & Bray, H. Tough to nip sexism in the bud. *Psychology Today*, December 1975, p. 58.

Haan, N., Smith, M. B., & Block, J. Moral reasoning of young adults: Political-social behavior, family background and personality correlates. *Journal of Social Psychology*, 1968, *10*, 182–201.

Haas, A. Male and female spoken language differences: Stereotypes and evidence. *Psychological Bulletin*, 1979, *86*, 616–626.

Haavio-Mannila, E. Convergence between East and West: Tradition and modernity in sex roles in Sweden, Finland, and the Soviet Union. In M. Mednick, S. S. Tangri, & L. Hoffman (Eds.), *Women and achievement: Social and motivational analyses*. New York: Halsted Press, 1975. Pp. 71–84.

Hacker, H. M. Women as a minority group twenty years later. In R. Unger & F. Denmark (Eds.), *Women: Dependent or independent variable?* New York: Psychological Dimensions, 1975. Pp. 103–112.

Hacker, H. M. Women as a minority group. *Social Forces*, 1951, *30*, 60–69.

Hall, J. A. Gender effects in decoding nonverbal cues. *Psychological Bulletin*, 1978, *85*, 845–857.

Hamburg, D. A., & Lunde, D. T. Sex hormones in the development of sex differences in human behavior. In E. E. Maccoby (Ed.), *The development of sex differences*. Stanford, Calif.: Stanford University Press, 1966. Pp. 1–24.

Hammer, E. F. Creativity and feminine ingredients in young male artists. *Perceptual and Motor Skills*, 1964, *19*, 414.

Hariton, E. B. The sexual fantasies of women. *Psychology Today*, 1973, *6*(10), 39–44.

Harlow, H. F. Sexual behavior in the rhesus monkey. In F. A. Beach (Ed.), *Sex and behavior*. New York: Wiley, 1965.

Harlow, H. F. The heterosexual affectional system in monkeys. *American Psychologist*, 1962, *17*, 1–9.

Harlow, H. F. The nature of love. *American Psychologist*, 1958, *13*, 673–685.

Harren, V. A., Kass, R. A., Tinsley, H. E. A., & Moreland, J. R. Influences of gender, sex-role attitudes and cognitive complexity on gender-dominant career choices. *Journal of Counseling Psychology*, 1979, *26*, 227–234.

Harren, V. A., Kass, R. A., Tinsley, H. E. A., & Moreland, J. R. Influence of sex role attitudes and cognitive styles on career decision making. *Journal of Counseling Psychology*, 1978, *25*, 390–398.

Harrentsian, D. The nature of female criminality. *Issues in Criminology*, 1973, 117–136.

Harris, L. J. Sex differences in the growth and use of language. In E. Donelson & J. E. Gullahorn (Eds.), *Women: A psychological perspective*. New York: Wiley, 1977. Pp. 79–94.

Harris, M. *Cannibals and Kings*. New York: Random House, 1977. (a)

Harris, M. Why men dominate women. *New York Times Magazine*, November 13, 1977, p. 46ff. (b)

Harrison, B. G. Feminist experiment in education. In J. Stacey, S. Bereaud, & J. Daniels (Eds.), *And Jill came tumbling after: Sexism in American education*. New York: Dell, 1974. P. 380.

Harrison, J. Male sex role and health. *Journal of Social Issues*, 1978, *34*(1), 65–86.

Hartford, T. C., Willis, C. H., & Deabler, H. L. Personality correlates of masculinity-femininity. *Psychological Reports*, 1967, *21*, 881–884.

Hartley, R. E. Sex role pressures and the socialization of the male child. *Psychological Reports*, 1959, *5*, 457–468.

Hartup, W. N. Peer interaction and social organization. In P. Mussen (Ed.), *Carmichael's manual of child psychology*, (Vol. 2). New York: Wiley, 1970.

Hatton, G. J. Biology and gender: Structure, sex and cycles. In E. Donelson & J. E. Gullahorn (Eds.), *Women: A psychological perspective*. New York: Wiley, 1977. Pp. 49–64.

Hayakawa, S. I. Popular songs versus the facts of life. *ETC Review of General Semantics*, 1955, *12*(1), 88–94.

Hayman, A. S. Legal challenge to discrimination against men. In D. David & R. Brannon (Eds.), *The forty-nine percent majority*. Reading, Mass.: Addison-Wesley, 1976. Pp. 297–321.

Heilbrun, A. B., Jr. Measurement of masculine and feminine sex role identities as independent dimensions. *Journal of Consulting and Clinical Psychology*, 1976, *44*, 183–190.

Heilbrun, A. B., Jr. Sex-role instrumental expressive behavior and psychopathology in females. *Journal of Abnormal Psychology*, 1968, *73*, 131–136.

Heiman, J. R. The physiology of erotica: Women's sexual arousal. *Psychology Today*, April 1975, pp. 90–94.

Helmreich, R., Beane, W., Lucker, G. W., & Spence, J. T. Achievement motivation and scientific attainment. *Personality and Social Psychology Bulletin*, 1978, *4*, 222–226.

Helmreich, R. L., & Spence, J. T. The Work and Family Orientation Questionnaire. JSAS *Catalog of Selected Documents in Psychology*, 1978, *8*, 35. (Ms. No. 1677)

Helmreich, R., Spence, J. T., Beane, W. E., Lucker, G. W., & Matthews, K. A. *Making it in academic psychology: Demographic and personality correlates of eminence*. Paper presented at the meeting of the American Psychological Association, New York, September 1979.

Helmreich, R. L., Spence, J. T., & Holahan, C. K. Psychological androgyny and sex role flexibility: A test of two hypotheses. *Journal of Personality and Social Psychology*, 1979, *37*, 1631–1644.

Helson, R. Women mathematicians and the creative personality. *Journal of Consulting and Clinical Psychology, 1971, 36, 210–220.

Henley, N. M. Body politics: Power, sex and nonverbal communication. Englewood Cliffs, N.J.: Prentice-Hall, 1977.

Henley, N., & Thorne, B. Womanspeak and manspeak: Sex differences and sexism in communication, verbal and nonverbal. In A. Sargent (Ed.), Beyond sex roles. St. Paul: West, 1977. Pp. 201–218.

Hennig, M., & Jardim, A. The managerial woman. New York: Anchor Press, 1977.

Hermans, H. J. M. A questionnaire measure of achievement motivation. Journal of Applied Psychology, 1970, 54, 353–363.

Hersh, S. My Lai 4. New York: Random House, 1970.

Herzog, E., & Sudia, C. Children in fatherless families. In E. M. Hetherington & P. Ricciuti (Eds.), Review of child development research, (Vol. 3). Chicago: University of Chicago Press, 1974.

Hess, R. D. Social class and ethnic influences upon socialization. In P. H. Mussen (Ed.), Carmichael's manual of child psychology, (3rd edition), Vol. 2. New York: Wiley, 1970. Pp. 457–557.

Hess, R. D., & Shipman, V. C. Cognitive elements in maternal behavior. In J. P. Hell (Ed.), Minnesota symposia on child psychology, (Vol. 1). Minneapolis: University of Minnesota Press, 1967. Pp. 57–81.

Hetherington, E. M. Effects of father absence on personality development in adolescent daughters. Developmental Psychology, 1972, 7, 313–326.

Hetherington, E. M., Cox, M., & Cox, R. Divorced fathers. Psychology Today, April 1977, pp. 42–46.

Hildebrandt, K. A., & Fitzgerald, H. E. Adults' perceptions of infant sex and cuteness. Sex Roles, 1979, 5, 471–481.

Hill, C. E., Hobbs, M. A., & Verble, C. A developmental analysis of the sex-role identification of school-related objects. Journal of Educational Research, 1974, 67, 205–206.

Hill, C. E., Tanney, M. F., Leonard, M. M., & Reiss, J. Counselor reactions to female clients: Type of problem, age of client, and sex of counselor. Journal of Counseling Psychology, 1977, 24, 60–65.

Hill, C. T., Rubin, Z., & Peplau, A. Breakups before marriage: The end of 103 affairs. Journal of Social Issues, 1976, 32, 147–168.

Hilton, T. A., & Berglund, G. W. Sex differences in math achievement: A longitudinal study. Journal of Educational Research, 1974, 67(5), 231–237.

Hite, S. The Hite report: A nationwide study of female sexuality. New York: Macmillan, 1976.

Hochreich, D. J. Sex-role stereotypes for internal-external control and interpersonal trust. Journal of Consulting and Clinical Psychology, 1975, 43(2), 273.

Hoffman, D. M., & Fidell, L. A. Characteristics of androgynous, undifferentiated, masculine and feminine middle-class women. Sex Roles, 1979, 5, 765–781.

Hoffman, L. R., & Maier, N. R. F. Social factors influencing problem solving in women. Journal of Personality and Social Psychology, 1966, 4, 382–390.

Hoffman, L. W. Maternal employment: 1979. American Psychologist, 1979, 34, 859–865.

Hoffman, L. W. Changes in family roles, socialization, and sex differences. American Psychologist, 1977, 32, 644–657.

Hoffman, L. W. Effects of maternal employment on the child: A review of the research. Developmental Psychology, 1974, 10, 204–228.

Hoffman, L. W. Early childhood experiences and women's achievement motives. Journal of Social Issues, 1972, 28, 129–155.

Hoffman, L. W., & Nye, F. I. Working mothers. San Francisco: Jossey-Bass, 1974.

Holahan, C. K. Stress experienced by women doctoral students, need for support, and occupational sex typing: An interactional view. Sex Roles, 1979, 5, 425–436.

Holahan, C. K., & Gilbert, L. A. Interrole conflict for working women: Careers versus jobs. Journal of Applied Psychology, 1979, 64, 86–90.

Hollender, J. Sex differences in sources of social self-esteem. Journal of Consulting and Clinical Psychology, 1972, 38, 343–347.

Holsendolph, E. TV cited on stereotypes. New York Times, January 17, 1979, p. c21.

Hopkins, J. R. Sexual behavior in adolescence. Journal of Social Issues, 1977, 33(2), 67–85.

Horn, J. Drinking buddies and confidants. Psychology Today, 1978, 11(11), 28.

Horn, J. Bored to sickness. *Psychology Today*, 1975, *9*(11), 92.

Horner, M. J. The measurement and behavioral implications of fear of success in women. In J. W. Atkinson & J. O. Raynor (Eds.), *Personality, motivation, and achievement*. Washington, D.C.: Hemisphere, 1978. Pp. 41–70.

Horner, M. J. Toward an understanding of achievement related conflicts in women. *Journal of Social Issues*, 1972, *28*, 157–176.

Horner, M. J. Femininity and successful achievement: A basic inconsistency. In J. M. Bardwick, E. Douvan, M. S. Horner, & D. Gutman (Eds.), *Feminine personality and conflict*. Belmont, Calif.: Brooks/Cole, 1970.

Horner, M. J. *Sex differences in achievement motivation and performance in competitive-noncompetitive situations*. Unpublished doctoral dissertation, University of Michigan, 1968.

Horner, M., & Fleming, J. Revised Scoring Manual for an Empirically Derived Scoring System for the Motive to Avoid Success. May 1977. (Obtainable from author).

Horney, K. On the genesis of the castration complex in women. 1922. In J. B. Miller (Ed.), *Psychoanalysis and women*. New York: Brunner/Mazel, 1973.

House, G. F. *Orientation to achievement: Autonomous, social comparison, and external*. Unpublished doctoral dissertation, University of Michigan, 1973.

Hudzinski, J. Sweeping social changes could bring end to family structure. *Asbury Park Press*, June 2, 1977, p. A24.

Hunt, M. *Sexual behavior in the 1970s*. Chicago: Playboy Press, 1974.

Hutt, C. *Males and females*. Baltimore: Penguin, 1972.

Hyde, J. S., Rosenberg, B. G., & Behrman, J. Tomboyism. *Psychology of Women Quarterly*, 1977, *2*, 73–75.

Hyland, D. A. Participation in athletics: Is it worth all the suffering? *New York Times*, January 26, 1978, p. S2.

Ickes, W., & Barnes, R. D. Boys and girls together—and alienated: On enacting stereotyped sex roles in mixed-sex dyads. *Journal of Personality and Social Psychology*, 1978, *36*, 669–683.

Ickes, W., & Barnes, R. D. The role of sex and self-monitoring in unstructured dyadic interactions. *Journal of Personality and Social Psychology*, 1977, *35*, 315–330.

Inderlied, S. D., & Powell, G. Sex-role identity and leadership style: Different labels for the same concept? *Sex Roles*, 1979, *5*, 613–625.

Institute for Social Research. Young people look at changing sex roles. *ISR Newsletter*, Spring 1979, p. 3.

Institute for Social Research. Earnings advantage enjoyed by white males not explained by differences in qualifications. *ISR Newsletter*, Spring 1978, p. 7.

Israel, J., & Eliasson, R. Consumption society, sex-roles and sexual behavior. *Acta Sociologica*, 1971, *14*, 68–82.

Ivey, M. E., & Bardwick, J. M. Patterns of affective fluctuation in the menstrual cycle. *Psychosomatic Medicine*, 1968, *30*, 336–344.

Jakubowski-Spector, P. Facilitating the growth of women through assertiveness-training. *The Counseling Psychologist*, 1973, *4*, 75–86.

Jancar, B. W. *Women under communism*. Baltimore: Johns Hopkins Press, 1978.

Janda, L. H., O'Grady, K. E., & Capps, C. F. Fear of success in males and females in sex linked occupations. *Sex Roles*, 1978, *4*, 43–50.

Jaquette, J. S. (Ed.). *Women in politics*. New York: Wiley, 1974.

Jennings, J. W., Geis, F. L., & Brown, V. The influence of television commercials on women's self-confidence and independent judgment. *Journal of Personality and Social Psychology*, in press.

Joesting, J. Comparison of women's liberation members with their nonmember peers. *Psychological Reports*, 1971, *29*, 1291–1294.

Johnson, D. D. Sex differences in reading across cultures. *Reading Research Quarterly*, 1973–1974, *9*, 67–86.

Johnson, M. *Research in teaching psychology of women*. Paper presented at the meeting of the American Psychological Association, New York, September 1979.

Johnson, P. B. Feminist people and power: Are we copping out? *SASP Newsletter*, 1979, *5*(3), pp. 3–4.

Johnson, P. B. *Working women and alcohol use: Preliminary national data*. Paper presented at symposium "Psychological

Issues Related to Women's Employment," *American Psychological Association* convention, Toronto, August 1978.

Johnson, P. B. Woman and power: Towards a theory of effectiveness. *Journal of Social Issues*, 1976, *32*(3), 99–110.

Johnson, P. B., & Goodchilds, J. D. How women get their way. *Psychology Today*, October 1976, pp. 69–70.

Jones, J. The conflicting role of the Black woman in White society. *American Journal of Orthopsychiatry*, 1971, *41*, 250.

Jones, W. H., Chernovetz, M. E., & Hansson, R. O. The enigma of androgyny: Differential implications for males and females? *Journal of Consulting and Clinical Psychology*, 1978, *46*, 298–313.

Jong, E. *Fear of flying*. New York: Signet, 1973.

Jongeward, D., & Scott, D. *Women as winners*. Reading, Mass.: Addison-Wesley, 1976.

Jorgenson, C., Davis, J., Opella, J., & Angerstein, G. *Hemispheric asymmetry in the processing of Stroop stimuli: An examination of gender, hand-preference, and language differences*. Paper presented at the American Psychological Association convention, New York, September 1979.

Jourard, S. *The transparent self*. New York: Van Nostrand, 1971.

Julty, S. A case of "sexual dysfunction". *Ms.*, November 1972, pp. 18–21.

Jung, C. G. *Two essays on analytical psychology*. New York: Meridian Books, 1956.

Juran, S. A measure of stereotyping in fear-of-success cues. *Sex Roles*, 1979, *5*, 287–297.

Kagan, J. Acquisition and significance of sex typing and sex role identity. In M. L. Hoffman & L. W. Hoffman (Eds.), *Review of child research*, (Vol. 1). New York: Russell Sage Fund, 1964. Pp. 137–169.

Kahn, A. From theories of equity to theories of justice: An example of demasculinization in social psychology. *SASP Newsletter*, 1979, *5*(3), pp. 12–13.

Kahn, R. L. The work module: A time for lunchpail lassitude. *Psychology Today*, February 1973, pp. 35–39ff.

Kahne, H., & Kohen, A. Economic perspectus on the role of women in the American economy. *Journal of Economic Literature*, December 1975, 1249–1292.

Kandel, D. B. Similarity in real-life adolescent friendship pairs. *Journal of Personality and Social Psychology*, 1978, *36*, 306–312.

Kanowitz, L. *The Equal Rights Amendment*. Talk given at Yongsan Army Base, Seoul, Korea, April 5, 1976.

Kanter, R. M. *Men and women in the corporation*. New York: Basic Books, 1977.

Kanter, R. M. Why bosses turn bitchy. *Psychology Today*, May 1976, pp. 56–59ff.

Kaplan, A. Clarifying the concept of androgyny: Implications for therapy. *Psychology of Women Quarterly*, 1979, *3*, 223–230.

Kaplan, A. Androgyny as a model of mental health for women: From theory to therapy. In A. Kaplan & J. Bean (Eds.), *Beyond sex-role stereotypes*. Boston: Little, Brown, 1976. Pp. 352–362.

Kaplan, A., & Bean, J. P. From sex stereotypes to androgyny: Considerations of societal and individual change. In A. Kaplan & J. Bean (Eds.), *Beyond sex-role stereotypes*. Boston: Little, Brown, 1976. Pp. 383–392.

Kaplan, J. Women athletes and their fears about femininity. *New York Times*, June 5, 1977, p. S2.

Karr, R. G. Homosexual labeling and the male role. *Journal of Social Issues*, 1978, *34*(3), 73–83.

Kaschak, E. Sex bias in student evaluation of college professors. *Psychology of Women Quarterly*, 1978, *3*, 235–243. (a)

Kaschak, E. *Another look at sex bias in students' evaluation of professors: Do winners get the recognition that they have been given*. Paper presented at the Western Psychological Association convention, San Francisco, April 1978. (b)

Kasl, S. V., & Cobb, S. Blood pressure changes in men undergoing job loss: A preliminary report. *Psychosomatic Medicine*, 1970, *6*, 95–106.

Kass, R. A., Tinsley, H. E. A., Harren, V. A., & Moreland, J. R. *Cognitive and attitudinal influences on career decision making*. Paper presented at the American Psychological Association convention, Toronto, August 1978.

Katz, B. L. Women's liberation auxiliaries? *The National Observer*, December 29, 1973, p. 8.

Katz, L., Bowermaster, J., Jacobson, E., & Kessell, L. *Sex role socialization in early childhood.* Urbana, Ill.: ERIC Clearinghouse on Early Childhood Education, 1977.

Katz, P. The development of female identity. *Sex Roles*, 1979, *5*, 155–178.

Kaufman, B. L. Catholic bishops attack racism, leave "sexist" language in Mass. *Courier News*, November 17, 1979, p. A14.

Kelber, M. The United Nation's dirty little secret. *Ms.*, November 1977, *6*(5), 51ff.

Kelly, J. A., & Worell, J. New formulations of sex roles and androgyny: A critical review. *Journal of Consulting and Clinical Psychology*, 1977, *45*, 1101–1115.

Kelly, J. A., & Worell, L. Parent behaviors related to masculine, feminine, and androgynous sex role orientations. *Journal of Consulting and Clinical Psychology*, 1976, *44*, 843–851.

Kelly, J. A., Caudill, M. S., Hathorn, S., & O'Brien, C. G. Socially undesirable sex-correlated characteristics: Implications for androgyny and adjustment. *Journal of Consulting and Clinical Psychology*, 1977, *45*, 1185–1186.

Kenworthy, J. A. Androgyny in psychotherapy: But will it sell in Peoria? *Psychology of Women Quarterly*, 1979, *3*, 231–240.

Keogh, B. K. Pattern copying under three conditions of an expanded spatial field. *Developmental Psychology*, 1971, *4*, 25–31.

Kessler, S. J., & McKenna, W. *Gender: An ethnomethodological approach.* New York: Wiley, 1978.

Key, M. R. The role of male and female in children's books—dispelling all doubt. 1971. In R. Unger & F. Denmark (Eds.), *Women: Dependent or independent variable?* New York: Psychological Dimensions, 1975. Pp. 56–70.

King, M. C. The politics of sexual stereotypes. *The Black Scholar*, March-April 1973, pp. 12–23.

Kinsey, A. E., Pomeroy, W. B., & Martin, C. E. *Sexual behavior in the human male.* Philadelphia: Saunders, 1948.

Kinsey, A. E., Pomeroy, W. B., Martin, C. E., & Gebhard, P. H. *Sexual behavior in the human female.* Philadelphia: Saunders, 1953.

Kipnis, D. Inner direction, other direction and achievement motivation. *Human Development*, 1974, *17*, 321–343.

Kissler, G. D. *Nonprojective analysis of need for achievement among male and female workers.* Paper presented at the Western Psychological Association convention, San Francisco, April 1978.

Klemesrud, J. Women executives: View from the top. *New York Times*, March 11, 1979, p. 50.

Klerman, G. L. The age of melancholy? *Psychology Today*, April 1979, *12*(11), 36–42, 88.

Koeske, R. K., & Koeske, G. F. An attributional approach to moods and the menstrual cycle. *Journal of Personality and Social Psychology*, 1975, *31*, 473–478.

Kohlberg, L. A cognitive-developmental analysis of children's sex-role concepts and attitudes. In E. E. Maccoby (Ed.), *The development of sex differences.* Stanford, Calif.: Stanford University Press, 1966. Pp. 82–173.

Kolata, G. B. !Kung hunter-gatherers: Feminism, diet and birth control. *Science*, 1974, *185*, 932–934.

Komarovsky, M. *Dilemmas of masculinity: A study of college youth.* New York: Norton, 1976.

Komarovsky, M. Patterns of self-disclosure in male undergraduates. *Journal of Marriage and the Family*, 1974, *36*, 677–687.

Komarovsky, M. Cultural contradictions and sex roles: The masculine case. *American Journal of Sociology*, 1973, *78*, 873–874.

Komarovsky, M. Cultural contradictions and sex roles. *American Journal of Sociology*, 1946, *52*(3), 184–189.

Komisar, L. Right wingers and the ERA. *Do It NOW*, August 1977, p. 1.

Komisar, L. Violence and the masculine mystique. *Washington Monthly*, July 1970.

Korda, M. *Male chauvinism: How it works.* New York: Random House, 1973.

Kotelchuck, M. The infant's relationship to the father: Experimental evidence. In M. E. Lamb (Ed.), *The role of the father in child development.* New York: Wiley, 1976. Pp. 329–344.

Kravetz, D. Consciousness-raising groups in the 1970s. *Psychology of Women Quarterly*, 1978, *3*, 168–186.

Kravetz, D., & Sargent, A. G. Consciousness-raising groups: A resocialization process for personal and social change. In A. Sargent (Ed.), *Beyond sex roles.* St. Paul: West, 1977. Pp. 148–156.

Kreinberg, N. Furthering the mathematical competence of women. *Public Affairs Report*. Bulletin of the Institute of Governmental Studies, 1976, *17*(6).

Kreps, J. M. (Ed.). *Women and the American economy: A look to the 1980s.* Englewood Cliffs, N.J.: Prentice-Hall, 1976.

Kristal, J., Sanders, D., Spence, J. T., & Helmreich, R. Inferences about the femininity of competent women and their implications for likability. *Sex Roles*, 1975, *1*, 33–140.

Krulewitz, J. E. *Sex differences in the perception of victims of sexual and nonsexual assault.* Paper presented at the American Psychological Association convention, Toronto, August 1978.

Kulik, J. A., & Harackiewicz, J. Opposite-sex interpersonal attraction as a function of the sex roles of the perceiver and the perceived. *Sex Roles*, 1979, *5*, 443–452.

Kupke, T., Lewis, R., & Rennick, P. Sex differences in the neuropsychological functioning of epileptics. *Journal of Consulting and Clinical Psychology*, 1979, *47*, 1128–1130.

Lacher, M. R. B. On advising undergraduate women: A psychologist's advice to academic advisers. *Journal of College Student Personnel*, 1978, *19*, 488–493.

Ladner, J. A. *Tomorrow's tomorrow: The Black woman.* Garden City, N.Y.: Doubleday, 1971.

Lakoff, R. *Language and woman's place.* New York: Harper & Row, 1975.

Lamb, M. E. Paternal influences and the father's role: A personal perspective. *American Psychologist*, 1979, *34*, 938–943.

Lamb, M. E. (ed.). *The role of the father in child development.* New York: Wiley, 1976. (a)

Lamb, M. E. The role of the father: An overview. In M. E. Lamb (Ed.), *The role of the father in child development.* New York: Wiley, 1976. Pp. 1–61. (b)

Lamb, M. E., & Lamb, J. E. The nature and importance of the father-infant relationship. *The Family Coordinator*, 1976, *25*, 379–386.

Landers, A. D. The menstrual experience. In E. Donelson & J. Gullahorn (Eds.), *Women: A psychological perspective.* New York: Wiley, 1977. Pp. 65–78.

Lando, H. A. Sex differences in response to differing patterns of attack. *Personality and Social Psychology Bulletin*, 1976, *2*, 286–289.

Larrance, D., Pavelich, S., Storer, P., Polizzi, M., Baron, B., Sloan, S., Jordan, P., & Reis, H. T. Competence and incompetence: Asymmetric responses to women and men on a sex-linked task. *Personality and Social Psychology Bulletin*, 1979, *5*, 363–366.

LaRue, L. The Black Movement and Women's Liberation. In S. Cox (Ed.), *Female psychology: The emerging self.* Chicago: SRA, 1976. Pp. 216–225.

Laws, J. L., & Schwartz, P. *Sexual scripts: The social construction of female sexuality.* Hinsdale, Ill.: Dryden, 1977.

Lederer, W. J., & Jackson, D. D. *The mirages of marriage.* New York: Norton, 1968.

Lee, R. B. The !Kung Bushmen of Botswana. In M. G. Bicchieri (Ed.), *Hunters and gatherers today.* New York: Holt, Rinehart & Winston, 1972.

Lefcourt, H. *Locus of control: Current trends in theory and research.* Hillside, N.J.: Lawrence Erlbaum Associates, 1976.

Lehne, G. K. Homophobia among men. In D. David & R. Brannon (Eds.), *The forty-nine percent majority.* Reading, Mass.: Addison-Wesley, 1976. Pp. 66–88.

Lenney, E. Androgyny: Some audacious assertions toward its coming of age. *Sex Roles*, 1979, *5*, 703–719. (a)

Lenney, E. Concluding comments on androgyny: Some intimations of its mature development. *Sex Roles*, 1979, *5*, 829–840. (b)

Lenney, E. Women's self-confidence in achievement settings. *Psychological Bulletin*, 1977, *84*, 1–13.

Lerman, H. What happens in feminist therapy. In S. Cox (Ed.), *Female psychology: The emerging self.* Chicago: SRA, 1976. Pp. 378–384.

Lesser, G. L., Kravitz, R. N., & Packard, R. Experimental arousal of achievement motivation in adolescent girls. *Journal of Abnormal and Social Psychology*, 1963, *66*, 59–66.

Lester, D. Sex differences in suicidal behavior. In E. S. Gomberg & V. Franks (Eds.), *Gender and disordered behavior: Sex differences in psychopathology.* New York: Brunner/Mazel, 1979. Pp. 287–300.

Lester, M. Rape: A report. *New York Times Magazine*, January 26, 1976, pp. 4–16.

Levenson, H., Burford, B., Bonno, B., & Davis, L. Are women still prejudiced against women? A replication and extension of Goldberg's study. *Journal of Psychology*, 1975, *89*, 67–71.

Levine, S. One man's experience. *Ms.*, February 1973, p. 14.

Levinson, D. *The seasons of a man's life.* New York: Knopf, 1978.

Levinson, R. Sex discrimination in employment. *Psychology Today*, March 1976, p. 21.

Lévi-Strauss, C. The family. In H. Shapiro (Ed.), *Man, culture, and society.* New York: Oxford University Press, 1956. Pp. 261–285.

Levitin, R. E., Quinn, R. P., & Staines, G. L. A woman is 58% of a man. *Psychology Today*, March 1973, pp. 89–91.

Levy, J. Cerebral lateralization and spatial ability. *Behavioral Genetics*, 1976, *6*, 171–188.

Levy, J., & Reid, M. Variations in cerebral organization as a function of handedness, hand posture in writing, and sex. *Journal of Experimental Psychology: General*, 1978, *107*, 119–144.

Lewis, M. Parents versus children: Sex-role development. *School Review*, 1972, *80*(2), 229–240.

Lewis, M., & Brooks-Gunn, J. *Social cognition and the acquisition of self.* New York: Plenum, in press.

Lewis, M., & Weinraub, M. Origins of early sex-role development. *Sex Roles*, 1979, *5*, 135–153.

Lewis, R. A. Emotional intimacy among men. *Journal of Social Issues*, 1978, *34*(1), 108–121.

Lichenstein, G. How women are faring at the Twentieth Air Academy. *New York Times Magazine*, September 11, 1977, pp. 104–106.

Lindsey, K. Sexual harassment on the job and how to stop it. *Ms.*, November 1977, *6*(8), 47–51ff.

Lipman-Blumen, J., & Bernard, J. (Eds.). *Sex roles and social policy: A complex social science equation.* Beverly Hills, Calif.: Sage, 1979.

Lipman-Blumen, J., & Leavitt, H. Vicarious and direct achievement patterns in adulthood. *The Counseling Psychologist*, 1976, *6*, 26–32.

Lipson, E. R. In the Carter administration, big jobs for young lawyers. *New York Times*, May 1, 1977, Sec. 3, p. 1ff.

Lockheed, M. E. (Ed.). *Research on women's acquisition of professional and leadership roles.* Proceedings of the AERA/SIG: Research on Women Symposium "Socialization Into Professional Roles." Princeton, N.J.: Educational Testing Service, 1975. (a)

Lockheed, M. E. Female motive to avoid success: A psychological barrier or a response to deviancy? *Sex Roles*, 1975, *1*, 41–50. (b)

Lockheed, M. E., & Hall, K. P. Conceptualizing sex as a status characteristic and applications to leadership training strategies. *Journal of Social Issues*, 1976, *32*, 111–124.

Locksley, A., & Colton, M. E. Psychological androgyny: A case of mistaken identity? *Journal of Personality and Social Psychology*, 1979, *37*, 1017–1031.

Locksley, A., & Douvan, E. Problem behavior in adolescents. In E. S. Gomberg & V. Franks (Eds.), *Gender and disordered behavior: Sex differences in psychopathology.* New York: Brunner/Mazel, 1979. Pp. 71–100.

Loeb, R. C., & Horst, L. Sex differences in self and teacher's reports of self-esteem in preadolescents. *Sex Roles*, 1978, *4*, 779–788.

Loeffler, E. *Sex-role stereotypes and psychological judgments of mental health and mental illness.* Paper presented at the Eastern Psychological Association convention, Washington, D.C., March 1978.

Loevinger, J. The meaning and measurement of ego development. *American Psychologist*, 1966, *21*, 195–206.

Loevinger, J., & Wessler, R. *Measuring ego development*, (Vol. 1). San Francisco: Jossey-Bass, 1970.

Lombardo, J. P., & Levine, L. J. *Self-disclosure: A function of sex or sex role?* Paper presented at the Eastern Psychological Association convention, Washington, D.C., March 1978.

LoPiccolo, J., & Heiman, J. Cultural values and the therapeutic definition of sexual function and dysfunction. *Journal of Social Issues*, 1977, *33*(2), 166–183.

Lott, B. Behavioral concordance with sex role ideology related to play areas, creativity and parental sex typing of children. *Journal of Personality and Social Psychology*, 1978, *36*, 1087–1100.

Lowenthal, M. F., Thurner, M., & Chiriboga, D. *Four stages of life*. San Francisco: Jossey-Bass, 1975.

Luce, G. G. *Body time*. New York: Pantheon, 1971.

Lunneborg, P. W. The vocational interest inventory: Development and validation. *Educational and Psychological Measurement*, 1979, in press.

Lynn, D. B. *Daughters and parents: Past, present and future*. Monterey, Calif.: Brooks/Cole, 1979.

Lynn, D. B. *The father: His role in child development*. Monterey, Calif.: Brooks/Cole, 1974.

Lynn, D. B. *Parental and sex role identification: A theoretical formulation*. Berkeley: McCutchan, 1969.

Lynn, D. B. A note on sex differences in the development of masculine and feminine identification. *Psychological Review*, 1959, *66*, 126–135.

Lynn, N. Women in American politics: An overview. In J. Freeman (Ed.), *Women: A feminist perspective*. Palo Alto, Calif.: Mayfield, 1975. Pp. 364–385.

MacArthur, R. S. Sex differences in field dependence for the Eskimo. *International Journal of Psychology*, 1967, *2*, 139–140.

Maccoby, E. E. Sex differences in intellectual functioning. In E. E. Maccoby (Ed.), *The development of sex differences*. Stanford, Calif.: Stanford University Press, 1966. Pp. 25–55.

Maccoby, E. E., & Jacklin, C. M. *The psychology of sex differences*. Stanford, Calif.: Stanford University Press, 1974.

Maccoby, M. The corporate climber. *Fortune*, December 1976, pp. 98–101; 104–108.

Maffeo, P. A. Thoughts on Stricker's "Implication of research for psychotherapeutic treatment of women." *American Psychologist*, 1979, *34*, 690–695.

Mahoney, T. A., & Blake, R. H. *Occupational pay as a function of sex stereotypes and job content*. Paper presented to the National Academy of Management, August 1979.

Maier, N. R. F., & Casselman, G. C. The SAT as a measure of problem-solving ability in males and females. *Psychological Reports*, 1970, *26*, 927–939.

Major, B. Sex-role orientation and fear of success: Clarifying an unclear relationship. *Sex Roles*, 1979, *5*, 63–70.

Makosky, V. P. *Fear of success, sex-role orientation of the task, and competitive conditions as variables affecting women's performance in achievement-oriented situation*. Paper presented at the Mid-West Psychological Association convention, Cleveland, 1972.

Malamuth, N. M., Feshbach, S., & Jaffe, Y. Sexual arousal and aggression: Recent experiments and theoretical issues. *Journal of Social Issues*, 1977, *33*(2), 110–133.

Malamuth, N. M., Huber, S., & Feshbach, S. Testing hypotheses regarding rape: Exposure and sexual violence, sex differences and the "normality" of rapists. *Journal of Research in Personality*, in press.

Malinowski, B. *The sexual life of savages*. London, England: Routledge, 1932.

Mancini, J. A., & Orthner, D. K. Recreational sexuality preferences among middle-class husbands and wives. *Journal of Sex Research*, 1978, *14*(2), 96–106.

Mandel, W. M. Soviet women in the work force and professions. *American Behavioral Scientist*, 1971, *15*, 255–280.

Marini, M. M. Sex differences in the determination of adolescent aspirations: A review of research. *Sex Roles*, 1978, *4*, 723–753.

Marolla, J. A., & Scully, D. H. Rape and psychiatric vocabularies of motive. In E. S. Gomberg & V. Franks (Eds.), *Gender and disordered behavior: Sex differences in psychopathology*. New York: Brunner/Mazel, 1979. Pp. 301–318.

Marshall, D. S. Too much in Mangaia. *Psychology Today*, 1971, *4*(February), 43–44ff.

Martin, D. *Battered wives*. San Francisco: Glide, 1976.

Marwell, G., Rosenfeld, R., & Spilerman, S. Geographic constraints on women's careers in academia. *Science*, 1979, *205*, 1225–1231.

Maslow, A. H. *Toward a psychology of being*. Princeton, N.J.: Van Nostrand, 1962.

Maslow, A. H. Self-esteem (dominance-feeling) and sexuality in women. *Journal of Social Psychology*, 1942, *16*.

Massengill, D., & DiMarco, N. Sex-role stereotypes and requisite management characteristics: A current replication. *Sex Roles*, 1979, *5*, 561–570.

Masters, W. H., & Johnson, V. *Homosex-*

uality in perspective. Boston: Little, Brown, 1979.

Masters, W. H., & Johnson, V. *The pleasure bond: A new look at sexuality and commitment.* Boston: Little, Brown, 1974.

Masters, W. H., & Johnson, V. *Human sexual inadequacy.* Boston: Little, Brown, 1970.

Masters, W. H., & Johnson, V. *Human sexual response.* Boston: Little, Brown, 1966.

Maynard, J. The liberation of the total woman. *New York Times Magazine,* September 28, 1975, p. 10ff.

McArthur, L. Z., & Eisen, S. V. Achievements of male and female storybook characters as determinants of achieving behavior by boys and girls. *Journal of Personality and Social Psychology,* 1976, *33,* 467–473.

McCandless, B. R. *Adolescents: Behavior and development.* Hinsdale, Ill.: Dryden, 1970.

McClelland, D. C., Atkinson, J. W., Clark, R. A., & Lowell, E. G. *The achievement motive.* New York: Appleton-Century-Crofts, 1953.

McCoy, N. L. Innate factors in sex differences. In A. Sargent (Ed.), *Beyond sex roles.* St. Paul: West, 1977.

McDaniel, E., Guy, R., Ball, L., & Kolloff, M. *A spatial experience questionnaire and some preliminary findings.* Paper presented at the American Psychological Association convention, Toronto, August 1978.

McGlone, J. Sex differences in functional brain asymmetry. *Cortex,* 1978, *14,* 122–128.

McGrady, M. *The kitchen sink papers.* New York: Doubleday, 1976.

McGuinness, D., & Pribram, K. The origins of sensory bias in the development of gender differences in perception and cognition. In M. Bortner (Ed.), *Cognitive growth and development—Essays in honor of Herbert G. Birch.* New York: Brunner/Mazel, 1978.

McMillan, J. A., Clifton, A. K., McGrath, C., & Gale, W. S. Women's language: Uncertainty of interpersonal sensitivity and emotionality? *Sex Roles,* 1977, *3,* 545–559.

Mead, M. Some theoretical considerations of the problem of mother-child separation. *American Journal of Orthopsychiatry,* 1954, *24,* 471–483.

Mead, M. *Sex and temperament.* New York: William Morrow, 1935.

Meislen, R. J. Poll finds more liberal beliefs on marriage and sex roles, especially among the young. *New York Times,* November 27, 1977, p. 75.

Melges, F. T. Postpartum psychiatric syndromes. *Psychosomatic Medicine,* 1968, *30,* 95–108.

Mellen, J. Hollywood rediscovers the American Woman. *New York Times,* April 23, 1978, Sect. 2, p. 1ff. (a)

Mellen, J. *Big bad wolves: Masculinity in the American film.* New York: Pantheon, 1978. (b)

Mellen, J. *Women and their sexuality in the new film.* New York: Dell, 1973.

Men's studies bibliography. MIT: Human Studies Collection, Humanities Library, 3rd. ed., 1977.

Messé, L. A., & Watts, B. *Self-pay behavior: Sex differences in reliance on external cues and feelings of comfort.* Paper presented at the meeting of the American Psychological Association, New York, September 1979.

Meyer-Bahlburg, F. L. Aggression, androgens and the XYY syndrome. In R. C. Friedman et al. (Eds.), *Sex differences in behavior.* New York: Wiley, 1974. Pp. 433–454.

Michaud, G. E. Pennsylvania study pinpoints women's offenses. *Do It NOW,* August 1977, p. 2.

Milgram, S. Some conditions of obedience and disobedience to authority. *Human Relations,* 1965, *18,* 57–76.

Miller, F. D., & Zeitz, B. A woman's place is in the footnotes. *Personality and Social Psychology Bulletin,* 1978, *4,* 511–514.

Millett, K. *Sexual politics.* New York: Doubleday, 1970.

Milton, C., Pierce, C., & Lyons, M. *Little sisters and the law.* Washington, D.C.: American Bar Association Commission on Correctional Services and Facilities, 1977.

Minuchin, P. Sex role concepts and sex typing in childhood as a function of school and home environment. *Child Development,* 1965, *36,* 1033–1048.

Mischel, H. N. Sex bias in the evaluation of professional achievements. *Journal of Educational Psychology,* 1974, *66*(2), 157–166.

Mischel, W. *Personality and assessment.* New York: Wiley, 1968.

Mischel, W. A social learning view of sex differences in behavior. In E. E. Maccoby (Ed.), *The development of sex differences.* Stanford, Calif.: Stanford University Press, 1966. Pp. 56–81.

Mitchell, G. D. Attachment differences in male and female infant monkeys. *Child Development*, 1968, *39*, 611–620.

Moely, B. E., Skarin, K., & Weil, S. Sex differences in competition-cooperation behavior of children at two age levels. *Sex Roles*, 1979, *5*, 329–342.

Molinoff, D. D. Life with father. *New York Times Magazine*, May 22, 1977, pp. 13–17.

Monahan, L., Kuhn, D., & Shaver, P. Intrapsychic versus cultural explanations of the fear of success motive. *Journal of Personality and Social Psychology*, 1974, *29*, 60–64.

Money, J. *Sex determinants and sex stereotyping: Aristotle to H-Y androgen.* Invited address, Western Psychological Association convention, San Francisco, April 1978.

Money, J. Developmental differentiation of femininity and masculinity compared. In Farber & Wilson (Eds.), *Man and civilization: The potential of women.* New York: McGraw-Hill, 1963.

Money, J., & Ehrhardt, A. A. *Man and woman, boy and girl.* Baltimore: Johns Hopkins University Press, 1972.

Monge, R. H. Developmental trends in factors of adolescent self-concept. *Developmental Psychology*, 1973, *8*, 382–393.

deMonteflores, C., & Schultz, S. Coming out: Similarities and differences for lesbians and gay men. *Journal of Social Issues*, 1978, *34*(3), 59–72.

Montgomery, C. L., & Burgoon, M. An experimental study of the interactive effects of sexes and androgyny on attitude change. *Communication Monographs*, 1977, *44*(2), 130–135.

Moore, D. M. (Ed.). *Battered women.* Beverly Hills, Calif.: Sage, 1979.

Moos, R., Kopell, B., Melges, F., Yalum, I., Lunde, D., Clayton, R., & Hamburg, D. Variations in symptoms and mood during the menstrual cycle. *Journal of Psychosomatic Research*, 1969, *13*, 37–44.

Morgan, M. *The total woman.* New York: Pocket Book, 1975.

Morin, S. F., & Garfinkle, E. M. Male homophobia. *Journal of Social Issues*, 1978, *34*(1), 29–47.

Mosher, D. L., & Abramson, P. R. Subjective sexual arousal to films of masturbation. *Journal of Consulting and Clinical Psychology*, in press.

Moss, H. Sex, age, and state as determinants of mother-infant interaction. *Merrill-Palmer Quarterly*, 1967, *13*, 19–36.

Moulton, J., Robinson, G. M., & Elias, C. Sex bias in language use. *American Psychologist*, 1978, *33*, 1032–1036.

Moyer, K. E. Sex differences in aggression. In R. C. Friedman et al. (Eds.), *Sex differences in behavior.* New York: Wiley, 1974. Pp. 149–163.

Ms. June 1979.

Ms. The death of Rosie Jimenez. December 1978.

Ms. August 1977, p. 43.

Muenchow, S. H. New divorce ethic: Sparing the child. *APA Monitor*, 1977, *8*(6), 6ff.

Mundy, J. Women in rage: A psychological look at the helpless heroine. In R. Unger & F. Denmark (Eds.), *Woman: Dependent or independent variable?* New York: Psychological Dimensions, 1975.

Munroe, R. L., & Munroe, R. H. A cross-cultural study of sex, gender and social structure. *Ethnology*, 1969, *8*(2), 206–211.

Murdock, G. P., & Provost, C. Factors in the division of labor by sex: A cross-cultural analysis. *Ethnology*, 1973, *12*, 203–225.

Mussen, P. H. Early sex-role development. In D. A. Goslin (Ed.), *Handbook of socialization theory and research.* Chicago: Rand McNally, 1969.

Mussen, P. H. Long-term consequences of masculinity of interests in adolescence. *Journal of Consulting and Clinical Psychology*, 1962, *26*, 435–440.

Myers, A. M., & Lips, H. M. Participation in competitive amateur sports as a function of psychological androgyny. *Sex Roles*, 1978, *4*, 571–588.

Myers, B. J., Weinraub, M., & Shetler, S. *Preschoolers knowledge of sex role stereotypes: A developmental study.* Paper presented at the American Psychological Association convention, New York, September 1979.

Nadelman, L. Sex identity in American children: Memory, knowledge, and preference tests. *Developmental Psychology*, 1974, *10*, 413–417.

Nagel, S., & Weitzman, L. J. Double standard of American justice. *Society*, March 1972, pp. 18–25.

Nash, S. C. Sex role as a mediator of intellectual functioning. In M. A. Wittig & A. C. Petersen (Eds.), *Sex-related differences in cognitive functioning: Developmental issues*. New York: Academic Press, 1979. Pp. 263–302.

Nash, S. C. The relationship among sex-role stereotyping, sex-role preference, and sex differences in spatial visualization. *Sex Roles*, 1975, *1*, 15–32.

Nassi, A. J., & Abramowitz, S. I. Raising consciousness about women's groups: Process and outcome research. *Psychology of Women Quarterly*, 1978, *3*, 139–156.

National NOW Times. December 1977, p. 5; January 1978, p. 11; August 1978, pp. 2, 15; October 1978, p. 6; April 1979, p. 4; June 1979, p. 2.

National Women's Political Caucus, Inc. *Womens Political Times*, Summer 1978, *3*(2), 7.

Nemy, E. Networks: New concepts for top-level women. *New York Times*, April 29, 1979, p. 60. (a)

Nemy, E. Women's movement sets its sights on the future of the family. *New York Times*, November 20, 1979, p. B11. (b)

Neugarten, B. L., & Gutman, D. L. Age, sex-roles and personality in middle-age: A thematic apperception study. In B. L. Neugarten (Ed.), *Middle age and aging: A reader in social psychology*. Chicago: University of Chicago Press, 1968.

Newark Star Ledger. Women soldiers less costly than men. July 25, 1977, p. 7.

Newcombe, N., & Arnkoff, D. B. Effects of speech style and sex of speaker on person perception. *Journal of Personality and Social Psychology*, 1979, *37*, 1293–1303.

Newcombe, N., & Arnkoff, D. B. *Speech styles and sex stereotypes*. Paper presented at the meeting of the Association of Women in Psychology, Pittsburgh, March 1978.

New York Times. (Editorial) On sex and the draft. January 27, 1980, p. E18.

New York Times. Army combat role for women opposed. November 18, 1979, p. 28.

New York Times. Women's enrollment in universities surges, Census study reports. November 13, 1979, p. A27.

New York Times. Impact of female cadets assessed by West Point. October 10, 1979, p. C17.

New York Times. Increase foreseen in wives at work. September 25, 1979, p. B9.

New York Times. Survey finds "male stronghold" persists in schools. September 5, 1979, p. A16.

New York Times. Census study shows divorce-trend rise. July 2, 1979, p. A14.

New York Times. More choose to live outside marriage. July 1, 1979, p. E7.

New York Times. Pentagon finds three services falter in drives for recruiting women. April 22, 1979, p. 48.

New York Times. Rape-case comment leads to censure. March 29, 1979, p. B4.

New York Times. College women and self-esteem. December 10, 1978, p. 85.

New York Times. New report on rape shows underreporting. August 26, 1978.

New York Times. Polls find 58% favor rights proposal; men give greatest support. July 16, 1978, p. 24.

New York Times. More women sought for military. November 6, 1977.

New York Times. Women call for combat service. September 2, 1977.

New York Times. Study links stress to weekend. August 25, 1977, p. L50.

New York Times. New edition of the Bible to eliminate many masculine references. June 5, 1977.

New York Times. Dropout rate of women physicians studied. October 11, 1976.

New York Times. White males said to dominate federal advisory committees. September 19, 1976.

Nicholls, J. G. Causal attributions and other achievement-related cognitions: Effects of task outcomes, attainment value, and sex. *Journal of Personality and Social Psychology*, 1975, *31*, 379–389.

Nielson Television 78. Chicago: A. C. Nielson, 1978.

Nieto-Gomez, A. Heritage of La Hembra. In S. Cox (Ed.), *Female psychology: The emerging self*. Chicago: SRA, 1976. Pp. 226–235.

Nikelly, A. *Psychological androgyny: Achieving male liberation*. Paper presented at the meeting of the American Psychological Association, New York, September 1979.

Nirenberg, T. D., & Gaebelein, J. W. Third party instigated aggression: Traditional versus liberal sex role attitudes. *Personality and Social Psychology Bulletin*, 1979, *5*, 348–351.

Nordheimer, J. The family in transition: A challenge from within. *New York Times*, November 27, 1977, p. 1ff.

Norton, E. H. Black women as women. *Social Policy*, 1972, *3*, 2–3.

NOW Legal Defense and Education Fund. A fund-raising appeal. Author, 1978.

Oakley, A. *Sex, gender and society.* New York: Harper & Row, 1972.

O'Connell, A. Barriers to research in psychology. *Division 35 Newsletter*, October 1977, *4*(4), 7–9.

Ogilvie, B. C., & Tutko, T. Sport: If you want to build character, try something else. *Psychology Today*, October 1971, p. 61ff.

Olds, D. E. *Masculinity, femininity, achievement conflicts and health.* Paper presented at the meeting of the American Psychological Association, New York, September 1979.

Olds, D. E., & Shaver, P. *Masculinity, femininity, academic performance, and health: Further evidence concerning the androgyny controversy.* Paper presented at the Eastern Psychological Association convention, Philadelphia, April 1979.

O'Leary, V. *Toward understanding women.* Monterey, Calif.: Brooks/Cole, 1977.

O'Leary, V. Some additional barriers to occupational aspirations in women. *Psychological Bulletin*, 1974, *81*, 809–826.

O'Leary, V., & Donoghue, J. M. Latitudes of masculinity: Reactions to sex-role deviance in man. *Journal of Social Issues*, 1978, *34*(1), 17–28.

Olesker, W., & Balter, L. Sex and empathy. *Journal of Counseling Psychology*, 1972, *19*, 559–562.

Olstad, K. Brave new man: A basis for discussion. In J. W. Petras (Ed.), *Sex: male; gender: masculine.* Port Washington, N.Y.: Alfred, 1975. Pp. 160–178.

O'Malley, P. M., & Bachman, J. G. Self-esteem and education: Sex and cohort comparisons among high school seniors. *Journal of Personality and Social Psychology*, 1979, *37*, 1153–1159.

O'Neil, J. M., Meeker, C. H., & Borgers, S. B. A developmental, preventative, and consultative model to reduce sexism in the career planning of women. *JSAS Catalog of Selected Documents in Psychology*, 1978, *8*. (Ms. No. 1684)

O'Neil, J. M., Ohlde, C., Barke, C., Prosser-Gelwick, B., & Garfield, N. *Research on a career workshop to reduce sexism with women.* Paper presented at the meeting of the American Psychological Association, New York, September 1979.

Oppenheimer, V. K. The sex labeling of jobs. In M. S. Mednick, S. S. Tangri, & L. W. Hoffman (Eds.), *Women and achievement: Social and motivational analyses.* New York: Halsted, 1975. Pp. 307–325.

Oppenheimer, V. K. *The female labor force in the U.S.* Population Monograph Series, No. 5. Berkeley: University of California Press, 1970.

Orlinsky, D., & Howard, K. The effects of sex of therapist on the therapeutic experience of women. *Psychotherapy: Theory, research, and practice*, 1976, *13*, 82–88.

Orlofsky, J. L. Parental antecedents of sex-role orientation in college men and women. *Sex Roles*, 1979, *5*, 495–512.

Ortner, S. B. Is female to male as nature is to culture? In M. Z. Rosaldo & L. Lamphere (Eds.), *Women, culture, and society.* Stanford, Calif.: Stanford University Press, 1974.

Ouellette, P. L., & White, K. M. *Occupational preferences: Children's projections for self and opposite sex.* Paper presented at the Eastern Psychological Association convention, Washington, D.C., March 1978.

Paige, K. E. Women learning to sing the menstrual blues. *Psychology Today*, 1973, *7*, 41–43ff.

Paige, K. E. The effects of oral contraceptives on affective fluctuations associated with the menstrual cycle. *Psychosomatic Medicine*, 1971, *33*, 515–537.

Paige, K. E., & Paige, J. M. The politics of birth practices: A strategic analysis. *American Sociological Review*, 1973, *38*, 663–676.

Parke, R. D., & O'Leary, S. E. Father-mother-infant interactions in the newborn period. In K. Riegel & J. Meacham (Eds.), *The developing individual in a changing world.* The Hague, Netherlands: Mouton, 1976.

Parke, R. D., & Sawin, D. B. Fathering:

It's a major role. *Psychology Today*, 1977, *11*(6), 108–112.

Parlee, M. B. Conversational politics. *Psychology Today*, May 1979, *12*(12), 48–56.

Parlee, M. B. The sexes under scrutiny: From old biases to new theories. *Psychology Today*, 1978, *12*(6), 62–69.

Parlee, M. B. The premenstrual syndrome. *Psychological Bulletin*, 1973, *80*, 454–465.

Parlee, M. B. Comments on "Role of activation and inhibition in sex differences in cognitive abilities." *Psychological Review*, 1972, *79*, 180–184.

Parsons, J. E., Ruble, D. N., Hodges, K. L., & Small, A. W. Cognitive-developmental factors in sex differences in achievement-related expectancies. *Journal of Social Issues*, 1976, *32*(3), 47–61.

Parsons, T., & Bales, R. F. *Family, socialization and interaction process*. Glencoe, Ill.: Free Press, 1955.

Pawlicki, R. E., & Almquist, C. Authoritarianism, locus of control and tolerance of ambiguity as reflected in membership and nonmembership in a women's liberation group. *Psychological Reports*, 1973, *32*, 1331–1337.

Pedersen, D. M., Shinedling, M. M., & Johnson, D. L. Effects of sex of examiner and subject on children's quantitative test performance. *Journal of Personality and Social Psychology*, 1968, *10*, 251–254.

Pedhazur, E. J., & Tetenbaum, T. J. Bem Sex Role Inventory: A theoretical and methodological critique. *Journal of Personality and Social Psychology*, 1979, *37*, 996–1016.

Peevers, B. H. Androgyny on the TV screen: An analysis of sex-role portrayal. *Sex Roles*, 1979, *5*, 797–809.

Peplau, L. A. Impact of fear of success and sex-role attitude on women's competitive achievement. *Journal of Personality and Social Psychology*, 1976, *34*, 561–568.

Peplau, L. A. *The impact of fear of success, sex-role attitude and opposite-sex-relationship on women's intellectual performance: An experimental study of competitiveness in dating couples*. Unpublished doctoral dissertation, Harvard University, 1973.

Peplau, L. A., Rubin, Z., & Hill, C. T. Sexual intimacy in dating relationships. *Journal of Social Issues*, 1977, *33*(2), 86–109.

Peplau, L. A., Rubin, Z., & Hill, C. T. The sexual balance of power. *Psychology Today*, November 1976, p. 142ff.

Perez, S., & O'Connell, A. N. *Fear of success and causal attributions of success and failure in males and females*. Paper presented at the Eastern Psychological Association convention, Philadelphia, April 1979.

Perloff, R. M., Brown, J. D., & Miller, M. M. *Mass media and sex-typing: Research perspectives and policy implications*. Paper presented at symposium "Policy Implications of the Research on the Effects of TV Viewing," American Psychological Association convention, Toronto, August 1978.

Perry, D. G., & Bussey, K. The social learning theory of sex differences: Imitation is alive and well. *Journal of Personality and Social Psychology*, 1979, *37*, 1699–1712.

Persky, H., Smith, K. D., & Basu, G. K. Relation of psychological measures of aggression and hostility to testosterone production in men. *Psychosomatic Medicine*, 1971, *33*, 515–537.

Petersen, A. C. Hormones and cognitive functioning in normal development. In M. A. Wittig & A. C. Petersen (Eds.), *Sex-related differences in cognitive functioning: Developmental issues*. New York: Academic Press, 1979. Pp. 189–214.

Petersen, A. C. Physical androgyny and cognitive functioning. *Developmental Psychology*, 1976, *12*, 524–533.

Petersen, A. C., & Wittig, M. A. Sex-related differences in cognitive functioning: An overview. In M. A. Wittig & A. C. Petersen (Eds.), *Sex-related differences in cognitive functioning: Developmental issues*. New York: Academic Press, 1979. Pp. 1–17.

Phelps, S., & Austin, N. *The assertive woman*. San Luis Obispo, Calif.: Impact Press, 1975.

Pheterson, G. S., Kiesler, S. B., & Goldberg, P. Evaluation of the performance of women as a function of their sex, achievement and personal history. *Journal of Personality and Social Psychology*, 1971, *19*, 114–118.

Pheterson, G. S., Kiesler, S. B., & Goldberg, P. *Female prejudice against men*. Unpublished manuscript, Connecticut College, 1969.

Phillips, D., & Segal, B. Sexual status and psychiatric symptoms. *American Sociology Review*, 1969, *34*, 58–72.

Phillips, E. B. Magazine heroines: Is *Ms.* just another member of the *Family Circle?* In G. Tuchman, A. K. Daniels, & J. Benét (Eds.), *Hearth and home: Images of women in the mass media.* New York: Oxford University Press, 1978. Pp. 116–129.

Phillips, S., King, S., & DuBois, L. Spontaneous activities of female versus male newborns. *Child Development,* 1978, *48*(3).

Pietropinto, A., & Simenauer, J. *Beyond the male myth: What women want to know about men's sexuality.* New York: Times Books, 1977.

Pifer, A. *Women working: Toward a new society.* 1976 Annual Report. Carnegie Corp. of America (437 Madison Avenue, N.Y. 10022).

Pines, A. The influence of goals on people's perceptions of a competent woman. *Sex Roles,* 1979, *5*, 71–76.

Pines, A., & Soloman, T. *The social psychological double bind of the competent woman: Sex role and mental health stereotypes.* Paper presented at the Western Psychological Association convention, San Francisco, April 1978.

Pingree, S. The effects of nonsexist TV commercials and perceptions of reality on children's attitudes about women. *Psychology of Women Quarterly,* 1978, *2*, 262–277.

Platt, J. Women's roles and the Great World Transformation. In G. Streatfield (Ed.), *Women and the future.* Binghamton, N.Y.: Center for Integration Studies, 1976.

Pleck, J. H. The male sex role: Definitions, problems and sources of change. *Journal of Social Issues,* 1976, *32*(3), 155–164. (a)

Pleck, J. H. My male sex role and ours. In D. David & R. Brannon (Eds.), *The forty-nine percent majority.* Reading, Mass.: Addison-Wesley, 1976. Pp. 253–264. (b)

Pleck, J. H., & Sawyer, J. (Eds.). *Men and masculinity.* Englewood Cliffs, N.J.: Prentice-Hall, 1974.

Polatnick, M. Why men can't rear children: A power analysis. *Berkeley Journal of Sociology,* 1973–1974, *18*, 45–86.

Polk, B. B. Male power and the Women's Movement. In S. Cox (Ed.), *Female*

psychology: The emerging self. Chicago: SRA, 1976. Pp. 400–413.

Poloma, M. Role conflict and the married professional woman. In C. Safilios-Rothschild (Ed.), *Toward a society of women.* Lexington, Mass.: Xerox College Publishing, 1972. Pp. 187–199.

Polyson, J. Sexism and sexual problems: Societal censure of the sexually troubled male. *Psychological Reports,* 1978, *42*, 843–850.

Pope, K. S., Levenson, H., & Schover, L. R. Sexual intimacy in psychology training. *American Psychologist,* 1979, *34*, 682–689.

Porter, C. H. Social security. *WEAL Washington Report,* August 1979, *8*(4), 1–2.

Porter, N., Geis, F., & Walstedt, J. *Are women invisible as leaders?* Paper presented at the American Psychological Association convention, Toronto, August 1978.

Porter, S. Myths about ERA confusing issue. *New Brunswick Home News,* May 11, 1977, p. 40.

Powell, G. N. *Factor analysis of the BSRI revisited: A comprehensive study.* Paper presented at the meeting of the American Psychological Association, New York, September 1979.

Powell, G. N., & Butterfield, D. A. *Sex and sex role identification: An important distinction for organizational research.* Paper presented at the American Psychological Association convention, San Francisco, August 1977.

Powers, E., & Bultena, G. Sex differences in intimate friendships of old age. *Job, Marriage and the Family,* 1976, *38*, 739–747.

Preston, R. C. Reading achievement of German and American children. *School and Society,* 1962, *90*, 350–354.

Proctor, E. B., Wagner, N. M., & Butler, J. C. The differentiation of male and female orgasms: An experimental study. In N. M. Wagner (Ed.), *Perspectives in human sexuality.* New York: Human Sciences, 1974.

Psychology Today. Silent sexism. February 1979, p. 98.

Psychology Today. Male bonding in the nursery. February 1979, pp. 23–24.

Psychology Today. The life-giving properties of marriage. January 1977, pp. 20–22.

Psychology Today. High school is a tough place for girls. December 1976, pp. 36–37.

Purkey, W. W. *Self-concept and school achievement*. Englewood Cliffs, N.J.: Prentice-Hall, 1970.

Rabin, A. I. Motivation for parenthood. *Journal of Projective Techniques & Personality Assessment*, 1965, *29*, 405–411.

Radloff, L. Sex differences in depression: The effects of occupation and marital status. *Sex Roles*, 1975, *1*, 249–265.

Rainwater, L. Sexual and marital relations. *Family design*. Chicago: Aldine, 1965.

Ramey, E. R. Sex hormones and executive ability. *Annals of the N.Y. Academy of Sciences*, 1973, *208*, 237–245.

Ramey, E. R. Men's cycles (they have them too, you know). *Ms.*, Spring 1972, pp. 8–14.

Ramey, J. *Intimate friendships*. Englewood Cliffs, N.J.: Prentice-Hall, 1976.

Rapoport, R., Rapoport, R., & Bumstead, J. (Eds.). *Working couples*. New York: Harper & Row, 1978.

Rebecca, M., Hefner, R., & Olenshansky, B. A model of sex role transcendence. *Journal of Social Issues*, 1976, *32*(3), 197–206.

Reinartz, K. F. The paper doll: Images of American women in popular songs. In J. Freeman (Ed.), *Women: A feminist perspective*. Palo Alto, Calif.: Mayfield, 1975. Pp. 293–308.

Reinisch, J. M., Gandelman, R., & Spiegel, F. S. Prenatal influences on cognitive abilities: Data from experimental animals and human genetic and endocrine syndromes. In M. A. Wittig & A. C. Petersen (Eds.), *Sex-related differences in cognitive functioning: Developmental issues*. New York: Academic Press, 1979. Pp. 215–239.

Reinisch, J. M., & Karow, W. A. Prenatal exposure to synthetic progestins and estrogens: Effects on human development. *Archives of Sexual Behavior*, 1977, *6*(4), 257–288.

Reis, H. T., & Jelsma, B. A social psychology of sex differences in sport. In W. Straub (Ed.), *Sport psychology: An analysis of athlete behavior*. Ithaca, N.Y.: Mouve-

ment, 1978. Pp. 178–188.

Rensberger, B. New debate on why man first walked erect. *New York Times*, January 30, 1979, pp. C1–2.

Renwick, P. A., & Lawler, E. E. What you really want from a job. *Psychology Today*, 1978, *11*(12), 53–65ff.

Revell, J. E. WACS in combat. *The Army Times Magazine*, February 9, 1976, pp. 7–12; February 23, 1976, pp. 9–13.

Rhodes, B. The changing role of the Black woman. In R. Staples (Ed.), *The Black family*. Belmont, Calif.: Wadsworth, 1971. Pp. 145–149.

Richardson, M. S., Merrifield, P., & Jacobson, S. *A factor analytic study of the Bem Sex Role Inventory*. Paper presented at the meeting of the American Psychological Association, New York, September 1979.

Richardson, N. Assertiveness training for men and women. In A. Sargent (Ed.), *Beyond sex roles*. St. Paul: West, 1977. Pp. 336–352.

Ricks, F., & Pyke, S. Teacher perceptions and attitudes that foster or maintain sex role differences. *Interchange*, 1973, *4*, 26–33.

Riddle, D. I., & Morin, S. F. Removing the stigma: Data from individuals. *APA Monitor*, November 1977, pp. 16, 28.

Riddle, D. I., & Sang, B. Psychotherapy with lesbians. *Journal of Social Issues*, 1978, *34*(3), 84–100.

Riesman, D. Listening to popular music. In B. Rosenberg & D. M. White (Eds.), *Mass culture: The popular arts in America*. New York: Free Press, 1957. Pp. 410–412.

Riess, B. F., & Safer, J. M. Homosexuality in females and males. In E. S. Gomberg & V. Franks (Eds.), *Gender and disordered behavior: Sex differences in psychopathology*. New York: Brunner/Mazel, 1979. Pp. 257–286.

Rivlin, L. Lilith. *Ms.*, December 1972, pp. 92–97ff.

Roache, J. P. Confessions of a house husband. *Ms.*, November 1972, *1*, 25–27.

Roberts, S. V. The women talk and the candidates listen hard. *New York Times*, December 16, 1979, p. E4.

Roberts, S. V. How Social Security penalizes women. *New York Times*, November 19, 1979, p. E20.

Robertson, N. Do female scientists face

bias? Columbia sociologist says 'No.' *New York Times*, December 17, 1979, p. D12.

Roby, P. Structural and internalized barriers to women in higher education. In C. Safilios-Rothschild (Ed.), *Toward a sociology of women*. Lexington, Mass.: Xerox College Publishing, 1972.

Rohrbaugh, J. B. Femininity on the line. *Psychology Today*, August 1979, p. 30ff.

Roman, M., & Haddad, W. The case for joint custody. *Psychology Today*, 1978, *12*(4), 96–105.

Rose, R. M., Gordon, T. P., & Bernstein, I. Plasma testosterone levels in the male rhesus: Influence of sexual and social stimuli. *Science*, 1972, *178*, 643–645.

Rose, R. M., Holaday, J. W., & Bernstein, I. Plasma testosterone, dominant rank, and aggressive behavior in male rhesus monkeys. *Nature*, 1971, *231*, 366–368.

Rosenbach, W. E., Dailey, R. C., & Morgan, C. B. Perceptions of job characteristics and affective work outcomes for women and men. *Sex Roles*, 1979, *5*, 267–277.

Rosenberg, B. G., & Sutton-Smith, B. *Sex and identity*. New York: Holt, Rinehart & Winston, 1972.

Rosenberg, M. The biological basis for sex role stereotypes. *Contemporary Psychoanalysis*, 1973, *9*, 374–391.

Rosenfeld, L. B., Civikly, J. M., & Herron, J. R. *Anatomical sex and self-disclosure: Topic, situation and relationship considerations*. Paper presented at the International Communications Association convention, Philadelphia, May 1979.

Rosenkrantz, P., Vogel, S. R., Bee, H., Broverman, I. K., & Broverman, D. M. Sex role stereotypes and self-concepts in college students. *Journal of Consulting and Clinical Psychology*, 1968, *32*, 287–295.

Rosenthal, R. *Experimenter effects in behavioral research*. New York: Appleton-Century-Crofts, 1966.

Rosenthal, R., & DePaulo, B. M. Sex differences in eavesdropping on nonverbal cues. *Journal of Personality and Social Psychology*, 1979, *37*, 273–285.

Rosenthal, R., Hall, J. A., DiMatteo, M. R., Rogers, P. L., & Archer, D. *Sensitivity to nonverbal communication: The PONS test*. Baltimore, Md.: Johns Hopkins University Press, 1979.

Rosenthal, R., & Jacobson, L. *Pygmalion in the classroom: Teacher expectation and pupil's intellectual development*. New York: Holt, Rinehart & Winston, 1968.

Rossi, A. G. Equality between the sexes: An immodest proposal. In S. Lifton (Ed.), *The woman in America*. Boston: Beacon Press, 1964.

Rossi, A. G. Sex equality: The beginnings of ideology. *The Humanist*, Sept.-Oct. 1969.

Rossi, A. S. Barriers to the career choice of engineering, medicine, or science among American women. In J. A. Matfield & C. G. Van Aken (Eds.), *Women and the scientific professions*. Cambridge, Mass.: M.I.T. Press, 1965. Pp. 51–127.

Rothbart, M. K., & Maccoby, E. E. Parents' different reactions to sons and daughters. *Journal of Personality and Social Psychology*, 1966, *4*, 337–343.

Rotkin, K. F. The phallacy of our sexual norm. *RT: A Journal of Radical Therapist*, 1972, *3*(11).

Rotter, G. S. The effect of sex identification upon teacher evaluation of pupils. 1967. In R. Unger (Ed.), *Sex-role stereotypes revisited. Psychological approaches to women's studies*. New York: Harper & Row, 1975.

Rotter, J. B. Generalized expectancies for internal versus external control of reinforcement. *Psychological Monographs: General and Applied*, 1966, *80*(1), 1–28.

Roy, M. (Ed.). *Battered women*. New York: Reinhold, 1977.

Rubenstein, J. L., & Howes, C. Caregiving and infant behavior in day care and in homes. *Developmental Psychology*, 1979, *15*, 1–24.

Rubin, J. Z., Provenzano, F. J., & Luria, Z. The eye of the beholder: Parents' views on sex of newborns. *American Journal of Orthopsychiatry*, 1974, *44*, 512–519.

Ruble, D. N. Premenstrual symptoms: A reinterpretation. *Science*, 1977, *197*, 291–292.

Ruble, D. N., & Higgins, E. T. Effects of group sex composition on self-presentation and sex-typing. *Journal of Social Issues*, 1976, *32*(3), 125–132.

Russell, C., Waller, A., James, A., & Ames, E. W. *Maternal influence on infants' play with sex-stereotyped toys*. Paper presented at the Western Psychological Association convention, San Francisco, April 1978.

Russo, N. F. The Motherhood Mandate. *Journal of Social Issues*, 1976, *32*(3), 143–153.

Saario, T. N., Jacklin, C. N., & Tittle, C. K. Sex role stereotypes in the public schools. *Harvard Educational Review*, 1973, *43*(3), 386–416.

Sadd, S., Lenauer, M., Shaver, P., & Dunivant, N. Objective measurement of fear of success and fear of failure: A factor analytic approach. *Journal of Consulting and Clinical Psychology*, 1978, *46*, 405–416.

Sadd, S., Miller, F. D., & Zeitz, B. Sex roles and achievement conflicts. *Personality and Social Psychology Bulletin*, 1979, *5*, 352–355.

Safilios-Rothschild, C. Women as change agents: Toward a conflict theoretical model of sex role change. In J. Lipman-Blumen & J. Bernard (Eds.), *Sex roles and social policy: A complex social science equation.* Beverly Hills, Calif.: Sage, 1979. Pp. 287–301.

Safilios-Rothschild, C. *Love, sex, and sex roles.* Englewood Cliffs, N.J.: Prentice-Hall, 1977.

Safilios-Rothschild, C. A cross-cultural examination of women's marital, educational, and occupational options. In M. S. Mednick, S. S. Tangri, & L. W. Hoffman (Eds.), *Women and achievement: Social and motivational analyses.* New York: Halsted, 1975. Pp. 48–70.

Sanday, P. R. Female status in the public domain. In M. Z. Rosaldo & L. Lamphere (Eds.), *Women, culture, and society.* Stanford, Calif.: Stanford University Press, 1974. Pp. 189–207.

Sanday, P. R. Toward a theory of the status of women. *American Anthropologist*, 1973, *75*, 1682–1700.

Sarri, R. C. Crime and the female offender. In E. S. Gomberg & V. Franks (Eds.), *Gender and disordered behavior: Sex differences in psychopathology.* New York: Brunner/Mazel, 1979. Pp. 159–203.

Savage, J. E., Jr., Stearns, A. D., & Friedman, P. Relationship of internal-external locus of control, self-concept, and masculinity-femininity to fear of success in Black freshmen and senior college women. *Sex Roles*, 1979, *5*, 373–383.

Savell, J. M., Woelfel, J. C., Collins, B. E., & Bentler, P. M. A study of male and female soldiers' beliefs about the "appropriateness" of various jobs for women in the Army. *Sex Roles*, 1979, *5*, 41–62.

Sawyer, J. On male liberation. *Liberation*, Aug.–Oct. 1970, *15*(6–8), 32–33.

Scarf, M. The more sorrowful sex. *Psychology Today*, 1979, *12*(11), 44–52, 89–90.

Schacter, S., & Singer, J. E. Cognitive, social and physiological determinants of emotional state. *Psychological Review*, 1962, *63*, 379–399.

Schlafly, P. *The power of the positive woman.* New Rochelle, N.Y.: Arlington House, 1977.

Schmeck, R., Jr. Bias charged in medical diagnoses. *New York Times*, May 29, 1979, p. 23.

Schmidt, G. Male-female differences in sexual arousal and behavior during and after exposure to sexually explicit stimuli. *Archives of Sexual Behavior*, 1975, *4*, 353–364.

Schmidt, G., & Sigusch, V. Women's sexual arousal. In J. Zubein & J. Money (Eds.), *Contemporary sexual behavior: Critical issues in the 1970's.* Baltimore: Johns Hopkins Press, 1973. Pp. 117–143.

Schmidt, G., Sigusch, V., & Schafer, S. Responses to reading erotic stories: Male-female differences. *Archives of Sexual Behavior*, 1973, *2*, 181–199.

Schneider, F., & Rall, M. *Attitudes toward male and female political candidates.* Paper presented at the American Psychological Association convention, Washington, D.C., August 1976.

Schneider, J. W., & Hacker, S. S. Sex role imagery and the use of the generic "man" in introductory texts. *American Sociologist*, 1973, *8*(8), 12–18.

Schofield, M. *The sexual behavior of young people.* London, England: Penguin, 1968.

Schreiber, C. T. *Changing places.* Boston: MIT Press, 1979.

Schumer, F. Gender and schizophrenia. In E. S. Gomberg & V. Franks (Eds.), *Gender and disordered behavior: Sex differences in psychopathology.* New York: Brunner/Mazel, 1979. Pp. 321–353.

Scott, H. Women in Eastern Europe. In J. Lipman-Blumen & J. Bernard (Eds.), *Sex roles and social policy: A complex social science equation.* Beverly Hills, Calif.: Sage, 1979. Pp. 177–197.

Scott, R., Richards, A., & Wade, M.

Women's studies as change agent. *Psychology of Women Quarterly*, 1977, *1*, 377–379.

Seaman, B. *Free and female*. Greenwich, Conn.: Fawcett Crest, 1972.

Sears, R. R. Relation of early socialization experiences to self-concepts and gender role in middle childhood. *Child Development*, 1970, *41*, 267–289.

Segal, J., & Yahraes, H. Bringing up mother. *Psychology Today*, 1978, *12*(6), 90–96.

Segal, P. N. Choosing women judges. *National NOW Times*, August 1979, p. 4.

Seiden, A. M. Gender differences in psychophysiological illness. In E. S. Gomberg & V. Franks (Eds.), *Gender and disordered behavior: Sex differences in psychopathology*. New York: Brunner/Mazel, 1979. Pp. 426–449.

Seiden, R. Suicide: Preventable death. *Public Affairs Report*, 1974, *15*, 1–5.

Seidenberg, R. *Marriage between equals*. Garden City, N.Y.: Anchor Press, 1973.

Seidman, C. Women athletes gained recognition and also respect. *New York Times*, December 30, 1979, p. S7.

Seligman, M. E. Depression and learned helplessness. In R. J. Friedman & M. M. Katz (Eds.), *The psychology of depression: Contemporary theory and research*. Washington, D.C.: Winston, 1974.

Sells, L. W. High school mathematics as the critical filter in the job market in developing opportunities for minorities in graduate education. *Proceedings of the Conference on Minority Graduate Education*. Berkeley: University of California, May 1973.

Serbin, L. A., & Connor, J. M. Sex-typing of children's play preferences and patterns of cognitive performance. *Journal of Genetic Psychology*, in press.

Serbin, L. A., O'Leary, K. D., Kent, R. N., & Tonick, I. J. A comparison of teacher response to the pre-academic and problem behavior of boys and girls. *Child Development*, 1973, *44*, 796–804.

Sexton, P. *The feminized male*. New York: Random House, 1969.

Shafran, R. B. *Differential patient expectations and preferences regarding male and female therapists*. Paper presented at the meeting of the American Psychological Association, New York, September 1979.

Shapiro, L. Letter to the editor. *Mother Jones*, August 1977, p. 3.

Shaver, P., & Freedman, J. Your pursuit of happiness. *Psychology Today*, August 1976, pp. 26–32.

Sheehy, G. *Passages: Predictable crises of adult life*. New York: Bantam, 1976.

Shepherd, H. A. Men in organizations: Some reflections. In A. Sargent (Ed.), *Beyond sex roles*. St. Paul: West, 1977. Pp. 387–394.

Sherfey, M. J. *The nature and evolution of female sexuality*. New York: Aronson, 1974.

Sherman, J. Cognitive performance as a function of sex and handedness: An evaluation of the Levy hypothesis. *Psychology of Women Quarterly*, 1979, *3*, 378–390.

Sherman, J. *Sex-related differences in cognition: An essay on theory and evidence*. Springfield, Ill.: Charles C Thomas, 1978.

Sherman, J. Social values, femininity and the development of female competence. *Journal of Social Issues*, 1976, *32*, 181–195.

Sherman, J. Problems of sex differences in space perception and aspects of intellectual functioning. *Psychological Review*, 1967, *74*, 290–299.

Sherman, J., & Fennema, E. Distribution of spatial visualization and mathematical problem-solving scores: A test of Stafford's X linked hypotheses. *Psychology of Women Quarterly*, 1978, *3*, 157–167.

Sherman, J., Kaufacos, C., & Kenworthy, J. A. Therapists: Their attitudes and information about women. *Psychology of Women Quarterly*, 1978, *2*, 299–313.

Shields, S. Functionalism, Darwinism and the psychology of women: A study in social myth. *American Psychologist*, 1975, *30*, 739–754.

Shinar, E. H. Person perception as a function of occupation and sex. *Sex Roles*, 1978, *4*, 679–693.

Shinedling, M., & Pedersen, D. M. Effects of sex of teacher versus student on children's gain in quantitative and verbal performance. *Journal of Psychology*, 1970, *76*, 79–84.

Shinn, M. Father absence and children's cognitive development. *Psychological Bulletin*, 1978, *85*, 295–324.

Short, J. F., Jr., & Strodtbeck, F. L. Why gangs fight. In D. S. David & R. Brannon (Eds.), *The forty-nine percent majority: The male sex role.* Reading, Mass.: Addison-Wesley, 1976. Pp. 131–137.

Shostak, A. B. Middle-aged working class Americans at home: Changing expectations of manhood. *Occupational Mental Health*, 1972, *3*, 2–7.

Shostak, A. B. *Blue collar life.* New York: Random House, 1969.

Signorella, M. L., Vegega, M. E., & Mitchell, M. E. *Selected sex-related variables in published research: Implications for the study of psychological sex differences.* Paper presented at the Eastern Psychological Association convention, Philadelphia, April 1979.

Silvern, L. E. Children's sex-role preferences: Stronger among girls than boys. *Sex Roles*, 1977, *3*, 159–171.

Silvern, L. E., & Ryan, V. L. Self-related adjustment and sex-typing on the Bem Sex Role Inventory: Is masculinity the primary predictor of adjustment? *Sex Roles*, 1979, *5*, 739–763.

Simon, R. J. *Women and crime.* Lexington, Mass.: Lexington Books, 1975.

Simpson, G. H. Injuries and pain: A former player hurts and regrets. *New York Times*, November 26, 1978, p. S2.

Sistrunk, F., & McDavid, J. W. Sex variables in conforming behavior. *Journal of Personality and Social Psychology*, 1971, *17*, 200–207.

Slaby, R. G., & Frey, K. S. Development of gender constancy and selective attention to same-sex models. *Child Development*, 1975, *46*, 849–856.

Slobogin, K. Stress. *New York Times Magazine*, November 20, 1977, pp. 48–50ff.

Snow, K. Women in the American novel. In J. Freeman (Ed.), *Women: A feminist perspective.* Palo Alto, Calif.: Mayfield, 1975. Pp. 279–292.

Snow, R. B. NWPC finds judicial selection unfair. *Women's Political Times*, April 1979, *4*(2), 13.

Snyder, M., Tanke, E. D., & Berscheid, E. Social perception and interpersonal behavior: On the self-fulfilling nature of social stereotypes. *Journal of Personality and Social Psychology*, 1977, *35*, 656–666.

Solmon, L. C. Attracting women to psychology: Effects of university behavior and the labor market. *American Psychologist*, 1978, *33*, 990–999.

Solomon, N. S., & Jassin, L. A. ERA and the law. *Do It NOW*, May 1977, p. 2.

Spence, J. T. The thematic apperception test and attitudes toward achievement in women: A new look at the motive to avoid success and a new method of measurement. *Journal of Consulting and Clinical Psychology*, 1974, *42*, 427–437.

Spence, J. T., & Helmreich, R. L. The many faces of androgyny: A reply to Locksley and Colton. *Journal of Personality and Social Psychology*, 1979, *37*, 1032–1046. (a)

Spence, J. T., & Helmreich, R. L. On assessing "androgyny." *Sex Roles*, 1979, *5*, 721–738. (b)

Spence, J. T., & Helmreich, R. *Masculinity and femininity: The psychological dimensions, correlates and antecedents.* Austin: University of Texas Press, 1978.

Spence, J. T., & Helmreich, R. Who likes competent women? Competence, sex-role congruence of interests, and subjects' attitude toward women as determinants of interpersonal attraction. *Journal of Applied Social Psychology*, 1972, *2*(3), 197–213.

Spence, J. T., Helmreich, R. L., & Holahan, C. K. Negative and positive components of psychological masculinity and femininity and their relationship to self-reports of neurotic and acting out behaviors. *Journal of Personality and Social Psychology*, 1979, *37*, 1673–1682.

Spence, J. T., Helmreich, R., & Stapp, J. Ratings of self and peers on sex role attributes and their relation to self-esteem and conceptions of masculinity and femininity. *Journal of Personality and Social Psychology*, 1975, *32*, 29–39.

Spence, J. T., Helmreich, R., & Stapp, J. The Personal Attributes Questionnaire: A measure of sex role stereotyping and masculinity and femininity. *JSAS Selected Documents in Psychology*, 1974. (Ms. No. 617)

Sprafkin, J. N., & Liebert, R. M. Sex-typing and children's television preferences. In G. Tuchman, A. K. Daniels, & J. Benét (Eds.), *Hearth and home: Images of women in the mass media.* New York: Oxford University Press, 1978. Pp. 228–239.

Stafford, R. E. *Gender differences resulting from heredity components on the X-chromosome.* Paper presented at the Symposium "Determinants of Sex Differences in Cognitive Functioning," American Psychological Association convention,

Washington, D.C., September 1976.

Stafford, R. E. Hereditary and environmental components of quantitative reasoning. *Review of Educational Research*, 1972, *42*, 183–201.

Stafford, R. E. Sex differences in spatial visualization as evidence of sex-linked inheritance. *Perceptual and Motor Skills*, 1961, *13*, 428.

Staines, G. L., Tavris, C., & Jayaratne, T. E. The Queen Bee Syndrome. *Psychology Today*, January 1974, pp. 55–60.

Stake, J. E. The ability/performance dimension of self-esteem: Implications for women's achievement behavior. *Psychology of Women Quarterly*, 1979, *3*, 365–377.

Stapp, J. Minorities and women: Caught in an academic revolving door. *APA Monitor*, 1979, *10*(11), p. 14.

Starer, R., & Denmark, F. Discrimination against aspiring women. *International Journal of Group Tensions*, 1974, *4*, 65–70.

Starr, P. Hollywood's new ideal of masculinity. *New York Times*, July 16, 1978, Sec. 2, p. 1ff.

Stars & Stripes. Chances of being injured are 1 in 4. March 25, 1976, p. 8.

Stars & Stripes. Claims women slighted. January 27, 1976.

Stars & Stripes. Kids prefer TV over dad. December 6, 1975.

Stauffer, S. A. et al. *The American soldier: Combat and its aftermath, Vol. 2 of studies in social psychology in World War II*. Princeton, N.J.: Princeton University Press, 1949.

Stein, A. H., & Bailey, M. M. The socialization of achievement motivation in females. *Psychological Bulletin*, 1973, *80*, 345–366.

Stein, P. J., & Hoffman, S. Sports and male role strain. *Journal of Social Issues*, 1978, *34*(1), 136–150.

Steinem, G. The myth of the Masculine Mystique. *International Education*, 1972, *1*, 30–35.

Steinmann, A., & Fox, D. J. Attitudes toward women's family role among Black and White undergraduates. *Family Coordination*, 1970, *19*, 363–368.

Stericker, A., & Johnson, J. Sex-role identification and self-esteem in college students: Do men and women differ? *Sex Roles*, 1977, *3*, 19–26.

Sternglanz, S. H., & Serbin, L. A. Sex role stereotyping in children's TV programs. *Developmental Psychology*, 1974, *10*, 710–715.

Stevens-Long, J., Cobb, N. J., & Goldstein, S. *The influence of televised models on toy preference in children*. Paper presented at the American Psychological Association convention, Toronto, August 1978.

Stewart, V. Social influence on sex differences in behavior. In M. Teitelbaum (Ed.), *Sex differences: Social and biological perspectives*. New York: Anchor Press, 1976.

Stockard, J., & Johnson, M. M. The social origins of male dominance. *Sex Roles*, 1979, *5*, 199–218.

Stoller, R. J. *Sex and gender: On the development of masculinity and femininity*. New York: Science House, 1968.

Stone, E. Mothers and daughters: Taking a new look at Mom. *New York Times Magazine*, May 13, 1979, pp. 14–17ff.

Stone, I. F. Machismo in Washington. In J. Pleck & J. Sawyer (Eds.), *Men and masculinity*. Englewood Cliffs, N.J.: Prentice-Hall, 1974. Pp. 130–133.

Stone, P. Childcare in twelve countries. In A. Szalai (Ed.), *The use of time*. The Hague, Netherlands: Mouton, 1972. Pp. 249–264.

Stricker, G. Implications of research for psychotherapeutic treatment for women. *American Psychologist*, 1977, *32*, 14–22.

Strommen, E. A. Friendship. In E. Donelson & J. Gullahorn (Eds.), *Women: A psychological perspective*. New York: Wiley, 1977.

Suchner, R. W. Sex ratios and occupational prestige: Three failures to replicate a sexist bias. *Personality and Social Psychology Bulletin*, 1979, *5*, 236–239.

Suelzle, M. Women in labor. *Transaction*, Nov.-Dec. 1970, pp. 50–58.

Sugg, R. S. *Motherteacher: The feminization of American education*. Charlottesville: University Press of Virginia, 1978.

Suter, L. E., & Miller, H. P. Income differences between men and career women. *American Journal of Sociology*, 1978, *78*, 962–974.

Sutherland, S. T. The unambitious female: Women's low professional aspirations. *Signs*, 1978, *3*, 774–794.

Suziedelis, A. *Differentiation of 'masculinity and feminity' among adolescent girls*.

Paper presented at the American Psychological Association convention, San Francisco, August 1977.

Swanson, M. A., & Tjosvold, D. The effects of unequal competence and sex on achievement and self-presentation. *Sex Roles*, 1979, *5*, 279–285.

Sweet, J. A. *Women in the labor force.* New York: Harcourt Brace Jovanovich, 1973.

Symons, D. *The evolution of human sexuality.* Oxford, England: Oxford University Press, 1979.

Tangri, S. S. Determinants of occupational role innovation among college women. *Journal of Social Issues*, 1972, *28*(2), 177–199.

Tanner, J. M. Sequence, tempo, and individual variation in the growth and development of boys and girls aged 12–16. In J. Kagan & R. Coles (Eds.), *Twelve to sixteen: Early adolescence.* New York: Norton, 1972. Pp. 907–930.

Tauber, M. A. Parental socialization techniques and sex differences in children's play. *Child Development*, 1979, *50*, 225–234.

Tavris, C. Masculinity. *Psychology Today*, January 1977, pp. 34–42ff.

Tavris, C. Who likes Women's Liberation and why: The case of the unliberated liberals. *Journal of Social Issues*, 1973, *29*(4), 175–194.

Tavris, C., & Offir, C. *The longest war: Sex differences in perspective.* New York: Harcourt Brace Jovanovich, 1977.

Taylor, M. C. Race, sex, and the expression of self-fulfilling prophecies in a laboratory teaching situation. *Journal of Personality and Social Psychology*, 1979, *37*, 897–912.

Taylor, S. P., & Smith, I. Aggression as a function of sex of victim and male subjects' attitude toward women. *Psychological Reports*, 1974, *35*, 1095–1098.

Taynor, J., & Deaux, K. Equity and perceived sex differences: Role behavior as defined by the task, the mode, and the action. *Journal of Personality and Social Psychology*, 1975, *32*, 381–390.

Taynor, J., & Deaux, K. When women are more deserving than men: Equity, attribution and perceived sex differences. *Journal of Personality and Social Psychology*, 1973, *28*, 360–367.

Thomas, A. H., & Stewart, N. R. Counse-lor ratings to female clients with deviate and conforming career goals. *Journal of Counseling Psychology*, 1971, *18*, 352–357.

Thomopoulos, E., & Huyck, M. H. *Love and labor: Happy wives, worried mothers.* Paper presented at the American Psychological Association convention, Washington, D.C., 1976.

Thompson, N. L., McCandless, B. R., & Strickland, B. B. Personal adjustment of male and female homosexuality and heterosexuality. *Journal of Abnormal Psychology*, 1971, *78*, 237–240.

Throop, W. F., & MacDonald, A. P. Internal-external locus of control: A bibliography. *Psychological Reports*, Monograph Supplement *1*, Vol. 28, 1971.

Tidball, E. M. Perspective on academic women and affirmative action. *Educational Record*, 1973, *54*, 130–135.

Tiger, L. *Men in groups.* New York: Random House, 1969.

Time. Custody: Kramer vs. Kramer. February 4, 1980, p. 40.

Time. Comes the Revolution. July 26, 1978, pp. 54–59.

Time. Changing American political views. January 27, 1976, p. 18.

Time. Testing the creed. October 27, 1975, p. 60.

Tobias, S. *Overcoming math anxiety.* New York: Norton, 1978.

Tobias, S. Math anxiety: Why is a smart girl like you counting on your fingers? *Ms.*, 1976, *5*(Sept.), 56–59ff.

Tolchin, M. U.S. search for women and Blacks to serve as judges is going slowly. *New York Times*, April 22, 1979, p. 1.

Tolson, A. *The limits of masculinity: Male identity and women's liberation.* New York: Harper & Row, 1977.

Toth, R. C. Field performance of women soldiers shows little difference. *Easton Express*, October 20, 1977, p. 10.

Touhey, J. C. Effects of additional women professionals on ratings of occupational prestige and desirability. *Journal of Personality and Social Psychology*, 1974, *29*, 86–89.

Townsend, R. C. The competitive male as loser. In A. Sargent (Ed.), *Beyond sex roles.* St. Paul: West, 1977. Pp. 228–242.

Treadway, C. R., Kane, F. J., Jr., Jarrahi-Zadeh, A., & Lipton, M. A psychoendocrine study of pregnancy and piresperium. *American Journal of Psychiatry*, 1969, *125*, 1380–1386.

Tresemer, D. W. *Fear of success*. New York: Plenum Press, 1977.

Tresemer, D. W. Fear of success: Popular but unproven. *Psychology Today*, 1974, 7(10), 82–85.

Troll, L. E., & Turner, B. F. Sex differences in problems of aging. In E. S. Gomberg & V. Franks (Eds.), *Gender and disordered behavior: Sex differences in psychopathology*. New York: Brunner/Mazel, 1979. Pp. 124–156.

Tuchman, G., Daniels, A. K., & Benét, J. (Eds.). *Hearth and home: Images of women in the mass media*. New York: Oxford University Press, 1978.

Tung, R. L. *Occupational stress profiles of male versus female administrators*. Paper presented at the meeting of the American Psychological Association, New York, September 1979.

Tunnell, G. *Age and sex effects on social desirability of sex-role characteristics*. Paper presented at the American Psychological Association convention, New York, September 1979.

Unger, R. K. *Sex-role stereotypes revisited: Psychological approaches to women's studies*. New York: Harper & Row, 1975.

Unger, R. K., & Denmark, F. L. (Eds.). *Woman: Dependent or independent variable?* New York: Psychological Dimensions, 1975.

Unger, R., Raymond, B. J., & Levine, S. Are women a minority group? Sometimes! *International Journal of Group Tensions*, 1974, *4*, 71–81.

Unger, R. K., & Siiter, R. Sex role stereotypes: The weight of a "grain of truth." In R. Unger (Ed.), *Sex-role stereotypes revisited: Psychological approaches to women's studies*. New York: Harper & Row, 1975. Pp. 10–13.

U'ren, M. B. The image of women in textbooks. In V. Gornick & B. Moran (Eds.), *Women in a sexist society: Studies in power and powerlessness*. New York: Basic Books, 1971. Pp. 318–346.

U.S. Bureau of the Census. *Statistical abstract of the United States*. Washington, D.C.: U.S. Government Printing Office, 1979; 1977.

U.S. Commission on Civil Rights. *Window dressing on the set: Women and minorities on television*. Washington, D.C.: U.S. Government Printing Office, 1977.

U.S. Department of Health, Education, and Welfare. *Vital statistics of the U.S. 1975* (Vol. 2). Washington, D.C.: U.S. Government Printing Office, 1977.

U.S. Department of Labor, Bureau of Labor Statistics. *Employment and earnings, February 1979*. Washington, D.C.: U.S. Government Printing Office, 1979. (a)

U.S. Department of Labor, Bureau of Labor Statistics. *Employment & earnings, November 1979*. Washington, D.C.: U.S. Government Printing Office, 1979. (b)

U.S. Department of Labor, Bureau of Labor Statistics. *Employment in perspective: Working women*. Report 547. Washington, D.C.: U.S. Government Printing Office, 1978.

U.S. Department of Labor, Women's Bureau. *Women in the labor force, April 1976–1977*. Washington, D.C.: U.S. Government Printing Office, 1977. (a)

U.S. Department of Labor, Women's Bureau. *Occupations of employed women, April 1977*. Washington, D.C.: U.S. Government Printing Office, 1977. (b)

U.S. Department of Labor, Women's Bureau. *U.S. working women: A datebook*. Washington, D.C.: U.S. Government Printing Office, 1977. (c)

U.S. Department of Labor, Women's Bureau. *Women workers today*. Washington, D.C.: U.S. Government Printing Office, 1976. (a)

U.S. Department of Labor, Women's Bureau. *The earnings gap between women and men*. Washington, D.C.: U.S. Government Printing Office, 1976. (b)

U.S. Department of Labor, Women's Bureau. *Mature women workers: A profile*. Washington, D.C.: U.S. Government Printing Office, 1976. (c)

U.S. Department of Labor, Women's Bureau. *1975 handbook on women workers*. Bulletin 297. Washington, D.C.: U.S. Government Printing Office, 1975.

U.S. News & World Report. SAT scores continue to drop. October 20, 1975, p. 54.

Vandenberg, S. G., & Kuse, A. R. Spatial ability: A critical review of the sex-linked major gene hypothesis. In M. A. Wittig & A. C. Petersen (Eds.), *Sex-related differences in cognitive functioning: Develop-*

mental issues. New York: Academic Press, 1979. Pp. 67–95.

Van den Berghe, P. Academic gamesmanship. In D. David & R. Brannon (Eds.), *The forty-nine percent majority.* Reading, Mass.: Addison-Wesley, 1970. Pp. 124–131.

Van Dusen, R. R., & Sheldon, E. B. The changing status of American women: A life cycle perspective. *American Psychologist*, 1976, *31*, 106–117.

Vanek, J. Time spent in housework. *Scientific American*, 1974, *231*(14), 116–120.

Van Keep, P. A., & Kellerhals, J. M. The aging woman. *Acta Obstietrica et Gynecologica*, Scandinavica Supplement, 1975, *51*, 17–27.

Vaughn, L. S., & Wittig, M. A. *Occupation, competence, and role overload as evaluation determinants of successful women.* Paper presented at the meeting of the American Psychological Association, New York, September 1979.

Vecsey, G. Quest for equality in Church dividing Catholic women. *New York Times*, October 2, 1979, p. A12.

Vener, A. M., & Snyder, C. The preschool child's awareness and anticipation of adult sex roles. *Sociometry*, 1966, *29*, 159–168.

Veroff, J. Process versus impact in men's and women's achievement motivation. *Psychology of Women Quarterly*, 1977, *1*, 283–292.

Veroff, J., & Feld, S. C. *Marriage and work in America.* New York: Van Nostrand Reinhold, 1970.

Veroff, J., Wilcox, S., & Atkinson, J. W. Achievement motivation in high school and college age women. *Journal of Abnormal and Social Psychology*, 1953, *48*, 108–119.

Vogel, S. R. Discussant's comments. Symposium: Applications of androgyny to the theory and practice of psychotherapy. *Psychology of Women Quarterly*, 1979, *3*, 255–258.

Waber, D. P. Cognitive abilities and sex-related variations in the maturation of cerebral cortical functions. In M. A. Wittig & A. C. Petersen (Eds.), *Sex-related differences in cognitive functioning: Developmental issues.* New York: Academic Press, 1979. Pp. 161–186.

Waber, D. P. Sex differences in mental abilities, hemispheric lateralization, and rate of physical growth at adolescence. *Developmental Psychology*, 1977, *13*, 29–38.

Waber, D. P. Sex differences in cognition: A function of maturation rate? *Science*, 1976, *192*, 572–574.

Waldman, E., & McEaddy, B. J. Where women work: An analysis by industry and occupation. *Monthly Labor Review*, 1974, *97*, 3–12.

Waldron, I. Why do women live longer than men? *Journal of Human Stress*, 1976, *2*, 1–13.

Wallace, M. *Black macho and the myth of the superwoman.* New York: Dial Press, 1979.

Walstedt, J. J. A content analysis of sexual discrimination in children's literature, 1973. In R. Unger (Ed.), *Sex-role stereotypes revisited: Psychological approaches to women's studies.* New York: Harper & Row, 1975. Pp. 36–38.

Ward, W. D. Process of sex role development. *Developmental Psychology*, 1969, *9*(2), 163–168.

Waterman, A., & Whitbourne, S. K. *Androgyny and psychosocial development among college students and adults.* Paper presented at the meeting of the American Psychological Association, New York, September 1979.

Watson, N. *Sex role identity and defensively high self-esteem.* Paper presented at the meeting of the American Psychological Association, New York, September 1979.

Watts, B. L., Messé, L. A., & Vallacher, R. R. *Toward understanding sex differences in pay allocation: Agency, communion and reward distribution behavior.* Paper presented at the meeting of the American Psychological Association, New York, September 1979.

WEAL. Arms and the woman: Equal opportunity in the military. *WEAL Washington Report*, 1977, *6*(2), 1–6.

WEAL. Women and politics. *WEAL Washington Report*, December 1976, *5*, p. 1ff.

Webb, A. P. Sex role preference and adjustment in early adolescence. *Child Development*, 1963, *34*, 609–618.

Weiss, M. Unlearning. In J. Pleck & J. Sawyer (Eds.), *Men and masculinity.* Englewood Cliffs, N.J.: Prentice-Hall, 1974. Pp. 162–170.

Weissman, M. M., & Klerman, G. L. Sex differences and the epidemiology of depression. In E. S. Gomberg & V. Franks (Eds.), *Gender and disordered behavior: Sex differences in psychopathology.* New York: Brunner/Mazel, 1979. Pp. 381–425.

Weisstein, N. Woman as nigger. *Psychology Today*, October 1969, p. 22ff.

Weitz, S. *Sex roles: Biological, psychological and social foundations.* New York: Oxford University Press, 1977.

Weitzman, L. J. Sex-role socialization. In J. Freeman (Ed.), *Women: A feminist perspective.* Palo Alto, Calif.: Mayfield, 1975. Pp. 105–144.

Weitzman, L. J., Eifler, D., Hokada, E., & Ross, C. Sex role socialization in picture books for preschool children. *American Journal of Sociology*, 1972, 77, 1125–1150.

Weitzman, L. J., & Rizzo, D. Images of males and females in elementary school text books. New York: NOW Legal Defense & Education Fund, 1974.

Welch, R. L. Androgyny and derived identity in married women with varying degrees of non-traditional role involvement. *Psychology of Women Quarterly*, 1979, 3, 308–315.

Weston, L. C., & Ruggiero, J. A. Male-female relationships in best-selling "Modern Gothic" novels. *Sex Roles*, 1978, 4, 647–655.

Wetzsteon, R. The feminist man? *Mother Jones*, November 1977, pp. 52–59.

White, L. A. Erotica and aggression: The influence of sexual arousal, positive affect, and negative affect on aggressive behavior. *Journal of Personality and Social Psychology*, 1979, 37, 591–601.

White, M. S. Measuring androgyny in adulthood. *Psychology of Women Quarterly*, 1979, 3(3), 293–307.

White, M. S. Psychological and social barriers to women in science. *Science*, October 23, 1970, pp. 413–416.

Whiting, B., & Edwards, C. P. A cross-cultural analysis of sex differences in the behavior of children aged three through eleven. *Journal of Social Psychology*, 1973, 91(Second Half), 171–188.

Widom, C. S. *Self-esteem, sex-role identity and feminism in female offenders.* Paper presented at the American Psychological Association convention, San Francisco, August 1977.

Wiggins, J. S., & Holzmuller, A. Further evidence on androgyny and interpersonal flexibility. *Journal of Research in Personality*, in press.

Wiggins, J., & Holzmuller, A. Psychological androgyny and interpersonal behavior. *Journal of Consulting and Clinical Psychology*, 1978, 46, 40–52.

Wilborn, B. L. The myth of the perfect mother. In L. Harmon, J. Bert, L. Fitzgerald, & M. F. Tanney (Eds.), *Counseling women.* Monterey, Calif.: Brooks/Cole, 1978. Pp. 241–249.

Williams, J. H. Sexual role identification and personality functioning in girls: A theory revisited. *Journal of Personality*, 1973, 41(1), 1–8.

Williams, R. M., Jr. *American society: A social interpretation.* New York: Knopf, 1970.

Williamson, N. E. *Sons or daughters: A cross-cultural survey of parental preferences.* Beverly Hills, Calif.: Sage, 1976.

Wills, T. A., Weiss, R. L., & Patterson, G. R. A behavioral analysis of the determinants of marital satisfaction. *Journal of Consulting and Clinical Psychology*, 1974, 42, 802–811.

Wilson, E. O. *On human nature.* Cambridge, Mass.: Harvard University Press, 1978.

Wilson, F. R. *Concurrent validity of four androgyny instruments.* Paper presented at the meeting of the American Psychological Association, New York, September 1979.

Wilson, J. Hollywood flirts with the New Woman. *New York Times*, May 29, 1977, Section 2, p. 1ff.

Winick, C. *The new people and desexualization in American life.* New York: Pegasus, 1968.

Winter, D., Stewart, A., & McClelland, D. Husband's motive and wife's career level. *Journal of Personality and Social Psychology*, 1977, 35, 154–166.

Wise, L. L. *The role of mathematics in women's career development.* Paper presented at the American Psychological Association convention, Toronto, August 1978.

Witelson, S. F. Sex and the single hemisphere: Specialization of the right hemisphere for spatial processing. *Science*, 1976, 193, 425–427.

Witkin, H. A., Dyk, R. B., Faterson, H. F., Goodenough, D. R., & Karp, S. A. *Psycho-*

logical differentiation. New York: Wiley, 1962.

Witt, S. H. Native women today: Sexism and the Indian woman. In S. Cox (Ed.), *Female psychology: The emerging self.* Chicago: SRA, 1976. Pp.2 49–259.

Wittig, M. A. Genetic influences on sex-related differences in intellectual performance: Theoretical and methodological issues. In M. A. Wittig & A. C. Petersen (Eds.), *Sex-related differences in cognitive functioning: Developmental issues.* New York: Academic Press, 1979. Pp. 21–66.

Wittig, M. A., & Petersen, A. C. (Eds.). *Sex-related differences in cognitive functioning: Developmental issues.* New York: Academic Press, 1979.

Wolman, C., & Frank, H. The solo woman in a professional peer group. *American Journal of Orthopsychiatry,* 1975, *45,* 164–171.

Women Employed. *Women in the economy: Preferential mistreatment.* Chicago, Ill.: Author, 1977.

Women in Transition, Inc. *Women in transition.* New York: Scribner, 1975.

Women on Words and Images. *Channeling children.* Princeton, N.J.: Author, 1975. (a)

Women on Words and Images. *Dick and Jane as victims; An update.* Princeton, N.J.: Author, 1975. (b)

Women on Words and Images. *Doctor, lawyer, Indian chief. . . ? Sex stereotyping in career education materials.* Princeton, N.J.: Author, 1975. (c)

Women on Words and Images. *Dick and Jane as victims.* Princeton, N.J.: Author, 1972.

Worden, O., Chesler, M., & Levin, G. Racism, sexism, and class elitism: Change agents' dilemmas in combatting oppression. In A. Sargent (Ed.), *Beyond sex roles.* St. Paul: West, 1977. Pp. 451–469.

Worell, J. Sex roles and psychological well-being: Perspectives on methodology. *Journal of Consulting and Clinical Psychology,* 1978, *46,* 777–791.

Wortis, R. P. The acceptance of the concept of the mother-role by behavioral scientists: Its effects on women. *American Journal of Orthopsychiatry,* 1971, *41,* 733–746.

Wrightsman, L. *Social psychology (2nd ed.).* Monterey, Calif.: Brooks/Cole, 1977.

Wyckoff, H. Sex role scripts in men and women. In C. Steiner (Ed.), *Scripts people live.* New York: Grove Press, 1974. Pp. 196–208.

Yates, G. G. *What women want: The idea of the movement.* Cambridge, Mass.: Harvard University Press, 1975.

Youssef, N. H., & Hartley, S. F. Demographic indicators of the status of women in various societies. In J. Lipman-Blumen & J. Bernard (Eds.), *Sex roles and social policy: A complex social science equation.* Beverly Hills, Calif.: Sage, 1979. Pp. 83–112.

Zanna, J. J., & Pack, S. J. On the self-fulfilling nature of apparent sex differences in behavior. *Journal of Experimental Social Psychology,* 1975, *11,* 583–591.

Zedlow, P. B. Effects of nonpathological sex-role stereotypes on student evaluations of psychiatric patients. *Journal of Consulting and Clinical Psychology,* 1976, *44,* 304.

Zeitz, B. *A Fishbein-Ajzen model of achievement motivation.* Paper presented at the meeting of the American Psychological Association, New York, September 1979.

Zuckerman, M., & Wheeler, L. To dispel fantasies about the fantasy-based measures of fear and success. *Psychological Bulletin,* 1975, *83,* 932–946.

NAME INDEX

SUBJECT INDEX

Basow, Susa

SEX-ROLE ST

Monterey, (

384 pages